Mastering Art Law

Carolina Academic Press Mastering Series
Russell Weaver, Series Editor

For other titles, please go to caplaw.com.

Mastering Administrative Law, Second Edition
Linda D. Jellum

Mastering Adoption Law and Policy
Cynthia Hawkins DeBose

Mastering Alternative Dispute Resolution
Kelly M. Feeley, James A. Sheehan

Mastering American Indian Law, Second Edition
Angelique Wambdi EagleWoman, Stacy L. Leeds

Mastering Appellate Advocacy and Process, Revised Printing
Donna C. Looper, George W. Kuney

Mastering Art Law, Second Edition
Herbert Lazerow

Mastering Bankruptcy
George W. Kuney

Mastering Civil Procedure, Third Edition
David Charles Hricik

Mastering Constitutional Law, Second Edition
John C. Knechtle, Christopher J. Roederer

Mastering Contract Law
Irma S. Russell, Barbara K. Bucholtz

Mastering Corporate Tax, Second Edition
Gail Levin Richmond, Reginald Mombrun, Felicia Branch

Mastering Corporations and Other Business Entities, Second Edition
Lee Harris

Mastering Criminal Law, Second Edition
Ellen S. Podgor, Peter J. Henning, Neil P. Cohen

Mastering Criminal Procedure, Volume 1: The Investigative Stage, Third Edition
Peter J. Henning, Cynthia E. Jones, Ellen S. Podgor,
Karen McDonald Henning, Sanjay K. Chhablani

Mastering Criminal Procedure, Volume 2: The Adjudicatory Stage, Third Edition
Peter J. Henning, Cynthia E. Jones, Ellen S. Podgor,
Karen McDonald Henning, Sanjay K. Chhablani

Mastering Elder Law, Second Edition
Ralph C. Brashier

Mastering Employment Discrimination Law, Second Edition
Paul M. Secunda, Jeffrey M. Hirsch, Joseph A. Seiner

Mastering Environmental Law
Joel A. Mintz, Tracy D. Hester

Mastering Family Law
Janet Leach Richards

Mastering First Amendment Law
John C. Knechtle

Mastering Income Tax, Second Edition
Gail Levin Richmond, Christopher M. Pietruszkiewicz

Mastering Intellectual Property
George W. Kuney, Donna C. Looper

Mastering Labor Law
Paul M. Secunda, Anne Marie Lofaso, Joseph E. Slater, Jeffrey M. Hirsch

Mastering Legal Analysis and Drafting
George W. Kuney, Donna C. Looper

Mastering Legislation, Regulation, and Statutory Interpretation, Third Edition
Linda D. Jellum

Mastering Negotiable Instruments (UCC Articles 3 and 4) and Other Payment Systems, Second Edition
Michael D. Floyd

Mastering Negotiation
Michael R. Fowler

Mastering Partnership Taxation
Stuart Lazar

Mastering Professional Responsibility, Second Edition
Grace M. Giesel

Mastering Property Law, Revised Printing
Darryl C. Wilson, Cynthia Hawkins DeBose

Mastering Sales
Colin P. Marks, Jeremy Kidd

Mastering Secured Transactions: UCC Article 9, Second Edition
Richard H. Nowka

Mastering Tort Law, Second Edition
Russell L. Weaver, Edward C. Martin, Andrew R. Klein, Paul J. Zwier, II, John H. Bauman

Mastering Trademark and Unfair Competition Law
Lars S. Smith, Llewellyn Joseph Gibbons

Mastering Trusts and Estates
Gail Levin Richmond, Don Castleman

Mastering Art Law

SECOND EDITION

Herbert Lazerow
University of San Diego School of Law

Carolina Academic Press
Durham, North Carolina

Library of Congress Cataloging-in-Publication Data

Names: Lazerow, Herbert I., author.
Title: Mastering art law / by Herbert Lazerow.
Description: Second edition. | Durham, North Carolina : Carolina Academic Press, LLC, [2020] | Series: Carolina academic press mastering series | Includes index.
Identifiers: LCCN 2020016382 (print) | LCCN 2020016383 (ebook) | ISBN 9781531019044 (paperback) | ISBN 9781531019051 (ebook)
Subjects: LCSH: Law and art--United States. | Artists--Legal status, laws, etc.--United States. | Cultural property--Protection--Law and legislation--United States.. | Museums--Law and legislation--United States.
Classification: LCC KF4288 .L39 2020 (print) | LCC KF4288 (ebook) | DDC 344.73/097--dc23
LC record available at https://lccn.loc.gov/2020016382
LC ebook record available at https://lccn.loc.gov/2020016383

Carolina Academic Press
700 Kent Street
Durham, NC 27701
Telephone (919) 489-7486
Fax (919) 493-5668
www.cap-press.com

Printed in the United States of America

To

My parents, the giants on whose shoulders I stand,
Julius Lazerow (1909–1994) and Beatrice Lillian Lazerow née Kimmelman
(1906–2002);

Erica, Forrest and Athena Davis, Shana Lazerow, and Chris
and Calder Underwood,
who have taught me far more than they can appreciate;

Michael G. Kammen (1936–2013),
Newton C. Farr Professor of American History and Culture at Cornell,
my cousin, my rival, my idol, my best man;

and the person truly responsible for this book,
Jane Frances Lazerow née Goding,
wife and best friend,
who will recognize her words in a few places, and her ideas in many more.

Contents

Table of Cases

Table of Constitutions, Statutes, Regulations, Rules, Rulings and Treaties

(Except as indicated, all items are United States federal items)

Table of Secondary Authorities

Series Editor's Foreword

The Carolina Academic Press Mastering Series is designed to provide you with a tool that will enable you to easily and efficiently "master" the substance and content of law school courses. Throughout the series, the focus is on quality writing that makes legal concepts understandable. As a result, the series is designed to be easy to read and is not unduly cluttered with footnotes or cites to secondary sources.

In order to facilitate student mastery of topics, the Mastering Series includes a number of pedagogical features designed to improve learning and retention. At the beginning of each chapter, you will find a "Roadmap" that tells you about the chapter and provides you with a sense of the material that you will cover. A "Checkpoint" at the end of each chapter encourages you to stop and review the key concepts, reiterating what you have learned. Throughout the book, key terms are explained and emphasized. Finally, a "Master Checklist" at the end of each book reinforces what you have learned and helps you identify any areas that need review or further study.

We hope that you will enjoy studying with, and learning from, the Mastering Series.

Russell L. Weaver
Professor of Law & Distinguished University Scholar
University of Louisville, Louis D. Brandeis School of Law

Preface

Resources

The casebooks in the area are:

RICHARD B. CUNNINGHAM, ARCHAEOLOGY, RELICS, AND THE LAW (Carolina Academic, 2d ed. 2005).

LEONARD D. DUBOFF & MICHAEL D. MURRAY, ART LAW (Kluwer, 2d ed. 2017).

PATTY GERSTENBLITH, ART, CULTURAL HERITAGE, AND THE LAW (Carolina Academic, 4th ed. 2019).

ROBERT C. LIND, ROBERT M. JARVIS & MARILYN E. PHELAN, ART AND MUSEUM LAW (Carolina Academic 2002).

JOHN HENRY MERRYMAN, ALBERT E. ELSEN & STEPHEN K. URICE, LAW, ETHICS AND THE VISUAL ARTS (Kluwer Law Int'l 5th ed. 2007).

ANNE-MARIE RHODES, ART LAW & TRANSACTIONS (Carolina Academic 2011).

The major treatises are:

ALEXANDRA DARRABY, ART, ARTIFACTS, ARCHITECTURE AND MUSEUM LAW (West, annual, included in Westlaw).

LEONARD DUBOFF, CHRISTY KING & MICHAEL MURRAY, DESKBOOK OF ART LAW (Lexis, updated periodically, included in Lexis).

RALPH E. LERNER & JUDITH BRESLER, ART LAW (Practicing Law Institute, 4th ed. 2012).

Request

No work of law is ever complete because the law is a living organism. I hope that the readers of this volume will help prepare subsequent editions by e-mailing me their suggestions at lazer@sandiego.edu.

Acknowledgments

First Edition

I have been blessed with helpful research associates. Arien Koorn USD 2010, Jennifer Scott USD 2011, and Rachel Weitzman of USD's Class of 2015 did preliminary spadework. Lindsey Hertzig and Kerry Swendt of USD's Class of 2015 enabled this work to be published on time by preparing first drafts of some materials, suggesting ways that chapters might be organized, and reviewing my convoluted prose to assure that it would be intelligible to law students.

The University of San Diego financed the activities of my research associates, as well as providing me with research grants to help push the work toward completion.

My colleagues Lawrence Alexander, David Brennan, Nancy Carol Carter, Derrick Cartright, Walter Heiser, Adam Hirsch, Judge David Laro, William Lawrence, Pierre Legrand, Lisa Ramsey, Maimon Schwarzschild, Christopher Wonnell and Sally Yard have generously discussed specific legal or practical problems with me or read drafts.

Marshall Becker of Westchester State, Charles Craver of George Washington, William Dodge of Hastings, Patty Gerstenblith of DePaul, Philadelphia sculptor Harold Kimmelman (1923–2013), Jan Kosel of Golden Gate, Jennifer Kreder of Northern Kentucky, Michael Murray of Valparaiso, and William Wang of Hastings have all shared their insights, and Jane Ginsburg of Columbia went far beyond the call of duty in critiquing drafts of several chapters.

Second Edition

In the midst of the coronavirus pandemic, Linda Silberman of NYU spent time reading and making helpful suggestions on the sections treating choice of law and proving foreign law, for which I am grateful.

Mastering Art Law

Chapter 1

What Is Art? Why Does Anyone Care?

Roadmap

After reading this chapter, you should understand:

- Definition of art: There is no universal definition of "art" or "artist"; courts define these terms differently depending on the purpose for which the term is being defined.
- One definition of art is creativity of a human being that is fixed in tangible form.
- Tariff law defines art as requiring handmade creativity.
- Copyright law requires less creativity, permits mass-produced items, and does not necessarily exclude functional items.
- First Amendment law is concerned with whether the work expresses a message.
- Housing law may exclude commercially successful artists and amateurs to benefit artists whose income is low by allowing them to reside where they may both live and work.
- Income tax considers the originality and uniqueness as well as the aesthetic value of an item in considering whether its maker is an artist.
- Reasons for different rules for art and artists: Art is aesthetically pleasing, conveys messages, and educates about past societies. Artists are often treated specially because they have unequal bargaining power, and because there is often market failure in the art market.

---

1. Introduction: Why Define Art?

Art law is not a unified discipline, like Torts or Contracts. Instead, it is a field that studies the legal problems of an industry. The industry is composed of a number of different players: artists, critics, collectors, gallery operators, auctioneers, and museums, as well as the myriad state, federal, and international government officials who regulate the industry, such as local police, customs officers, trade officials, attorneys general, and tax collectors. Their legal problems fall within a large number of domains, including constitutional law, torts, contracts, agency, copyright, trademark, moral rights, tax, property, nonprofit organizations, international law, and civil procedure.

In each area, general rules developed without art in mind apply to art law problems in the absence of specific rules targeted at art. If a special rule is to be tailored to the needs of the art world, it is incumbent upon its advocates to make a case for the proposition that art requires a special rule.

If special rules are enacted, it then becomes necessary to draw a line between cases that fall within the special case of art law and those governed by the general rules in the field. For example, if metal imported into the United States is subject to duty at a positive rate, 10% for example, and art can be imported without paying a tariff, one must distinguish between metal sculpture that is classified as art, and other pieces of metal that are not classified as art.

2. Defining "Art" and "Artist"

It is not possible to provide a universal definition of "art" or the "artist." While there is a core component of creativity involved in all definitions of art, the degree of creativity varies considerably, and creativity alone is usually not sufficient to distinguish art from other items.

What one can say definitively about judicial treatment of art is that courts have almost universally tried to avoid distinguishing good art from mediocre art from bad art. Justice Oliver Wendell Holmes Jr. said, "[I]t would be a dangerous undertaking for persons trained only to the law to constitute themselves final judges of [art]." *Bleistein v. Donaldson Lithographic Co.*, 188 U.S. 239 (1903).

Art is defined differently depending on the purpose for which it is being defined. Below are some examples; more examples could have been provided.

A. Art Defined by Artists and Art Critics

Artists and critics have offered a number of different definitions of art. The most inclusive definition is "Art is what the artist says it is." Whatever the validity of that definition, its indeterminacy and dependence on pronouncement by an interested party render it of little use to the law. The definition pursued by Marcel Duchamp, "Art is anything used or produced by an artist" is no more helpful because it requires us to define "artist." I would think it overbroad in including the artist's fingernail pairings, but Piero Manzoni in 1961 created 90 small sealed cans, signed and dated, labeled "Merda d'Artista." supposedly containing his excrement, which he sold by weight at the price of gold and which have been exhibited in major museums. Gauguin said "Art is either plagiarism or revolution." More cynical is Andy Warhol's definition, "Art is what you can get away with," and in a tele-film, a fictional Alfred Steiglitz tells a fictional Georgia O'Keeffe, "Work doesn't become art until some rich person comes along and buys it." Putting them together, the philosopher Arthur Danto said that art was whatever the art world—artists, art historians, critics, curators, dealers and collectors—accepted as art.

i. Creativity of a Human Being Fixed in Tangible Form

An alternate art definition is to suggest that the essence of art is the creativity or originality of a human being that is fixed in tangible form.

The requirement of a human being means that things created entirely by nature do not qualify as art, no matter how aesthetically pleasing. On the other hand, there is no limit to the number of tools a person can use to assist her in creating the work. A computer program whose movements are randomly generated is no less an acceptable tool than a paintbrush.

Originality or creativity serves the function of separating copies from originals. An exact copy is not art, no matter how much skill is required to make it.

On the other hand, full originality is rare if not non-existent. Every work of art builds to a greater or lesser extent on the works that have preceded it. For example, there was a tradition in the Renaissance of doing portraits in profile. Some artist conceived the idea of doing a three-quarters view portrait, an original idea for the time. But the rest of that portrait probably followed the conventional format of the time with respect to composition, color, density of paint, and medium.

A standard example of originality is Picasso's construction of his *Bull's Head* sculpture. He conceived the idea of combining a bicycle seat and a set of bicycle handlebars to represent a bull's head. Combining the two elements required relatively little skill. Conceiving the idea showed great creativity.

But creativity alone is insufficient to create art. If Picasso had told people about his idea, it would not have been art. He had to actually fuse his two ingredients in tangible form to create art.

Fixation in a tangible form should be taken in its broadest sense. It not only includes paper, canvas and sculpture, but also computer programs, which are more or less permanent even though the work disappears from the screen when the electricity is removed.

Having enumerated the three qualities of being man-made, creative and tangibly fixed, we have certainly described art, but we have not significantly differentiated it from other human activities like science or carpentry.

We can postulate that different levels of originality exist, but it is rare that we can evaluate those levels, especially since at the time that the work is produced we lack the judgment of history on it.

ii. Different Levels of Art

Art writers often try to draw distinctions between different levels of art. Typically, they will talk about the fine arts like drawing, painting, printmaking and sculpture, as compared to crafts like ceramics, stained glass, jewelry or furniture making. A third classification might be industrial design of manufactured items. They are sometimes distinguished by comparing items that are purely decorative with those having a non-decorative function, or comparing handmade items with those that are mass-produced. Others suggest that the decorative arts should be a separate classification. Attempts to apply those categories consistently have not been overwhelmingly successful. And one might note that the very word "art" derives from the Italian "arte," which in the Renaissance described an association of craftsmen who banded together to set standards: a guild. Indeed, the thought of an artist as anything but a craftsman is a decidedly post-Renaissance concept.

B. Art Defined by Tariff Law

Paintings, drawings, prints, and sculptures appear today in chapter 97 of the Harmonized Tariff Schedule, a uniform system to classify items for customs duty purposes. Most of the world's major trading nations adhere to this classification, which permits each country to assign its own tariff rate to each classification. The United States assigns a zero rate to chapter 97 items.

More than a century ago, the Convent of the Sacred Heart imported stained or painted (it is not clear which) glass windows depicting biblical subjects for their chapel. "Works of art, ..." including paintings imported for religious use or sculptures, were charged a 15% duty; stained or painted manufactured window glass was assessed at 45%. In *United States v. Perry*, 146 U.S. 71 (1892), the court held that the glass did not qualify as paintings despite the fact that the windows were prepared by recognized artists, in part because in the catalogues by which such items were sold, no distinction was drawn between those done by artists and those executed by artisans. The court suggested that art could be divided into four categories: fine arts such as paintings and statues; minor objects of art like statuettes, vases, drawings and etchings; *objets d'art*, which are primarily ornamental and incidentally useful, like stained glass and tapestry; and objects that are primarily useful but are made to be ornamental, like carpets and furniture. Congress, the court said, had accorded favorable treatment only to the first group, fine arts.

It was not the task of the *Perry* court to define art. The question before it was whether the window glass was a painting. Several other options lay open to the court. It could have responded that the windows were not a painting, but only the makings of a painting, like canvas and paint; it could have decided that a painting is any two-dimensional surface upon which a recognizable form could be placed, as *Tiffany v. United States*, 66 Fed. 736 (C.C.S.D.N.Y. 1895), affirmed for fans of silk and bone upon which artists had painted; or it could have held that nothing is a painting unless it contains paint. Each of those plus the court's decision are linguistically acceptable interpretations of the law.

Decorated marble mantelpieces were held not to be art. The court extensively reviewed the education and professional history of the person who was the foreman of the shop that made them, and determined that both indicated that he was an artisan, not an artist. It then decided based on the fact that the appearance of the items was primarily a mantelpiece rather than a decorative work. *Consmiller v. United States*, 3 Ct. Cust. App. 298 (1912).

Taking its cue from *Perry*, the court in *United States v. Olivotti & Co.*, T.D. 36309, 7 Ct. Cust. App. 46 (1916), held that a marble font and two marble seats produced by a professional sculptor, the former decorated with carvings resembling leaves, were not sculptures. The court admitted that they were beautiful, but said that many beautiful crafts were not included in the expression "works of art." Adopting a dictionary definition of sculpture, the court said it must imitate natural objects in their true proportions.

The law had changed by the time Marcel Duchamp arrived in the United States with a load of modern art for the Armory Show, including Constantine Brancusi's abstract metal sculpture *Bird in Flight*. In *Brancusi v. United States*, 54 Treas. Dec. 428 (Cust. Ct. 1928), the court interpreted a statute that would have admitted *Bird* free of duty if it met the definition of sculpture, but charged 40% duty if it was admitted as simply metal. The law read:

> Original paintings in oil, mineral, water, or other colors, pastels, original drawings and sketches in pen, ink, pencil, or water colors, artists' proof etchings unbound, and engravings and woodcuts unbound, original sculptures or statuary, including not more than two replicas or reproductions of the same; but the terms "sculpture" and "statuary" as used in this paragraph shall be understood to include professional productions of sculptors only, whether in round or in relief, in bronze, marble, stone, terra cotta, ivory, wood, or metal, or whether cut, carved, or otherwise wrought by hand from the solid block, or mass of marble, stone, or alabaster, or from metal, or cast in bronze or other metal or substance, or from wax or plaster, made

> as the professional productions of sculptors only; and the words "painting" and "sculpture" and "statuary" as used in this paragraph shall not be understood to include any articles of utility, nor such as are made wholly or in part by stenciling or any other mechanical process; and the words "etchings," "engravings," and "woodcuts" as used in this paragraph shall be understood to include only such as are printed by hand from plates or blocks etched or engraved with hand tools and not such as are printed from plates or blocks etched or engraved by photochemical or other mechanical processes.

The court begins by finding that the work was produced by a professional sculptor. This appears to be a matter of questionable relevance, since the law requires (twice) that it be a professional production of a sculptor, not that it be the product of a professional sculptor. The unexpressed reasoning must be that the standard of professional production refers to the kind of sculpture that would be produced by a professional sculptor, not by an amateur, so the fact that this sculpture was produced by a professional means that it is a professional production.

The court finds this a work of art, even though it was not necessary because that term was omitted from this statute, probably because it was a term used in the predecessor statute. It rejects the "nature imitation" test, pointing out that the definition of art changes with time and the influence of new schools, one of which attempts to portray abstract ideas rather than natural objects. The object is purely ornamental, rather than functional, so it is being used for decorative purposes, as is sculpture.

What is missing from the court's opinion is any sense that the tariff law has a purpose. Initially, tariffs were imposed to raise revenue, but such income quickly became a tiny part of the federal government's revenue. The main purpose of tariffs in modern times is to protect domestic industries, such as the stained glass industry, from foreign competition. The statute draws a clear distinction between individually produced items and manufactured items, by excluding from duty-free entry non-sculptural reproduction and bound copies of prints, both products of the publishing industry; more than three copies of a sculpture, indicating mass production; articles of utility; works made by stenciling or manufacturing; and prints not made and printed by hand. Once it was determined that the item was a sculpture, it also fit the purpose of the statute because it was entirely made by hand rather than in a manufacturing process.

Brancusi and other art controversies are discussed in MICHAEL KAMMEN, VISUAL SHOCK: A HISTORY OF ART CONTROVERSIES IN AMERICAN CULTURE (2006).

One should not believe that *Brancusi* was the end of the discussion. Several decades of litigation ensued causing difficulties with many of the newer schools of art. European Union Commission Regulation No 731/2010 of 11 August 2010 concerning the classification of certain goods in the Combined Nomenclature, 2010 O.J. L 214, note 6, overruling a British court decision, holds that a video-sound installation and a neon light installation are not art under chapter 97 of the Harmonized Tariff Schedule, but are instead the electronic equipment of their components, and comments that they are only artworks when turned on, and they are not turned on when imported. It is entirely possible that these items are not art, but the means of displaying art. That is a technical question that one cannot determine from the regulation's description. If they are equally suited to perform other functions, perhaps the regulation is correct. One must remember that a frame is a way of displaying art, and no one suggests that the frame is in a different tariff classification than the art.

The definition of sculpture allows the original and two reproductions to enter the United States duty free. In *Gregory v. United States*, 32 Cust. Ct. 228 (1954), the sculptor who made the mold for the statue died. The statue imported was cast by the sculptor's wife, also a professional sculptor. It was the tenth reproduction cast, but the first imported into the United States. The court stated that the reproduction did not need to be made by the professional sculptor who made the mold because the making of the mold was the important creative work. But the person in charge of the casting needed to be a professional sculptor. In discussing whether the tenth reproduction qualified, the court adverted to the purpose of the rule. It was intended " ... to cover original works of fine art and not commercial objects produced in great numbers." When more than two reproductions are made, "the sculptures become articles of trade, which ... do not belong to that class of fine art of a rare and special genius...." Therefore, only the original and the first two copies are admitted duty free.

Another provision of the tariff laws allowed the duty-free import of an "artistic antiquity." There was no doubt that the diamond in question was more than a century old, the definition of an antiquity. It was held not to be artistic because the beautiful stone was cut in a typical artisanal fashion, showing considerable skill, but none of the originality that separates the craftsman from the artist. *Mayers, Osterwald & Mulfeld, Inc. v. Bendler*, 18 C.C.P.A. 117 (1930).

The originality of a work of art copied from another seems greatly enhanced by moving it to a different medium with different technical challenges. A mosaic made in Italy after a photo of La Farge's Ascension was held to be an original, based in part on the testimony of the creators that they used the photo as a source of ideas, but made their own creative judgments. *Elder & Co. v. United States*, C.D. 3525, 61 Cust. Ct. 50 (1968). In reaching this conclusion, the court made no comparison of the similarities and differences between the painting and the mosaic.

Most recently an importer of new, highly decorated, extra-large (but usable) beer steins from Brazil for sale at auction, primarily to collectors, for advertising purposes, succeeded in establishing that the steins should be classified as "art and ornamental articles," rather than "mugs or other steins," because the predominant use of the items in the United States was for advertising rather than for the serving of beverages. *G. Heilman Brewing Co. v. United States*, 14 C.I.T. 614 (1990).

The difficulty lurking unspoken in the background of all these cases is valuation. In each case, the work has a higher value if it is art than if it is not art. To take *Brancusi* as an example, *Bird in Flight* at the time might have had a value of $10,000, but its value as metal probably did not exceed $200. Yet the importer who classifies the work as art and places the $10,000 value on it is stuck with that value even though the court might decide that it is not art, but metal. By contrast, an importer who values the work as metal and assigns a $200 value to it when it is in fact art has made a false valuation statement on a Customs form, thereby committing a federal criminal offense. He has also subjected the work to civil forfeiture to the United States.

C. Art Defined by Copyright Law

Art is defined for copyright law somewhat differently. A modest requirement of originality remains; there is less stress on being non-functional; and mass production is not a factor. In *Mazer v. Stein*, 347 U.S. 201 (1954), plaintiff manufactured glass statuettes of Balinese dancers that he had copyrighted and that he used as lamp bases. Defendant produced identical lamp bases. The court held that the issuing of the copyright was proper because the statuettes showed sufficient originality. The fact that the statuettes were mass produced and were functional did not disqualify them from copyright. The purpose of copyright is to encourage the production of new designs by according designs with sufficient originality a long monopoly from copying.

While that is the definition for purposes of obtaining a copyright, copyright law also provides moral rights for certain artists. Moral rights are accorded only to a much smaller universe of art. Any photo, movie or video qualifies for copyright, but only a still photographic image produced solely for exhibition qualifies for moral rights, and then only if it is the only copy, or part of a limited edition of 200 or fewer copies signed and consecutively numbered by the author. 17 U.S.C. § 101.

Whether an object is art or something else (in this case a swimsuit) is a matter of fact, rather than a matter of law. Acceptable evidence includes expert testimony, the artist's intent, custom in both the art world and the fashion world and marketability as art or as fashion. *Poe v. Missing Persons*, 745 F.2d 1238 (9th Cir. 1984).

D. Art Defined by the First Amendment

New York City has an ordinance requiring a vendor's permit to sell items on the street, but exempts newspapers and other print media from acquiring a permit. As the number of permits that can be issued is limited, the wait for the permit is roughly five years. Following the decision holding the distinction between print and visual media unconstitutional in *Bery v. City of New York*, 97 F.3d 689 (2d Cir. 1996), the city signed a consent decree promising that it would not enforce its permitting law against persons selling art. Cases followed trying to determine whether items sold were art. A deck of cards with pictures of leading players in the Vietnam war was held not to be art because insufficiently expressive, *People v. Saul*, 3 Misc. 3d 260, 776 N.Y.S.2d 189 (NYC Crim. Ct. 2004); coasters with photographs of scenes was art, *People v. Lee*, 19 Misc. 3d 791, 860 N.Y.S.2d 845 (NYC Crim. Ct. 2008); and, most surprisingly, a trained artist who painted individualized pictures on clothing while standing on the sidewalk with the client present did not produce art protected by the First Amendment. *Mastrovincenzo v. City of New York*, 435 F.3d 78 (2d Cir. 2006). All three cases could have been decided in the opposite way. Saul was making a political statement, Lee was just selling coasters, and Mastrovincenzo was making an artistic statement.

The most important factor to consider when determining whether art is being produced (and the *Mastrovincenzo* court specifically declined to define "art," but had to decide whether the work fell within the First Amendment or not) is whether the work was expressive of a message. One might be tempted to say that all artworks contain a message, but sometimes counsel does not adequately spell out for the court what the message is, and sometimes the court is too dense to grasp the message. But the more important message is that the right of freedom of speech is concerned with robust debate, and privileges speech more as the speech engages in debate.

The *Mastrovincenzo* court saw its mandate as deciding whether Mastrovincenzo was primarily engaged in artistic expression or primarily selling a product, even though it is standard First Amendment dogma that the desire to make a profit does not negate the protection of speech.

E. Art Defined by Local Housing Law

In New York City, persons are generally not permitted to reside in lofts zoned industrial or commercial. However, New York Mult. Dwell. L. §§ 275-278 permits artists to reside in these lofts. An artist is "a person who is regularly engaged in the fine arts, such as painting and sculpture or in the performing or creative arts, including choreography and filmmaking, or in the composition of music on a professional basis, and is so certified by the city department of cultural affairs...." § 276. Marhoffer was denied certification as an artist for the purpose of housing on the grounds that he was a commercial photographer. The court held the distinction between the three categories mentioned and commercial photographers to be an appropriate standard appropriately applied so that the benefits of the statute are not extended either to commercial artists or to amateurs. *Matter of Marhoffer*, N.Y.L.J.1/14/1985 at 13 (Sup. Ct. 1985) and N.Y.L.J. 10/31/1990 (Sup. Ct. 1990). While the underlying reasoning is less than clear, it appears that the ability to both live and work in a loft is a substantial economic benefit that the city wants to extend only to persons whose income is normally low, thus excluding both commercially successful artists and persons engaging in art as a hobby who presumably have other sources of income.

F. Art for Income Tax Purposes

Most businesses cannot immediately deduct the cost of producing their inventory. They must capitalize that cost, which means that it becomes part of the cost of the inventory which can only be recouped for tax purposes when the inventory is sold. But writers, photographers and artists need not follow that rule; they can currently deduct their costs. An artist is a person who creates a "picture, painting, sculpture, statue, etching, drawing, cartoon, graphic design, or original print edition." In making that determination, one should consider "[t]he originality and uniqueness of the item created ..." and "[t]he predominance of aesthetic value over utilitarian value of the item created...." INTERNAL REVENUE CODE OF 1986, § 263A(a), (h).

G. Conclusion

There is no universal legal definition of "art" or "artist". The definition will vary with the purpose for which the term is used. All definitions examined seem to require creativity, but the amount of creativity varies. Other conditions also vary depending on whether the term is defined to prevent imports from competing with domestic firms, to establish a right to prevent copying, to provide a subsidy to a supposedly impoverished group, to stimulate real estate prices, to assure that government does not interfere with communication, or to provide a special tax rule for people for whom the normal rule would be inappropriate because of different business conditions.

3. Why Should Art Differ from Other Tangible Personal Property? Why Should the Artist Differ from Other Persons?

Arguments for the unique nature of art fall under the heading of education in several senses, and of unequal bargaining power.

A. Benefits of Exposure to Art

Exposure to art heightens the senses. It makes one more likely to produce art. It gives one the tools to appreciate art. It spills over into functional items by creating demand that they be produced in aesthetically pleasing forms.

Because the artist is trained to observe, he is equipped to assess the world around him more astutely than others. The mirror the artist holds up to the world increases everyone's perception.

B. Education About the Past

Art is also the gateway to the past. Artifacts tell us much about the way our ancestors lived because most often these items had functions in the societies in which they appeared. In this respect, archaeology and historic preservation are twinned. Societies that had the written word may leave both written and artifact records; our knowledge of societies without writing, or whose writing has yet to be deciphered, depends on artifacts alone.

C. Conveying Messages

Art shares the written word's ability to convey messages. While those messages are pictorially coded, the pictorial message is particularly strong. Portraits may convey the wealth, power or knowledge of the subject. Genre scenes may instruct by delivering moral or practical messages like the dangers of alcohol or the potential of swindle. Still life paintings may comment on mortality.

D. Unequal Bargaining Power

Arguments for the unique nature of the artist usually spring from arguments that the artist is not compensated well enough in our society, or that her bargaining power is so minimal that she is disproportionately oppressed by others. Improving the artist's compensation and bargaining power will encourage more people to produce art as a profession, increasing its supply.

E. Market Failure

The underlying assumption of many of these arguments is that a market failure exists. Insufficient art is created or displayed; insufficient artifacts are discovered or made the subject of educational programs; there are not enough messages being conveyed pictorially; and inequalities of bargaining power in the art world are not being redressed.

Checkpoints

You should have learned that:

- There is no universal definition of "art" or "artist"; courts define these terms differently depending on the purpose for which the term is being defined.
- One definition of art is creativity of a human being that is fixed in tangible form.
- Tariff law defines art as requiring handmade creativity because such items are unlikely to compete with domestic products.
- Copyright law requires less creativity, permits mass-produced items, and does not necessarily exclude functional items in determining what is entitled to a copyright monopoly.
- First Amendment law requires that a work express a message to be entitled to constitutional protection as speech.
- Housing law may exclude commercially successful artists and amateurs to benefit artists whose income is low by allowing only professional fine artists to reside where they may both live and work.
- Income tax considers the originality and uniqueness as well as the aesthetic value of an item in considering whether its maker is an artist.
- Five reasons have been advanced justifying different rules for art and artists than for others. Art is aesthetically pleasing, conveys messages, and educates about past societies. Artists are often treated specially because they suffer from unequal bargaining power, and because there is often market failure in the art market.

Chapter 2

Freedom of Expression

Roadmap

After reading this chapter, you should understand:

- First Amendment Purposes: There are five main policy reasons behind the First Amendment: Communication to further self-governance, to seek truth and allow ideas to compete on the open market, to help humans reach their full potential, to help balance stability and change, and to promote tolerance.
- Rational Basis Scrutiny is applied to a law that does not infringe a fundamental right. The government need only show that there is some rational basis for the law.
- Strict Scrutiny applies to laws that infringe a fundamental right. The government must show a compelling interest the law serves and that there is no less restrictive means to achieve the law's purpose.
- What is considered speech: Speech is oral or written communication of ideas. Conduct is speech when it is expressive.
- Obscenity: The First Amendment does not protect obscenity. A work of art is obscene only if: (1) "the average person, applying contemporary community standards" would find that the work, taken as a whole, appeals to the prurient interest, (2) the work depicts or describes, in a patently offensive way, sexual conduct specifically defined by the applicable law, and (3) the work, taken as a whole, lacks serious literary, artistic, political, or scientific value.
- Child Pornography: The First Amendment does not protect child pornography because the government has a compelling interest in protecting children.
- Regulation by the Government: The government can limit sale and display of artwork through licensing and sign ordinances.
- Public Forum: A space traditionally available for speech and assembly, such as public streets, sidewalks, and parks.
- Limited Public Forum: A space not traditionally available for speech and assembly, but made available for that purpose by government decision.
- Nonpublic forum: Spaces not defined as public or limited public forums.
- Government as a manager: The government can sometimes limit display of art when it is acting in a managerial capacity.

- Government as funder: The government need not provide funds for the arts, but it cannot use its position as funder or landlord to dictate the content of the art displayed.
- Government as funder: Programs in which the government gives grants to fund museums and artists may take into account "general standards of decency and respect for the diverse beliefs and values of the American public" in making grants as long as those criteria do not constitute an absolute bar that would eliminate protected speech.
- Government as buyer: There are no constitutional limits restricting the government's choice of subject matter or content when it purchases art.

1. Introduction

The First Amendment is a short amendment. It states "Congress shall make no law respecting an establishment of religion, or prohibiting the free exercise thereof; or abridging the freedom of speech, or of the press; or the right of the people peaceably to assemble, and to petition the Government for a redress of grievances." Leaving aside religion, our concern in this chapter is with the intersection of art and government, such as whether a government can restrict the sale or display of art, or confer benefits on artists or museums that have strings attached to them. In later chapters we will discuss whether the government must shape private rights of action to protect free speech in areas such as copyright or trademark infringement, defamation, the right of publicity, the right of privacy or moral rights.

The usual remedy for the artist where state or local officials abridge his freedom of speech is an action under 42 U.S.C. § 1983, alleging that defendants have deprived plaintiff of constitutional rights under color of law. *Nelson v. Streeter*, 16 F.3d 145 (7th Cir. 1994).

2. First Amendment Purposes

There is little legislative history telling us the meaning of the First Amendment's few words. Most of its activity has come during the twentieth century. Interpretation of its meaning often comes from the purpose or purposes assigned to it. While they do not necessarily conflict, different commentators have seen the First Amendment with the following aims.

A. Enhanced Self-Governance

This goal assumes that communication is a necessary element of representative government. Candidates must communicate with the public to seek their votes; private individuals must communicate with other private individuals and their representatives. Representatives must communicate with their constituents and with each other. This communication is in a political context, but the courts have never confined the First Amendment to political speech, perhaps because of the difficulty of distinguishing political speech from other kinds of speech. Instead, freedom of speech applies to "public issues" defined as information about matters that would help members of society cope with their problems. While this might involve politics, it might also involve individual decision-making about matters unrelated to government, such as family practices.

B. Truth-Seeking Permits the Marketplace of Ideas to Function

One view of freedom of speech is that it is designed to reach truth. To do that, ideas compete, much like products. Freedom of speech permits all ideas to compete, with the most persuasive idea prevailing. A concomitant is that the government does not have a monopoly on the truth, so should not be able to limit the "truth" available to the public. This is not a distinctly political theory; it applies to all ideas. Critics have noted that not all ideas compete, and the objectively best idea does not always win.

C. Personal Autonomy

A more expansive theory is that of personal autonomy. It holds that humans are expressive beings. In order to reach their full potential, they must be able to express themselves. Here the emphasis is on self-fulfillment, rather than persuasion or ideas. Critics note that humans engage in many activities that denote their personal autonomy, and that there is no reason to give speech priority among those activities.

D. Balancing Stability and Change

Suppressing speech may be seen as a way to ensure stability and avoid violent change. This masks social discontent. When it eventually explodes (as it sometimes does), change is likely to be sharper than if changes were honestly debated.

E. Promoting Tolerance

Protection of speech has the value of promoting tolerance. This is especially important in a pluralistic society where people can be expected to have widely divergent views. Unlike the self-governance argument above, it is not the ideas that are protected, but their expression. This view has been criticized on grounds that there should be a limit to tolerance of speech, especially if it is intolerant speech.

The first three justifications for freedom of speech are frequently cited; the last two less so, but may be important in an individual case.

3. Economic Result of Prioritizing Expression: Subsidy for Expression

In some circumstances, the economic result of a holding that free speech trumps some other value is to give the speaker a subsidy. A photo of a celebrity on the cover of a magazine may sell magazines. If coupled with a news article about the celebrity, the magazine obtains the use of the celebrity's image free. By contrast, if the seller of artwork wants to use a celebrity's image to advertise his product, the seller must pay for the right of publicity.

To hold that a public figure cannot recover for defamation in the absence of actual malice permits more speech that damages public figures than would be the case if the same rules applied to public figures as applied to ordinary citizens. Subsidizing the media is not the purpose of free speech, but it can be a result of it.

4. First Amendment Methodology: Degree of Scrutiny

Because freedom of speech is such a fundamental right, the constitutionality of laws that regulate it may be subject to different levels of scrutiny.

A. Rational Basis Review

The constitutionality of most laws is determined under the rational basis test. Under rational basis review, the person challenging the constitutionality of the law must prove that the legislation is not directed at a legitimate government purpose. Alternatively, if the purpose is a legitimate one for that government to pursue, the challenger must prove that there is no rational basis to conclude that the law in question would achieve that purpose. This is a heavy burden. The challenger rarely wins under rational basis review.

B. Strict Scrutiny

By contrast, where the statute impinges on a fundamental right, such as regulating the content of speech, it is often subjected to strict scrutiny. Under the strict scrutiny test, the state must establish that it has a compelling interest, and the means chosen by the statute are necessary to achieve that interest. The state must also show that there are no other ways to achieve the end that restrict the fundamental right less. Yet the cases have been relatively silent on the compelling state interest in banning speech, and in discussing alternatives.

C. Intermediate Scrutiny

A compromise position is intermediate scrutiny, where some discretion is given to the state to enact a law, but not as much as under the rational basis test. The test for intermediate scrutiny is whether the law furthers an important government interest in a way that is substantially related to that interest. This level of review is more common where the law is a content-neutral regulation of speech.

5. What Is Speech?

A. Positive Tests

Oral or written communication of ideas, information or emotions are speech and, subject to the qualifications below, are protected by the First Amendment.

i. Conduct

Conduct can be speech, or it may not be speech. It is speech when it is communicative. For example, conduct was communicative when the flag was used in sculptures protesting the Vietnam War. *United States ex rel. Radich v. Criminal Court of New York*, 385 F.Supp. 165 (S.D.N.Y. 1974). The courts struck down statutes that criminalized opposition to government by displaying any flag, badge, banner or device, or that criminalized disrespect to the flag, in two cases. In one case the state could not justify the law on any ground other than suppressing dissent, *Stromberg v. California*, 283 U.S. 359 (1931). In the other the action of the defendant did not result in destruction or damage to the flag, the display was in a private art gallery whose windows were not likely to assault the eyes of passersby, and under the facts of the case there was no reasonable likelihood of a breach of the peace from use of the flag in this artwork. *United States ex rel. Radich v. Criminal Court of New York*, 385 F.Supp. 165 (S.D.N.Y. 1974). Interestingly, the person prosecuted was the gallery owner who displayed the art, a United States flag in the shape of a phallus emerging from a cross. The artist who created the artwork was not prosecuted.

Burning your draft card a generation ago communicated a protest against the war in Vietnam (though the court doubted that this was communicative, it discussed the case as though it were), but the court still upheld the constitutionality of a law criminalizing the intentional forging, altering, intentional mutilation or destruction of a draft card. The court established a four-part test for situations where the law was constitutional, but also infringed freedom of expression:

1. the rule is within the constitutional power of the government;
2. the law furthers an important government interest;
3. that governmental interest is unrelated to suppressing free expression; and
4. the incidental restriction on free expression is no greater than essential to further that interest.

While this purports to be four criteria, the first criterion applies to every statute alleged to be unconstitutional. Without the power to enact the law, the law cannot stand.

The court found that the government had a valid purpose in issuing and requiring people not to destroy their draft cards. The smooth administration of the Selective Service System enabled Congress to raise an army, a power within the constitution's legislative purview. The requirement that one keep one's draft card facilitated quick determination of persons who failed to register, or emergency mobilizations, and deterred deceptive use of the card. The restriction was not directed specifically toward expression, as it likewise criminalized the private destruction of the cards. The court perceived no alternate means that would restrict speech less than prohibiting their destruction. *United States v. O'Brien*, 391 U.S. 367 (1968). One should note that there are many effective alternative protest means that do not fall afoul of the statute, like burning a copy or a photo of your draft card.

Twenty years later, the court held unconstitutional a Texas statute that prohibited defacing an American flag in a way that the person knows would offend at least one person observing it. The court distinguished *O'Brien* on grounds that communication was an essential element of the crime; if no one observed the defacing, there was no offense. *Texas v. Johnson*, 491 U.S. 387 (1989). The same result followed for a U.S. law that did not require specific communication on the grounds that burning a flag is essentially communication. *United States v. Eichman*, 486 U.S. 310 (1990).

Even if the person's actions constitute communicative speech, the protections that speech receives may be reduced by the circumstances. Soldiers in a combat zone, incarcerated prisoners, and school students do not give up all their First Amendment rights, but they may have reduced speech protections because of the perceived need for the orderly administration of those institutions. Compare Tinker v. Des Moines Independent Community School Dist., 393 U.S. 503 (1969), where students suspended for wearing black armbands to school to protest the Vietnam war were ordered reinstated because the court did not believe that their suspension was necessary to the good order of the school, with Morse v. Frederick, 551 U.S. 393 (2007), allowing suspension of a student who held a banner reading "Bong Hits 4 Jesus" at a school outing, saying that schools can prohibit speech encouraging drug use.

ii. Art

Applied to art, communication is by pictures, because until recently, art had no words. Pictures can communicate only the object depicted, or they can represent concepts or actions. Certain representations are widely accepted, such as a red rose for romantic love, a doorway or teenager for transitions, or a skull, insect, or rotting fruit for mortality. Other symbols may be peculiar to a school or group of artists. Beautiful landscapes communicated the majesty of the American continent and a wish that nature be left in its pristine state for the Hudson River school. Vertiginous perspective may signal the loneliness and insignificance of man for surrealists. Some representations are personal to particular artists.

Alternatively, as Freud once observed, "Sometimes a cigar is just a cigar."

If all conduct is communicative, then it follows that all conduct is protected by the First Amendment. This goes too far. Distinguishing communicative conduct from non-communicative conduct is often difficult. Communicative conduct is conduct where the actor intends to communicate a particularized message, and where there is a strong likelihood that the message will be understood by those apprised of the conduct. Thus, the representations detailed above are likely to be sufficiently particularized to merit protection, while the artist with more personalized represenations might need to argue forcefully for the likelihood that viewers will understand the message.

B. Negative Tests

Certain categories of speech are not protected by the First Amendment. Advocacy of imminent illegal action or fighting words thrown at a hostile audience are seldom encountered in the art world. Likewise, the First Amendment will not protect from criminal prosecution or civil liability a person who obtains money by falsely claiming that the painting he is selling is by Rembrandt. The main areas of art law interest are in the field of sexually explicit matters.

i. Obscenity

a. Introduction

Obscenity often comes (un)dressed as art. Art with sexual content is protected art, and artists have been depicting nudes of both sexes for millenia, sometimes *in flagrante delicto*. When the art slides over the line to become obscenity, that art is not protected by the First Amendment. This apparently seems so self-evident that few commentators or courts have chosen to seriously justify it. Mostly justifications are referred to as asides like "void of exposition of ideas" or " ... such slight social value as a step to truth that any benefit ... is clearly outweighed by the social interest in order and morality." *Chaplinsky v. New Hampshire*, 315 U.S. 568 (1942). Such a statement assumes that the only underlying purposes of the First Amendment are self-government and the search for truth, and do not explain why suppressing the sale or advertising of obscenity contributes to either order or morality. If it could be proven that the viewing of obscenity frequently led the viewer to commit crimes, that might justify prohibiting its sale. But how can that justification be squared with a person's constitutional right to possess obscene matter? *Stanley v. Georgia*, 394 U.S. 497 (1969).

b. What Is Obscenity?

1. Historical Background: Britain Without a Written Constitution

What could the government prohibit in a country that lacks a First Amendment to its constitution? In a lovely mid-Victorian opinion filled with paternalism, the court stated that an obscene book could be seized and its seller prosecuted. The standard for obscenity was whether the work would suggest to anyone thoughts of a libidinous character. The court specifically references young people of both sexes, though it appears that such a libidinous appeal to a young person of either sex would be sufficient to classify a work as obscene. *Regina v. Hicklin*, (1867–68) L.R. 3 Q.B. 360 (April 29, 1868). The Victorian test was whether the most susceptible members of society would be sexually inspired. Very little is probably required to induce a teenaged boy to think about sex.

2. *United States Law*

Obscenity is afforded no First Amendment protection. It can be prohibited by the government. To determine if a work of art is obscene the court uses a three-prong obscenity test: (1) whether "the average person, applying contemporary community standards" would find that the work, taken as a whole, appeals to the prurient interest, (2) whether the work depicts or describes, in a patently offensive way, sexual conduct specifically defined by the applicable law, and (3) whether the work, taken as a whole, lacks serious literary, artistic, political, or scientific value. *Miller v. California*, 413 U.S. 15 (1973); *Roth v. United States*, 354 U.S. 476 (1957). If the trier of facts finds all three criteria, the work is obscene.

A. Contemporary Community Standards. The first *Miller* test applies two artificial standards. We must imagine the sensibilities of the "average person" and "contemporary community standards." The average person calls on the trier of fact to consider neither the most libertine nor the most prudish person in the community, but a hypothetical average person in that community. Would that average person consider the work offensive using contemporary community standards?

But what community? Not a national community, but a local community. Use of a local community creates a nonuniform national standard. What might be obscene in Salt Lake City might not be obscene in San Francisco. Artists who wish to display their artwork at any museum in the country, or sell their art on the internet, must adopt the strictest standard that would exist in any community nationwide. Alternatively, the artist could produce a different product aligned with each community's standards, but must assure that work designed for San Diego is not exhibited in a community with stricter standards. The product must be tailored to its market. This will not work with the internet, as the internet is the same in all communities. The only feasible solution for the artist selling over the internet is to conform to the strictest community's standards.

i. Imported Property. But which local community? Suppose that I import a painting from Europe. It may first arrive in the United States at the port of New York, Los Angeles, San Diego or any number of ports of entry. I may be unable to predict at which port of entry it will arrive. A customs official may seize it as obscene. The painting is addressed to me in San Diego. Both the majority and the concurring opinions in such a case thought that the local community whose standards determine whether imports are obscene was the port of entry into the United States, not the place to which the imported item is addressed. That decision was taken on the basis of statutory interpretation, rather than constitutional law. It was based in part on practical grounds, as large amounts of putatively obscene materials are seized at each port of entry and their cases consolidated. That court case cannot be subdivided and portions sent to the courts for the residences of each of the addressees, who in this case were located in 48 of the 50 states. The decision was justified in part by the fact that the offense in that case was importing obscene material, and the place of importation was the port of entry. *United States v. Various Articles of Obscene Merch.*, 562 F.2d 185 (2d Cir. 1977). If the purpose of refusing to protect obscenity under the First Amendment is because of an anticipated harm, that harm might be either to the viewer, or to someone who would be harmed by the viewer. In either case, the harm is likely to occur at the place to which the obscene material is addressed, rather than the port of entry. Most ports of entry are large cities with more permissible community standards than the country as a whole.

ii. Artwork Created Domestically. Assuming that there is no import, the question remains, which local community's standards do you use? Your author lives in a 100-home subdivision, called La Jolla Shores Heights, which in turn is part of a 35,000-person area named La Jolla. La Jolla is part of the city of San Diego. The city of San Diego is in the county of San Diego and the San Diego-Carlsbad-San Marcos Metropolitan Statistical Area, which is separated from the Los Angeles-Long Beach-Anaheim Metropolitan Statistical Area's urban sprawl only by the fortuitous location of the Camp Pendleton Marine Base. All are located in the State of California. Which is the local community to determine whether a painting I am trying to sell from my house is obscene? In discussing which community standards to use, the court stated that the court should get an approximate average of the community standards of the entire area covered by the court. *United States v. Various Articles of Obscene Merch.*, 562 F.2d 185 (2d Cir. 1977). This means that if my case is tried in the state Superior Court, it would be the community standards of San Diego County, the geographic limits of the court; if tried in the federal court, the Southern District of California covers both San Diego and Imperial counties, so it would be the community standards of a larger and more diverse area.

iii. The Problem of Averages. Of course, one cannot average standards. Standards do not have a mathematical nature. The task is to find the average person in the community, and apply that person's standards.

iv. The Internet and Local Standards. The internet seems inimical to government attempts to regulate obscenity because of the obligation to define obscenity by contemporary local community standards. Any attempt to set a national standard for the internet causes problems. In *Reno v. American Civil Liberties Union*, 521 U.S. 844 (1997), the Court struck down the Communications Decency Act of 1996, 47 U.S.C. §§ 230, 560–561, that criminalized making available indecent material on the internet knowing that it could be accessed by persons under 18 because, among other reasons, the law did not allow for local community standards. Instead, the law set a national standard. The law's restriction does not apply to only one geographic area; a person could be reading these materials anywhere in the world.

v. Material as a Whole. The first test requires that the material be looked at as a whole, but it does not define what the "whole" means. That requirement is intended to assure that portions of the work are not taken out of context, as in *Wojnarowicz v. American Family Ass'n*, 745 F. Supp. 130 (S.D.N.Y. 1990), where defendant enlarged particularly salacious portions of an artwork, thereby presenting an inaccurate impression of the entire work. It is not clear that the whole work is always circumscribed by a single frame, but that was the holding in *Cincinnati v. Contemporary Arts Center*, 57 Ohio Misc.2d 15, 566 N.E.2d 214 (Ohio Mun. 1990). The museum displayed Robert Mapplethorpe photographs in an art gallery. The court determined that each individual photograph was a whole. Looking at the entire exhibit of photographs was not looking at the work as a whole. If five of the photographs were found to be obscene, they could not be rescued by a finding that the show as a whole was not obscene. On the other hand, the court's finding that five of the photographs were obscene did not taint the remaining 170 photos exhibited.

The court did not set forth a rule that all work within a single frame is the work as a whole. That was the result in this case because there was no evidence that more than one work was part of an integrated artistic plan. The works had been sold separately, and borrowed from different owners for the show. There was no evidence that they were produced to be shown together, as would have been the case for a triptych altarpiece. There was no evidence that scholarly opinion regarded the 175 works in the show as a single, unified work. The catalogue of the show omitted some pieces, and made no effort to show the photographs in relation to each other.

City of St. George v. Turner, 813 P.2d 1188 (Utah App. 1991), *aff'd* 860 P.2d 929 (Utah 1993) presents conflicting views about what constitutes the work "as a whole." The defendant, who was both the owner of the record store and the artist who prepared the work, testified that one of two separate sheets hanging together was prepared four years before the other, and that each sheet was a separate work. He also testified that each sheet was separate from the record store. The dissenting judge evaluated each sheet separately, while the majority believed that the entire record store was the work because of stylistic similarity between all works in the store.

Taking the work as a whole may make it either more or less obscene. *United States v. 113 Prints*, 128 F.Supp.280 (D.C. Md. 1955) involved a challenge to the seizure by customs of 113 prints of erotic portions of classical paintings and sculptures on cards that were unbound. They were accompanied by an extensive German scholarly text that was separable from the prints. The court held the prints obscene, considering them in isolation from the text because the text and the prints could be separated, despite the fact that the text was meant to be read with the prints and would have been difficult to understand without them. The court did not follow its reasoning to its logical conclusion and consider each print as a separate work on the grounds that each print could be separated from each of the others, finding some of them obscene and others not obscene. The court further commented, in response to the argument that many of the original sculptures of which the prints were reproductions had been displayed without incident in many museums, that the museum displays were in the context of other art products of antiquity without sexual content, whereas the 113 prints represented a concentration of work focusing on the erotic.

It thus appears that what is the work "as a whole" very much depends on the surrounding facts. Context is important.

vi. Burden of Proof. The burden of proof in these cases may be important. The government does not have the burden of proving what community standards might be, but it would be a foolish government attorney who did not come to trial with experts and sociological survey evidence as to what this community accepts.

The fact that comparably suggestive material is readily available from other stores in the locality is not conclusive of community standards (and may not be admissible in some jurisdictions), but a wise lawyer challenging the constitutionality of an obscenity statute would certainly wish to introduce evidence of availability. Perhaps more persuasive than the ability to buy comparable material would be finding it in the collection of the public library or the local museum.

vii. What is the Prurient Interest? The first test also requires that the material appeal to a prurient interest. This boils down to whether the obscene materials are designed to appeal to a lewd, leering, and perverted interest in sex. Material that appeals to a person's normal, natural and healthy interest in sex is not obscene. This distinction between healthy and perverted interest in sex will usually require competing testimony by perversion experts, as it is unlikely that either the judge or the jurors will admit that they are perverts, and will likely lead to unpredictable results. Before the matter goes to a jury, the judge is obligated to determine whether the material sufficiently depicts hard-core sexual conduct. In *City of St. George v. Turner*, 813 P.2d 1188 (Utah App. 1991), *aff'd* 860 P.2d 929 (Utah 1993), the court held that crudely drawn, blurry and indistinct drawings of female genitals are too sketchy and abstract to appeal to a shameful or morbid interest in sex. A dissenting judge disagreed, believing that it was within the exclusive province of the jury to determine what would appeal to the prurient interest in that community.

B. Specified Conduct Displayed Offensively. The second test for pornography has two requirements. The law must specifically define the sexual conduct to be prohibited, and that conduct must be displayed in an offensive way. The court enumerates a non-exclusive list of things that a state can prohibit, such as depictions of intercourse, masturbation, excretion and genitalia. But a state cannot prohibit all depictions of these things because the depiction may or may not be obscene. It is only obscene if it is depicted in a patently offensive way. Rabelais said that Gargantua was conceived when his parents "played the animal with two backs," certainly a depiction of intercourse, but unlikely to be viewed as patently offensive today. It might be wondered if there is a difference between "displayed in an offensive way" in the second test and "contemporary community standards" in the first test.

The Supreme Court criticized the vagueness of a similar standard in *Reno v. American Civil Liberties Union*, 521 U.S. 844 (1997), which invalidated provisions of the Communications Decency Act of 1996 criminalizing transmission of any indecent or offensive message knowing that it might be received by a person under eighteen. It distinguished the second test from the statute overturned there by pointing out that the second test has another requirement, that of a statute that specifically defines the conduct prohibited.

It also pointed out that where the standard for violation is difficult to ascertain, there are special First Amendment problems because people have a tendency to be overly cautious and not exercise their full rights. This has a chilling effect on free speech. The chilling effect is even clearer when the sanctions are criminal.

The "offensive way" language directly contradicts most First Amendment jurisprudence. Generally, the fact that an audience is likely to be outraged or incensed is not a criterion permitting the government to ban speech unless the speech reaches the status of "fighting words." "First Amendment rights are not subject to the heckler's veto." *Nelson v. Streeter*, 16 F.3d 145 (7th Cir. 1994). From that one must deduce that the offense must be an objective offense, not one dependent on any particular audience.

C. Serious Artistic Value. Even if the work meets the first and second tests, it will still not be obscene if, taken as a whole, the work has serious literary, political, scientific or artistic value. In the case of artwork, that is likely to be serious artistic value. This is another area ripe for expert testimony. Again, one considers the work as a whole, so one horrendous section may be saved by the rest of the work.

This third test does not depend on contemporary community standards. The courts set a national floor for value. *Reno v. American Civil Liberties Union*,

521 U.S. 844 (1997). It is unlikely that the court meant to make the standard timeless, but it is clear that it meant to prevent one locality from restricting a work that had serious artistic value, at least for most of the country.

i. What You Can and Cannot Do with Obscene Materials. A person has a constitutional right to possess obscene materials. *Stanley v. Georgia*, 394 U.S. 497 (1969). However, there is no constitutional right to sell or deliver obscenity. *United States v. Reidel,* 402 U.S. 351 (1971). Which leads to the interesting question, how is one to possess them if no one has the right to sell or deliver them? If one is an artist, one could create them. We have no guidance from the courts about whether there is a constitutional right to create obscenity. One might argue that creation is the first step toward sale or delivery, but it is also the first step toward possession. While this is an interesting conundrum, it is not very practical; few artists will create obscenity if they can neither sell nor deliver it.

The court has made it clear that it is not unconstitutional for a state to ban obscenity even if that obscenity is never shown to a minor. The rationale is that obscenity could have a corrupting effect on adults that might lead to antisocial behavior, so states can ban its display under the police power. *Paris Adult Theatre I v. Slaton*, 413 U.S. 39 (1973).

Classifying something as obscene clearly goes to the content of the item. But since obscenity is not protected speech, obscenity does not qualify for First Amendment protection.

ii. Child Pornography

A government may restrict artistic depictions of children's sexual parts or sexual activity even more than it can restrict obscenity. The court's description in one case was a photograph that "depicts a nude male adolescent posed in a sexually explicit position." If this involved an adult, it probably would not have been defined as obscene under the test above because of a lack of lewdness. *Osborne v. Ohio*, 495 U.S. 103 (1990).

The government regulation must pass strict scrutiny. That is usually pretty easy because the governmental interest is strong and the alternatives do not seem very effective, but let's begin with the paradigm case. New York passed a statute prohibiting the promotion of a sexual performance by a child. A child is defined as someone under the age of 16. Sexual performance includes "actual or simulated sexual intercourse, deviate sexual intercourse, sexual bestiality, masturbation, sado-masochistic abuse or lewd exhibition of the genitals." The court upheld the constitutionality of the statute. The state's compelling interest was the protection of the physical and psychological well-being of children. The court said that being involved in child pornography damages a child physically, emotionally and mentally and noted that nearly all states had criminalized it. It also found the sale and distribution of child pornography further harms the child because the depiction may have an indefinite life, and the money to be made from the distribution encourages people to subject more children to abuse for profit. When there is advertising of the materials, the advertising simply increases the danger. To the extent that child pornography has any artistic value, it is modest, and could be met by portraying a person who is in fact older, but looks younger. *Ferber v. New York*, 458 U.S. 747 (1982).

Ferber held constitutional a prohibition on the advertising and distribution of child pornography rather specifically defined. In a later case, the court added that a prohibition on possession of child pornography was constitutional for the reasons set forth above and because it was a way of attacking the potential indefinite life of the harm to the child by inducing persons to destroy the pornography in order to escape prosecution. *Osborne v. Ohio*, 495 U.S. 103 (1990). Thus a clear distinction emerges between obscenity and child pornography: a person has a constitutional right to possess obscene material, but can be criminally prosecuted for possessing child pornography.

The government cannot criminalize depictions of persons who are in fact adults but appear to be children, or computer-generated images of children that are not real children. Despite the argument that simulated child pornography made it easier to convince children to engage in abusive sexual contact and the argument that it would make real child pornography easier to prosecute, the court held statutes criminalizing the possession of computerized images or adults who look like children unconstitutional. *Ashcroft v. Free Speech Coalition*, 535 U.S. 234 (2002). The court also questioned, but did not decide, whether a statute that pegged the age of majority for child porn purposes at an age greater than the age for statutory rape or the age at which marriage was permitted in the jurisdiction, could survive constitutional challenge. It did not say why the question was raised, but it was probably because a person old enough to be permitted to engage in sexual activity is a person that the jurisdiction defines as not being likely to be damaged by participating in the creation of pornography.

Nonetheless, the government can constitutionally ban both the pandering and solicitation of child pornography, so that a person may be punished for soliciting or advertising child pornography, even if there is in fact no such pornography in the possession of either the inquirer or the promoter. *United States v. Williams*, 553 U.S. 285 (2008). Presumably, an attempt to extend that provision to inquiring about computer-generated images that resemble child pornography would be unconstitutional.

It is appropriate to note some of the substantial differences between obscenity and child pornography. Obscenity involves speech that is worthless; child pornography involves speech that is usually the result of harm to a child. Obscenity requires material that appeals to a prurient interest; child pornography does not. Obscenity requires that it be a prurient interest of an average member of the local community; child pornography may appeal to the prurient interest of the most perverted member of a community. Obscenity considers the whole work; child pornography does not. Even the most lewd work can be redeemed from obscenity by artistic value; artistic value never enters the calculus for child pornography.

iii. National Security

Initially, the government could criminally punish a speaker if the speech had a tendency to harm public welfare. This rather broad test gave way to Justice Holmes' test that speech could only be punished if it created a clear and present danger that it would bring about evils that Congress has the right to prevent. His dictum that no one has the right to falsely yell "Fire!" in a crowded theater with impunity was not really relevant to the case, and the case itself, which involved a prosecution for advocating resisting the draft, resulted in a conviction, but it paved the way for a tightening of the requirements for punishing speakers. *Schenck v. United States*, 249 U.S. 47 (1919).

By the Vietnam War, resistance to the draft was widespread. Advocacy of anti-government action was common, as well as slogans like "Don't trust anyone over 30." The current strict test, that speech could not be punished unless it is directed to and likely to incite imminent lawless action, was enunciated in *Brandenburg v. Ohio*, 395 U.S. 444 (1969), overturning a criminal syndicalism law that merely required advocacy of force or the violation of law. The test requires that the speaker advocate lawlessness now, and that there is a reasonable likelihood that lawlessness will quickly break out as a result. The likely result is that speech cannot be punished unless it incites a riot, so most visual artists are quite safe from criminal prosecution as a result of expressing themselves in their usual media.

6. Government and Protected Work: Government as Regulator

The fact that work is protected by the First Amendment because it is speech and it does not fall within obscenity, child pornography or any of the other categories discussed above does not necessarily free it from the government. The state may still have interests in the work or its production, display or sale that must be balanced against the interests of the artist or the owner.

One might distinguish situations based on the role that the government is assuming in the particular transaction. The government may act as regulator; as promoter of culture, usually by making display space available for the art; as buyer, lessee or donee of the art; as lessor or underwriter of a museum; or as talent developer through the provision of grant money. In general, whatever its role, the government may impose reasonable restrictions on the time, place and manner that art is displayed or sold, but the emphasis must be placed on the reasonableness of the restrictions.

It is clear that a governmental unit can neither prohibit nor criminalize the exhibition of art that qualifies as speech.

The more difficult question is whether the government can limit its sale or display.

A. Of Vendors

Many cities have ordinances organizing sales on public streets, and collecting revenue while doing so. New York's ordinance has been particularly litigated because New York has limited the number of vendor's licenses to less than 1,200, so there is a five-year wait to obtain a vendor's license. A person who sells print media, such as a newspaper, is not required to obtain a license; a person who sells art must compete with other non-food vendors, such as sellers of t-shirts or CDs, for a permit.

Artists who wish to enjoin enforcement of the licensing system face formidable procedural challenges. A preliminary injunction will not normally issue unless the party seeking the injunction would suffer irreparable harm in its absence. This is not a major hurdle, because any invasion of free speech rights is considered irreparable harm. *Brooklyn Inst. of Arts & Sciences v. New York*, 64 F. Supp. 2d 184 (E.D.N.Y. 1999). The more serious difficulty is that the artists in *Bery v. New York*, 97 F.3d 689 (2d Cir 1996), were seeking to enjoin the implementation of a municipal ordinance requiring licensing to sell art on the street. To receive a preliminary injunction, they needed to show a likelihood of success on the merits at trial.

The artists convinced the court that the system was not content neutral, as it discriminated between communication by print and communication by art, so the court should apply strict scrutiny to the ordinance. The court was not very clear about why this law was not content neutral, and it might appear to the casual observer that the discrimination here was not based on content, but on the medium used. The point was not important in that case because the court analyzed the ordinance under the rules for content neutral regulation.

Content neutral regulation can be imposed to restrict the time, manner and place of speech if two conditions are satisfied. First, It must be narrowly tailored to implement an important government interest. Second, it must allow alternate means of communicating the message.

The important government interest here is keeping the city's streets safe and free from congestion. That could be done by regulating where vendors could set up in relationship to the street or the width of the sidewalk. Those rules also existed.

The court in *Bery* found that there was no alternate means of communicating the message. Commercial galleries were generally not available to the plaintiff artists because of the subject matter of their art, and they would disdain commercial galleries because of their message and because it reaches a different audience. The court confirmed a consent decree in which the city promised not to enforce its licensing law on sellers of art.

The matter did not end there. Subsequent cases took up the question of whether the work sold was sufficiently expressive to warrant First Amendment protection. 4" x 4" tiles with cork on one side and stock photographs on the other side of Marilyn Monroe, sports arenas, and retail shops were expressive because they were not usable as coasters, *People v. Lee*, 19 Misc. 3d 791, 860 N.Y.S.2d 845 (Crim. Ct. NYC 2008); decks of playing cards showing pictures and names of military and political figures involved with the war in Iraq were not. *People v. Saul*, 3 Misc 2d 260 (NYC Crim. Ct. 2004). Most surprising, the court held that a trained artist who painted in graffiti style on t-shirts and hats did not do so primarily for expressive purposes. The dissenting judge thought distinguishing whether something was communicative based on it being painted on wearing apparel rather than on canvas or board was artificial. *Mastrovincenzo v. City of New York*, 435 F.3d 78 (2d Cir. 2006).

One might well wonder at the court's obsession with trying to define art as "expressive conduct," in light of the fact that cases have protected entertainment forms such as topless dancing under the First Amendment. *Doran v. Salem Inn, Inc.*, 422 U.S. 922 (1975). Yet the problem in these cases comes down to pigeon-holing: if not protected by the First Amendment, these so-called artists are selling goods on the street without the required license. Given the long wait for a license, the temptation is great to re-characterize anything possible as art. To defend against the complete gutting of the licensing regulation, the courts have engaged in a "primary purpose" test trying to determine whether the peddler was primarily selling ideas or merchandise. Unlike Justice Mosk's opinion in *Comedy III Productions, Inc. v. Gary Saderup, Inc.*, 25 Cal. 4th 387, 21 P.3d 797 (2001), discussed under the Right of Publicity below, the courts have not suggested any criteria for making this decision. Possible criteria might include the professional training of the seller, the seller's intention, or comparison of the cost with similar items that lack the art.

Bery was an easy case because the art was produced on a traditional artistic medium that was not similar to non-artistic merchandise. It was not produced at the moment of sale, but had been made earlier. The court assumes that it is the artists themselves who are the vendors, but nothing in the opinion requires this. *Mastrovincenzo* was produced on the spot by a trained artist on articles of clothing. In both cases, it appears that the works were unique. In *Lee* and *Saul*, the images were presumably pre-printed and mass-produced on playing cards or coaster-like items, with results the opposite of what one would expect. The playing cards with faces of the major players in the war in Iraq are held to be insufficiently expressive to be protected by the First Amendment, while the almost-coasters with stock photos are held to be expressive because the judge makes a finding of fact that they are not really usable as coasters. If there are principles at work here, they need to be articulated.

B. Sign Ordinances

Another area that has fomented much litigation is the conflict between free speech and the community's desire to regulate its aesthetics. These cases typically arise where the local government regulates advertising billboards or signage on buildings. A community often limits the size of a billboard or the proximity of one billboard to another. Such regulations are normally constitutional because of the strong governmental interest in allowing the community to determine its own aesthetics, and because these regulations do not restrict the content of the billboards. Likewise, it is common for local governments to regulate the signage permitted to be attached to a building by limiting its size and the number of signs permitted based on the amount of street frontage that the building occupies. Usually, these ordinances require the property occupier to obtain a permit before erecting the sign or billboard. Building owners sometimes avoid these restrictions by purchasing a truck, painting it with the desired advertising, and parking it more or less permanently in the desired location.

These forms of regulation are constitutionally permitted provided that the ordinance is stated in sufficiently objective terms to determine that the regulation is in fact content neutral. In *City of Indio v. Arroyo*, 143 Cal. App.3d 151, 191 Cal. Rptr. 565 (1983), the court struck down an ordinance giving the city planner wide discretion to assure the sign's compatibility with the aesthetics of the building and the surrounding area. The planner was directed to consider compatible design, simplicity and sign effectiveness in making his determination. The ordinance was challenged by the owner of the building who commissioned a mural on its wall and who disclaimed the political motivation behind the mural. The court allowed the owner to assert the First Amendment right despite the owner's apparent lack of interest in making a political statement, on analogy to a newspaper owner's ability to assert freedom of speech rights in advertisements purchased in his papers. After commenting that the ordinance seemed directed at commercial advertising and was overbroad when applied to a mural, the court held that the unlimited discretion granted to the planning director made the ordinance unconstitutional on its face.

7. Government as Promoter of Culture

There are numerous cases where government officials have made space available for artistic endeavors, then revoked permission to use that space once the officials had seen the work. As the decision is clearly based on the content of the work, one might assume that such government action would be unconstitutional. The cases are not so clear.

A. Public Forum, Limited Public Forum, or Nonpublic Forum

The court has distinguished three types of space owned by the government. A public forum and a limited or designated public forum receive much First Amendment protection; a nonpublic forum receives much less. Courts do not consistently apply this analysis, and often do not even discuss the kind of forum involved.

A public forum is defined as space traditionally available for speech and assembly, such as public streets, sidewalks and parks. Perhaps the archetypical public forum would be the Roman forum, where speakers have debated public issues since the days of the Republic. The internet is not a public forum because it is not a traditional forum. *United States v. American Library Ass'n, Inc.*, 539 U.S. 194 (2003). To limit expressive activity in a public forum, the law must be either a content-neutral time, place and manner restriction, or it must pass strict scrutiny.

Art and other forms of expression can be limited by reasonable time, place and manner restrictions. The restriction is permitted if the regulation furthers an important or substantial governmental interest and the governmental interest is unrelated to the suppression of free expression, i.e. the restriction is content neutral. Restrictions on speech and expression cannot be greater than essential to the furtherance of the governmental interest. Problems with these restrictions generally arise in determining if a restriction is content neutral, and if the restriction on speech is no greater than essential to the furtherance of that interest.

A limited or defined public forum is a space not traditionally available for speech and assembly, but that is made available for that purpose by government decision. For example, the lobby of a government building made available for art exhibits would be a limited public forum. An airport terminal is not a limited public forum, even though it has been made accessible for many people at the same time and even though it may display artwork, because it was made available for transportation purposes, rather than for communication. This is a distinction that does not work well, as all limited public fora are primarily designed for other purposes.

The government can decide to remove the limited public forum from its availability for speech and assembly, but otherwise its regulation must conform to the requirements of regulation of a public forum.

All other spaces are nonpublic fora. Buildings such as the jail, the police station or city hall are nonpublic fora unless the government invites the public to speak and assemble there. Even in nonpublic fora, the government may not discriminate on grounds of content, but it is not held to the other restrictions on government action.

B. Open Corridors

A space in the lobby of Chicago's Daley Civic Center was made available for citizens to display art. John Sefick submitted a general description of the work he proposed to display, which was accepted. When the work was installed, it verbally satirized the mayor. It was first covered with a blanket, and later removed. The court commented that a public agency is not obligated to provide display space, but if it does, it must make the space available to all points of view. The city argued that the removal was not based on content, but was based on the fact that Sefick did not fully disclose in his application what he would exhibit. The court found that the predominant reason for revocation was content, as Sefick's two previous works also varied from their proposal, and held the removal unconstitutional. In doing so, the court did not analyze the type of forum involved, but applied the rules for public, rather than nonpublic, fora. *Sefick v. City of Chicago*, 485 F.Supp. 644 (N.D. Ill. 1979).

The largest number of cases have not referred to artwork that the government official in charge of the space finds objectionable because of politics or the words the viewers hear. In most cases, there is the visual display of nudity that falls short of obscenity. A typical case involves a faculty art show at a state college where a faculty member submits nudes in suggestive positions. The show is not presented in a locked art gallery, but in a public space through which persons who have no interest in art must pass in their ordinary business.

In the most famous of these cases, *Piarowski v. Illinois Community College*, 759 F.2d 625 (7th Cir. 1985), Judge Posner believed that he had to balance the managerial discretion of the public entity against the free speech rights of the artist. He noted that the college also had free speech rights, in this case the right not to have the speech of the chair of the art department attributed to the college as its official speech. But the case was ultimately easy because the college had an enclosed art gallery on the fourth floor of the same building to which it offered to move either the offending pieces, or the entire show, but the artist declined both offers. The court held that under those circumstances, removing the offending works was not a First Amendment violation.

In a similar case where suggestive nudes were placed along a passageway in the Student Union where people, including children, passed in their daily routines and where no alternative space was offered in which the offending work could be exhibited, the court unduly minimized the artist's expressiveness, dwelt on the college's right to provide an orderly place, and seemed to find the trump card in the privacy right of passersby not to be confronted by visual images. *Close v. Lederle*, 424 F.2d 988 (1st Cir 1970).

But the college did not ban all visual images from the corridor. It may have banned only those images to which people objected, a clear First Amendment violation because freedom of speech cannot depend on the reaction of the listener. Or it may have banned those paintings that college officials thought would reasonably offend someone or be inappropriate for children, a decision which appears to be content-based.

As to whether the art is sufficiently expressive to warrant First Amendment protection, the court conveniently disregarded the titles of the works. A painting of a naked teenager may have limited expressive content (absent fuller description than the court provided), but that content increases significantly when you know that titles are "I'm only 12 and already my mother's lover wants me" and "I am the only virgin in my school."

These cases taken together raise the question of whether sound or vision is more intrusive to the person passing through the space, and the opinions generally think that the visuals are more intrusive. That judgment may be questioned. It may depend on the volume and clarity of the sound compared to the size and clarity of the visual presentation.

i. Alternative Space

One may question the role of alternative space. Where the government offers to display the work in an alternative space, it should be a comparable alternative space. Granted that a space on a public corridor is more advantageous than a space in an enclosed room because it will be seen by more people, just as being displayed in the MoMA annex in Queens will not attract the crowd that display in the main museum building in Manhattan would, this factor should seldom be determinative unless the artist can establish that the lack of attention from the casual crowd would cause significant harm to him. On the other hand, if conditions in the enclosed gallery are significantly worse than those in the corridor, such as defects in illumination or lack of places to sit, the alternative space may not be comparable.

ii. The Argument for Free Speech Rights of the Government

An analogous case is *Claudio v. United States*, 836 F. Supp. 1230 (E.D.N.C. 1993). Claudio requested permission under a statute designed to make space in public buildings available for cultural purposes to exhibit a painting for a month in the entrance lobby of the Raleigh Federal Building near the security station. There was no discussion of the content of the painting. Claudio created a painting in the shape of a cross that depicted a naked woman with a coat hanger and a fetus, presumably depicting an abortion. It is unclear whether the artist was taking a stand for or against legalized abortion. As soon as the art was unveiled, people began gathering in front of the painting, impeding ingress to the building and the operation of the security station. The government revoked Claudio's revocable license for the exhibit. The court held that the government could revoke the license because the artwork was in the direct line of vision of anyone who entered the building and could not be avoided as people passed through security, basically relying on a "captive audience" theory. The court recognized the balancing of the right to freedom of expression and one's right to be left alone. The court decided the work did not leave people alone and its removal did not violate the artist's First Amendment protection. It also commented that the work might be interpreted as speech by the government because of its attachment to the government building, then went on to declare (without providing any authority) that the lobby of the federal building was a nonpublic forum, despite the federal statute that invited applications for use by the general public.

The supposed conflict between the free speech rights of the artist and the free speech rights of the government in most cases strikes me as non-existent. The exhibited artist clearly has free speech rights, but the government in these cases is arguing a negative speech right—the right not to have speech imputed to it that it does not believe. The line of reasoning goes that the display of art is the approval of that art, even more so where the artist is a government employee. It is doubtful if most people think that the display of art endorses that art, except that a display by a museum or in a place where there is a competition for the display space implies a judgment about artistic quality. How significant the artistic superiority of the displayed piece may be is hidden from the general public, because the public does not know what art might have been competing for that display space.

Nor should the fact that the art was produced by a government employee attribute that content to the government. No one in academia would suggest that the government should display only artworks with whose message it agrees. There are so many instances to the contrary that the general public should not believe it either.

Courts have yet to determine whether the government may remove art that is protected speech from an enclosed gallery where there are no involuntary spectators.

iii. Government Management Obligations

There is, however, one aspect of these cases that does not get much mention. In most of these cases, the display of art is not the principal governmental use of the space. In *Claudio*, the principal use of the display space was as an entry hall to maintain security over the building; in *Close* and *Piarowski*, the principal use of the space was either as a passageway or a food court. The government has a managerial interest in assuring that the principal use of the space is predominant.

The conflict that seems more genuine is between the artist's right to freedom of speech and the audience's right to not listen. In most cases, the audience can exercise its right to not listen by simply moving away. In the case of a space devoted to other uses, members of the audience may not simply move away without neglecting the other business for which they came. Still, one retains the ability to look away if there is something that is visually displeasing.

In *Serra v. U.S. General Services Admin.*, 847 F.2d 1045 (2d Cir. 1988), the court looked at whether the removal of government-owned artwork from federal property violated the freedom of expression of the artist. The artwork in question was commissioned by the U.S. under its requirement that it devote .5% of the construction cost of a new building to artwork. Unlike the previous cases where the installation was temporary, it must have been the assumption of both Serra and the GSA that the art would be permanently placed in the plaza, though the contract does not so specify. The artwork was a large solid steel arc 12 feet tall and 120 feet long that was installed in a way that blocked a third of Federal Plaza in Manhattan from the remainder of the plaza, forcing pedestrians who wanted to go from one side to the other to walk around it. The sculpture initially received negative feedback from the community, but was kept in place for six years before removal. The court said that Serra relinquished his free expression rights when he sold the art to the government, a questionable conclusion, and added that the government was free to display or remove the sculpture as it saw fit, a more reasonable conclusion. In this instance the government was working in a managerial capacity. The principal purpose of the space was to provide access from one part of the plaza to the other.

Alternatively, assuming that Serra retains some First Amendment rights, the court held that the removal of the work was a reasonable time, place and manner restriction. The government had an interest in keeping the plaza unobstructed which, because of the size of the sculpture, could only be done by its removal. The court found that the removal left Serra with alternate ways of expressing his opinion. Indeed, the opinion had been expressed for six years, and there were numerous photographs of the sculpture in place so the public could see (but not experience) the effect of the piece. The court added that the burden was on Serra to show that there were barriers to delivering Serra's message created by the removal. Finally, the court stated that there was no evidence that the removal was content-based. Rather, the objections were based on aesthetics (it is ugly) or convenience (one must walk around it to get from one place to another, a longer route).

While this may be a reasonable decision, it is hard to see it as a time, place or manner restriction. The time is never, the place is nowhere, and the manner is not at all. The sculpture reposes in storage, cut into a number of shorter pieces. This would have violated Serra's moral rights under the Visual Artist's Rights Act had the piece been sold after the 1990 effective date of that act (see the chapter on Moral Rights below).

All of these cases could have been avoided by perfect foresight. The government can decide which art to show and which art to buy. Careful administration of the program would permit the choice of art that was wanted and that would not interfere with other government uses of the space.

8. Government as Buyer, Lessee, Displayer or Donee

The government is often the buyer, lessee, displayer or donee of art. The purchase may be voluntary, or may result, as the *Serra* case did, from rules that require the devotion of a certain percentage of the construction cost of government buildings to the purchase of art for the building. When governments operate museums, decisions must be made about acquisitions, loans for temporary shows, what work to show when, or whether to accept gifts of art offered to the museum. Even where the government does not believe it is operating a museum, every government owned or operated facility can function as a museum if it displays art. The government may certainly establish standards based on the quality of the art. But may the government impose content-based standards? For instance, can the local airport authority refuse to buy art showing aircraft disasters?

There are no cases restricting the government's right to buy, lease or display art based on its content. The general attitude is that the government has the same rights of selection as does a private party.

The government may establish standards for the acceptance of artworks, and may entrust those standards to an administrative agency. In *Silvette v. Art Comm'n of Virginia*, 413 F.Supp. 1342 (E.D. Va. 1976), Virginia law provided that purchases of art could only be made, and donations could only be accepted, by the governor, after receiving the advice of the Art Commission. Silvette, who represented himself, painted a portrait of Dr. Richard Morton for Morton Hall at the College of William and Mary that he proposed to donate. The commission's advice to the governor referred entirely to the quality of the painting, relating to technical aspects of composition, color and shading. But this case does not discuss whether those standards may include content-based considerations, as neither the commission nor the governor assigned any content reasons for recommending refusal or refusing the donation. Despite losing his case, Silvette's portrait of Dr. Morton now hangs in Morton Hall as a result of a 1976 amendment exempting from the law the acquisition of portraits by museums operated in conjunction with state university art departments.

9. Government as Lessor or Underwriter

The government sometimes leases a building to an art museum, or provides funds to help finance the operation of a museum. There is general agreement that the government has no obligation to do so. It need not lease property to a museum, nor need it decide to supply it with funds. It is also clear that a government can decide to not renew a museum's lease, or to reduce or eliminate the annual funding it has provided in the past.

Like other landlords, a government can refuse to renew a lease for any reason, or for no reason. What it cannot do is refuse to renew the lease for a prohibited reason. One prohibited reason is to control the content of the work shown at the museum. *Brooklyn Inst. of Arts & Sciences v. New York*, 64 F. Supp. 2d 184 (E.D.N.Y. 1999); *Cuban Museum of Arts and Culture, Inc. v. City of Miami*, 766 F. Supp. 121 (S.D. Fla. 1991). Likewise, a city cannot cut off funding for a museum in order to induce the museum to make content-based decisions about the art that it shows. These decisions are perfectly consistent with modern landlord-tenant law, which would prohibit a landlord from suppressing complaints to the housing inspectors by threatening to refuse to renew the lease of a tenant who files a complaint. In other words, the government cannot engage in retaliatory eviction or retaliatory fund-cutting. *Esperanza Peace and Justice Ctr. v. City of San Antonio*, 316 F.Supp.2d 433 (W.D.Tex. 2001). Interestingly, the politicians in each of these cases who were so outraged by the activities they were funding saw no reason to appeal adverse trial court decisions. The political moment had passed.

However, advance planning can provide many opportunities for governments supporting museums to influence what is displayed in them. The leases of some museums require that a preliminary list of shows to be mounted be submitted to the government. There are no cases on the constitutionality of that requirement. It is also not unusual for representatives of governments supplying funds or premises to hold seats on the boards of trustees of those museums.

Whatever arrangements may be made between a museum and a government, only the parties to an agreement can challenge its violation. For example, citizens of New York who were denied free admission to the Metropolitan Museum of Art had no standing to challenge that denial as a violation of an agreement with the city, *Grunewald v. Metropolitan Museum of Art*, 125 A.D. 3d 438, 3 N.Y.S.3d 23 (2015).

10. Government as Talent Developer

The government develops artistic talent through grants from the National Endowment for the Arts (NEA) and similar state bodies. Usual NEA procedure is to solicit applications for grants. Grants are awarded based on the reputation of the artist and the evaluation of the merit of the project to be funded. As a result of controversy developing about some of the projects funded, Congress passed a law that required that NEA take into consideration "general standards of decency and respect for the diverse beliefs and values of the American public" in making grants. Four artists who had previously been denied grants under earlier law joined with an art organization to challenge the constitutionality of the law as written. While the dissenters and concurrers thought the law prohibited grants to projects that challenged decency and respect for diverse beliefs, the court construed the statute to only require that decency and respect be taken into consideration. The court admitted that the criteria of decency and diverse beliefs were both vague, but thought them no less vague than the other criteria for making awards, like artistic excellence. The court was unwilling to invalidate the law on grounds that the NEA might use those new standards to make content-based decisions, and was likewise unwilling to invalidate the law on its face as being too vague. What seemed to be uppermost in the court's mind was that the program received many more applications than it could fund, so it must rely on a large number of subjective factors in deciding what to fund. The court distinguished a case holding unconstitutional a public university's decision to fund newspapers for student organizations except organizations with religious affiliation. The court expressly reserved the case where it could be proven that NEA rejected a grant to penalize disfavored viewpoints. Apart from attaching unconstitutional conditions, the government has wide latitude to determine what activities it will fund and what activities it will not fund. *National Endowment for the Arts v. Finley*, 524 U.S. 569 (1998).

Justices Scalia and Souter agree that the law requires that content of the proposed work be taken into account. Justice Scalia finds that irrelevant. He states that the denial of funding is no abridgement of freedom of speech. The speaker is as free as he always was to speak. He is only deprived of government funds to permit him to do so. Justice Souter thought the content discrimination key because the provision originated in disagreement with some of the viewpoints that NEA had funded.

In *United States v. American Library Ass'n, Inc.*, 539 U.S. 194 (2003), Congress required that libraries who wished to receive federal funds for internet upgrade attach filters to prevent library patrons from accessing child or adult pornography. The court held that this did not violate the First Amendment rights of either library patrons or the libraries, and that the government can subsidize some activities of its grantees and not others.

One suspects that there are government restrictions on content or authorship that the court would find unconstitutional, even though the government is only providing money. Perhaps a racial or religious restriction on recipients of grants, or on artists whose work is displayed at a supported museum, or on persons depicted in artworks, would be unconstitutional. Such a case has yet to arise.

Checkpoints

- There are five main policy reasons behind the First Amendment: Communication to further self-governance; to seek truth and allow ideas to compete on the open market; to help humans reach their full potential; to help balance stability and change; and to promote tolerance.
- Rational Basis Scrutiny is applied to a law that does not infringe a fundamental right. The government need only show that there is some rational basis for the law. If rational basis scrutiny is applied, laws are usually held constitutional.

- Strict Scrutiny applies to laws that infringe a fundamental right. The government must show a compelling interest the law serves and that there is no less restrictive means to achieve the law's purpose. Reasonable restrictions on the time, place and manner of expression are constitutional.
- Speech is oral or written communication of ideas. Conduct is speech when it is expressive. Neither obscenity nor child pornography is speech protected by the First Amendment.
- A work of art is obscene only if: (1) "the average person, applying contemporary community standards" would find that the work, taken as a whole, appeals to the prurient interest, and (2) the work depicts or describes, in a patently offensive way, sexual conduct specifically defined by the applicable law, and (3) the work, taken as a whole, lacks serious literary, artistic, political, or scientific value.
- The government has a compelling interest in protecting the health and safety of children. Child pornography may be defined as the depiction of a child's sexual organs or of a child engaged in sexual activity.
- The government can limit sale and display of artwork through licensing and sign ordinances, but its limits must be content-neutral. The government can place reasonable time, place and manner restrictions on display and sale.
- The government can limit expressive activity in a public forum if the law is either a content-neutral time, place and manner restriction, or the law passes strict scrutiny. A public forum is a space traditionally available for speech and assembly, such as public streets, sidewalks, and parks. A limited public forum is a space not traditionally available for speech and assembly, but made available for that purpose by government decision, and is subject to the same rules as long as it is made available. A nonpublic forum is any other space, and persons have no right to use it.
- The government can sometimes limit display of art when it is acting in a managerial capacity, when necessary to keep traffic moving or to prevent exposure in passageways.
- The government need not provide funds for the arts, but it cannot use its position as funder or landlord to dictate the content of the art displayed.
- Programs in which the government gives grants to fund museums and artists may take into account "general standards of decency and respect for the diverse beliefs and values of the American public" in making grants as long as those criteria do not constitute an absolute bar that would eliminate protected speech.
- There are no constitutional limits restricting the government's choice of subject matter or content when it purchases art.

Chapter 3

Defamation

Roadmap

After reading this chapter, you should understand:

- Definition of defamation: The tort of defamation requires a person to publish (communicate) something false and damaging about another to a third person. As related to art, what constitutes defamation depends on context. Criticisms as well as falsely identifying an artist as the creator of an artwork can be defamatory.
- Publication: Communication of a defamatory statement to a third person is publication. This communication to a third party is necessary to establish defamation because it is how one's reputation becomes damaged.
- Opinions in art reviews and even opinions expressed through artwork are not considered defamatory.
- Damages: Proving damages in defamation cases can be challenging. In defamation per se a successful plaintiff is entitled to general damages for loss of reputation as well as special damages if proven. Other types of defamation require proof of special damages for recovery.
- Defamation per se: Four circumstances lead to defamation per se: accusations of criminal activity involving moral turpitude or a crime punishable by imprisonment; allegations that a person has a repulsive disease; statements that one is unfit for his occupation; and allegations of sexual misconduct.
- Strict liability: Normally, no fault need be proven because defamation is a strict liability tort. A defamation recovery by a public official or a public figure, or a recovery against the media, requires proof of fault.
- Single Publication Rule: All recovery for a defamatory statement must be sought in one lawsuit. Worldwide damages may be recovered in this lawsuit and the lawsuit bars future suits for that specific defamatory statement.
- Statute of Limitations: Once a third person reads or hears a defamatory statement the statute of limitations begins running.
- Defense to defamation: Qualified privilege to tell a third party with a need to know unless the statement was made with actual malice. Absolute privilege in a legal proceeding within the scope of their duties, or to make a report of the proceedings.

- First Amendment: The public is permitted to criticize public officials and public figures without being subject to defamation liability unless there is actual malice.
- Costs of defamation: Regardless of outcome, a defendant artist often is injured due to the high costs of defending against such a suit and the common lack of insurance.

1. What Is Defamation?

The tort of defamation may be heard in the art world. Defamation requires that one person "publish" something false and injurious about a second person to a third person. The essence of the tort is damage to the reputation of the person defamed, but there is an incidental (and uncompensated) detriment: the person to whom the falsehood is published refrains from the benefit he would otherwise have derived from the person defamed. However, no case has been found in which the hearer of the defamatory remark has recovered from the defamer.

In the art world, one is always talking about artists and their works. Sometimes the talk is filled with praise, but it is often laced with criticism. The criticism may be defamation.

A. Publication

Publication is the communication of the statement to a third person. Publication is important because without publication, there is no offense of defamation. No one's reputation is lowered in the eyes of a third person. It is also important as the statute of limitations begins to run from the date of publication.

B. Defamatory Statement

The classic definition of a defamatory statement is one that exposes the victim to "hatred, contempt or ridicule." False accusation of criminal conduct qualifies as defamation. A person accused of stealing art, or of forging it, has been the victim of a defamatory statement. Immoral conduct is included. Indeed, under some circumstances, falsely stating that a person has been the victim of criminal or immoral conduct may be defamatory if it alters the behavior of others toward that person. Anything that reduces the person's esteem in the community or deters others from dealing with him can be defamatory.

What is defamatory depends very much on context. It may require consideration of the statement in its entirety or, if many people are likely to notice only part of the statement, just that part. Seemingly defamatory words may be overruled by their frequent use in a non-defamatory context. For example, blackmail is a crime, but it is common to speak of developers blackmailing a city council, in the sense that the developers have driven a hard bargain. The question of what amounts to defamation has been framed as whether the statement would lower the victim's esteem in a substantial and respectable group, even though that group is a small minority of the population. A statement that an artist is not the creator of a work of art, if false, is defamatory. What about a statement that an artist is the creator of a work of art? One can argue that the statement does not defame the purported creator because it attributes to that person a greater body of work than he has produced. On the other hand, it may be a doubly defamatory statement. If the work in question is deemed not to rise to the normal standard of the artist to whom it is attributed, it defames him. In context, it certainly implies that the person who is the true creator of the work did not create it. Such a statement may defame the true creator even though it does not mention the true creator by name.

C. Fact or Opinion

A false statement of fact may be defamatory; a statement of one's opinion will not be. That is especially true when that opinion is too outrageous to be believed by a reasonable person. Usually, statements in a review of an art show will not be defamatory because they will be clearly signaled as the opinion of the reviewer.

An artwork itself may be either a statement of fact or an opinion. In *Silberman v. Georges*, 91 A.D.2d 520, 456 N.Y.S.2d 395 (1982), defendant's painting "Mugging of the Muse" depicted plaintiff artists about to attack a young woman wearing a red bath towel, perhaps a muse of art (though in Greek mythology, there were only nine muses and none of them had painting or sculpture in her jurisdiction) while a blue-winged cherub looks on. Reversing a verdict for plaintiffs, the court held that the painting was a statement of opinion by defendant about the effect plaintiffs' artistic approach would have on art, not a statement of fact that plaintiffs had committed a crime. The title of the painting and the cherub convinced the court that the painting was an allegory. As an alternate holding, the court also stated that no special damages were proven.

2. Damages

Damages in defamation are problematic. Some damages may be easy to prove. The artist who is fired from her job because of a defamatory remark has damages equal to the capitalized value of the loss of the salary and other benefits she would have received from working. Other damages are more difficult to prove. An artist who depends on referrals for commissions cannot easily prove who did not refer clients to him because of a defamatory remark; she may not know everyone to whom the remark was communicated, and establishing that she would have received specific commissions in the absence of the remark is next to impossible. Whether for that reason or not, the common law divided defamation into libel and slander per se, for which general damages involving the diminution of reputation were available as well as special damages if they could be proven, and other forms of defamation, for which the victim could recover only if he could show the special damages referred to above.

Defamation per se involves one of four circumstances: (1) charges of criminal activity involving moral turpitude or crimes for which, if convicted, the punishment might be imprisonment; (2) allegations that the person has a loathsome disease; (3) statements that the person is unfit for his chosen business; and (4) charges of sexual misconduct.

At common law, defamation was regarded as a strict liability tort; no fault need be proven. That is still the case for defamation of a person who is not a public figure by someone who is not the media. Those cases are relatively rare today. Today most defamation cases involve the defamation of public officials or public figures, or defamation in the media. For defamation of a private individual in the media, plaintiff must prove some fault on the part of the media, such as negligence.

3. Single Publication Rule

Mass media and the internet have complicated the concept of publication. Newspapers are read everywhere, not just in the state in which they are published; television reception is often interstate, or distribution by networks makes it so; and items on the internet can usually be accessed from anywhere in the world. The legal system would not want a different lawsuit for every jurisdiction in which the same defamatory statement is published. Consequently, the "single publication" rule provides that all recovery for a single defamatory statement must be brought in a single suit; that worldwide damages are recoverable in that suit; and that the result of that suit bars other suits for that statement by *res judicata*. The statute of limitations on the defamation action begins to run when the first person reads or hears the defamatory statement; there is not a separate running of the statute for each person to whom the statement is published. Plaintiff can recover for worldwide damages, even though the statute of limitations may have expired in some of the jurisdictions in which publication was made before the suit is brought. In a case where a short statute of limitations has expired in some jurisdictions, plaintiff will sue in a jurisdiction with a longer statute of limitations that has not expired, and get full recovery.

4. Defenses: Privileges

A person sued for defamation may have potential defenses. If the defendant communicates information to a third party who is a normal recipient of the type of information communicated, the defendant will have a qualified privilege to make the statement unless it is made with actual malice. Actual malice is either knowing that the statement is false or acting in reckless disregard of the truth. Thus, where a potential employer asks plaintiff's former employer about her performance as a graphic artist, the former employer would have a qualified privilege to answer. Likewise, an artistic consultant who is asked by his principal about the skill or honesty of an artist he is thinking about commissioning has a qualified privilege to answer.

Persons who participate in the legal process, such as judges, lawyers, witnesses, and complainants, have a complete defense to allegations of defamation—they have an absolute privilege within the scope of their duties. So do the media who make a complete report of what is said in court, or who prepare a fair summary of it.

A. Public Figures

The rule for defamation of public officials and public figures has taken on constitutional status. Those individuals cannot sue for defamation unless the defamer acts with actual malice as defined above. The First Amendment requires that the public be free to criticize public officials, politicians and, to a lesser extent, other public figures, such as cultural trendsetters. While few artists qualify as public officials, many qualify as public figures. The line between persons who are public figures and persons who are not is unclear, but anyone who has secured a bit of fame or notoriety may qualify as a public figure. *New York Times Co. v. Sullivan*, 376 U.S. 254 (1964).

B. Practicalities

As a potential defendant, whether the artist ultimately wins or loses the case, the artist usually loses financially. Defending a defamation case can be quite costly. Unlike persons in the business of bringing information to the public, like newspapers, magazines and broadcasters, most artists have no insurance covering the costs of defending defamation suits. Also, the time the artist spends helping to defend the suit is time not devoted to artistic pursuits.

For the related cause of action of product disparagement, see the chapter on Authentication.

Checkpoints

You should have learned that:

- A defamation action lies for statements of fact communicated to third parties about another person that are false and cause injury. This may include statements falsely attributing or denying credit to the creator of an artwork, or any statement detrimental to reputation or status.
- Opinions, either spoken or communicated through art, are not defamatory.
- Libel and slander per se allow for general damages because proving actual damages can be difficult.
- Other forms of defamation require proof of special damages to recover.
- Defamation per se arises from allegations of: criminal activity involving moral turpitude or crimes punishable by imprisonment; a loathsome disease; unfitness for his business; and sexual misconduct.
- Defamation of a private person by someone other than the media requires no proof of fault.
- Defamation of public officials or public figures, or defamation by the media, requires proof of fault.
- The Single Publication Rule forces recovery from a defamatory statement to be addressed in a single lawsuit.
- A defendant who communicates information to a person with a need to know has a qualified privilege unless communicated with actual malice.
- Statements made by persons in legal proceedings have an absolute privilege.
- Public officials and public figures may be criticized unless there is actual malice.
- Defending a defamation case is expensive and seldom covered by insurance that most artists have.

Chapter 4

Publicity and Privacy Rights

Roadmap

After reading this chapter, you should understand:

- Right of Publicity: Defined as the right to control the use of your name and image. This may include control over one's voice, signature, or mannerisms. Some states require that an image have special value in order to have a cause of action while others only consider the value of the image in calculating damages. Some states extend the right of publicity of images of deceased persons to their transferees or survivors.
- Authentication: If someone attaches a personality to something, like an artwork or brand, without consent, truth is not normally a defense to a breach of right of publicity action.
- Photos: Selling a photograph of someone commercially or to help sell a product can invoke the subject's right of publicity. If he has a right of publicity, the seller must secure the subject's consent as well as the consent of the photographer or person who holds the copyright to the photo.
- The First Amendment: Some argue the right of publicity should not apply to a work of art because of First Amendment protections.
- Exceptions to right of publicity: "Newsworthiness" is an exception to the right of publicity because of First Amendment protections, such as photographs taken of famous people participating in newsworthy events and then used by the media. State statutes may provide this exception or there may be a defense similar to fair use available. What is "newsworthy" can be hard to determine.
- Courts have provided several tests to balance the right of publicity and the First Amendment. These tests determine whether a work that uses an image is artistic and transformative, making the art more than just the identity of the image.
- Right of Privacy: The right to avoid undue disclosure of your name or image to the public.
- The right of privacy involves three privacy rights: the right to be free from unreasonable intrusions on one's seclusion, the right to not be publicized in a false light, and the right to be free from unreasonable publicity given to one's private life.
- Celebrities have fewer privacy rights than most people. They have more in Europe than in the United States.

1. Introduction

The rights of publicity and privacy are often confused. The right of publicity is the right to control the use of your name and image. The right of privacy is the right to avoid undue disclosure of your name or image to the public. Both rights historically emerged from advocacy of a right of privacy at the end of the nineteenth century. What New York calls the right of privacy is in fact the right of publicity. Semantic confusion aside, both rights are creatures of state, rather than federal, law, and both have their origins in case law, though are now to some extent embodied in statutes. While both rights sound in tort, the right of privacy is a true tort, compensation for a noncommercial injury, while the right of publicity is more like unfair competition or an intellectual property right akin to trademark violation, because it involves the appropriation of someone else's property for your own profit.

2. Right of Publicity

A. Defined

The right of publicity is designed to protect a person's personality in the sense that politicians, entertainers and other public figures create a public image. While its precise formulation differs from state to state, it provides a right to damages for the use of the person's name or likeness on products or in advertising for goods or services without the person's consent. In many states it includes the use of a person's voice, signature or image, and in one state it extends as far as the person's distinctive appearance, gestures or mannerisms.

Justification for the liability is that a person's image only has value to the extent that it is recognized by others. To gain that recognition, people invest enormous amounts of time and capital. They become proficient at something, and publicize that fact. They develop a following. If that value could be used by anyone who pleases, there would be less incentive on the part of people to develop it. How much less can be questioned; most people who have developed their images reap substantial contractual and career benefits from the services they provide, so that they might develop the image even if it were not legally protected. One can also regard recovery for violation of the right of publicity as analogous to recovery for theft. In both cases, the appropriator is taking something of value from the owner without paying for it, and using it for his own profit. In the case of theft, the property is tangible; in the right of publicity, the property is intangible. Another analogy frequently made is to patent and copyright laws, which protect the owners of copyrights and patents from their use by others. *Zacchini v. Scripps-Howard Broadcasting Co.*, 433 U.S. 562 (1977). The court in that case states three rationales: do not take the valuable property of others, reward people who improve their abilities that build reputation, and encourage people to invest time and money in endeavors that build reputation.

Thus far, the beneficiaries of the right of publicity have been individuals or groups of identified individuals like a band. No case has been found according a right of publicity to an artificial entity such as a corporation, partnership or trust.

B. The Thing Protected: Must the Personality Have Value?

One can argue that in order to bring an action for violation of the right of publicity, a plaintiff must first establish that he has a personality that has value. This is because the essence of the offense is the appropriation of plaintiff's property, his image, without paying for it. RESTATEMENT THIRD, UNFAIR COMPETITION §§46–49. But a person need not be a celebrity to bring an action for violation of the right of publicity in most states. (Most such actions are probably brought by celebrities because the likely damages are higher.) This rule avoids the necessity of drawing a line between celebrities and non-celebrities. Most states do not require that the image appropriated have special value in order to support a cause of action. *See Hoepker v. Kruger*, 200 F.Supp.2d 340 (S.D.N.Y. 2002). Instead, the value of the person's image enters into the calculation of damages. If the person's image had little value, its appropriation added little value to defendant's product or advertising.

While the ultimate result may be the same, there is a significant difference between the two groups of states. In a state that requires a personality with special value, if plaintiff's image has no special value, the case will be dismissed on the pleadings; in other states, the case will go to trial and the value of plaintiff's image will be used to calculate the damages awarded. In the second group of states, the defendant's legal costs will be much higher, thus pressuring the defendant to settle.

One can argue that the defendant, by appropriating plaintiff's identity, testifies that the plaintiff's identity has value in selling defendant's product. It may be true that defendant chose the photograph of plaintiff because plaintiff presented a more appealing appearance than the ninety other photographs that defendant took. It may also be true that whatever value has been created, has been created by defendant. In one case, plaintiff advertised that he had lost the right to rent because he had eight children. Defendant real estate firm's employee contacted plaintiff and arranged for him to buy a home. A newspaper printed a story about the case, and defendant reproduced the story as an advertisement for its real estate services. The court denied defendant's motion for summary judgment. It would appear that the actual identity of plaintiff is irrelevant to the ad, though it gives the ad a sense of truthfulness. It was defendant's action in helping plaintiff that created the value of the ad. *Canessa v. J. I. Kislak, Inc.*, 97 N.J. Super. 327, 235 A.2D 62 (Law Div. 1967). On the other hand, it might be observed that artists usually pay models, even if they are not celebrities, and advertisers likewise usually pay persons who record testimonials on their behalf, even if they are not celebrities.

C. The Post-Mortem Personality

The question has been raised as to whether a person's right of personality survives his death. Initially, some states held that the right of publicity terminates on the person's death, as does the right of privacy and other personal rights. While most states have not spoken to the question, the vast majority that have dealt with it now extend the right of publicity to "deceased personalities," or to be more precise, their transferees or survivors.

The longevity of the post-mortem right varies from ten to one hundred years from the date of death. In one state the right is unlimited, and in another it lasts as long as the right is exploited. Plaintiff is entitled to profits from the unauthorized use, and, in states with statutory rights that provide this, a successful plaintiff may also recover punitive damages, attorney fees, and costs.

As the Restatement makes clear, the purpose of this right is to prevent one person from appropriating the trade values of another. That requires that plaintiff prove that his name or image has trade value. Likewise, the post-mortem right is often conditioned on proving that the image had commercial value at the time of the person's death. The easiest way to do this is to prove that the executor or administrator included the personality right in the filed inventory of the estate or, even better, included it in the assets of the decedent's estate for federal or state tax purposes. While a requirement that the right of publicity had value at the time of death seems inconsistent with allowing a person whose image has no special value to sue, the two rules can coincide in the same jurisdiction.

D. Requirement of Previous Commercialization

Initially, as a compromise between the existence and non-existence of a post-mortem right of publicity, some courts stated that a post-mortem right would only be recognized if decedent had commercialized the right before death. Cases and statutes have generally rejected this view, and accord the right whether it was actually commercialized before death or not. *The Martin Luther*

King, Jr., Center for Social Change, Inc. v. American Heritage Products, Inc., 250 Ga. 135, 296 S.E.2d 697 (1982) authorized an injunction to prevent commercial production of a statuette of King even though he had not commercially exploited his right of publicity while alive.

E. Right of Publicity Used in Authentication

Right of publicity problems may arise in a number of ways related to the visual arts. One way is if a person selling an artwork that he owns represents that the work is by an artist who has a right of publicity. If the representation is true, there is no violation of the right of publicity. The transfer of the artwork from the creator implies that the artist is willing to have his name associated with the work, so there is consent. If the representation is not true, there is a violation of the right of publicity. In addition to a suit from the purchaser for breach of warranty, the seller may need to defend an action for breach of the right of publicity, defamation and breach of his moral rights by the artist whose name has been improperly attached to the artwork.

Truth is not normally a defense to violation of the right of publicity. For example, if the maker of a brand of paints advertises that a famous artist uses those paints, the maker may be liable regardless of whether the named artist does or does not use the paints. Defendant has appropriated the artist's personality without his consent. The falseness of the statement may also expose defendant to other suits both by the artist and by others who are deceived.

F. Selling an Individual's Photo Without His Consent

A second way in which right of publicity cases may arise in the visual arts is when a picture of a person is sold without his consent. This may occur when a photograph of the person is transferred to a t-shirt, a mug or notecards that are offered for sale; when it is used in advertising; when it is incorporated into an artwork that is for sale; or when a street photographer develops a photo of an unsuspecting passerby. Consequently, when someone wants to use a photograph for commercial purposes, he must secure the consent of the photographer or other person who holds the copyright on the photo, and also the consent of the person who has been photographed if that person has a right of publicity.

If the street photographer photographs a person on the street and the photograph is offered for sale at an art gallery, the street photographer is violating that person's right of publicity. The same is true when someone places a photograph on an item sold commercially, or uses a famous person's photograph to try to sell a product.

The California statute contains an exclusion. Use of an image in a "... single and original work of art ..." is not considered a product. CALIF. CIV. CODE § 3344.1(a)(2). If a single photograph is made of the person, there is no violation of the right of publicity. If two prints of that photographic image are made for sale, both violate the right of publicity.

More broadly a New York trial court held that creation of an artwork, even if it is intended for sale, does not constitute a product so as to fall afoul of the New York statutory right of publicity. Thus an artist did not violate Cheryl Tiegs' right of publicity (called the right of privacy in New York) by planning to make twenty bronze busts of her likeness from a plaster cast that she consented to have placed on her head to demonstrate that it would not harm an elephant if a cast was made of the elephant's head. *Simeonov v. Tiegs*, 602 N.Y.S.2d 1014 (N.Y.City Civ. Ct. 1993). The court states that this is art, an expression of the sculptor, and entitled to First Amendment protection. It construed the statute in this way to avoid a conflict with the First Amendment. The court did not detail what creative process was involved in taking the plaster cast. While this case should have made little impact because it is a report only of a trial court, and because of its complicated set of facts where the right of publicity was introduced as a defense to a suit for damaging the cast, it has been repeatedly cited, often for the proposition that the First Amendment bars any application of the right of publicity to a work of art.

G. Newsworthiness and Freedom of Expression

i. Newsworthiness

Photographs of famous people are frequently taken and used in the news media in connection with some newsworthy event in which the famous person has participated. The use of such photos does not violate the right of publicity. Sometimes there is an express exclusion by statute; sometimes this is established as a kind of fair use, analogous to the fair use defense to copyright infringement. Sometimes a parody defense succeeds. *Cardtoons, L.C. v. Major League Baseball Players Ass'n*, 95 F.3d 959 (10th Cir. 1996). In all cases, the exception to the right of publicity is likely to be motivated by concerns about infringing the values expressed by the First Amendment's guarantee of freedom of speech. The First Amendment is concerned with encouraging a lively debate about ideas, and personal self-expression. Artwork is protected to some extent by the First Amendment.

However, there is a difference between state law concerns, such as construction of a statute exempting newsworthy items from the right of publicity or a decision that the common law right of publicity does not extend to newsworthy items, and a decision that the First Amendment restricts the right of publicity. The former is state law and can be changed by the state legislature or the state courts. The latter prevents state law from encroaching on freedom of speech. In *Ali v. Playgirl, Inc.*, 447 F.Supp. 723 (S.D.N.Y. 1978), judicial interpretation of the New York statute had established that the right of publicity was not violated if the use was newsworthy. The court held that a nude drawing of the boxer Mohammad Ali accompanied by a clearly fictional poem was not newsworthy because it had no informational content. The newsworthiness concept is designed to assure that the public will continue to receive news and commentary on matters of public interest.

Exactly what falls within the concept of "newsworthiness" is not entirely clear. This is further discussed below under the right of privacy, but newsworthiness may be different under the right of publicity. The Supreme Court stated as much in *Zacchini v. Scripps-Howard Broadcasting Co.*, 433 U.S. 562 (1977), where it held that broadcasting the entire act of a human cannonball was not protected by the First Amendment from liability for breach of the right of publicity. It also stated that reporting on plaintiff's act, with or without plaintiff's photo, would be a different case. The Ohio Supreme Court had held that the First Amendment prevented recovery of damages for the broadcast under Ohio's right of publicity. However, the Supreme Court held that the First Amendment was not an impediment to liability in this case, leaving the Ohio Supreme Court to determine whether the Ohio right of publicity extended to these matters.

It is difficult to know what to make of *Zacchini* because it is not a typical right of publicity case. Defendant did not use plaintiff's name or likeness, but it gave the public for free what they would have paid Zacchini to see. To be more precise, Zacchini performed at a state fair. Patrons paid to enter the fair. That admission charge included the right to watch Zacchini's show. Presumably, the fair paid Zacchini to perform, so the connection between broadcasting Zacchini's act and a decline in Zacchini's revenue is somewhat attenuated. Defendant gave away plaintiff's business as part of defendant's presentation, rather than using his image, but both acts involve unjust enrichment of defendant by using something built by plaintiff. The uncertainty is compounded because defendant is a television broadcaster, a prime example of a news reporter, a non-commercial enterprise, but also a presenter of entertainment, a commercial enterprise. The court stated that defendant could have reported on Zacchini's act, with or without pictures, and that would have been protected by the First Amendment.

ii. Balancing the Right of Publicity and the First Amendment

a. Transformation

Courts have balanced the right of publicity and the First Amendment differently. The leading case is *Comedy II Productions, Inc. v. Gary Saderup, Inc.*, 25 Cal. 4th 387, 21 P.3d 797 (2001), where defendant Saderup sold lithographs and t-shirts with images of The Three Stooges from a charcoal drawing he had made. The trial court ordered damages and attorney's fees, and enjoined defendant from selling any image of The Three Stooges except his original drawing. The Court of Appeal affirmed the damages but struck the injunction. On behalf of the California Supreme Court, Justice Stanley Mosk characterized the area as a conflict between restraining unjust enrichment by the use of an image carefully cultivated by a celebrity, and restraining both a marketplace of ideas and the right to self-expression inherent in human dignity. After declining to import the fair use doctrine of copyright law into the right of publicity, he proposed a balancing test that ultimately requires the court to decide whether the use to which the celebrity's image is being put is transformative. If so, a First Amendment interest is likely implicated, and the defendant is not profiting largely from exploiting the celebrity's image. He suggested that transformation can exist with parody, factual reporting, fictionalized storytelling, or social criticism. An artist can use the celebrity's image as a starting point, but must go further. In a difficult case, the question is whether the marketability of the challenged work derives primarily from the fame of the celebrity or from something else like the skill or reputation of the artist. While agreeing that all portraits require skill and judgment, the court affirmed the decision because the principal economic factor in the sales of the t-shirts was the identity of The Three Stooges, not the skill with which they were portrayed.

It is clear that the transformation required here is considerably more than the originality required to qualify for a copyright. But it is unclear what would have been transformative enough. The court refers to works where Andy Warhol used photographs of entertainment personalities in different colors and slightly distorted, and said that this was transformative because it was social commentary on celebrity. Quaere as to whether Saderup might have prevailed had his lawyer been more creative in finding his t-shirts to be social commentary, or whether this test is reserved for famous artists, those whose work commands outstanding prices because of the artist's fame.

b. Expression

A second test that courts have stated is the "expression" test. Extending the *Simeonov* case, courts have held that art is pure expression, and as such it trumps any claim made by the right of publicity.

In a case using New York law, the artist Barbara Kruger found a photograph by a German photographer of plaintiff peering through a magnifying glass. Kruger cropped and enlarged it, transferred it to a silkscreen and added three blocks of red color in which she inserted the words "It's a small world, but not if you have to clean it." The court stated that this qualified as pure expression under the New York test, and was also transformative under the California test. Reproducing it in the exhibition catalogue is pure speech to facilitate discussion of the work. Alternatively, its reproduction three times among hundreds of photos in the book qualified for the "fleeting use" or *de minimis* exception. Its reproduction on a large street poster advertising the show was an ancillary use to the first amendment exercise, as a speaker must be allowed to advertise his speech. For the sale of souvenir items on which copies of the artwork had been placed, the court asked whether the purpose of doing that was to flaunt plaintiff's image or for artistic purposes, and found that the museums were selling art just as much by selling refrigerator magnets as by selling tickets to an exhibition. *Hoepker v. Kruger*, 200 F.Supp.2d 340 (S.D.N.Y. 2002). The court does not state whether the cropping, the enlarging, the silkscreening, the blocks of red color, the words, or a combination of them all was the transformative element. Thus the court proceeds from approval of an artistic use to approval of considerably more commercial uses. One of the problems with this case for plaintiff's counsel is that it is unclear that the plaintiff's image is recognizable, since it is distorted by the magnifying glass, and nothing else identifying plaintiff is used.

Defendant created a painting, and limited edition prints from it, of Tiger Woods' 1997 record-setting victory at the Masters tournament. It contains three different views of Woods, two caddies, the Augusta Clubhouse, the Masters leaderboard, and the heads of six great golfers from the past. The court stated that the panorama presented was much more than simply Woods' image. It had a message, that Woods would someday join the past golfing greats. It portrayed a historic event (though the court does not say that the event was newsworthy, nor does it suggest that defendant's work was conveying news). The court stated that it was using fair use as a defense, on analogy to the fair use defense in copyright law, and concluded that the informational and creative content of defendant's use outweighed any loss to the market for Woods' image. It also found the use transformative. *ETW Corp. v. Jireh Publ'g, Inc.*, 332 F.3d 915 (6th Cir. 2003).

c. Artistic Relevance

Another test for balancing the right of publicity with the First Amendment is set forth in *Rogers v. Grimaldi*, 875 F.2d 994 (2d Cir. 1989). This test requires that there be artistic relevance for the use of the name or image in the work, and that the use does not explicitly mislead the viewer about either the source or the content of the work. For further discussion, see the Trademark chapter below.

H. Choice of Law

One is not necessarily safe as an artist or a museum if one lives in a state that does not have a right of publicity. Placing material on the internet distributes it everywhere, and the law chosen to govern the case may be the law of the residence state of the person whose right of publicity is alleged to be invaded.

3. Right of Privacy

The right of privacy contains three related privacy rights.

A. Offensive Intrusions on Seclusion

One is the right to be free from unreasonable intrusions on your seclusion if the invasion would be highly offensive to a reasonable person.

i. Trespassory Intrusions

If defendant installed a camera in plaintiffs house and made the resulting video into an artwork, there would have been a violation of plaintiff's right of privacy if it were highly offensive to a reasonable person. (It would also be a trespass, and possibly intentional infliction of emotional distress, but those offenses are outside the scope of this work.) The law of trespass makes the intrusion unreasonable. People have the right to expect that others will not trespass to obtain videos of them.

One might well ask why one would sue under the right of privacy when an action for trespass would lie, especially given that one must prove that the invasion of privacy was highly offensive to a reasonable person; no such proof is required for trespass. It may have been thought that damages would not be available in trespass for mental distress or for the subsequent publication of private information obtained, though there would seem to be no reason for that doubt. Those damages are surely foreseeable; indeed, the publication is often the very reason for the trespass.

Both trespass and invasion of privacy will lie whether the entry is forcible, stealthy, or by deceit. So when an investigative reporter feigns a need for treatment to enter plaintiff's house and secretly photographs plaintiff in an embarrassing position, his publication is liable for invasion of privacy. *Dietemann v. Time, Inc.*, 449 F.2d 245 (9th Cir. 1971). Later cases involving investigative reporters or testers have gone the other way. *Desnick Eyes Services v. ABC*, 44 F.3d 1345 (7th Cir. 1995); *Food Lion v. ABC*, 887 F.Supp. 811 (M.D.N.C. 1995). The paparazzo who hires a helicopter to overfly a person's walled estate and take photos with a telephoto lens is surely as much a trespasser as if he had vaulted the wall.

ii. Non-Trespassory Intrusions

The question is more complicated where there is no trespass but there is an invasion of privacy. It is unreasonable to expect complete privacy in a public space, but contemporary community standards regard eavesdropping on others in public or taking their pictures without consent as beyond the pale.

B. False Light

A second branch of privacy is where a person is publicized in a false light. While the artist who does this is likely to be liable in defamation, he may also be liable for violating the person's right of privacy. No cases have been found involving the visual arts, and there are few successful false light privacy cases that do not also constitute defamation.

C. Unreasonable Publicity Given to Private Life

The third and most important branch of privacy is unreasonable publicity given to a person's private life. Most people regard any publicity given to their private lives as unreasonable. The courts do not always agree.

i. Newsworthiness

There is a large exception for the publication of things deemed newsworthy. While newsworthiness has a larger scope than "hot news" to include seemingly private information about persons who have ever been in the public eye, it does not encompass everything a large part of the public wishes to know. The courts seem to accord a broad discretion to publishers to make a good faith determination of newsworthiness. Many of the cases that have held defendants liable under this branch of the right of privacy involve situations where the media acquired the knowledge disclosed through trespass, theft, or deceit, so alternate remedies existed. In a few cases, media outlets have been held liable for publicizing facts available in public records, but in many more recovery has been denied because of the newsworthiness of the facts. Since the overwhelming number of cases under this rubrique have involved the disclosure of facts, visual artists are not usually implicated. The visual arts would be involved in the publication of photos or other representations.

ii. Celebrities

In the United States, a sharp line can be drawn between the ordinary citizen and the celebrity. But both the ordinary citizen and the celebrity are protected from harassing behavior that interferes with their daily lives, like staking out their homes and in-your-face obstruction.

California has tried to draw a line between public figures and their children. It imposes serious criminal penalties on persons harassing the children or wards of persons because of their occupation if it leads to reasonable emotional distress in the children. California also provides a civil action for damages, attorneys' fees, recovery of profits made and injunctions. CALIF. PENAL CODE § 11414.

In the United States, any photograph or drawing of a public figure in a public place can be published. See *Gallela v. Onassis*, 487 F.2d 986 (2d Cir. 1973), where the photographer's outrageous behavior was enjoined, but not the publication of its fruits.

D. European Convention of Human Rights

Europe has tried to define a zone of privacy, even for celebrities. Article 8(1) of the European Convention of Human Rights provides that "Everyone has the right to respect for his private and family life, his home and his correspondence." In holding that Princess Caroline of Monaco had the right not to have photos of her daily life engaging in sports or shopping published, the court drew a distinction between publishing facts properly debatable in a democratic society relating to politicians in their official functions and facts that would not be an appropriate part of that debate. The court was clear that a person without official government functions did not lose her right of privacy merely by being born royal, and therefore a celebrity. One is left unclear about the extent of protection afforded to politicians or persons holding elective or appointive office. *Von Hannover v. Germany*, [2004] E.C.H.R. 59320/00 (Grand Ch.).

In *Google Spain SL v. Agencia Española de Protección de Datos (AEPD)* of 13 May 2014, #C131/12, the European Court of Justice held that a person residing in the European Union has the right to have links to data about him removed from search results even if posted by third parties, except that the interest of the public in information may outweigh the privacy interests of the subject. The source of this right is the European Union privacy directive and articles 7 and 8 of the European Charter of Human Rights. Search engines are not obligated to de-link all information—only that which is ancient, irrelevant, excessive or unnecessarily defamatory. Google has de-linked about 40% of the items requested. It is unlikely that persons will ask for de-linking many items of visual art, though one can certainly imagine its use in the case of the posting of embarrassing photographs of unwilling subjects, such as revenge porn. Failure to de-link after request by a European resident when the search engine should delete carries a penalty of two percent of the enterprise's worldwide income, payable to the government involved.

For further guidance, see J. THOMAS MCCARTHY, THE RIGHTS OF PUBLICITY AND PRIVACY (2d ed. 2019).

Checkpoints

You should have learned that:

- The right of publicity and privacy are often confused; the right of publicity involves the right to control commercial use of your name and image whereas the right of privacy focuses on the right to prevent undue intrusion or disclosure. The right of publicity aims to provide recovery for someone whose valuable image has been used without out permission or compensation.
- Some states' rights of publicity require that a person's appropriated image have a special value in order to bring a lawsuit, while others only weigh special value in calculating damages.
- In states that extend the right of publicity to deceased persons, the longevity of that right can range from a few years to unlimited years. This post-mortem right is often dependent on plaintiff proving that the deceased person's appropriated image was valuable at the time of death.
- A statement that attaches another person's image to something requires consent of that person to avoid a right of publicity action, regardless of the statement's truth.
- One must secure the consent of someone with a right of publicity before using a photograph of him commercially. One court has held that the First Amendment bars the application of the right of publicity to a work of art.

- Exceptions to the right of publicity include a fair use type defense and express statutes that exclude the media's use of photos of famous people at "newsworthy" events. These exceptions arise out of a concern of First Amendment infringements. While "newsworthiness" is an exception to the right, determining what is newsworthy can be a challenge.
- Several tests balance the right of publicity and the First Amendment. These include determining if art that involves an image of a celebrity is transformative. If so, it may implicate the First Amendment and shield the art from right of publicity claims. Another test requires use of an image in a piece of work to have artistic relevance and to not mislead the viewer of the work about the content or source of the work.
- Some tests consider art pure expression that supersedes any right of publicity claims.
- The right of privacy aims to protect individuals from undue disclosure of his image to the public.
- The right of privacy contains the right to be free from unreasonable intrusions on one's seclusion. This is available if the invasion, trespassory or not, would be highly offensive to a reasonable person.
- Individuals also have a right to not be publicized in a false light. Often violations of this privacy right constitute defamation as well.
- The most important privacy right is the right to be free from unreasonable publicity given to one's private life. A broad exception to this right is the publication of newsworthy things which is often left to the discretion of publishers.
- Celebrities are protected from overly interfering behavior. While photographs of public figures in public places may be freely published, California imposes serious penalties on those who harass children of celebrities. Europe has also created privacy for celebrities which prevents publishing their daily life activities unrelated to their celebrity functions.

Chapter 5

Copyright

Roadmap

After reading this chapter, you should understand:

- Constitutional scope: Federal Copyright law is authorized by the Constitution. Courts have granted copyright ability to artists and artwork, although the Constitution only refers to authors and writing.
- Purpose: To encourage the production of copyrightable works by providing the author with a monopoly on the work for a period of time.
- Copyright grants exclusive rights for the period of the copyright to reproduce the work; to use it to prepare a derivative work; to sell, lease, or lend it; and to publicly display it.
- First sale doctrine: The owner of the physical item, even if he does not own the copyright, has the right to sell, lease, lend and display that physical item.
- Obtaining a copyright is now automatic if it is an original work in a copyrightable subject matter that is fixed in a medium of expression.
- Originality: The work needs to be a creation of the author and at least minimally creative. Facts cannot be copyrighted.
- Idea-expression dichotomy: Ideas cannot be copyrighted; all that can be copyrighted is the expression of an idea.
- Scènes á faire doctrine: The necessary steps in expressing an idea are not protected by copyright.
- Functional elements of a design are not copyrightable; only the expressive element of the design can be copyrighted.
- Government copyright: The United States government may not be an original copyright holder, but state and foreign governments may. A copyright may be transferred to the federal government.
- Joint ownership: All authors of a joint work are tenants in common of its copyright.
- Work made for hire: If a work is made by an employee in his scope of employment, the copyright belongs to the employer.
- Transferring a work and its copyright: Transferring the work does not transfer the copyright unless such an intent is expressed.

- Suing for infringement may not begin until the copyright is registered.
- Infringement defined: Copying a work's protected expression.
- Proving an infringement: Plaintiff must prove that defendant had access to the copyrighted work and that something was copied.
- *De Minimis*: Minimal copying may not violate copyright laws.
- Vicarious infringement: Occurs when a person has the right to control the action of another and fails to prevent infringement when he profits by it.
- Derivative work: Must be done with permission of the copyright holder. Derivative works may be copyrighted if they demonstrate sufficient originality.
- Fair use is not infringement. Purposes of fair use include criticism, comment, news reporting, teaching, scholarship, or research.
- Fair use factors: To determine if a use is fair, consider the purpose of the use, the nature of the copyrighted work, the proportion of the copyrighted work that is used and the effect of the use on the potential market for the copyrighted work.
- Remedies: A successful plaintiff is entitled to ordinary damages, an injunction, and costs. Statutory damages and attorneys' fees may be awarded if the copyright is registered before the infringement.

1. Constitutional Authority: Copyrights and Patents

Federal copyright law is authorized by Article I, §8 of the constitution, which grants Congress the power "To promote the Progress of Science and useful Arts, by securing for limited Times to Authors and Inventors the exclusive Right to their respective Writings and Discoveries...." The words specify "Authors" and "Writings," neither of which seems to include artists or artwork. Congress, the courts and most commentators believe that under the constitution an artist is an author, and writings include works of art. One of the categories of copyrightable objects enumerated in the current statute is "pictorial, graphic and sculptural works." *Burrow-Giles Lithograph Co. v. Sarony*, 111 U.S. 53 (1884), upheld the copyrightability of photographs against a challenge that they were not "writings," saying that writings included all forms of writing, printing, engraving, etching that allowed an artist to express herself in visible form. The court supported this by the fact that early copyright acts drafted by people who signed the constitution included maps, charts, engravings and etchings. An "author" is any person who originates a writing. So an artist is an author who can receive a copyright, which accords the artist certain exclusive rights to her artwork. Justice Douglas wished to re-raise the issue of whether statuettes used as lamp bases and other applied art constituted writings that were constitutionally eligible for copyright in *Mazer v. Stein*, 347 U.S. 201 (1954), despite the fact that neither party had argued that point, but the court was not disposed to re-examine the question.

Patents and copyrights promote the progress of science and useful arts by providing the author or the inventor with a monopoly for a limited time. The right to use that contribution may be acquired from the patent or copyright holder for that time, usually for a fee. When the limited time expires, the contribution falls into the public domain and can be used by anyone without permission or charge.

Congress has chosen to provide those rights in different ways. For patents, Congress has conferred on the inventor a very strong right, prohibition of use, that lasts for a short duration: it lasts only twenty years. For copyrights, Congress grants a much weaker right, the right to prohibit copying, adaptation, distribution, public performance and public display, but it lasts for the life of the author plus seventy years. Independent generation is a complete defense to copyright infringement; it is no defense to patent infringement.

2. Copyright and the Business Model

The stated purpose behind copyright is to encourage the production of copyrightable works by providing the author with a monopoly on the work for a period of time. That monopoly is crucial to the business model of most publishers and distributors of copyrightable material. The business model used by most publishers, artists and movie studios involves the production of numerous different works. The works that sell well subsidize the works that do not sell well. Absent copyright, competing content providers could wait to see what sells well, then rush it into print in competition with the original publisher, depriving him of some of the profits of work that sells well, without shouldering the costs of new work that does not sell well.

Another way to think about this business model is that the lower the cost of duplication, the more important copyright is. When Johannes Gutenberg printed his bible in 1455, he had no copyright, nor had he any need for it. Anyone who wanted to print competing bibles would incur exactly the same expenses that Gutenberg had paid, so it would be difficult for a new entrant to undercut Gutenberg's price. Today digital reproduction places the cost of duplicating a work at close to zero, so copyright is essential to the economic health of authors, and especially of their publishers.

The reader has probably noted a disconnect in the previous several paragraphs. The focus of the constitution was on the author, but the focus of the business model was not that of the author primarily, but on the distributor: publisher or movie producer. In fact, most copyrights rest with the distributor, because the artist often sold his copyright for a fixed sum or a percentage royalty as a necessary condition to having his work published or distributed. When you add the fact that a work produced by an employee in the scope of his employment belongs to the employer, it is easy to see that the primary direct beneficiary of copyright has traditionally been the distributor.

So the stated "deal" enshrined in the copyright law is that government provides the author a monopoly for a limited time, and the public benefits because the author is thereby induced by the prospect of personal gain to create more works, and the publisher to whom the copyright will be assigned is induced to publish a wider variety of works than he otherwise would have.

3. The Copyright Trade-Off: Protecting the Past or the Future

Every copyright bestows a benefit on the author and a detriment on everyone else. According to Kohelet, the supposed author of Ecclesiastes 1:9, "there is nothing new under the sun." Each creative person looks intently at the work around him. It was said that no one looked at Matisse's work as carefully as Picasso, and vice versa. While the artist is not copying extant work, he does base his work in part on what exists. Inspiration is good; copying is bad. This would not be a problem if copyright infringement were limited to direct copying. Today copyright infringement includes the preparation of works derivative of the copyrighted item. So the broader the copyright protection of an existing art, the less scope is provided for current and future artists to produce work. One of the roles of the fair use doctrine discussed below is to mediate between the copyright holder and the future artist.

The role of copyright in the life of the artist is quite differential, depending on what the artist produces. For the artist who produces images that are reproduced in large numbers, copyright is essential. You will note that most of the cases described in this chapter involve photographs. For the artist who produces unique items, copyright is much less important because that artist earns his income from the sale of relatively unique items. Part of the sale price is the rarity value. But even where the artist produces unique items, copyright may be an additional source of income from the sale of reproductions, and from the use of the image on mugs, notecards, etc., or in commercial publicity.

4. Rights Conferred by Copyright

The rights conferred by copyright, in the case of the visual artist, are the exclusive right for the period of the copyright to reproduce the work; to use it to prepare a derivative work; to sell, lease, or lend it; and to publicly display it. 17 U.S.C. § 106. This is balanced by the "first sale" doctrine under which the owner of the physical item, even if he does not own the copyright, has the right to sell, lease, lend and display that physical item. The owner of a lawfully made copy, including the physical original, can also display it publicly " … either directly or by the projection of no more than one image at a time, to viewers present at the place where the copy is located." 17 U.S.C. § 109. That means that a museum that does not own the copyright can make and show a slide or an enlarged poster of a copyrighted painting it owns on the museum premises, but it cannot show that slide by any technological means in another building unless it also brings the original physical item to that place and keeps it there while the slide or poster is being displayed.

Except as otherwise indicated, the analysis below refers to the current copyright law. However, previous copyright laws are not dead. Previous law may govern some aspects of the case if the work was produced before the effective date of the 1976 Act. A work produced in 1970 that was not properly copyrighted could not be infringed today even if the same actions would have produced a valid copyright today. If a United States work had fallen into the public domain under previous law, current law will generally not revive the copyright. (The copyrights in many foreign works may have been restored in 1995 under our international obligations.) Given the long duration of copyrights, most current students will need to consult previous copyright law throughout their working lives.

5. Obtaining a Copyright: The Old Rules, from 1909

A. Substantive Rules

There were three substantive requirements to obtain a copyright. The work to be copyrighted had to be a copyrightable subject matter; it had to show some originality; and it had to be fixed in a medium of expression. For more discussion of these three subjects, see below. A copyright lasted for twenty-eight years from the date of publication, and could be renewed for another twenty-eight years.

B. Formal Rules

Before the work was published, a copyright notice needed to be affixed to the work specifying the name of the copyright holder and the year. The famous Picasso sculpture in Daley Square Chicago lost its potential copyright protection because it was published by public display of the maquette, distributing photos of it for publicity purposes, printing souvenir booklets, and permitting the printing of a postcard, all without a copyright notice. *Letter Edged in Black Press, Inc. v. Public Building Commission of Chicago*, 320 F.Supp. 1303 (N.D. Ill. 1970).

In order to renew a copyright, the artist filed an application with the Copyright Office, a branch of the Library of Congress. The renewal required an artist to send his application, a fee and two copies of the copyrighted work. This registration was also a pre-requisite to suing for copyright infringement.

6. Obtaining a Copyright: Current Rules

By contrast, after 1977 (or in some cases after 1990), a copyright automatically attaches upon creation if the three substantive rules above are met: it must be an original work in a copyrightable subject matter that is fixed in a medium of expression. No copyright notice is required (though one is advisable to forestall the defense of innocent infringement and provide the name of the copyright owner), nor is an application, nor must one send copies to the Library of Congress (though registration is advisable because neither statutory damages nor attorneys' fees are available in cases where the copyright registration has not been submitted before the infringing act).

The copyright lasts for the life of the author plus seventy years or, in the case of an author that is a corporation, pseudonymous or anonymous, or the work is made for hire, ninety-five years from the date of the work's first publication, or one hundred twenty years from the work's completion, whichever first occurs. 17 U.S.C. § 302.

A. Copyrightable Subject Matter and Production Methods

Copyright law lists a number of categories of things that can be copyrighted, and defines things that cannot be copyrighted. Those non-copyrightable aspects of works serve two functions. They are excluded in determining whether a work is sufficiently original to justify copyright, and the copying of those items is generally ignored in determining whether there has been copyright infringement.

i. Listed Subject Matters

17 U.S.C. § 102(a) lists eight different types of copyrightable subject matter. Most visual artwork falls within the heading of pictorial, graphic and sculptural works. Architecture falls in the category of architectural works. While there is a category for literary works, it is doubtful that the work of any visual artist, even one who uses as many words as Jenny Holzer does, would fall in that category because of the pictorial aspects of the works.

Pictorial, graphic and sculptural works are defined to include works of fine, graphic and applied art, photographs, prints and art reproductions, maps, globes, charts, diagrams, models and technical drawings (including architectural plans). All these categories are very broad, but they are limited in a number of ways.

ii. Idea v. Expression

It is often said that ideas cannot be copyrighted; all that can be copyrighted is the expression of an idea. When a photographer creates a portrait of a celebrity seen from the right side, the copyright in the photograph does not prohibit other photographers from re-using the idea and photographing other celebrities in the same position. Nor is it copyright infringement for other photographers to make their own portraits of the same celebrity.

The result is that copyright does not preclude anyone from using an idea. If the idea appears in a copyrighted work, anyone may still use the idea. It is the expression of the idea that may not be copied; the user must express the idea in his own way.

Ideas remain in the public domain. Put differently, the patent is the exclusive means of securing a monopoly over the functionality of an item, while a copyright protects its nonfunctional design from copying. The difference between a patent and a copyright is that a patent requires a much higher level of creativity, an advance in the state of the technology, than does a copyright. Permitting a copyright holder a monopoly over the functionality of anything would suppress the implementation of technology.

The noncopyrightability of an idea may have broader reach. If the only way to express an idea is to copy a previous artist's expression, the expression merges into the idea, so that all that remains is the idea, which cannot be copyrighted. Supposedly for that reason (though this is questionable) and because of specific exclusion, invented typefaces cannot be copyrighted. *Eltra Corp. v. Ringer*, 579 F.2d 294 (4th Cir. 1978).

Neither a person nor an animal nor a plant can be copyrighted.

iii. Scènes á Faire

In most of the decided cases involving photographs, defendant has produced a new photograph, and the question is whether that photograph copies too many copyrighted elements from plaintiff's photograph. The scènes á faire doctrine holds that not only is an idea uncopyrightable, the necessary steps in expressing that idea are likewise not protected by copyright.

In *Kaplan v. Stock Market Photo Agency, Inc.*, 133 F.Supp.2d 317 (S.D.N.Y. 2001), both plaintiff and defendant produced photos conveying the idea of an exasperated businessman contemplating suicide by jumping from a building. They both showed the scene from the eyes of the businessman looking down and perched on a roof or a ledge overlooking other buildings and a city street, their shoes extended over the edge, dressed in typical businessperson attire. The other buildings and the street were different, and the court refused summary judgment for plaintiff on grounds that the only similarities were the items necessary to express the idea of a businessman looking down and thinking about jumping.

By contrast, where two photographers shot photos used in commercials featuring the same athlete, Kevin Garnett, the court refused to grant either party summary judgment. The athlete was wearing the same jewelry (demanded by plaintiff) and shirt, and the photo was shot from a similar angle. The court did not extend Mannion's copyright to the athlete or the cloudy sky background, but did believe that copyright protection extended to the shirt and jewelry that plaintiff photographer had demanded and the camera angle. It thought that a reasonable jury might or might not find substantial similarity and copying between the two photos. It also despaired of making sense out of the idea-expression doctrine where photographs are concerned, a thought with which law students might well concur. *Mannion v. Coors Brewing Co.*, 377 F.Supp.2d 444 (S.D.N.Y. 2005).

iv. Usefulness

What is copyrightable about the expression is its form, not its function or utility. In *Mazer v. Stein*, 347 U.S. 201 (1954), a glass statuette was designed that was used as a lamp base. There was a copyright in the statuette, but not in the way the base held up the shade. If the functional elements of a design cannot be separated from the expressive elements, the item is not copyrightable because copyright should not provide a monopoly over something that is useful– that is the function of the patent law, with its higher creative requirements and shorter monopoly term.

Sometimes a work of art embodies both decorative and functional elements. Some cases separate the functional elements from the decorative ones. A mannequin's function is to display clothes or wigs or makeup. A copyright would not prevent another boutique from copying the way clothes hang on a mannequin. But a mannequin may also have an original facial expression or skin tone. In *Pivot Point Int'l, Inc. v. Charlene Products, Inc.*, 372 F.3d 913 (7th Cir. 2004), the court held that the facial modeling on plaintiff's copyrighted mannequin was protected from copying because it was separable from the function of the mannequin. In this case, the mannequin was a head on a stand that permitted students in beauty schools to practice styling hair and applying makeup. The facial features had no relationship to the hair, and arguably little relationship to the makeup application.

Some cases seem to reflect a primary influence test. A bicycle rack supposedly inspired by abstract expressionist sculpture was not copyrightable because the design was so dictated by its necessary function of holding bikes that decorative elements could not be separated from the functional elements. *Brandir Int'l, Inc. v. Cascade Pacific Lumber Co.*, 834 F.2d 1142 (2d Cir. 1987). *Brandir* may have reached the correct result in that case, but its logic was questionable. The court sought to follow the designer's thoughts to determine whether the design mostly reflected his independent artistic judgment or was primarily constrained by functional concerns. Often this path of inquiry will be unavailable because the designer is unavailable, or because there is insufficient evidence of the evolution of his concepts. Even when such evidence is available, it is not clear why the designer's thought process, which will always contain a mixture of the functional and the aesthetic, should be determinative, rather than the appearance.

Some courts have tried to draw a distinction based on physical separability. Under this doctrine, only design items that are physically separable from functional items are protected by copyright. For example, the shape of outdoor lighting fixtures could not be copyrighted because it was not physically separate from the portion of the fixtures that provided the lighting, and that was true even though the fixtures had shapes not required by their functions of directing or shielding light. One of the corollaries of this doctrine is that the overall shape of a useful item cannot be protected by copyright because it contains the functional elements. *Esquire, Inc. v. Ringer*, 591 F.2d 796 (D.C. Cir. 1978). Under this doctrine, the statuettes in *Mazer* would be protected if they could be physically removed from the lamps as an independent object. If the shade and the cord were removed, the statuette could function independently.

Other courts have permitted copyright when a design element is conceptually separable from function. Conceptual separability has been difficult to define. Some courts have used a primary purpose test, asking whether the primary purpose of the item was decorative or functional. In *Kieselstein-Cord v. Accessories by Pearl*, 632 F.2d 989 (2d Cir. 1980), the court ruled that copyright was appropriate to the ornamental surface of belt buckles despite the fact that the buckles functioned to hold the belt in position. The design was unrelated to the function of the buckles. The court suggested that one test might be whether the article could be marketed as an aesthetic object in a context where its utility would not be demanded. Such a counterfactual sounds good, but proving it might be extremely difficult unless the item were actually marketed in that way. In this case it was not marketed that way, but there was evidence that some consumers used the belt buckles as jewelry, thereby dispensing with the use of their parts designed to hold a belt.

Another test might be whether the design appeared to the average observer to be more dictated by its function, or whether it appeared to be more decorative.

The truth is that all these cases of applied art and industrial design involve a mixture of design and functionality. Perhaps it would be better to focus on the ultimate reason for asking the question, which is to prevent copyright protection from conferring a monopoly on functional developments that do not show a sufficient advancement in the art to qualify for a patent. This might more easily be achieved by asking the question directly, or by classifying every functional element as an idea that would not be protected by copyright, rather than an expression. This simple approach to the question is foreclosed because the law requires barring a "useful article" from copyright protection except when "such design incorporates pictorial, graphic, or sculptural features that can be identified separately from, and are capable of existing independently of, the utilitarian aspects of the article." 17 U.S.C. § 101.

The Supreme Court established a two-part test in a case where plaintiff had copyrighted 200 designs that plaintiff had applied to cheerleader uniforms. First, look at the useful item and ask whether there is an element that appears to have pictorial, graphic or sculptural qualities. Next, ask if the element is capable of existing on its own. The court held that the arrangement of colors, shapes, stripes and chevrons was capable of existing on its own, in part because plaintiff had applied it to other forms of clothing that were not cheerleader's uniforms. Star Athletica L.L.C. v. Varsity Brands, Inc., 137 S. Ct. 1002 (2017).

Architecture is by definition functional. Architectural works are "the design of a building..., architectural plans, or drawings." Buildings include habitable structures and those used by people, such as gazebos. They do not include walls, highways or bridges unless, like Florence's *ponte vecchio*, they contain shops or living quarters. Architectural works do not require fine decisions about conceptual separability because separability is part of the definition of pictorial, graphic, and sculptural works, and architectural works are their own separate category. The work must have original design elements to deserve copyright. If those design elements are not functionally required, the work is eligible for copyright, but the functional elements cannot be copyrighted.

v. Copyrightable Element Can Be Combination of Non-Copyrightable Elements

In many of the cases above, there were some aspects of the work protected by copyright, and other aspects not so protected. Even in a work consisting entirely of items not protected, the juxtaposition of non-protected elements may be protected by copyright as long as it is sufficiently original. That protection does not extend to the unprotectable elements; it only extends to the juxtaposition. Such a thin copyright provides some protection, but very little. In *Satava v. Lowry*, 323 F.3d 805 (9th Cir. 2003), plaintiff and defendant both made glass-in-glass sculptures depicting jellyfish. The court commented on many things not subject to copyright, such as jellyfish, their bells, their tentacles, depiction in clear glass because that is the most natural depiction, the fact that the fish almost fill their glass because that is standard in glass-in-glass sculpture, and the fact that the combination of these unprotectable elements was insufficiently original for copyright. It held that there was copyright in some of the hues used, distinctive curls of some tendrils and some unique bell shapes, but that was insufficient to justify the lower court in enjoining defendant from producing jellyfish glass-in-glass sculptures without proof that defendant was copying protectable elements of plaintiff's sculptures.

Compare that with *Mattel, Inc. v. Goldberger Doll Mfg. Co.*, 365 F.3d 133 (2d Cir. 2004), where plaintiff alleged that defendant had copied the face from two Barbie dolls. The court noted that while successful dolls had full faces, upturned noses, bow lips, large, widely spaced eyes and slim figures, that formula did not permit one doll manufacturer to copy the precise rendition of those features from another. A grant of summary judgment was reversed, leaving it to the jury to determine whether defendant copied from plaintiff.

vi. Other Things That Can or Cannot Be Copyrighted

Copyright is not denied to a work because it contains sexual elements, or even if it is obscene. In *Mitchell Bros. Film Group v. Cinema Adult Theater*, 604 F.2d 852 (5th Cir. 1979), defendant showed the pornographic film "Behind the Green Door" without permission of the copyright owner. The court rejected a defense that such a film was not entitled to a copyright. In addition to the fact that there was no such exception in the statute, the court worried that because obscenity is determined by applying local community standards, such a rule would produce nonuniform copyrights, protected in one community but not in another. This would seriously undermine the law's goal of providing a uniform national copyright law.

Copyright is not available for any work of the United States government. 17 U.S.C. § 105. Because work of the United States government cannot be copyrighted, there is no copyright in work prepared by a United States government employee within the scope of his employment under the work made for hire doctrine. The work is in the public domain.

However, the federal government is not prohibited from acquiring copyrights by transfer, such as assignment, sale or bequest. The federal government commissions many works of art for its buildings. If the federal government employs an artist as an independent contractor, but includes in the contract commissioning the art an assignment of the copyright to the United States, one might wonder if the assignment is valid, or whether it is void as subverting the purpose of the law providing that the United States cannot take an initial copyright. Clearly, the federal government could at a later time buy the copyright from the artist.

This rule about original copyrights only applies to the federal government. It does not apply to state governments or subsidiary bodies such as counties, cities, or special-purpose districts. However, longstanding caselaw stands for the proposition that state as well as federal statutes, ordinances, regulations and judicial decisions are inherently in the public domain, so cannot be protected by copyright.

None of the governmental disqualification rules apply to foreign governments.

Titles, at least short titles, cannot be copyrighted. They are usually so short that alternate forms of expression are difficult to find. Allowing a copyright would seriously inconvenience subsequent artists painting similar subject matter. They would be unable to title their still lives "Still Life," though one might wonder whether such a descriptive title is sufficiently original to justify a copyright.

vii. Computer-Generated Art

With the advent of computer-generated visual art, one must ask whether a computer can be an author under the copyright law. While there is no law on this point, granting a copyright to a computer would not serve the function of copyright in inducing the computer to produce the work. Computers cannot be induced.

If the computer cannot be an author, who is the author of a painting produced by computer? Where the computer operator makes significant choices so that it can be said that he provided the originality, he is clearly the author. One might add that he is also the one who fixes the product in a tangible medium.

This would include situations where the artist is using the computer as if it were a brush. One might call this computer-assisted work. Where the computer operator makes no significant choices, such as where the program operates with randomly-generated instructions to create the painting, one might argue that the author is the programmer who created the program. The programmer certainly has the copyright in the program, but it is not so clear that he would have a copyright in the work produced by the program. Neither the programmer nor the user makes decisions of the design in which the work will be fixed.

B. Fixation

i. Work in Progress

A work is copyrighted when it is fixed in a tangible medium of expression if it is original and a copyrightable subject matter. The work need not be finished to be protected by copyright. In *Massachusetts Museum of Contemporary Art Foundation, Inc. v. Büchel*, 593 F.3d 38 (1st Cir. 2010), the court held that where a number of elements of the installation work had been put in place by the artist or his assistants sufficient to communicate the work on more than a transitory basis, the work was fixed and copyright attached. This has the curious result of suggesting that each brushstroke added to a painting results in a different copyright because each brushstroke is a new fixing of the work. Each brushstroke might be a bit too transitory. Perhaps a better statement of the rule would be that a new copyright arises when the work is fixed for a reasonable period of time.

ii. Fixed on Computer

Computers have raised new questions about fixation for two reasons. Our usual concept of fixation is that it is permanent and readable by the naked eye. Something that is fixed only on a computer screen does not stay when the power is turned off. It may be fixed as a series of 0s and 1s on a flash drive, but the flash drive cannot be read without the aid of a machine. An early case had held that preparing a piano roll did not fix a work because the notes could not be read by the human eye, only by using a player piano. Congress reversed that result by statute, providing that a work is fixed if it can be perceived either by humans directly, or with the aid of any machine or device that currently exists or that might be invented at a later time, like the flash drive. It is clear that Congress intended to give a very broad interpretation to fixation. So the fact that a machine is required to perceive the work, to reproduce it, or to otherwise communicate it, is not a hindrance.

The second computer problem relates to permanence. A computer game has many possibilities. The direction in which the game goes depends in part on the user and in part on the program's response to each user decision. This means that once the first several screens are passed, duplicating the same screen is unlikely. It has been argued that computer games are insufficiently fixed to be copyrighted. *Williams Electronics, Inc. v. Arctic Int'l, Inc.*, 685 F.2d 870 (3d Cir. 1982), held that video games were sufficiently fixed to be copyrighted because the program anticipated the many alternatives that would appear in playing the game. The same argument can be made against a computer that, with the help of an operator, generates a painting, at least before the painting has been printed. One would expect the same affirmation that putting the painting into machine language is sufficient to fix it in a tangible medium.

iii. Performance Art and Temporary Art

There is usually little problem with fixation in the visual arts. Paintings, drawings and sculpture are fixed by definition. A form of art called a happening, such as an event where a group of women of different ages meet for two hours to discuss what it means to be a woman, would not be fixed until it was recorded in some way.

Temporary art, such as that practiced by Christo and Jeanne-Claude in erecting a running fence for a long distance but a short period of time, stands on a different footing. Though it has been argued that such art is not fixed because it is not permanent, the art is in fact fixed in a permanent medium, in this case wire, supports and cloth. It simply is not intended to be permanent. But a work is fixed under the statute if it "is sufficiently permanent or stable to permit it to be perceived, reproduced, or otherwise communicated for a period of more than transitory duration." 17 U.S.C. § 101. A temporary work can be perceived for that long a time. In addition, such a work is sufficiently fixed to support copyright if a work-in-progress is fixed. The purpose of encouraging the creation of original works does not require that the works endure. If the original copy of a drawing is destroyed, its copyright nonetheless remains. Copyright is distinct from the physical object, including the physical object in which it was first fixed. Likewise, when a work intended to be temporary is destroyed, its copyright remains.

iv. Purpose of Fixation Requirement

One might ask why fixation is required. The paradigm copyright violation is the copying of the copyrighted item. Without fixation, it would be difficult to determine whether the copyrighted item had been copied because one would not have the original with which to compare the copy.

C. Originality

Originality is usually not a problem for works of art because of the small amount of creativity required. The work needs to be a creation of the author, rather than a copy, and at least minimally creative. In *Bleistein v. Donaldson Lithographic Co.*, 188 U.S. 239 (1903), a poster advertising the circus conceived by the lithographers' employees was sufficiently original. The fact that its purpose was commercial did not disqualify it, and the court refused to decide whether it was good art or not. Numerous cases comment that there must be some originality, but the originality threshold is very low. However, photographs that tried to be close to exact copies of old master paintings were not sufficiently original to qualify for copyright in *Bridgeman Art Library v. Corel Corp.*, 36 F. Supp. 2d 191 (S.D.N.Y. 1999). This does not mean that there is no contract remedy available for reproducing them; it simply means that copyright is not an available remedy. One might argue that the exact copy should not be absolutely barred from copyright protection. Where considerable creativity is required to produce an exact copy, one can argue that the required creativity is enough to support a copyright. The problem with this argument is that the originality would be in designing or executing the process, an idea, whereas the copyright is granted for originality in the expression.

For some years, it was thought that the investment of considerable labor was sufficient for originality. *Feist Publications, Inc. v. Rural Telephone Service Co.*, 499 U.S. 340 (1991), held that a telephone directory was insufficiently original, being a compilation of facts (the persons' names, addresses and phone numbers) arranged in alphabetical order, first by surname, then by given name. Facts are not copyrightable, nor is alphabetical order, which is not original. So the phone book could not be copyrighted despite the massive work required to produce it because it is a series of facts arranged in alphabetical order.

In some cases, however, reproductions can be original. This is especially true when moving from one medium to another. Renderings of paintings done as mezzotints were held to be sufficiently original because they had more than a trivial variation from the original, on the analogy to translations of literary works. *Alfred Bell & Co. v. Catalda Fine Arts*, 74 F.Supp. 973 (S.D.N.Y. 1947).

It is often stated that the purpose of originality is only to denote that a copy of another's expression cannot be copyrighted. It is true that copies are not eligible, and many cases have been won or lost on the judge's opinion of whether the work claiming copyright is a substantial copy of some other work, such as the plastic bank that was held by a divided court to be too similar to a metal Uncle Sam bank in the public domain in *L. Batlin & Son v. Snyder*, 536 F.2d 486 (2d Cir. 1976).

The originality requirement disqualifies other things, like common geometric shapes, from copyright. While a square may not be copyrightable, the paintings of Josef Albers, showing concentric squares in different colors, would be. No protection would be given to the square, but protection might be given to the squares-within-squares and the color combinations.

The determination of originality should not be a determination of value or quality of what is produced. In *Bleistein*, Justice Holmes warned: "[I]t would be a dangerous undertaking for persons trained only to the law to constitute themselves final judges of the worth of pictorial illustrations...." Courts and the copyright office have generally followed that admonition.

7. Who Owns the Copyright?

A. Joint Authorship

All authors of a joint work are considered tenants in common of its copyright. That means that each can use it or license others to do so, but the co-tenant licensing the copyright must account to the other authors of the joint work for their share of the fees received from third parties. One co-tenant cannot grant an exclusive license of the copyright because that would preclude his co-tenants from using or licensing the copyrighted item. *Davis v. Blige*, 505 F.3d 90 (2d Cir. 2007).

A joint work is a work prepared with the intention that the contributions of the multiple authors, each of which has sufficient originality to merit copyright, will merge into inseparable or interdependent parts of a unitary whole. The easiest way to find a joint authorship is if the authors agree in writing. Alternatively, they could agree orally; they could consent to attach all their names to the credits; or they could follow a course of conduct indicating that intention.

Intent must be distinguished from hope. An artist may hope that his painting will be incorporated into a company's snappy advertisements, but that is insufficient. She must intend it. While she need not be part of that collaboration, she must intend it. Proving this is often difficult. A contemporaneous writing by the artist might be useful. More useful would be proof that the artist sent reproductions of the painting to a number of potential advertisers with the suggestion that it be used in advertising with appropriate promotional words prepared by others.

It is easier to find joint authorship if the contributions of the joint authors are relatively contemporaneous. Indeed, there is some suggestion that the older cases permitting joint authorship when the contributions of the joint authors are made separately and years apart are no longer valid.

The statute does not require this, but one circuit requires each joint author to contribute some copyrightable content. A requirement of copyrightable content may be justified in a number of ways. It is certainly more in conformity with the spirit of the copyright laws in encouraging original contributions, though one might argue that the ability to assign a copyright to someone who was not a co-creator already contradicts that spirit. It has the advantage of being an objective criterion subject to more concrete proof than the question of whether there was intent to create a joint work. If the rule is widely known, it will encourage parties to such an endeavor to specify their respective rights by contract as a substitute for the automatic rights that copyright conveys. The principal result of such a rule is that where one person provides only the ideas, that person is not a joint author. In *Johannsen v. Brown*, 797 F.Supp. 835 (D. Or. 1992), defendant suggested to plaintiff that he create a work like Grant Wood's American Gothic, substituting skeletons for the farmers and a guitar for the pitchfork, to promote interest in the rock group the Grateful Dead. Defendant was not a joint author, though he contributed invaluable ideas, because he did not contribute anything copyrightable to the work. Nothing he contributed was fixed. Most circuits have yet to adopt this requirement. What is clear is that there is no requirement that the contributions of joint authors be equal.

The number of joint authorships of visual artwork is small. The most common form of joint authorship involves one person writing the music and another the lyrics to a song. The paintings in the Brancacci Chapel in Florence's Santa Maria del Carmine were done by Masolino da Panicale (1383?–1477?) and Masaccio (1401–1428), who were probably joint authors, and finished sixty years later by Filippino Lippi (1457?–1504). Filippino Lippi would not today be considered a joint author because the earlier painters did not contemplate joint authorship when they performed their work. Likewise, Lorenzo Ghiberti (1378–1455) reported that twenty-one persons, including Michelozzo (1396?–1472) and Donatello (1386?–1466), worked on his doors for Florence's Baptistery that Michaelangelo called "The Gates of Paradise" (1425–52), but none did so as part of a joint enterprise, rather than as being subject to Ghiberti's direction. A classic example of joint authorship is found in the work of Jan Breugel the Elder (1568–1625) and Peter Paul Rubens (1577–1640), who did several paintings in which one painted the landscape and the other the figures in it.

The Supreme Court in *Community for Creative Non-Violence v. Reid*, 490 U.S. 730 (1989), suggested that there might have been a joint authorship between the person who supplied the concepts for the work and the sculptor who actually produced it. As a proposition, this seems dubious in a circuit requiring that each joint author provide something that is copyrightable because concepts are not copyrightable. A person who only supplied concepts could not be a joint author. But it is possible that the person who provided the concepts and also supplied the base for the sculpture might have contributed sufficient originality through the base to qualify for the issuance of a copyright. Alternatively, it is possible that the concepts were embodied in a design. Because the parties settled, we never discovered if this case involved joint authorship.

Joint authorship must be distinguished from co-ownership. Joint authorship is created as set forth above; co-ownership occurs whenever the copyright is transferred in undivided shares to more than one person, whether that transfer be by assignment, will, intestate succession, divorce, or by the exercise of termination of transfer provisions. If the author is a resident of a community property state, such as California, where products of the personal services of a person belong equally to that person and that person's spouse, there is co-ownership. Co-ownership may arise if the copyright holder assigns an undivided one-half share to someone else. In joint authorship, the duration of the copyright is the life of the surviving joint author plus seventy years. Co-ownership does not change the life of the copyright from its original duration of either the life of the author plus seventy years or the fixed term provided for some works.

B. Work Made for Hire

If a work is made for hire, the copyright belongs to the hirer. A work made for hire is a work prepared by an employee within the scope of his employment, or a work specially ordered if there is a written contract deeming it a work made for hire and it meets certain subject matter requirements.

It is common in the motion picture and television industries that contracts with independent contractors provide that the eventual work is a work made for hire, and the production company owns the copyright.

The question of whether a work is made for hire is important in determining who owns the copyright and for other reasons. We have already seen that the work made for hire doctrine attributing the copyright in federal government work to the employer results in no copyright in the work, and that the duration of copyright on a work made for hire differs from the duration of other copyrights.

i. Employee Rules

There has been little litigation involving the rights of admitted employees because the law is clear, even if the facts are frequently unclear. For example, faculty members in university visual arts departments are expected to publish as part of their jobs. That publication normally takes the form of producing paintings, sculptures or photographs. Faculty members are university employees and these works are produced within the scope of their employment, so these are works made for hire.

The reason there is little controversy over teachers is two-fold.

First and most important, most university employee policies permit the employee to keep copyrights (but not patents) developed as work made for hire. Such a policy (or even an express contractual provision) does not change the copyright from a work made for hire to a copyright secured by the employee. It is instead an assignment of the copyright from the employer to the employee. In *Carter v. Helmsley-Spear, Inc.*, 71 F.3d 77 (2d Cir 1995), the contract specifically provided that the artists held the copyright, which did not prevent the court from holding that this was a work made for hire.

Second, it appears that there was an exception for teachers under the 1909 Copyright Act. That exception to the work made for hire doctrine covered the teacher's lecture notes and may have covered the teacher's publications. Whether that teacher's exception has survived the 1976 Act is a matter of some dispute, its principal proponents being two well-respected federal judges who were formerly full-time law professors.

a. Employee Defined

Some difficulty has arisen in determining whether persons are employees or not. There is no definition in the copyright law. In *Community for Creative Non-Violence v. Reid*, 490 U.S. 730 (1989), the court said that a person is an employee for purposes of copyright if he would have been an employee under the common law of agency, and enumerated thirteen factors a court should consider in deciding that question. Those factors are: (1) the right of the hiring party to control the way in which the task is accomplished; (2) who has the skill required; (3) who provides the tools; (4) where the work is done; (5) the length of the relationship between the parties; (6) whether the hiring party has the right to assign other tasks to the person hired; (7) whether the hired party has discretion over when and how to work; (8) the method of payment; (9)

whether the hired party may hire assistants and, if so, who pays them; (10) whether the work is part of the regular business of the hiring person; (11) whether the hiring person is in business; (12) whether the hiring person provides the hired person normal employee fringe benefits such as health insurance and especially retirement contributions; and (13) whether the hiring person withholds or otherwise treats the hired person as an employee for tax purposes.

That case involved the production of a sculpture to be placed on a base provided by the commissioning party by a sculptor commissioned by an organization wanting to dramatize the plight of the poor. The sculptor had the required skill, provided his own tools, did not work on the hirer's premises, could not have been assigned other tasks, could decide when and how to work, was paid a lump sum, not on the basis of time invested, could hire assistants but would be responsible for paying them, received no fringe benefits, and was not subjected to income tax withholding by the hirer. Under those circumstances, the court held that the individual was an independent contractor rather than an employee.

A test that employs thirteen factors without any weighting of the factors makes it difficult to predict the outcome in many cases. In *Aymes v Bonelli*, 980 F.2d 857 (2d Cir. 1992), the court pointed out that the significance of each factor needs to be weighed with the facts of the case, and suggested that the factors are not all of equal weight, the important factors being #1, 2, 6, 12 and 13, perhaps the most important being normal fringe benefits and tax treatment. In *Carter v. Helmsley-Spear, Inc.*, 71 F.3d 77 (2d Cir 1995), the hiring party had the right to control the way the art was produced; the artists had the skills; the hirer provided the tools and the raw materials; the work was done on the hirer's premises; the relationship was long-term; the hired persons were in fact assigned other tasks; payment did not appear to be by the job; there were normal employee fringe benefits, and the hirer withheld income tax as though the artists were employees. The court held this a work made for hire.

b. Scope of Employment

A work is made for hire by an employee only if the work is created within the scope of his employment. Taking the example of the art professor, her paintings would be produced within the scope of her employment, but if she were also hired on a contract to produce a logo for the university, the logo would not have been prepared in the scope of her employment; it was produced under an independent contract. The university should have provided in the contract for assignment of the copyright. On the other hand, if the employee were a high school teacher whose employment does not require that she publish, it is unclear whether the publication would be within the scope of her employment. That may depend on other factors such as whether the publication was developed during time for which she was paid by the school district by being released from her regular duties.

ii. Independent Contractor Rules

The number of times when a work not prepared by an employee within the scope of his employment can be a work made for hire is very limited. Such a work must fall within a small number of categories, and there must be a written agreement signed by both parties agreeing that the work is a work made for hire. The categories where a work made for hire by an independent contractor might be permitted that are of interest to the visual artist are movies, discussed above, supplementary works, contributions to compilations and collective works, and instructional texts. A separately-published book of illustrations for a novel would be a supplementary work; an artist hired to prepare one illustration for a volume of drawings on the Adam-and-Eve story would be contributing to a compilation, as would a freelance photographer whose picture is published in a newspaper or magazine; and the flow charts illustrating decision-making processes would be instructional texts. Otherwise, a painting, drawing, print, sculpture or photograph generally does not fall within one of the categories that can be a work made for hire by an independent contractor.

There is little that can be said about the written agreement required, except that both parties must sign it. This is different from the statute of frauds or the transfer of certain rights in a copyright, which need only be signed by the party to be charged. The statute does not state whether the written agreement needs to be integrated into the agreement commissioning the work, or whether it need be signed before the work is completed.

8. Transferring the Copyright

Under pre-1978 state law, the transfer of an artwork was an implied transfer of the copyright in the work unless the copyright was specifically reserved. The 1976 Copyright Act reverses this rule. There is no transfer of the copyright unless it is expressly transferred with the work. 17 U.S.C. § 202.

California has a mirror-image rule. Just as federal law provides that transferring the work does not transfer the copyright unless such an intent is expressed, in California the transfer of a copyright does not transfer ownership of the copyrighted work unless the intent to transfer ownership of the work is evidenced by a writing signed by the owner. This is not a generalized statute of frauds for artwork; it only applies when there is a transfer of a copyright or an interest in a copyright. CALIF. CIV. CODE § 988; *Chamberlain v. Cocola Assocs.*, 958 F.2d 282 (9th Cir. 1992).

The result is that a copyright owner may not have the right to digitally photograph the work after he sells it so that he can effectively exploit his copyright without the permission of the buyer. Likewise, the owner of the physical work may not use the perfect digital image he makes of the work to produce and sell posters of it without the consent of the copyright owner.

The transfer of an exclusive right or an assignment can only be made in writing, 17 U.S.C. §§ 101, 204(a), whereas a nonexclusive right can be transferred orally or by conduct (though it is not good practice because both the exact scope of the rights being transferred and the consideration to be received may be difficult to prove, and because it makes it more difficult to record the transfer).

To protect oneself against subsequent transfers or security interests, the transferee of any right under a copyright should record the transfer with the Copyright Office of the Library of Congress promptly. 17 U.S.C. § 205.

Even where these transfers purport to endure for the full term of copyright and any renewals or extensions of it, the transfers may be revoked (unless it is a work made for hire) at any time during a period of five years beginning on the thirty-fifth anniversary of either the original transfer or, if the contract grants first publication rights, of the publication date, provided the author gives at least two years' advance notice. 17 U.S.C. § 203. The reasoning behind this provision is to give the author a second chance to exploit the copyright. The first assignee has thirty-five years to recoup his investment. If the copyright is not generating significant returns, the author is unlikely to exercise his right of revocation unless the author believes that the grantee has been insufficiently diligent in exploiting the copyright. Otherwise, no one else will bid higher for it. If the copyright does generate significant returns, such as for licensing the design for reproduction on napkins that sell well, the threat of termination may cause the assignee to increase the royalty promised.

We speak about "the copyright owner" and "the owner of the copyrighted work" as though they both could have but a single owner. But a copyright owner can divide the many rights he is given by the copyright system and assign each right to a different person so there might be a legion of copyright owners and licensees. It is more unusual to have divided ownership in the copyrighted work, but there are instances where a painting is owned by a group of people with fractional shares.

9. Infringement

An action for infringement of copyright in a work may not begin until the copyright holder has filed registration papers for the item with the Copyright Office of the Library of Congress and paid the appropriate fee. (The basic fee is $125; a bargain fee of $45 applies to online registration of a single author work that is not a work made for hire; other online registration $65; an eve-of-litigation registration costs $800 for expedited special handling.) The infringement may occur before the registration, but registration is a pre-requisite to bringing suit. Works first published abroad in the more than 170 countries with which the United States has copyright treaty relations are not subject to the requirement of pre-suit copyright registration.

Copying a work's protected expression infringes the copyright on the work. Two elements of infringement are access to the copyrighted work, and copying copyrightable elements.

A. Access

Plaintiff has the burden of proving that defendant had access to the copyrighted work. Sometimes there is direct evidence of this, as when plaintiff sends a copy to defendant and retains the signed postal receipt. More frequently, the plaintiff proves this access by establishing that both plaintiff and defendant had dealings with a third party, usually a publisher or an agent, who had the work and who showed it to defendant. Absent that, a plaintiff can prove access by showing that the work was widely distributed to the general public, in which case the court is accepting proof of reasonable opportunity to access the work, rather than actual access. Finally, some courts have allowed a plaintiff to prove access when the two works have substantial similarities that they do not share with any works in the public domain. *Crown Awards, Inc. v. Discount Trophy & Co., Inc.*, 326 Fed. Appx. 575 (2d Cir. 2009). Courts sometimes refer to this as "striking similarities."

B. Copying Copyrightable Elements

Plaintiff also has the burden of proving that something was copied.

Copying usually presents problems of proof, but occasionally the person who copies leaves a paper trail. In *Rogers v. Koons*, 960 F.2d 301 (2d Cir. 1992), Jeff Koons provided the artists who worked for him with a copy of Rogers' photo and wrote on it instructions to produce a sculpture as close to Rogers' photograph of a couple holding eight puppies as possible. In the more usual case, plaintiff can show infringement by demonstrating that the alleged infringer had access to the work and the similarities between the copyrightable parts of the copyrighted work and the alleged infringement were so great or so tell-tale that one may infer that the second work was copied from the first. *Crown Awards, Inc. v. Discount Trophy & Co., Inc.*, 326 Fed. Appx. 575 (2d Cir. 2009). The trier of fact may take into account variations that seem designed to disguise the fact of copying.

Proof of substantial similarity can be overcome by establishing that the defendant independently created his work. This is not often done, but can be accomplished where defendant has contemporaneous notes showing the progressive development of his work. While independent creation is often considered a defense to infringement, it more logically belongs with proof of copying. Alternatively, where the artist is accused of copying an item in his previous work the copyright in which he has transferred, one would expect that an artist with a distinctive style who paints the same subject matter twice would wind up with substantially similar items even though the second was not a copy of the first.

Plaintiff must also prove that what was copied was protected by copyright. (Recall that ideas and information are not protectable; only expression is protectable.) Most frequently plaintiff proves this by showing a substantial similarity between the works.

Some courts hold that proving substantial similarity conceptually has two components. First, courts dissect the works and compare their components and details to determine if there has been copying. But copying is not enough. Second, courts determine whether impermissible elements have been copied. It is not copyright infringement to copy elements of a work that are not protected by copyright, such as ideas, utilitarian elements, or elements in the public domain. Once the unprotected elements are eliminated, courts compare the two works asking if a reasonable person would believe that similarities between the copyright-protected elements of the two works indicate that defendant unlawfully appropriated protected material of substance and value. This method of dissection, often used effectively with software, risks losing the sense of the composition when applied to artwork.

In *Leigh v. Warner Bros., Inc.*, 212 F.3d 1210 (11th Cir. 2000), the court held that the protected elements of a copyrighted photograph of a cemetery statue were the selection of lighting, shading, timing, angle and film selection. The copyright of the statue did not belong to the photographer, and the eerie mood of the photograph was insufficiently original for copyright, as such a mood is typical of cemeteries. Eliminating the elements that did not qualify, there was similarity in some of the protected elements, but not in enough of them to establish copying, and the photographer's infringement suit failed.

Given that the subject matter is not protected by copyright and only the original elements are, it is often difficult to find original elements where the photographer does not arrange the scene, provide props or plan the lighting. In *Harney v. Sony Pictures TV, Inc.*, 704 F.3d 173 (1st Cir. 2013), the court found the placement of the father and daughter centrally in the photo a similarity, but the lighting and coloring were different, and the subject matter is not copyrightable, so the court affirmed the lower court's grant of summary judgment for defendant. Where the cartoonist Saul Steinberg accused Columbia Pictures of copying his near-sighted New Yorker cover view of the world for a poster advertising the movie "Moscow on the Hudson," the court said in granting summary judgment for plaintiff, "There is no dispute that defendants cannot be held liable for using the idea of a map of the world from an egocentrically myopic perspective." But it looked at style as one factor in expression. "Defendants' illustration was executed in the sketchy, whimsical style that has become one of Steinberg's hallmarks. Both illustrations represent a bird's eye view across the edge of Manhattan and a river bordering New York City to the world beyond. Both depict approximately four city blocks in detail and become increasingly minimalist as the design recedes into the background. Both use the device of a narrow band of blue wash across the top of the poster to represent the sky, and both delineate the horizon with a band of primary red." "Both artists chose a vantage point that looks directly down a wide two-way cross street that intersects two avenues before reaching a river. Despite defendants' protestations, this is not an inevitable way of depicting blocks in a city with a grid-like street system, particularly since most New York City cross streets are one-way." "[T]he Columbia artist's use of the childlike, spiky block print that has become one of Steinberg's hallmarks to letter the names of the streets in the "Moscow" poster can be explained only as copying." The court rejected defenses based on substantial dissimilarities between the works, and also that the copying involved only a small amount of the works. "No plagiarist can excuse the wrong by showing how much of his work he did not pirate." *Steinberg v. Columbia Pictures Ind., Inc.*, 663 F.Supp. 706 (S.D.N.Y. 1987).

An artist can use the same source to prepare more than one version of the same scene. In *Franklin Mint Corp. v. National Wildlife Art Exchange, Inc.*, 575 F.2d 62 (3d Cir. 1978), the watercolor artist used some of the same models he had used in creating a first painting of cardinals (whose copyright he had transferred to plaintiff) to create a second such painting. He convinced the court that he did not copy the first painting because while there were substantial similarities between the two, there were also substantial differences, so there was no copyright infringement.

C. *De Minimis*

There is a possibility that some actual copying may be so minimal as to not violate the copyright laws, thereby not becoming actionable copying. Photocopying a cartoon for posting on your refrigerator is said to be one; copying a very small amount of the work is another. One court held that the action of the Register of Copyrights in requiring a compulsory license fee for on-air display in excess of three seconds establishes the *de minimis* limit for television programs, so exposure for twenty-five seconds was not *de minimis*. *Ringgold v. Black Entertainment Television, Inc.*, 126 F.3d 70 (2d Cir. 1997). But in the same circuit, appearance of the copyrighted pinball machine in the background of a film, sometimes out of focus, during parts of a three-minute scene, was held not to be copyright infringement as a matter of law, in part because the casual observer of the film would not perceive the copying. *Gottlieb Development v. Paramount Pictures Corp.*, 590 F.Supp.2d 625 (S.D.N.Y. 2008). The appearance of out-of-focus portraits shot in a movie at long distance and often obscured by actors so that an average viewer would be unable to make them out was held not to be copyright infringement because it was *de minimis*. *Sandoval v. New Line Cinema Corp.*, 147 F.3d 215 (2d Cir. 1998). When the courts speak about *de minimis*, it is unclear to what they are referring as minimal. In both cases, the entire copyrighted work was copied, so this is not the sort of case, properly discussed below under fair use, where only a small amount was copied. Minimal factors that seem to be important are the importance of the copyrighted work to the work into which it was copied, the ability of the average person to identify that a work has been copied, or the percent of the copying work in which the copied work appears.

10. Secondary Liability

It is not just the person who copies a copyrighted artwork who may be liable to the copyright owner. A contributory infringer is someone who does not infringe the copyright in the work himself, but encourages direct infringement by providing the means for infringement and turning a blind eye to it. That person may be liable as a contributory infringer. Vicarious infringement occurs when a person has the right to control the action of another and fails to prevent infringement when he profits by it. Copyright owners are motivated to sue secondary infringers where the direct infringers are a large number of individuals of questionable ability to respond in damages. Usually, the secondary infringers are a limited number of solvent businesses whom it is more efficient to sue, and from whom it is easier to collect. While most of the cases have involved music, a person who does not copy the work, but who knowingly displays a work that infringes copyright may be liable. The exact contours of this secondary liability are murky, but it should be a matter of concern to gallery owners, distributors of movies and videos, and website owners. (It would also concern online service and access providers but for 17 U.S.C. §512, which provides some of them a safe harbor if they comply with its requirements.) The question of the liability of the gallery owner who displays works that violate copyrights was raised, but not answered, in *Cariou v. Prince*, 714 F.3d 694 (2d Cir. 2013), because the case was remanded to the district court to determine whether five of the thirty works at issue were saved from copyright violation by the fair use doctrine, which would negate the copier's liability, as well as the gallery's secondary liability. The parties then settled.

A fringe detriment of secondary liability is that it is likely to induce people who provide artists with platforms for displaying their work to become art censors. Given the inherent unpredictability of the application of the fair use doctrine discussed below, gallery owners, movie distributors and website owners are much more likely to simply remove the work that is accused of violating a copyright than to pay to litigate the question of whether the copying was permitted by fair use.

11. Derivative Works

The preparation of a derivative work without permission of the copyright holder infringes the copyright. *Rogers v. Koons* was not actually a case of copying, but of taking a photograph and preparing a sculpture, a derivative work, of the same image.

A. Originality Required for a Derivative Work

Derivative works may be copyrighted if they demonstrate sufficient originality to distinguish them from the original copyrighted work. In *Gracen v. Bradford Exchange*, 698 F.2d 300 (7th Cir 1983), defendant was authorized by the copyright holder of the movie "The Wizard of Oz" to produce plates with designs based on the movie. Defendant held a contest for the best such designs, which was won by Ms. Gracen, but the parties could not reach agreement on a contract for her to produce cartoons for the china. Defendant hired another artist to produce the cartoons, showing that person Ms. Gracen's work, and Ms. Gracen sued for copyright infringement. It seemed clear to the court that Ms. Gracen was authorized to produce her derivative work by the license given from the copyright holder to defendant, but not at all clear that Ms. Gracen was authorized to receive a copyright on those derivative works. Setting that question aside, the court commented that Ms. Gracen's drawings did not show enough variation from the original movie stills to justify a copyright because more originality is required to copyright a derivative work than the original. Since her work did not qualify for a copyright, she could not recover from defendant for copyright infringement.

Two important aspects of *Gracen* were questioned in *Schrock v. Learning Curve Int'l, Inc.*, 586 F.3d 513 (7th Cir. 2009). One defendant, HIT, held the copyright to the Thomas & Friends train characters. It licensed Learning Curve to produce the Thomas toys. Learning Curve hired plaintiff photographer to take publicity shots of the toys. After plaintiff was no longer photographing for Learning Curve, Learning Curve made copies of plaintiff's photos, and plaintiff sued for copyright infringement. The court stated that no permission was required from the copyright holder for plaintiff to receive a copyright in his photos; a copyright would automatically issue if there was copyrightable subject matter, the work was fixed in a tangible medium (both of which were uncontested), plaintiff's work was sufficiently original and plaintiff was authorized to create a derivative work. The court then stated that the originality required for a derivative work was no more than the originality required for a non-derivative work: sufficient, non-trivial expressive variation to make it distinguishable from other copyrighted works or works in the public domain. The final result was a remand to determine first, whether HIT and Learning Curve had authorized the creation of a derivative work, and second, whether plaintiff Schrock had by contract authorized Learning Curve to use his copyright in the photos.

B. Derivative Works v. the First Sale Doctrine

A series of cases raise the question of whether the sale of a purchased copyrighted item can result in infringement by constituting a derivative work. Annie Lee produced notecards and lithographs. A.R.T. Co. purchased them at retail, attached them to ceramic tiles, protected them with transparent resin, and sold the resultant decorated tiles. Ms. Lee claimed that defendant produced a derivative work without permission; defendant claimed that it was simply reselling the work it purchased, which is not a copyright infringement because of the first sale doctrine. The first sale doctrine provides that, as an exception to the exclusive right of the copyright holder to distribute copies to the public, the first sale of the work exhausts the copyright holder's distribution right to that physical item, so that the item can be re-sold without the re-sale being a copyright violation. 17 U.S.C. § 109. The first sale doctrine is not an exception to the right of the copyright holder to prepare derivative works. At issue was the definition of derivative work as "a work based upon one or more preexisting works, such as a translation ... motion picture version, ... art reproduction, abridgment, condensation, or any other form in which a work may be recast, transformed, or adapted." While everyone agrees that changing the frame of an artwork does not create a derivative work, the Ninth Circuit held that gluing the work to a tile created a derivative work because it recast, transformed or adapted the work, while the Seventh Circuit dismissed out of hand the idea that gluing recast or adapted the work, then found no transformation because the image was exactly the same. *Mirage Editions, Inc. v. Albuquerque A.R.T. Co.*, 856 F.2d 1341 (9th Cir. 1988); *Lee v. A.R.T. Co.*, 125 F.3d 580 (7th Cir. 1997). The sale of a used book with the first purchaser's annotations in it would not constitute a copyright violation because of the additions to the original work, either because they are *de minimis*, or because this would constitute fair use. The Supreme Court's recent decision in *Kirtsaeng v. John Wiley & Sons, Inc.*, 133 S.Ct. 1351 (2013) strengthens the first sale doctrine, but does not resolve the problem because the books in that case were unchanged.

It is unclear whether copying a part of a copyrighted work is infringement by copying, or infringement by the preparation of a derivative work, or both. In *Wojnarowicz v. American Family Ass'n*, 745 F. Supp. 130 (S.D.N.Y. 1990), defendant copied "the dirty parts" of plaintiff's work to send to legislators and other influential persons to convince them that the work was pornography. The case was tried on the theory of violation of plaintiff's moral rights under New York law, but this might have been the creation of a derivative work. It is certainly a work based on a pre-existing work that recast the work.

12. Distribution

It is a copyright violation to distribute the copyrighted item without authorization. It does not frequently occur that there is distribution without a sale, but where a club commissioned a photographer to take photos of its "girls" for a promotional calendar but never paid for the photos, the free distribution of the calendars with the copyrighted photos was infringement. *Tangorre v. Mako's, Inc.*, 2003 WL 470577 (S.D.N.Y. 2003). The distribution right also includes the lending or leasing of the artwork.

The distribution right is separate from the reproduction right. An artist might find that his reproduction right is being violated by one person and his distribution right by another. If one activity is being carried on in the United States and another activity in a foreign country, it may be considerably easier to exercise rights in the United States than abroad.

13. Special Problems of Architecture

Architectural works are also subject to copyright. The general rules of copyright apply to architectural works except where a different rule has been established. In *Shine v. Childs*, 382 F.Supp.2d 602 (S.D.N.Y. 2005), plaintiff Yale architecture student alleged that his two building designs were used by one of the members of his evaluation jury in submitting a design for the Freedom Tower of the World Trade Center. The court reviewed the ordinary rules requiring originality, as well as the disqualification of functional elements. The court said that originality could be found in any non-functional design element, and it alternately could be found, if there was no individual design element that was original, in an original combination of design elements. Copying could be established by showing access (which was undisputed here) and probative similarity. It applied a test of "total concept and feel" of the copyrightable elements to the average observer, which is used to establish similarity between artistic works. The motion for summary judgment was granted for one design and denied for the other, because no reasonable jury could find substantial similarity in one case, but there was a conflict of evidence for the other. Nothing in this case would have been out of place in the discussion of copyright infringement of non-architectural works.

On the other hand, the statute provides that it is not copyright infringement to make or publish pictorial representations of a building visible from a public place. 17 U.S.C. § 120(a). Apparently, Congress did not want to condone trespass to represent a building that was not visible from a public space, but the statute does not limit the view that one can publish to an area visible from a public space. A sharp line is drawn between a building, that can legally be photographed, and a sculpture, which cannot. In *Leicester v. Warner Brothers Corp.*, 232 F.3d 1212 (9th Cir. 2000), a Batman movie was shot in an area of Los Angeles. The sculptor, Leicester, contended that the movie filmed his outdoor sculpture, Zanja Maja, commissioned by the building owner, but the court found that the areas filmed were part of the building, so there was no copyright violation in filming it.

A second exception to normal copyright treatment is that the owner of a building is privileged to alter or destroy it, regardless of the fact that he is thereby destroying or altering the element protected by copyright and possibly creating a derivative work which would normally violate the architect's copyright. The justification is that the ownership interest in the physical building outweighs the architect's copyright interest. One might ask how far the right to alter the building goes. It probably encompasses the right to produce plans based on the existing design altered to show the building scheme for the alteration. It may also permit the owner to build an addition in the style of the existing building.

14. Defense to Infringement: Fair Use

A. Requirements for Fair Use

The fair use defense began life as a judge-made defense after the founding of the republic; it was recently codified; and it may be required by the First Amendment.

The First Amendment protects freedom of speech and of the press. Copyright restrains speech and printing that duplicates or is substantially similar to a copyrighted work without permission. It has been argued that fair use reconciles these two conflicting principles. Specifically, fair use delimits the degree to which the First Amendment prevents the extension of copyright liability. While this is an interesting theory, it will never be confirmed; if fair use and the scope of the First Amendment in this area are co-extensive, the cases will always be decided on the nonconstitutional basis that defendant has satisfied fair use. It could be refuted if the court ever holds that a defendant has failed to establish fair use, but is nonetheless protected by the First Amendment.

The United States stands nearly alone in having an amorphous fair use defense. Most countries enumerate statutory defenses that might include fair dealing, but are much more specific than fair use.

The defendant has the burden of proving fair use. Fair use is a mixed question of law and fact. It is a defense resembling an equitable defense in that all the facts and circumstances are considered. It permits courts to avoid the rigid application of the remainder of copyright law when that would stifle the creativity that copyright law is designed to foster.

The statute states that the fair use of a copyrighted work "for purposes such as criticism, comment, news reporting, teaching (including multiple copies for classroom use), scholarship, or research, is not an infringement of copyright." 17 U.S.C. §107. One might think that means that any use for one of the six enumerated purposes would be a fair use, but that is not the case. One cannot copy a thousand page textbook solely because it will be used for teaching. Instead, this preamble gives a general flavor of the kinds of uses that courts have typically considered fair, but needs to be read in conjunction with the four factors the court must consider in deciding whether a use is fair, and other factors that the court might consider. The statute does not enumerate what other factors are permissible, but one might suggest good faith or custom. The four enumerated factors are:

1) the purpose of the use, especially whether it is commercial or nonprofit;
2) the nature of the copyrighted work;
3) the proportion of the copyrighted work that is used; and
4) the effect of the use on the potential market for the copyrighted work.

Applying those factors to the case above, the purpose of the use is teaching, by a nonprofit organization, a use that would favor fair use; the copyrighted work is a textbook, which would also favor fair use; all of it is being copied, which would disfavor fair use; and the copying will surely result in the loss of sales that otherwise would have occurred, which would disfavor fair use. The last two criteria argue against fair use, and they are precisely the underlying purpose of copyright. See *Encyclopedia Britannica Educational Corp. v. Crooks*, 542 F.Supp. 1156 (W.D. N.Y. 1982).

i. Purpose of the Use

The criterion of the purpose of the use seems to have two aspects.

The first aspect is set forth above: Is the use a favored use, such as criticism, comment, news reporting, teaching, scholarship, or research? These uses have one thing in common: each involves a context in which the work is transformed. News reporting adduces something occurring to the work; the other activities try to cast a new light on the work. Transformative uses tend to be creative and to be highly favored in First Amendment jurisprudence because they produce new work or adapt the work to new purposes. This transformative addition to the store of work outweighs the fact that the original author's work is being used without permission. By contrast, when work is not transformative, it is reproductive. Reproductive work violates the reason for copyright, without the counterbalancing blessing of adding to our store of original works. To succeed as fair use, it must adapt the work to new purposes. Transformation can occur either physically or in changing the mood the work conveys. Richard Prince's addition of a guitar and other materials to a peaceful portrait in nature changed the mood to hectic and provocative. *Cariou v. Prince*, 714 F.3d 694 (2d Cir. 2013). The concept of transformation is further discussed above in the chapter on the Right of Publicity.

Likewise, parody transforms a work by showing its style or substance in a different light. *Leibovitz v. Paramount Pictures Corp.*, 137 F.3d 109 (2d Cir. 1998). Parody does not automatically weight the first factor for defendant. If the parody is slight and the copying great, it may be insufficient.

It is not clear whether the parody must be of the copied work in order to weight this factor for defendant, or whether one might use the copied work to parody something else, like the banality of the lives of classes of society, or the treatment of women represented by a Barbie doll. *Rogers v. Koons*, 960 F.2d 301 (2d Cir. 1992) (must parody work); *Mattel, Inc. v. Walking Mountain Productions*, 353 F.3d 792 (9th Cir. 2003) (unclear whether parody of Barbie or society); *Cariou v. Prince*, 714 F.3d 694 (2d Cir. 2013) (need not comment on copied work). While parody of societal conditions, or social satire, is no less worthy of attention than parody of a work of art (and perhaps more worthy), there is no reason to violate someone's copyright to call attention to some societal defect. The only way to mock another work is to quote enough of it so the viewer knows what you are mocking.

A trump card for establishing fair use is parody. In the parody cases, the new use can be (and usually is) commercial (first criterion); it can take a highly expressive work, like the photo portrait of a pregnant Demi Moore, and use it in the same medium (second criterion); it can take a large portion of the original work if that is necessary to conjure up the parody (third criterion); and the change in message provides a fair chance of convincing the court that the parodist is not undermining the market for the original (fourth criterion). Also, parody need not be the sole or even the primary purpose of the work–it is sufficient if it is one of the purposes of it. The font of this elevation of parody is the Supreme Court's decision in *Campbell v. Acuff-Rose Music, Inc.*, 510 U.S. 569 (1994), where a song parody that used all of the music and some of the words of the original clarified the interpretation of fair use.

A good example of the influence of *Campbell* is found in two cases involving the appropriation artist Jeff Koons. In *Rogers v. Koons*, 960 F.2d 301 (2d Cir. 1992), decided before *Campbell*, the court found Koons' use of a photograph to create a sculpture not fair use because it did not parody the original work and it used all the copyrightable elements of the original, even though it probably did not usurp any existing market for the original photograph. (There was no discussion of whether postcards of Koons' sculpture would compete in the postcard market with postcards of Rogers' photograph, which were already being marketed.) The court said it was influenced by Koons' bad faith, shown when he bought a postcard of Rogers' work and tore off the copyright notice before giving it to his craftsmen to reproduce. The court's opinion did not mention this factor, but it surely did not help Koons that he had disobeyed the trial judge's order and shipped one copy of the sculpture out of the country.

By contrast, *Blanch v. Koons*, 467 F.3d 244 (2d Cir. 2006), uses *Campbell* as a guideline in holding that copying Blanch's photo for a shoe commercial as one of four pairs of legs in Koons' collage was fair use. The underlying purposes of Koons and Blanch were different, though his use was commercial. The court suggests that the transformation of the original trumps the commercial use to which it is put.

On the question of whether the parody must be of the original, the court contributes a novel insight. It points out that one might more properly refer to a criticism of something other than the original as satire, rather than parody. *Campbell* does not preclude fair use for satire, but satire has an additional hurdle to overcome. In parody, some parts of the original must be taken to link the comment to the original. In satire, the artist must demonstrate why the original must be taken. Koons did so by testifying that he needed a pair of legs of a type ubiquitous in the media, and veracity would be added by using something that actually appeared in the media. He regarded it as a short quotation. The court does not comment on why he needed this particular pair of legs, or indeed why he needed any copyrighted pair of legs. Nor was Koons disqualified by bad faith, as the court found that the failure to request a license was not bad faith because no license was needed if the use was fair. On the second factor, the court found Blanch's original creative, but Koons' transformative use neutralized that creativity. The third factor also went for Koons because he cut out what Blanch had claimed was her major contribution to her photo, a pose in an airplane cabin with the feet on the captain's lap. It might be noted that the part used became only a small part of Koons' work, one of four pairs of legs with other pictorial elements. The fourth factor also went for Koons because Blanch admitted that she never licensed her photos and had no plans to do so, so the court found that there was no potential market for the copyrighted work. But the court should have examined whether there was a general market for it, not whether the copyright holder chose to exploit it. Failure to exploit a market is not an invitation to infringement. One might add that the result was heavily influenced by Koons' ability to "talk the transformation talk" in his testimony.

Transformation may theoretically be counterbalanced by the commercial purpose of the copier, though no cases come to mind that have so held. Indeed, *Blanch* indicates to the contrary.

Another way to phrase the transformation question is to ask whether the work transforms the original, or merely replaces it, in all its actual and potential uses.

Usually, works of visual art are used for display or decoration. To the extent that a poster is used to decorate the set of a TV show, it is not transformative because it is used as it is, and for the same purpose as the original. *Ringgold v. Black Entertainment Television, Inc.*, 126 F.3d 70 (2d Cir 1997).

The second, and more usually encountered aspect, is whether the use is commercial or nonprofit. Nonprofit use is favored in establishing fair use. In most of the litigated cases involving the visual arts, the use of the copyrighted work has been to create advertising for a product, or works of art or entertainment for sale, neither of which is a nonprofit use.

The result of these two aspects of the "purpose" criterion may point in different directions. The use may be for news reporting in a profit-making enterprise, or for teaching at a proprietary school. Likewise, a parody might present commentary, but also be designed as advertising.

The desire to show comic book characters or other characters beloved during childhood in pornographic activities accounts for many fair use cases. Few of their authors have been able to establish fair use.

A finding that the new work transforms the copyrighted work is a strong predictor that the new work will be fair use; where the new work transforms only the use or purpose of the old work, the cases are in disarray.

ii. Nature of the Copyrighted Work

This criterion is somewhat difficult to understand. The implication of this factor is that an informational work may be more entitled to fair use than a work of entertainment.

Another possible distinction is between published and unpublished works. The right of the author to control the time and way that the work is presented to the public may be more important than protecting fair use. Put differently, the copier should not scoop the author.

Usually, the courts award the second criterion to the plaintiff because the work copied is creative. Indeed, the work must have some originality to qualify for a copyright. *Leibovitz* suggests that the weight to be given to the second criterion is slight, and that is confirmed in holdings.

iii. Portion of the Work Used (De Minimis)

De minimis may be thought of in two senses.

The first sense is that only a small portion of the copyrighted work has been used, and that portion, standing alone, is insufficient to constitute infringement. That argument is discussed above. Organizations of libraries have tried to define that portion of the work that is sufficiently minimal, such as photocopying a few pages of a long book, or 250 words of a poem. This advice, usually posted on photocopy machines, does not have the force of law. Nonetheless, there is an implication from the third criterion above that the smaller the percentage of the original that is used, the more likely the court will find it to be fair use. That is misleading, because we should be talking not about the percentage of the work, but how much of the copyrightable portion of the work is used. While using a small part of the original may be common with written works, it is unusual for works of visual art; normally, either the entire work is used, or most of it. One exception might be collage.

With parody, the parodist may take as much of the copyrighted aspects of the original as is necessary to permit the viewer to identify the parody with the original. The parodist can take more if what he is selling is principally the parody, rather than the original.

The second sense is the part that the copied portion plays in the finished work to which it is copied. In *Ringgold v. Black Entertainment Television, Inc.*, 126 F.3d 70 (2d Cir 1997), Faith Ringgold's mutilated poster was visible for only 27 seconds of a 5-minute segment of a 20-minute program. It was usually out of focus because the camera followed the action and the poster was background, and was partially obscured for some of that time. The court considered this even though the third criterion seems to be asking how much of the copyrighted work was used, not how significant the use of the copyrighted work was in the work to which it was copied. This second sense seems to duplicate the discussion above about whether a minimal copying is copyright infringement.

Despite dicta in opinions to the contrary, there may be no portion of a work that is so small that it guarantees a copier fair use status. Nor may there be any proportion that the copyrighted elements consist of the copied-to work so small that it is fair use. This is but one factor courts consider along with three other factors.

The amount may be assessed both quantitatively, in gross terms, and qualitatively, where the importance of the section taken, both to the original work and to the copy, are assessed.

In fact, it may be better to avoid fair use altogether by not infringing. The clear message here for prop managers is to take advantage of the first sale doctrine when possible. Use of a copyrighted prop in a stage play is not copyright infringement because of the first sale doctrine. Its use in a movie, television program or video is not protected by the first sale doctrine because it involves the display of the item and distribution of a copy of the copyrighted item.

iv. Effect on the Potential Market

This criterion requires the court to consider the effect of defendant's use and other uses in similar circumstances on the potential market for the copyrighted work. If the market for the copyrighted work is reduced, the incentives to create new work, the underlying purpose of copyright, is likewise reduced. Loss of revenue for the failure to pay a license fee for the use is not enough. Plaintiff must show that there is either an established or potential market for licensing the work that would be destroyed if defendant and others like defendant were able to use it for free. Plaintiff in *Ringgold* would satisfy this criteria if she could prove that she already had a market in licensing her posters to appear in movies or TV shows, or that there was a potential market for it that she had yet to exploit, but practically could. If Ringgold was already licensing her posters for movie use, she could prove that there was a market. If she proved that other poster makers customarily licensed their posters for movie use, she could prove that there was a potential market, even though she had never licensed a poster for TV use. Allegations that traditionally would be given little weight are the fact that fewer posters might be sold if they appear on TV, or that more posters would be sold because of the favorable publicity that appearance on TV provides.

Another form of injury considered under the fourth criteria is reputational. Every parody damages the object's reputation and by implication its author's, but that is not taken into consideration under the fourth criterion. However in one case, the copyright owner alleged damage to his reputation because the world would think that he licensed his art for commercial purposes and presented evidence to that effect. That damage was considered as one of the factors in determining that the use was not fair. *Steinberg v. Columbia Pictures Ind., Inc.*, 663 F.Supp. 706 (S.D.N.Y. 1987).

Parody provides a special case for the fourth criterion. There is usually no market for licensing the original work for parodies because the owner of the original work will not normally consent to such licensing. Owners perceive that a parody of a work decreases its value. The last thing an artist wants to see is a decrease in the value of his work. That may adversely affect the value of his other work. So one view of the fourth criterion is that parody substitutes for no market that the copyright owner would reasonably exploit.

Another way to look at it is as an example of market failure. Since the author of the infringing work would be unable to negotiate with the copyright owner a license to use the protected work at any price because the copyright owner is unwilling to be lampooned, the market failure would prevent the creation of the second work. Society's interest in having the second work created would be thwarted. The fair use doctrine permits the second work to be created without the consent of the copyright owner.

One is tempted to add that it also permits the use of the copyrighted work without any compensation to the copyright owner. Thus, the second work, whose value depends on the recognizability of the copyrighted work, need not share the profits from it with the copyright owner.

Though courts have stated that the fourth criterion by itself is not determinative, a review of the cases finds few situations where the result contradicts the leaning of the fourth criterion, except those cases finding the subsequent work transformative.

v. Internet Operation

The operation of the internet involves the frequent electronic copying and distribution of images. Internet browsers operate by webcrawlers that are programmed to find information (including images) that allow the preparation of algorithms permitting the browser to locate and reference the subject quickly. In the case of images, this is normally done by programing the webcrawler to copy the image, make a low resolution version of it, then delete the copy of the original image. This has been held to be a fair use. *Perfect 10, Inc. v. Google, Inc.*, 653 F.3d 976 (9th Cir. 2011).

B. Problems with the Four-Factor Test

At the end of the day, the four-factor test leaves us with four factors and an instruction to evaluate them. It provides no guidance as to how to evaluate the factors. The results in the cases have been unpredictable, though many litigated cases have established fair use.

C. An Alternate Rationale: Transaction Costs

Another way to look at the fair use defense is to view it as a device to avoid unreasonable transaction costs. Under this reasoning, fair use operates where the transaction costs of agreeing on a license make such an agreement unlikely. For instance, private parties have no easy way of negotiating a license to time shift network television programming. Researchers or teachers preparing a lesson might not have sufficient time to seek a license. And parodists would not receive licenses from copyright holders at any reasonable price because of the psychological damage of parody.

The problem with reasons based on transaction costs is that they assume that transaction costs are a permanent, structural matter. Doctrine based on transaction cost is likely to change more slowly than the economics of the situation. In fact, when a rule is based on avoiding transaction costs, it may remove incentives that the parties might have to find a way around transaction costs.

15. Remedies

A number of remedies are available for violation of a copyright. A successful plaintiff is entitled to ordinary damages or statutory damages, an injunction, costs and attorneys' fees. In rare cases, a willful violator may be prosecuted.

The availability of statutory damages in lieu of proving actual damages and the ability to collect reasonable attorneys' fees will induce most plaintiffs who could sue either for copyright violation or breach of contract to choose a copyright cause of action if they qualify for those remedies.

A. Actual Damages and Infringer's Profits

Successful plaintiffs may recover their actual damages and the profits made by the infringer, but may not engage in double counting. The copyright owner's damages and the profits made by the infringer cannot be the same. Take a case where the artist licenses the Art Institute of Chicago to sell a poster of her painting for $3 per poster sold. The infringer sells 1,000 copies of a poster of the same painting at a store across the street from the Art Institute, and sells 500 copies of the poster in New York City, for $10 each. Plaintiff's actual damages are $3,000, computed at $3 per poster sold in Chicago, because those are the royalties plaintiff lost from the infringement. The infringer's profits do not include any amount for the Chicago sales, as they have already been accounted for by the damages. As to the New York sales, plaintiff need only prove the amount of the sales, $5,000. That becomes the infringer's profits unless the infringer proves the amount of his deductible expenses, and the profits attributable to items other than the copyright. If the infringer proves that the cost of printing each poster is $5, and the profits of a reasonable printer would be 10% of cost, or $.50, the infringer's profits would be $4.50 per poster, or $2,250, so the total actual damages would be $5,250. 17 U.S.C. § 502.

In most cases, the infringer's gross revenue from the copyrighted product will be easily proven from the infringer's records inspected by plaintiff during discovery. The fight at trial is likely to be over the expenses that should be allocated to the product, and especially the profit that should be attributable to elements other than the copyrighted product. The greatest difficulty is experienced when the infringer produces many products, some infringing, some not. There are inevitably overhead expenses. To the extent that the infringer can show that they are due to the infringement, they can be offset. In the more usual case, the overhead cost of infringement cannot be isolated. The infringer cannot use them unless he can persuade the court that a proportional method of allocating these costs is reasonable. Expert testimony will often be relied upon, and any doubt resolved in favor of the copyright owner.

The infringer's profits include indirect profits. Where the infringement relates to producing an advertisement, indirect profits may include amounts received for the product or service that is advertised if plaintiff can demonstrate a causal relationship between the infringement and the profits. Simply introducing the infringer's gross receipts where some may be caused by infringement and others not so caused was insufficient where a major corporation copied a student artist's work into an ad. *Rainey v. Wayne State Univ.*, 26 F.Supp.2d 963 (E.D. Mich. 1998).

Where the artist whose copyright is infringed produces unique items, such as a sculpture, actual damages may be insufficient. If the infringer has not sold the sculpture, there are no profits to seek. Since the artist does not regularly license other artists to produce knock-offs of his sculpture, it is hard to measure lost revenue. So there are cases when actual damages are inadequate, and plaintiff will seek other remedies.

B. Statutory Damages

Alternatively, plaintiff may elect to seek statutory damages, but only if the work was registered with the Copyright Office before the infringement began or within three months after publication. 17 U.S.C. § 412. For the visual artist, this limitation often bars the use of statutory damages because artists and photographers who produce many works often do not register them, either because of the work required to register or the fees imposed.

Statutory damages are awarded by the trier of fact. For each work, they are between $750 and $30,000 as is just. The amount may go as high as $150,000 if the infringement was willful, meaning that the infringer knew that the work was subject to copyright and he copied it anyway. Evidence of willfulness would include situations where the infringer cut the copyright notice from the original before copying it, as in *Rogers*. 17 U.S.C. §§ 504, 412. For a defendant who proves that he was an innocent infringer, statutory damages can be as small as $200 per work infringed. Special damages may be nothing in a special case, but special cases are very limited indeed. 17 U.S.C. § 504(c)(2).

A plaintiff may elect statutory damages at any time during the litigation, so long as a judgment based on actual damages has not been issued.

Statutory damages are designed for situations where proof of actual damages may be difficult and to provide some remedy to discourage infringement, so plaintiff need introduce no evidence of damages. The wise plaintiff will introduce as much evidence of damages as he can amass to convince the trier of fact to increase the amount of statutory damages awarded.

Since statutory damages are assessed by the work infringed, one must define the work. A work is usually viewed as something that can stand alone in the marketplace. An individual painting would be a work even if it is part of a series.

The number of works infringed is important, as statutory damages are assigned by that measure. If an infringer makes one copy of a photograph, he has infringed one work. If the same infringer also puts that photograph on 500 mugs and 5,000 posters, he has still infringed only one work.

While the minimum and maximum amounts are computed by the work, judges are likely to determine a figure between the permitted amounts in part dependent on the number of times the work was infringed and the number of copies made during each infringement.

C. Injunction

A successful plaintiff may seek an injunction prohibiting further infringement, or a temporary injunction pending the resolution of the lawsuit. 17 U.S.C. § 502. While in theory an injunction requires that the remedy at law be inadequate, irreparable harm in its absence, a balance of hardships in favor of plaintiff and the public interest tilting his way, courts have until recently assumed the existence of those requirements once a finding of infringement (or likely success on the merits) was made. Recent cases call upon courts to separately and carefully examine each factor required.

This trend is both comforting and troubling. It is comforting because it tends to reduce the extent to which a plaintiff can blackmail a defendant into settling because of the enormous loss that might result from issuing an injunction. Imagine a film set to open that is accused of violating plaintiff's copyright by showing his painting on the wall in a number of scenes. Significant sums have been spent publicizing the opening of the movie on a particular date that would be lost if an injunction prevented the movie from opening then.

The trend is troubling because if an injunction does not issue, it demotes a copyright from being a property right, with exclusive control of use in the copyright owner, to a right that can be taken as long as one is willing to pay damages that the court will later assess.

An injunction is most likely to issue when the economic life of the copyrighted item is short, such as with fabric design.

A court that issues an injunction is likely to order the seizure and destruction, sale, or transfer to the copyright owner of any infringing copies in the possession of the infringer, or any equipment used to make those copies. 17 U.S.C. § 503. In the case of the copied sculpture discussed above, this may be the copyright owner's preferred remedy, so he can remove from the market a knock-off that might threaten the reputation of the original work.

D. Attorneys' Fees

A successful party may petition the court for attorneys' fees if the work was registered with the Copyright Office before the infringement began or within three months after publication. 17 U.S.C. § 412. Their award is not automatic, but is within the discretion of the court. 17 U.S.C. § 505. That discretion is more likely to be exercised in favor of a defendant when the court believes that the litigation was frivolous, unreasonable, or designed to harass. A court is very likely to award plaintiff attorneys' fees if the damages are small. In fact, attorneys' fees are usually awarded, though less frequently for defendants than for plaintiffs. But in *Mattel Inc. v. Walking Mountain Productions*, 353 F.3d 792 (9th Cir. 2003), the court awarded the prevailing defendant around $2 million in attorneys' fees because the grounds for the suit were unreasonable given the fair use doctrine and defendant's few sales, and the suit was pursued by Mattel in an unreasonable fashion, using Rambo-like litigation tactics.

The statute provides that an award of attorneys' fees can only be made if the copyright owner registers as required above. While this is understandable if the copyright owner is the prevailing party, it seems strange to deny attorneys' fees to the person accused of infringing on the grounds that his opponent failed to register his copyright, and there are few cases actually denying defendants attorneys' fees for that reason. It does create a situation where both parties may petition for attorneys' fees or neither may, so every case is a level playing field for attorneys' fees.

E. Costs

The prevailing party may also be reimbursed for his costs by the losing party. Costs can be extensive, as they include the costs of depositions, as well as filing and other fees. They are not usually ordered in the absence of bad faith or fault.

F. Criminal Liability

While rarely prosecuted, willful copyright violation is also a criminal offense.

G. State Immunity

In general, sovereigns are immune from suit.

i. Federal Government

The federal government has consented to be sued by a copyright owner for copyright infringement in the United States Court of Federal Claims. 28 U.S.C. 1498(b). This is a waiver of its sovereign immunity.

ii. State Governments

The Eleventh Amendment prohibits suing states in federal courts without their consent. This sets up a conflict with the copyright clause of the Constitution. *Chavez v. Arte Publico Press*, 204 F.3d 601 (5th Cir. 2000) held that the Eleventh Amendment overrides the copyright clause, so Congress cannot constitutionally subject states to suits for copyright infringement. Each state can decide to waive its sovereign immunity, but Congress cannot waive it for them.

As a practical matter, this is a significant holding. A person whose copyright has been infringed by a state cannot sue in state court because 28 U.S.C. § 1338 confers exclusive jurisdiction over copyright law on the federal courts. States and their subdivisions are significant users of copyrighted material, especially in schools that range from kindergarten, normally run by subunits of local governments, to graduate work in state universities and colleges. The copyright owner's only possible relief is to seek damages from the state official who authorized the copying, or from the official who actually did the copying. These individuals are less likely to have significant assets from which a judgment could be satisfied than the state would have.

iii. Foreign Governments

For possible actions against foreign states, see the chapter on International Litigation for Art Lawyers below where the Foreign Sovereign Immunities Act is discussed.

16. Pre-Emption

A. Of State Law

Federal copyright law broadly pre-empts state law. It completely pre-empts state copyright laws protecting copyrightable works fixed in a tangible medium. 17 U.S.C. § 301. Other state laws not specifically labeled copyright might or might not be pre-empted, depending on whether they are functionally equivalent. *Studza v. United Arab Emirates*, 281 F.3d 1287 (D.C. Cir. 2002), held that a suit seeking state law recovery for fraud, intentional interference with an advantageous contract relationship, and intentional infliction of emotional distress for using plaintiff's design and procuring a contract to build an embassy were not pre-empted by federal copyright law where each tort required proof of elements in addition to copying plaintiff's plans for the United Arab Emirates' embassy.

B. Of Federal Law

There is no statute specifically pre-empting other federal law. Quite the contrary. Other federal remedies are specifically preserved. 17 U.S.C. §301(d). It is not unusual for suits alleging copyright infringement to also allege violations of the Lanham Act, 15 U.S.C. §1125(a). For further discussion, see the Trademark chapter below. Where the trademark allegation is another way of alleging copyright infringement, that cause of action is unlikely to be successful if the copyright has expired. The Supreme Court strongly commented in *Dastar Corp. v. Twentieth Century Fox Film Corp.*, 539 U.S. 23 (2003) that the limited terms of copyright and patent were designed to be the sole protection for originality or creativity, and not the trademark laws which have potentially perpetual life.

For further guidance, see MELVILLE B. NIMMER & DAVID NIMMER, NIMMER ON COPYRIGHT or PAUL GOLDSTEIN, GOLDSTEIN ON COPYRIGHT.

Checkpoints

- Federal Copyright law is authorized by the Constitution. Courts have granted copyright ability to artists and artwork, although the Constitution only refers to authors and writing.
- Copyright is designed to encourage the production of copyrightable works by providing the author with a monopoly on the work for a period of time.
- Copyright grants exclusive rights for the period of the copyright to reproduce the work; to use it to prepare a derivative work; to sell, lease, or lend it; and to publicly display it.
- The first sale doctrine permits the owner of the physical item, even if he does not own the copyright, to sell, lease, lend and display that physical item.
- Copyright is now automatic if the work is an original work in a copyrightable subject matter that is fixed in a medium of expression.
- The work needs to be a creation of the author and at least minimally creative. Facts cannot be copyrighted.
- Ideas cannot be copyrighted; all that can be copyrighted is the expression of an idea.

- The scènes á faire doctrine prevents the necessary steps in expressing an idea from being protected by copyright.
- Functional elements of a design are not copyrightable; only the expressive element of the design can be copyrighted.
- The United States government may not be an original copyright holder, but state and foreign governments may. A copyright may be transferred to the federal government.
- All authors of a joint work are tenants in common of its copyright.
- If a work is made by an employee in his scope of employment, it is a work made for hire and the copyright belongs to the employer. Certain agreed works produced by an independent contractor are also works made for hire.
- Transferring a work does not transfer the copyright in it unless such an intent is expressed; transferring the copyright does not transfer the work unless such an intent is expressed.
- A suit for infringement may not begin until the copyright is registered.
- Infringement is copying a work's protected expression.
- Plaintiff must prove that defendant had access to the copyrighted work and that a copyrightable portion of it was copied.
- Minimal copying may not violate copyright laws.
- Vicarious infringement occurs when a person has the right to control the action of another and fails to prevent infringement when he profits by it.
- Derivative work must be done with permission of the copyright holder. Derivative works may be copyrighted if they demonstrate sufficient originality.
- Fair use is not infringement. Purposes of fair use include criticism, comment, news reporting, teaching, scholarship, and research.
- To determine if a use is fair, consider the purpose of the use, the nature of the copyrighted work, the proportion of the copyrighted work that is used and the effect of the use on the potential market for the copyrighted work.
- A successful plaintiff is entitled to ordinary damages, an injunction, and costs. Statutory damages and attorneys' fees may be awarded if the copyright is registered before the infringement.

Chapter 6

Trademarks and Related Actions

Roadmap

After reading this chapter, you should understand:

- Purposes: The Lanham Act protects the investment a business makes in the reputation of its trademarked products and services; prevents deception of the public about the source of goods or services; protects the owners of famous marks from having the meaning of their trademarks diluted; and prevents misrepresentations in commercial advertising.
- Effective marks: Marks must be distinctive, non-functional and used in the ordinary course of business. Names and descriptions are weak marks unless they have acquired secondary meaning attached to products.
- Trademark violation: The basic trademark violation is use of a mark on a product not made by the mark owner that results in public confusion about the product's source.
- Use by artists and art institutions: Artists and art institutions marketing work might wish to trademark their products to prevent others from marketing similar goods with the same mark.
- Dilution of famous mark: It is a trademark violation to blur or tarnish a nationally-known mark by using it on wildly different products or with unsavory connections.
- Trade dress: Where the appearance of a product has acquired a secondary meaning indicating the product's source, it can be a trademark violation to imitate the packaging or appearance in a way that causes confusion about the source of the goods.
- Fair use defenses to infringement: The fair use defenses to infringement require that the mark not be used to identify a product. Descriptive fair use is where the use of another's mark describes the producer, the product or its geographic origin. Nominative fair use is where another's mark is used only to identify the product.
- Fair use defense to dilution: If the use does not designate the source of goods, it may be fair use to comparatively advertize, parody, criticize or comment on another's trademarked product.
- Artistic relevance defense: It is a defense to trademark infringement that the use of the mark has artistic relevance in the artwork in which it is used.

- Noncommercial use defense to dilution: It is a defense to trademark dilution that the use is noncommercial. Noncommercial use is any use more than selling a product, like parody, satire, or editorializing.
- Remedies for trademark violation: Remedies include injunction, actual damages, and up to treble damages. Attorneys' fees may be awarded in exceptional cases.

1. Introduction: Basics of Trademark and Related Liabilities

It is not immediately obvious why people in the world of visual arts should have any interest in trademark law, but they do. Trademark law is law proscribing certain forms of unfair competition. Most specifically, it renders a person liable if that person uses someone else's trademark on a product the trademark owner did not produce.

There are state statutory trademarks, state common law trademarks, federal registered trademarks, and federal unregistered trademarks. Federal registered trademarks are most advantageous. In each case, in order to have a valid trademark, one must meet certain tests. This discussion focuses on federal registered trademarks because the requirements of different trademark protections often overlap. The federal registered trademark is the most advantageous for the holder. It carries a presumption of validity, and the rights it confers apply throughout the United States.

A. Purposes of Trademark Law

Trademark law has three theoretical purposes. The first is to protect the investment the businessperson has made in the reputation of the product or service he presents to the public. The second is to prevent deception of the public about the source (and therefore the quality) of goods or services and reduce consumer costs in assuring that they are buying quality goods. But since no consumer has any rights under trademark law, the consumer benefit is incidental to the businessperson benefit. The third is to protect certain trademark owners, those that have famous marks, from having the meaning of their trademarks diluted by others. Put differently, trademark protection induces producers to improve the quality of their products because they reap the benefit of public perception of quality by commanding higher prices. It benefits consumers because the trademark eliminates a need for consumers to repeatedly expend time and money to assure that they receive the quality they want; they can simply buy a familiar brand.

B. What Is a Trademark?

A trademark is a word, name, symbol, device or combination of those items. It must be used to identify and distinguish the source of one product or service from another. Lanham Act § 45, 15 U.S.C. § 1127. A trademark can include a product design, shape, color, sound, scent, packaging or other attribute, subject to the requirements that it be distinctive, non-functional, and actually used to denote the trademark owner's or his licensee's products or services. In some instances it will be called trade dress, especially when the reference is to design or packaging.

C. Trademark Infringement, Other Lanham Act Offenses, and Defenses

Trademark infringement occurs where plaintiff has a valid trademark, defendant uses that trademark without authorization, and that use results in likely confusion. The Lanham Act also prohibits the dilution of a famous mark. Dilution is said to occur when an unauthorized person uses the famous mark in a way that either tarnishes it by associating it with something disreputable, or blurs the mark by using it on a product unrelated to the product to which the mark owner has attached it. The Lanham Act also prohibits misrepresentations in commercial advertising about the goods or services of the advertiser or another.

Secondary trademark liability exists where a person intentionally induces someone to infringe a trademark, or has reason to know that someone is infringing a trademark and continues actions aiding that infringement.

The principal defenses encountered in the art world are artistic relevance, noncommercial use, and the fair use defenses.

D. Remedies

A successful plaintiff is likely to be granted an injunction against further violations, as well as monetary relief in the form of either actual damages or disgorgement of defendant's profits. Courts are authorized to increase damages up to three times actual damages "according to the circumstances of the case." Such an increase is neither routine nor rare.

A prevailing party may be awarded reasonable attorney's fees "in exceptional cases."

2. Trademarks and Related Actions in the Art World

A. Artists, Foundations and Museums Establish Their Trademarks

To be valid, a mark needs to be distinctive and nonfunctional, and it needs to be used for products or services.

i. Distinctiveness of the Mark

The mark needs to be distinctive; otherwise it will not do its job of signaling to the public that your product is made by a different manufacturer than another product. The word "prints" is an insufficiently distinctive trademark for someone who produces lithographs because it is a generic description of your product. It will not carve your lithographs out in the public's mind from the lithographs of anyone else.

A person's name can be a trademark. It is treated as a descriptive mark, a weak mark, unless it is a name that has secondary meaning. *Franklin Mint Co. v. Manatt, Phelps & Phillips*, 184 Cal.App.4th 313, 109 Cal.Rptr. 143 (2010). A name like Jane Artist Lithography could certainly be a trademark. To register a name of a living person as a federal trademark, the person named must consent to this use of his name, and the name must have acquired secondary meaning.

The problem with a descriptive mark is that standing alone it may be insufficiently distinctive. A mark that is not particularly distinctive can acquire distinctiveness and become a stronger mark through use, especially through advertising that associates it with a product in the public's mind. This is called creating "secondary meaning." In the case of an artist, that advertising might be directed toward galleries. It is important to consistently use the mark, both to satisfy the use requirements and to bolster the secondary meaning.

As an alternative to a descriptive name, a suggestive mark like Tide, an arbitrarily applied mark like Apple for computers, or a wholly fanciful mark like Chlorox, would be better, because one need not prove that the mark has secondary meaning. If you begin with a name that is distinctive, you need not create the distinction.

A trademark is strongest when it is used for a single product or line of products. One easily recognizes that "Picasso" is the producer of artwork. If

"Picasso" is used by many different companies for many different products, like perfumes, jewelry, automobiles, paintings, software, and makeup, the product lines and sources will be so diffused that "Picasso" will have much weaker secondary meaning to the public.

A person is usually entitled to use his own name in business, but not when it would cause confusion with another's long-standing use of that name. Where David Findlay had operated an art gallery for many years on East 57th Street specializing in French impressionists and post-impressionists, his brother was enjoined from using the name Findlay in connection with an art gallery opened next door selling the same kind of work. *David B. Findlay, Inc. v. Findlay*, 18 N.Y.2d 12, 218 N.E.2d 531, 271 N.Y.S.2d 652 (1966). The case is based on the use of a name in a location where it was guaranteed to cause confusion, rather than a trademark, and the court is none too clear about the nature of the cause of action, which it calls "unfair competition." The court made much of the extensive effort plaintiff had made to establish goodwill in this location, and the likelihood of public confusion. Some cases require proof of an intent to confuse the public. The rule is that a person is entitled to use his own name in business, subject to the limitation that it cannot cause confusion with a competing product, service or business.

ii. Non-Functionality of the Mark

The mark needs to be non-functional. It cannot enhance the product's utility. This prevents a trademark from becoming a drag on competition by assuring that all useful features of a product can be incorporated in similar products by all competitors (subject to constraints of patent law). It also assures that the developer of an invention does not effectively expand his patent protection from the statutorily-granted twenty years by using a trademark, which lasts as long as the mark is used. A mark is functional if it is essential to the use or purpose of the item or if it affects its cost or quality.

That sounds reasonable because we think of functionality in a physical sense. Trademark law calls that utilitarian functionality. Functional items include the shape of a shredded wheat biscuit, knurled markings to mask a weld mark on a bicycle, or the shape of wall-mounted lighting fixtures designed for an architectural style. But the specific color hues on different sides of a Rubix cube are non-functional (though some differentiation of the sides is a functional necessity).

Functionality has also been broadly applied in trade dress cases by a doctrine called aesthetic functionality. The test here is whether lacking the design puts one at a significant nonreputation-related competitive disadvantage. Some courts have resisted broad application by showing that there were alternate designs available. In *Hartford House, Ltd. v. Hallmark Cards, Inc.*, 846 F.2d

1268 (10th Cir. 1988), plaintiff sued for infringement of its trade dress and the court issued a preliminary injunction. Plaintiff established ten elements of similarity between its line of non-occasion greeting cards and defendant's which the court believed, in combination, gave the trade dress secondary meaning as identifying plaintiff as producer of the cards. Defendant alleged that the similarity between its greeting cards and plaintiff's was caused by aesthetic functionality. The court held those features non-functional because alternative design features of fold, color, shape, ink, illustrations and poetry could have been substituted, in part by showing that some of their competitors had in fact marketed cards with alternate designs. The result held that the trademark was valid and the competing cards infringing. Other courts have not paid much attention to alternate designs, and have held that "competitive necessity" constituted aesthetic functionality. The fact that other silverware makers would be at a competitive disadvantage was sufficient to find that a plaintiff's baroque design was functional in response to its claims to bar all other baroque designs.

iii. Using the Mark As a Mark

The person needs to adopt and use the trademark "in commerce", and it must be used as a trademark. If an artist is to adopt a trademark, the artist need not affix that trademark to every work produced, but it needs to be used "in the ordinary course of trade, and not made merely to reserve a right in a mark." Lanham Act § 1(a)(2). It would be good practice to use the mark on each artwork. Telling people that you are going to open a gallery with a specific name is probably insufficient use; one must actually open the gallery and use the selected name with it on signs or business cards. Failure to use a specific trademark consistently was one of the flaws that doomed the suit in *Rock and Roll Hall of Fame and Museum, Inc. v. Gentile Productions*, 134 F.3d 749 (6th Cir. 1998). Defendant had produced a poster with a picture of the museum's building. The museum sued, claiming that the image of the building was one of its trademarks. While the court found that the museum occasionally used images of its building as a trademark, it did not use the building image that Gentile photographed as a trademark. It also did not use any image of the building consistently.

A person's image could be a trademark, but trademark law does not protect an individual or an image; it protects the use of the trademark with specific goods. Not every use qualifies the image to be a trademark. If the image is not used with specific goods or services, it will not be a protected trademark. Tiger Woods' image was recognizable by a significant portion of the population, but the owner of the image had not used that image with specific goods or services.

The result was that the owner could not recover from an artist who placed Woods' image in a painting of great participants in the Masters golf tournament because the image had not been used as a mark. *ETW Corp. v. Jireh Publishing*, 332 F.3d 915 (6th Cir. 2003).

iv. Abandoning the Mark

A trademark can be abandoned. A living artist abandons a trademark when she ceases using it with intent to abandon it. A *prima facie* case of abandonment occurs when the trademark owner has not used the mark for three years. As a practical matter, the best way to rebut that *prima facie* case is to put forth a good reason for not using the trademark, and plans to resume using it in the reasonably foreseeable future. The wise trademark owner has strict contractual controls over the use of the mark with his licensees, and enforces those controls when a violation comes to its attention. This can be a serious problem when an artist, who has registered a trademark, dies. At that point, the artist will cease producing work with her trademark. The heir will not be producing work with the artist's trademark. The only opportunity to exert the trademark would be if the heir decides to offer some of the artist's work for sale, or if a third party presents a work with the artist's trademark to the market that the heir believes is a forgery and the heir sues to enforce the trademark.

v. Trademark Violation by Public Confusion

A traditional trademark violation is where one person uses the trademark of another in a way that is likely to cause public confusion about the source of the product—who produced it. To meet the public confusion standard, where defendant sells a painting with plaintiff's trademark that was not produced by plaintiff, the fact that the painting was not produced by plaintiff only needs to fool members of the general public. It need not rise to the level of fooling experts in that area of art. The wise plaintiff comes equipped with public surveys showing confusion in the mind of the public.

In *Dastar Corp. v. Twentieth Century Fox Film Corp.*, 539 U.S. 23 (2003), the court made it clear that it is the final production of the product that counts as the source. A person who puts together ingredients to make the final product is the source, not the person who made the ingredients he used.

Today, recovery can result when there is confusion created about sponsorship, affiliation or approval of a product or service. An heir or foundation established by the artist might sue a merchant selling a forgery on grounds that the merchant has represented to the public by using the artist's trademark that the heir or foundation has authenticated the work.

B. Artists, Galleries and Art Institutions Use Trademarks and Related Law

Suppose that you represent an artist who produces numbered and signed lithographs that he offers for sale under his registered trademark. You discover that a clever forger has imitated your client's style, forged his name, and sold many works. The buyers of those works might be able to recover from the forger, as discussed below in the chapter on Authentication. As the artist, your client's best chance to recover is under trademark law, as the forger is an unauthorized user of his trademark on goods that he did not produce, which results in public confusion. In limited cases, you might also be able to recover under the Visual Artists Rights Act discussed in the chapter on Moral Rights below. Once your client dies, his heir would not be able to recover under VARA, as those rights are personal to the artist and not inheritable.

A gallery or publisher that uses artists to create a series of prints may wish to protect that series with a trademark. One is liable for false commercial advertisements of your own product in interstate commerce, which would surely include falsely advertizing that a print you are selling was part of a named series of a publisher when in fact it was made by a person with no connection to the publisher.

Museum shops may wish to use trademark law in their merchandising efforts. Most such stores carry a significant range of products. A museum might want to adopt a trademark that would help it prevent competitors from marketing merchandise identically trademarked, such as a line of fine reproductions of old master paintings with the museum's trademark. Copyright law would not prevent a competitor from selling reproductions of the same paintings if those pictures were no longer protected by copyright, but the museum's trademark, whether a name or an image, would be protected. Whether this would be worthwhile would depend on how important the museum's trademark might be in the public eye as a guarantor of a quality reproduction.

C. Use of Trademark and Related Law Against the Artist or Gallery

i. Likelihood of Confusion: Competing Goods

Likelihood of confusion between the plaintiff's trademarked goods and the goods on which defendant has placed the trademark is essential to liability. Likelihood of confusion is determined based on a number of factors that differ somewhat from circuit to circuit. Typical tests consider these factors: the similarity of the marks used, the strength of plaintiff's mark, how closely the products or services compete, defendant's intent, and actual confusion.

The strength of the mark is an assessment of how recognizable it is to the public. A mark can be strong conceptually based on its distinctiveness, or it can be strong based on its wide market recognition.

Actual confusion presents some difference of opinion among the courts, some requiring significant evidence of confusion by surveys or expert witnesses or both.

The Rock and Roll Hall of Fame registered its name as a service mark. It constructed a unique building in Cleveland, which it used as an insignia on various items it sold. Defendant Gentile took a photo of the Hall from a public place, put it on a poster with the name of the Hall, and sold it to the public. The Hall thought that posters of its building were its exclusive merchandising opportunity, and it had used images of its building as a trademark. The court reversed the grant of an injunction stopping the sale of Gentile's posters. The court thought Gentile was not using the photo of the building as a trademark on the poster but as the goods themselves, so the first criterion was not met. Even if it could be construed as a trademark, the photo Gentile used did not duplicate the Hall's rendering of its building, so the marks were not similar. There was no discussion of the strength of the Hall's trademark or whether the Hall produced a competing poster. Gentile's intent was clearly not to use the Hall building as a mark. The court doubted that a reasonable consumer would think that the poster was produced by the Hall. None of the factors going in favor of the Hall, the court held for Gentile. *Rock and Roll Hall of Fame and Museum, Inc. v. Gentile Productions*, 134 F.3d 749 (6th Cir. 1998). The case reminds the artist that the content of the artwork produced can be important, as is the use of a mark as a mark. Had the artist produced a poster of the museum containing the museum's exact trademark and competing with a poster produced by the museum, he might have been held liable.

ii. False Endorsement: An End Run on the Right of Publicity

Other cases seem to be equivalent to right of publicity cases. In these cases, the image or trademark of plaintiff appears in an artwork, and the artist is sued on the theory that the appearance of the image or trademark falsely asserts to the public that plaintiff has produced or endorsed the artwork. The artists have often won these cases, either because the image was held not to be a trademark, as in *ETW* above, or because of defensive doctrines of fair use discussed below. Sometimes these cases involve the marketing of t-shirts with the images of famous people. These cases may be Pyrrhic victories for the artist, as the cost of defending the suit is often many times the profit on the items produced.

In some ways, trademarks may resemble the right of publicity discussed in the Publicity-Privacy chapter above. They both involve the unauthorized use of signifiers. But the differences are also significant. The signifier in the case of the right of publicity is the identity of a human being; the identity in a trademark is a signifier of a commercial source of goods or services, which may or may not be a human being. Trademarks require their exploitation; the right of publicity (mostly) does not. The right of publicity protects the identity of a person and the person's endorsements; trademark and related recoveries protect against the confusion of the source of goods and the dilution of the mark itself, and may also protect endorsements. Plaintiffs may prefer trademark recovery because a claim under a federal statute confers jurisdiction on the federal courts, or because of the possibility of enhanced damages and legal fees.

iii. False Advertising: An End Run on Defamation

A person can be liable under the Lanham Act, 15 U.S.C. §§ 1025(a)(1)(B), for false statements of fact in commercial advertising to influence consumers to buy defendant's goods or services. In *Gmurzynska v. Hutton*, 355 F.3d 206 (2d Cir. 2004), plaintiff art gallery alleged that defendant art gallery conspired with several art critics and a publisher to disparage plaintiff's expertise and products. The allegation was that when those experts were consulted by private collectors, the experts falsely disparaged plaintiff's expertise in Russian avant-garde art. A second conspiracy was alleged where the Sprengel Museum published a book questioning the authenticity of eight works sold by plaintiff based on opinions by other experts. Plaintiff alleged that the book and the critics' statements were false commercial advertising. The complaint was dismissed on the grounds that neither the conversations with the collector, nor the publication of the book constituted commercial advertising. Also, neither the Sprengel Museum nor the experts were selling products that competed with plaintiff gallery. But the named defendant, who ran the Hutton Gallery, certainly sold products that competed with defendants, and if the conspiracy could be proved, the acts of the co-conspirators would be attributed to each other. Nonetheless, the lack of commercial advertisement was fatal to the case. The message here is that galleries, auction houses and individual artists need to be especially careful about what they include in commercial advertisements.

The facts in Gmurzynska sound more like slander, discussed in the chapter on Defamation above. Plaintiffs may prefer trademark-type recovery so they can litigate in federal court, or because of the possibility of enhanced damages and legal fees.

iv. Dilution

Nothing quite delights the artist who wishes to *épater le bourgeoisie* like parodying or satirizing the tastes of the middle class by inserting real or fake trademarks into his artwork. The trademark owner may prevail on trademark infringement grounds if he can prove confusion about source in the public mind. Even if the parody is so good that few persons are likely to be confused about whether an industrial concern has produced the artwork, it may constitute another trademark violation called trademark dilution.

If the trademark is a famous mark (and such an artist would prefer such a target), a cause of action occurs when someone uses the trademark in a manner that is likely to dilute the trademark after it has become famous. A famous mark is a trademark that is nationally known, not just regionally known (though one should also consult state trademark laws to see if the applicable state law protects from dilution and requires more than state-wide fame). It does not appear that regional fame is enough. A second requirement for a famous mark is that it be famous "to the general consuming public." This seems to imply that the mark must be famous to most consumers, not just to experienced consumers of that particular product. For example, the trademarks Scott's or Ancestry.com are famous to philatelists and genealogists respectively, but largely unknown to the general consuming public.

There are two kinds of dilution. Blurring dilution can occur with the use of the mark on products that the trademark owner does not produce even if they are wildly different from the products the owner produces. It can also occur where the use of a similar, but not identical, mark makes the public unsure of just what the mark is. When the public thinks of a mark as signifying both products produced by the mark owner and products not produced by him, the mark is not as effective in identifying the mark owner's goods.

A second kind of dilution is by tarnishment, where the mark is used on unsavory products, such as pornography, drugs, or products of low quality. There might be liability for dilution when an artist makes fun of a famous mark by placing the mark in a pornographic or seedy context, as they often do.

It was tarnishment that was no doubt at the root of Mattel's complaint in *Mattel v. Walking Mountain Productions*, 353 F.3d 792 (9th Cir 2003). Defendant had produced photographs depicting Barbie dolls in suggestive or dangerous situations. Plaintiff sued for trademark infringement, false advertising, and dilution. The court did not discuss whether defendant's action was in fact dilution. It held that all the trademark (and copyright) causes of action were protected by fair use because they were a commentary on society.

The noncommercial use, artistic relevance, and fair uses defenses to dilution are discussed below.

v. Trade Dress, or Similarity of Styles

Artists may sometimes be liable for trade dress infringement. 15 U.S.C. § 1125(a) makes a person liable for the use in commerce of "any word, term, name, symbol, or device, or any combination thereof ... which (A) is likely to cause confusion ... as to the origin ... of his goods ..." The "symbol or device" language has been read to provide liability when one person uses a similar packaging to someone else, or when one person designs the goods themselves in a way that mimics someone else's design. This liability is called "trade dress."

To succeed, plaintiff must establish that his designs have secondary meaning. In *Diamond Direct, LLC v. Star Diamond Group, Inc.*, 116 F.Supp.2d 525 (S.D.N.Y. 2000), plaintiff was unable to prove that the designs of his diamond rings identified him as the source of the rings. His advertising was modest, there were no consumer surveys or unsolicited media coverage introduced, there was limited sales success, and the period of plaintiff's exclusive use of the design was short. The court granted defendant summary judgment because no reasonable jury could have found sufficient secondary meaning in the designs to constitute a trademark.

In an early case, plaintiff distributors of limited editions and fine art posters were able to obtain an injunction prohibiting another artist from marketing similar work in the same style showing two women in cafes with big hats because the first artist's style had become a trade dress identifying the source of the product. The court found that the similarity of the work was likely to lead to consumer confusion. *Romm Art Creations Ltd. v. Simcha Int'l Art, Inc.*, 786 F.Supp. 1126 (E.D.N.Y. 1992). The case seems comparable to Monet seeking an injunction to prevent Renoir from painting *plein air* scenes in the impressionist style, or Braque enjoining Picasso from producing cubist work depicting furniture.

The continued validity of the trade dress infringement theory when applied to the content of copyrighted artwork is questionable in light of the strong comments in *Dastar Corp. v. Twentieth Century Fox Film Corp.*, 539 U.S. 23 (2003) that the limited terms of copyright and patent were designed to be the sole protection for originality or creativity, and not the trademark laws which have perpetual life.

D. Defenses: Fair Use, Artistic Relevance, Noncommercial Use

It is perhaps fair to state that in trademark, aside from specific statutory designation as a defense, it is not always clear whether something is a defense or an element of the offense.

As with copyright, there are fair use exceptions to trademark liability. It would be convenient if fair use had the same content in trademark law that it has in copyright law, but that is not the case. The statutory provisions are very different, and the caselaw has not developed in tandem. Indeed, there are a number of different trademark fair use defenses extant.

i. Fair Use Defenses to Infringement

Two trademark fair use defenses that should seldom arise in art cases are descriptive and nominative fair use. These fair use defenses to infringement are of common law origin. Descriptive fair use has been incorporated by statute. It is trademark fair use to employ another's trademarked words as a descriptive term if they describe yourself, your product or its geographic origin, so long as they do not function as a trademark for your product. 15 U.S.C. § 1115(b)(4). Words on your donut package that describe the exterior as crispy and the interior as creamy would be a good descriptive fair use defense to a suit by KrispyKreme donuts.

A second fair use is nominative: to refer to products or their maker, usually a competitor, by using the words of the other person's trademark as an identifier, such as in advertising that compares your product to your competitor's product. Again, the words cannot function as a trademark for your product.

It is also to be noted that not all circuits recognize all forms of fair use trademark defenses.

Artists may frequently assert a fair use defense based on parody. Parody conveys both an idealized image of the trademark combined with elements that mock its idealized nature. There is no statutory fair use defense for parody to trademark infringement, but many cases have considered it, and the results are inconsistent.

If the treatment qualifies as parody, that infects other decisions required to find trademark infringement. If the parody is successful, that significantly reduces the likelihood of confusion. This was the line of reasoning in *Louis Vuitton Malletier S.A. v. Haute Diggity Dog, LLC*, 507 F.3d 252 (4th Cir. 2007). In trademark dilution by blurring cases, successful parody is unlikely to be blurring because most people will know that it is parody.

Parody may help in finding that defendant did not intend to use the trademark as a mark indicating origin, because the parody is an alternate reason for the use. In others, such as *Louis Vuitton*, use of the trademark functions both as parody and a designation of origin.

ii. Fair Use Defense to Dilution

There is a specific statutory fair use defense to dilution. Dilution fair use cannot involve use to designate the source of the user's goods or services. It includes use in comparative advertising, and use in identifying and parodying, criticizing or commenting on either the owner of the famous mark or his goods or services. It may include other uses. In *Louis Vuitton Malletier S.A. v. Haute Diggity Dog, LLC*, 507 F.3d 252 (4th Cir. 2007), defendant sold a dog chew toy called "Chewy Vuitton." The court held that defendant could not succeed with a fair use defense because it was using the name to identify the origin of its goods. But it held that successful parody would be evidence that some of the requirements to show dilution were not met, such as defendant's intent in using the parody, defendant's actual use of the parody, and its effect on the famous mark. "While a parody intentionally creates an association with the famous mark in order to be a parody, it also intentionally communicates, if it is successful, that it is *not* the famous mark, but rather a satire of the famous mark."

Other than having more specific statutory references, it is not clear that the fair use test for dilution produces different results in any case than the fair use test for infringement.

iii. Fair Use as Defense to Trademark-Related Actions

A fair use defense to some of the other trademark-related actions might exist, but I have found no cases. There would be no reason for a fair use defense to false advertising; anything false would not be fair. Whether a fair use defense is necessary for allegations that the mark use created confusion about sponsorship or approval is unclear. The falsity of the assertion might bar fair use. In *ETW Corp. v. Jireh Publishing*, 332 F.3d 915 (6th Cir. 2003), Tiger Woods' licensee sued the artist who placed his image in a painting three times celebrating his Masters Tournament championship. While the court is most unclear about its fair use analysis, it did state that this was fair use. Whether the reason related to the newsworthiness of the event or some other factor we will never know, and it probably does not matter because there were so many grounds for denying relief that the case is not a strong precedent.

For dilution, the courts' broad interpretation of the noncommercial use defense discussed below makes a fair use defense constitutionally unnecessary.

iv. Artistic Relevance Defense

Some courts have developed an "artistic relevance" test that is very favorable to the artist. It is not always clear whether artistic relevance is fair use, whether artistic relevance is a separate defense, or whether artistic relevance prevents what would otherwise be infringement from constituting infringement. I think the better interpretation is that, in the absence of intent to take financial advantage of plaintiff's trademark, artistic relevance should tip the balance of a case in favor of fair use. In *Rogers v. Grimaldi*, 875 F.2d 994 (2d Cir. 1989), defendant distributed a film by Fellini about two Italian dancers who imitated the work of Ginger Rogers and Fred Astaire, a famous American movie dancing pair, and titled the film "Ginger and Fred." Ginger Rogers sued for trademark infringement and invasion of her right of publicity. The court said, "[T]he [Lanham] Act should be construed to apply to artistic works only where the public interest in avoiding consumer confusion outweighs the public interest in free expression. In the context of allegedly misleading titles using a celebrity's name, that balance will normally not support application of the Act unless the title has no artistic relevance to the underlying work whatsoever, or ... unless the title explicitly misleads as to the source of the work." The court thus rejected plaintiff's proposed rule that the use could only be permitted if there were no possible alternative because that would too deeply restrict artistic expression, as well as defendant's proposed rule that the use should always be permitted, because that would provide insufficient protection where the sole purpose of the title was to take financial advantage of plaintiff's investment in her trademark. The title in this case had artistic relevance because of the activities of the characters, the defendants made no specifically misleading statements as to the source or endorsement of the film, and the small risk of confusion was greatly outweighed by the interests in artistic expression. While the court states that only a slight amount of artistic relevance is required, that was in a context of complete absence of evidence that defendants had intended to capitalize on plaintiff's trademark by stating that she had endorsed film. As to the right of publicity claim, the court held that the constitutional right of free expression prevented recovery in this case, though it was not clear whether the constitution providing that right was the Oregon constitution (which has been more broadly construed) or the United States constitution.

Rogers v. Grimaldi has been widely cited for two propositions. The first is that courts should balance avoiding consumer confusion with encouraging free expression. The second is that artistic relevance may be a determining factor in tipping a case against trademark infringement. But it is important to remember that there are two elements to the test. There must be some artistic relevance, though it may be slight, and the defendant cannot explicitly mislead as to the source of the product.

In *Univ. of Alabama Bd. of Trustees v. New Life Art, Inc.*, 683 F.3d 1266 (11th Cir. 2012), defendant produced paintings, prints, calendars, mugs and other mundane products like cups, towels, flags and t-shirts containing University of Alabama football scenes, including the University's trademarked uniforms and football colors. The court found that the use of the uniforms and colors were artistically necessary for a realistic depiction of scenes from Alabama football history in plaintiff's paintings, prints and calendars. There was no evidence that defendant ever stated University sponsorship for these artistic items, and summary judgment was granted defendant. For the mugs and mundane products, the district court had held against the artist, and the artist did not press his artistic relevance argument on appeal.

Rogers v. Grimaldi involved only the use of a trademark in a title as artistic relevance, but that was easily extended to the body of the artistic work in *U. of Alabama* and other cases.

"Artistic relevance" should only apply if the allegedly infringing work is an artwork, but whether it can be extended to the use of artwork on towels, flags or mugs has yet to be decided.

v. Noncommercial Use Defense to Dilution

There is a statutory defense to dilution for noncommercial uses. 15 U.S.C. § 1125(c)(4)(B). The purpose of that defense is to protect free speech. It seeks out fully constitutionally protected speech like parody, satire or editorials. The test evolved by the courts is whether the speech does more than simply propose a transaction. Speech whose only purpose is to sell goods does not qualify, but the fact that artwork is offered for sale does not disqualify the trademark used in that work from protection by the noncommercial use defense if it is providing commentary. This is an important defense for an artist because the use of a trademark in an artwork will usually be to provide commentary on it.

E. Remedies: Attorneys Fees

A prevailing party may be awarded reasonable attorney's fees "in exceptional cases." This is a different standard than prevails for attorney's fees in copyright. Different circuits formulate the concept of exceptional cases differently. One opinion deplored the variety of tests used by different courts to determine whether the case was exceptional, some involving bad faith, others differentiating between successful plaintiffs and successful defendants. It proposed a very narrow test. A case where plaintiff lost is exceptional where bringing the suit was abuse of process, which requires use of litigation for an improper purpose; a case where defendant lost is exceptional where defendant had no defense but persisted in the infringement to impose costs on plaintiff. The judge should look for either predatory suing or predatory defending. The court held the case exceptional under that standard where the judge found that the trademark claim was brought as part of an attempt to persuade defendant to lower the price it charged plaintiff for its infrared lamps. *Nightingale Home Healthcare, Inc. v. Anodyne Therapy, LLC*, 626 F.3d 958 (7th Cir. 2010). Adoption of those tests will result in little fee shifting because the standard will be difficult to meet. However, the Supreme Court held that a similar phrase in the patent law should not be so strictly interpreted. An exceptional patent case is simply one that stands out from others with respect to the substantive lack of strength of a party's litigating position (considering both the governing law and the facts of the case) or the unreasonable manner in which the case was litigated. District courts may determine whether a case is exceptional in the case-by-case exercise of their discretion, considering the totality of the circumstances. *Octane Fitness, LLC v. ICON Health & Fitness, Inc.*, 572 U.S. 545 (2014).

For further guidance, see J. THOMAS MCCARTHY, MCCARTHY ON TRADEMARKS AND UNFAIR COMPETITION.

Checkpoints

- The Lanham Act protects the investment a business makes in the reputation of its trademarked products and services; prevents deception of the public about the source of goods or services; protects the owners of famous marks from having the meaning of their trademarks diluted; and prevents misrepresentations in commercial advertising.
- Marks must be distinctive, non-functional and used in the ordinary course of business. Names and descriptions are weak marks unless they have acquired secondary meaning attached to products.
- The basic trademark violation is use of a mark on a product not made by the mark owner that results in public confusion about the product's source.
- Artists and art institutions marketing work might wish to trademark their products to prevent others from marketing similar goods with the same mark.
- It is a trademark violation to blur or tarnish a nationally-known mark by using it on wildly different products or with unsavory connections.
- Where the appearance of a product has acquired a secondary meaning indicating the product's source, it can be a trademark violation to imitate the packaging or appearance in a way that causes confusion about the source of the goods.

- The fair use defenses to infringement require that the mark not be used to identify a product. Descriptive fair use is where the use of another's mark describes the producer, the product or its geographic origin. Nominative fair use is where another's mark is used only to identify the product.
- If the use does not designate the source of goods, it may be a valid fair use defense to dilution to comparatively advertize, parody, criticize or comment on another's trademarked product.
- It is a defense to trademark infringement that the use of the mark has artistic relevance in the artwork in which it is used.
- It is a defense to trademark dilution that the use is noncommercial. Noncommercial use is any use more than selling a product, like parody, satire, or editorializing.
- Remedies for trademark violation include injunction, actual damages, and up to treble damages. Attorneys' fees may be awarded in exceptional cases.

Chapter 7

Moral Rights

Roadmap

After reading this chapter, you should understand:

- Moral rights distinguished from economic rights: Moral rights are a group of non-waivable rights artists have in the physicality and reputation of their works, while economic rights in those works, such as re-sale rights and copyright, involve only payments for use.
- Moral rights group together four distinct rights: The right of paternity or attribution, the right of integrity to prevent modification or destruction of the work, the right of divulgation to decide when the work is finished, and the right to repent, i.e., the right to take back the work.
- The right of divulgation and the right to repent are not protected in any United States jurisdiction.
- The right of paternity or attribution allows the artist to insist that his name be attached to works that he created, to remove his name from works he did not create, and to remove his name from works he created but that have been modified. It probably does not permit the artist to insist that the work be anonymous or pseudonymous.
- The right of integrity allows the artist to prevent the intentional modification or destruction of his work.
- The terms "prejudicial to his or her honor or reputation" and "work of recognized stature," which are necessary to find violation of the right of integrity, are easily satisfied, but do require that the work have some public recognition, though not necessarily praise from art professionals.
- A mental state is required for modification or destruction to be actionable: It must be intentional, or, in the case of destruction, grossly negligent, or, in the case of modification during conservation, grossly negligent.
- Fair use is a defense to a moral rights action.
- A work that is attached to a building but can be removed without damaging the work is subject to a special rule: If the owner gives the artist 90 days notice to remove the work and the artist removes it, the work belongs to the artist. If the artist does not remove the work, the owner may destroy it.

- A single work is modified if its elements are placed in different relationships with each other, but the question of whether a work with multiple pieces is a single work or many works is a question of fact. A site-specific work is not modified by being moved to another site or put in storage.
- Federal moral rights protect only "works of visual art," a limited class of artistic work that includes only paintings, drawings, and certain prints, sculptures and still photographs produced in limited quantities. Works of visual art must be copyrightable. Prints, sculptures and photos done in multiples must be signed and numbered by the artist, and photos must be produced for exhibition purposes.
- A work made for hire is not a "work of visual art," so it carries no moral rights.
- Useful items like advertising, containers, posters, maps, globes, charts or technical drawings are not works of visual art.
- Moral rights are personal to the artist: They cannot be transferred, and it is difficult to waive them.
- Federal law preempts state moral rights law during the lifetime of the artist for "works of visual art" only.
- The First Amendment guarantee of free speech may prohibit liability for moral rights where the work is modified or destroyed to communicate a message.

1. Introduction: What Are Moral Rights?

Moral rights and re-sale rights are sometimes classified together because they are both personal to the creator of the work and either difficult or impossible to waive. But re-sale rights are certainly economic rights, while moral rights are not normally conceived as economic rights. They are primarily preventive rights inherent in the artist, usually conferring a physical right about the work.

Moral rights are classified into four categories:

1. The right of paternity or attribution, comprising the right to have the creator's name attached to the artwork and to prevent the name of anyone who did not create the work from being attached;
2. The right of integrity, being the right to prevent modification of the work or its destruction;
3. The right of divulgation, which is the right to decide whether a work has been finished; and
4. The right to repent, which is the right to retake the work on payment of an indemnity and the right to modify the work after it has been sold.

Neither the right of divulgation nor the right to repent have found any purchase in United States federal law, or in the law of any state. *Mass. Museum of Contemp. Art Found. Inc. v. Büchel*, 593 F.3d 38 (1st Cir. 2010).

Curiously, moral rights were first created in France, a Civil Law jurisdiction whose law is primarily statute-based, by judicial decision that was later codified. Moral rights exist in the United States, a Common Law jurisdiction whose law is primarily judge-made, only as the creature of statutes, which have been enacted by the federal government and about a quarter of the states, mostly those that are highly populated. They protect only the rights of paternity and integrity. 17 U.S.C. §§ 101, 106A, 113, 301; CALIF. CIV. CODE §§ 987, 989; New York Arts & Cultural Affairs Law Title C § 14.03.

The theory of moral rights is that these are not economic rights. They are rights that are part of the personality of the creator of a work of art. To mistreat the artwork is to mistreat the artist. It is sometimes analogized to invasion of privacy. A second strain of theory sees moral rights as analogous to the right of publicity. The artist carefully builds a "persona" consisting of the entire corpus of his production, each of which (whether sold or not) contributes to his personality. A third theoretical strand is the public interest in preserving the artwork (right of integrity) and preventing fraud (right of paternity). This third strand is weakest when the public has no way to assert its rights, as under federal law, and strongest where it can, in California and some European countries.

Moral rights in the United States are principally provided by the Visual Artists Rights Act, 17 U.S.C. §§ 101, 106A, 113, 301. Some states have enacted similar laws that have survived preemption (at least in part) to the extent that they cover different types of artwork or different time periods.

2. The Right of Paternity or Attribution

The right of attribution can be thought of as two rights: the right to claim authorship of works that one has created, and the right to disclaim authorship of works one has not created.

This right of attribution may be motivated by fairness to the artist, increasing the amount of information about specific artworks available to the public, and helping insure the accuracy of that information. The fairness argument is easy to understand when work is misattributed; its counterpart is an action for misrepresentation. It is not so easy to understand in the case of a work presented without attribution. It must be based on the proposition that the creator of a work of visual art has a fairness claim to have his name associated with his work—a claim not made with respect to any other item of property, either real or personal.

A. Claiming Authorship—Attaching your Name

The right to claim authorship includes the right to have one's name attached to a work of visual art that the author has created. Thus, the artist who created a painting has the right to insist that a museum displaying the painting attribute that painting to her. The surest way to do this is for the artist to sign the painting herself.

Failing the artist's signature, what mode of attribution is required? The most traditional method is to affix a metal plaque to the frame of the painting, containing the artist's name and the title of the painting. That is more than is required by VARA, since VARA does not require that the title of the work be presented. Alternatively, the work might be attributed to the artist by a sign adjacent to the painting. Some museums do not have individual identifying signs, but may have an entire room devoted to a single artist that carries her name. Alternatively, each room might have a single placard containing the names of the creators of each work of art displayed within the room and some method of identifying which is which. It is doubtful that a system where the museum patron must request such a guide from a museum employee would meet the requirements of this provision. The system practiced in some museums (mostly museums that were formerly private homes) of simply not identifying the artist who created the work is a violation.

Likewise, a private owner of a work of visual art must identify the artist when the artwork is on display, even if the artwork is displayed in a private home. Presumably, no such identification is required when the work is in storage, though it is a good practice in order to avoid a situation where someone forgets to add the name of the artist when the work is put on display.

There is no requirement in VARA that a work ever be displayed.

There is no clue about how much identification is required. The provisions on removal refer to "use of his or her name," so providing the name would presumably be enough. There is no requirement that the title of the work be revealed, the dates of the artist's birth or death, the date when the work was created, the medium used, or the size. While it is common for museums, who are in the education business, to provide all that information, providing the name of the artist is sufficient to satisfy this part of VARA.

In fact, failure to attach the creator's name is unlikely. Much of the value of an original derives from its uniqueness and the fame of the artist. The failure to associate any artist's name with an original work of art is not in the economic interest of the owner. The time when the author's name is likely to be omitted from a work might be when the work is purchased for its decorative, rather than its artistic, value, for use in a commercial establishment like a hotel or an office. While it is hard to imagine why the author's name discretely attached to the work would be unduly distracting (and the owner can himself design the presentation of the name), an owner who insists on presenting the work without the author's name is well advised to obtain a written waiver from the artist.

B. Claiming Authorship—Removing the Names of Others

Can the artist who created the work require removal from the work of the names of persons who did not participate in its creation? There is no specific provision so requiring, but it is implied in the statement "to claim authorship of that work" that an artist who was the sole author of a work could claim sole authorship, which would require the owner to remove from the work the name of anyone who did not participate in its creation. If so, the right to claim authorship encompasses two rights: the right to have your name attached to the work, and the right to prevent the name of any non-creator from being attached to it.

Presumably, this would not prevent a museum from including on its signs the name of the person who donated the work as long as the museum clearly denominates the donors as benefactors so that it is not implied that the donor is the author of the work.

However real these rights might be with works of visual arts, the exclusion from the definition of work of visual art of reproductions renders the right much less valuable. For example, X might purchase an oil painting and its copyright from artist A. X clearly identifies A as the author of the painting, but X creates posters, reproductions, and magazine features with the image of the painting, attaching X's name to them as the creating artist. No violation of the right of attribution has occurred because neither posters, reproductions nor magazine features are works of visual art. This is a surprising conclusion. It does not protect the general public from being misled, and it is much more likely to be detrimental to the reputation of the author (or rather fail to improve the reputation of the author by its being attributed to her) because it will be much more widely circulated and viewed than a mislabeled original. For this reason, the right of attribution should apply to reproductions, and does apply in some states. New York Arts & Cultural Affairs Law § 14.03, 1-2.

C. Disclaiming Authorship

On the negative side, an author can have his name removed from work in two circumstances.

An author can "prevent the use of his or her name as the author of any work of visual art which he or she did not create; ...."

An author can also prevent the use of his name as author of a work of visual art "in the event of a distortion, mutilation, or other modification of the work which would be prejudicial to his or her honor or reputation;...." This is a counterpart to the right to prevent association of your name with a work you did not create. Most artists would not consider a work that has been mutilated or distorted to be their work.

Again, the limitation on this right to a "work of visual art" would not allow an artist to force removal of his name from a reproduction of his work that has been distorted because the reproduction is not a work of visual art.

The term "prejudicial to his or her honor or reputation" is important here, but is better discussed below in connection with the right of integrity.

D. Anonymity and Pseudonymity

The legislative history states that section "106A(a)(1) creates a right of attribution that extends ... to the right to publish anonymously or under a pseudonym." This and following quotes in this chapter are from H. R. Rep. No. 101-514, 101st Cong., 2d Sess. (1990) to PL 101-650 § 603(a), 104 Stat. 5128. But there is not a shred of evidence in the text of the statute that the right of attribution extends to either anonymity or pseudonymity. The plain meaning of the words does not suggest that the author has the right to prevent the use of her name on a work she did create, which would be a requirement for both anonymity and pseudonymity. Nor does it suggest that the author has the right to insist that some specific name other than her own be attached to a work that she created, which would be pseudonymity. If the statute read "the author shall have the right to *designate* authorship of that work," there would be textual support for anonymity and pseudonymity.

Indeed, a sudden decision by the author that a particular work which was sold as the work of the author should henceforth be anonymous or pseudonymous might devalue the work, as a substantial part of the value of an artwork derives from the name value of the artist. Giving the artist such a right would permit the artist to unforeseeably reduce the value of the owner's property, which should not be permitted.

The right to require that the work be anonymous or pseudonymous does not protect the public from false information, as does the right to insist that the artist's name be associated with the work or that the artist's name be removed from a work that she did not create.

A closer policy question is whether an artist, whose work is purchased as the work of the artist's pseudonym or anonymously, can prevent a purchaser from later attaching the artist's own name to the work when the artist becomes known. One can argue that attaching the artist's name confers an unbargained-for benefit on the owner, in a situation where the artist wishes to segregate this work (for whatever reason, perhaps a good professional reason) from the main body of his work. Given the balance of the equities, even in this situation the right of attribution should not extend to anonymity or pseudonimity without some hint in the text of the statute that the legislative intent was to include anonymity and pseudonimity.

E. Remedies for Violation of the Right of Attribution

An artist is entitled to an injunction to prevent violations of his right of attribution. It has been suggested that the artist may not be able to collect damages because the statute says only that the author has the right of attribution, whereas the provision on the right of integrity adds that any such action "is a violation of that right." This is an untenable verbal distinction upon which to base a denial of damages. The statute is quite specific that all the remedies for copyright infringement are available for moral rights infringement except where specifically excluded, and the only specific exclusion for moral rights is criminal prosecution.

Nor does there seem to be a policy reason to give the author the right to seek an injunction to enforce the right of attribution, but to deny him damages for the period before the injunction becomes effective. The injunction may obviate future violations, but will not compensate the author for past violations. He may have lost significant sales because the name was improperly used. But the only case to discuss this question so far, *Mass. Museum of Contemp. Art Found. Inc. v. Büchel*, 593 F.3d 38 (1st Cir. 2010), stated in dictum that damages were not available.

3. The Right of Integrity

The right of integrity encompasses the right to prevent modification of the work and the right to prevent its destruction. Different statements of the right to prevent modification and the right to prevent destruction appear in the statute. For modification to be actionable, the modification must be intentional, except that a modification resulting from conservation or public presentation that results from gross negligence is actionable. Destruction of the work is actionable if it is either intentional or grossly negligent. A modification is actionable if it is prejudicial to the author's honor or reputation, while a destruction is actionable if it is of a work of recognized stature.

A. "Prejudicial to his or her Honor or Reputation" and "Work of Recognized Stature"

i. "Prejudicial to his or her Honor or Reputation"

The term "prejudicial to his or her honor or reputation" appears twice in VARA. It is a condition to an action for distortion, mutilation or other modification of a work of visual art, and it is likewise a condition for permitting the author to remove his name from a work he has created, but which has been distorted, mutilated or modified. The term should be interpreted in the same way in both contexts, since it is the same action the statute is describing. An author can seek an injunction to prevent such modification (and presumably, if it is possible, to order restoration of any such modifications already made); and the author can seek damages for the modification and, if she chooses, have her name removed from the work, but only if the modification is sufficiently severe to be prejudicial to her honor or reputation.

"Prejudicial to honor" does not have a familiar ring in American law. It sounds the concerns of a different century and a different continent, where a gentleman's honor was a supreme quality, and duels were fought to preserve it.

"Prejudicial to reputation," on the other hand, is a term with which we are familiar from the law of defamation (though the legislative history expressly disclaims an analogy to defamation).

But it turns out that the term "honor or reputation" is taken directly from the Berne Convention, article 6bis(1). The bill as introduced contained no such requirement. Instead, it imposed a single requirement for redress of both modification and destruction: that it occur to a work of recognized stature. This requirement was removed in the House Committee version because "throughout history, many works now universally acknowledged as masterpieces have been rejected and often misunderstood by the general public at the time they were created," and the phrase "prejudicial to his or her honor or reputation" was substituted. The legislative history implies that "recognized stature" is a more difficult proof than harm to "honor or reputation." It suggests "focus on the artistic or professional honor or reputation of the individual as embodied in the work that is protected." This suggests that the author of a single work has a larger percentage of his honor or reputation invested in that work than does the author of a thousand works. It also suggests that the best of an author's work is more worthy of protection than the worst of his work, as his reputation is likely to increase if that work is not taken into account.

One might ask about the grammar of this particular clause. Does the phrase "which would be prejudicial to his or her honor or reputation" modify only the words "other modification," or does it modify "distortion, mutilation or other modification"? In addition to the placement of the phrase, one could argue that it only modifies "other modification." By definition any distortion or mutilation would be prejudicial because both of those words have contained within them a negative connotation. A modification might occur that might or might not be detrimental to the author's reputation, so it is only if the change is a modification that such detriment must be proven.

Though this argument may be appealing, it is essential that those words be read in the same manner as similar words contained in the provision guaranteeing integrity, as the wording is almost the same. The legislative history specifically requires that, and also makes it clear that the phrase "prejudicial to his or her honor or reputation" modifies all three terms. In addition, such an interpretation would require distinguishing between a "mutilation" and a "distortion," on the one hand, and a "modification" on the other, a distinction difficult to make.

The legislative history also suggests that the formula for determining whether there is harm to honor or reputation must be flexible, and that "the trier of fact must examine the way in which a work has been modified and the professional reputation of the author of the work." It further suggests that expert testimony might help, and "[w]hile no per se rule exists, modification of a work of recognized stature will generally establish harm to honor or reputation." This seems to imply a two-part test. First, the author attempts to prove that the work is a work of recognized stature. If he succeeds, any modification will *generally* harm his honor or reputation. If the author fails to establish that the work is of recognized stature, he can still try to prove that the particular modification harmed his honor or reputation. But what trial lawyer would rest his case without trying to prove both elements where proving one is not conclusive?

In fact, the requirement that the change harm honor or reputation has not proven to be a stumbling block. It appears that the courts presume that any modification is harmful to the author's honor or reputation, so this has not been a sticking point in any case. "An artist's professional and personal identity is embodied in each work created by that artist. Each work is a part of his/her reputation. Each work is a form of personal expression...." But if this is so, why impose the requirement at all? Is it not safe to say that any known or publicized modification will hurt the artist's honor and reputation because it will be known that someone disliked the work enough to modify it? Or could one contend that viewing the actual modified work will not damage the artist's honor and reputation if the viewer knows that the work has been modified? Or perhaps it is the degree of publicity that is significant. If no one knows that the work has been modified, there is no harm to reputation. It would appear that the better course of action would have been to stick with the requirement that the work be "of recognized stature," especially in light of the interpretation of that term, and eliminate the requirement for damage to honor or reputation.

ii. "Work of Recognized Stature"

Where a work has been destroyed, however, the statute states that there is no recovery unless the work was a "work of recognized stature." It has been suggested that its purpose was to protect serious art. This is "designed in part to make sure a doting mother doesn't sue her child's kindergarten teacher for throwing out her child's finger-painting."

A great deal of ink has been spent trying to define the tests of "prejudicial to honor or reputation" and "recognized stature" and trying to spin out the differences between the two tests. One commentator suggested that there was no need to prove prejudice to honor or reputation since that prejudice, the inability of the work to deliver the artist's meaning to the viewer, is always such an injury. Both tests are relatively easy to meet, as both serve a gate-keeping function of avoiding nuisance suits. Neither test is designed to require a high degree of reputation or standing. Nothing like museum quality is required. The two questions are: 1) is the work meritorious, and 2) is the work recognized by people. The reputation or standing can either be pre-existing, or can develop later in a proper case. It can result from the individual work, or from the full corpus of the artist's production in a proper case. It can be standing with experts or with the general public. *Carter v. Helmsley-Spear, Inc.*, 861 F.Supp. 303, 325 (S.D.N.Y. 1994) *rev'd on other grounds* 71 F.3d 77 (2d Cir. 1995); *Martin v. City of Indianapolis*, 192 F.3d 608 (7th Cir. 1999).

In fact, only a single case has held that the "reputation" or the "stature" test has been missed. In *Scott v. Dixon*, 309 F.Supp. 2d 395 (E.D.N.Y. 2004), plaintiff had produced (at least) two huge animal sculptures, one in the form of a deer 50 feet tall that was adjacent to and easily visible from a public road and that was discussed in the press, and the other in the form of a swan, that was the subject of the suit. The swan, made of steel, was 40 feet long and 10 feet high, and designed to fit in defendant's back yard. The sculpture was brought there in pieces and assembled there. The yard is surrounded by the house and a hedge 12 feet high. When defendant sold the house, the purchaser insisted that the swan be removed. Defendant at his expense had the sculpture cut up, removed and stored. The court found that due to rust, corrosion and changes in shape, the statue could not be restored to its previous form. Defendant offered the statue to plaintiff, but plaintiff asked defendant to pay to transport it to a museum in Massachusetts, which defendant refused to do. There was no evidence of either the general public or the art community ever seeing the Swan. There was only one mention of the Swan in a publication, and that was in connection with an article on defendant's home, called Swan's Way. There were frequent newspaper mentions of the deer. The district court held that Swan was not a work of "recognized stature." It admitted that a work by some artists (Picasso was cited) would be a work of recognized stature even if never seen by anyone, but it found that "[w]hile Plaintiff has achieved some level of local notoriety, that stature is not so great as to afford VARA protection to each and every work she creates." The court stated that the articles produced supported the proposition that the deer was a work of recognized stature.

The proposition that "reputation" and "recognized standing" are relatively low and comparable standards to meet is perfectly appropriate. "An artist's reputation depends on his artwork; if it is destroyed, he can't use it to attract potential clients, mount it in a retrospective show of his works, or reproduce it in exercise of his copyrights." The same can be said for the stature of a work, which depends in part on the identity of the artist. It is clear that both reputation and stature can be proven by both testimony of art experts and by testimony from members of the general public.

Also, in most cases, it is quite easy to prove "reputation" or "recognized standing." The proof will often come from the defendant himself. That proof consists of the fact that defendant spent a substantial sum of money to buy the art, and considerable care deciding which artwork to purchase or which artist to commission. (What defendant would testify that he did this thoughtlessly?) In the case of a public commission, there may have been a juried competition to select the artist or artwork, which provides further evidence of "reputation" or "stature." The fact that defendant is now arguing contrary to his previous actions makes his argument peculiarly unpersuasive, and almost an estoppel.

The argument that there is no "reputation" or "stature" may still be open to the recipient of a gift, one who purchased the art inexpensively, or a third party with no relationship to the art, who may find himself liable to the owner of the artwork on common law grounds and also liable to the artist under the right of integrity.

B. Modification or Destruction

One might well ask what the difference is between "mutilation, distortion or modification" (referred to as "modification") and destruction. Destruction would be the complete obliteration of the work. Complete incineration of paintings in a fire would be an example, as would the dismantling and selling for scrap of a metal sculpture. Modification would be the City of Pittsburgh re-painting Alexander Calder's black-and-white mobile in the green-and-grey colors of the city and motorizing it so that it moved constantly, or a hotel art consultant and interior decorator hiring a painter to cover a painting with varnish to dampen its colors. If one needs to draw a line between modification and destruction, destruction is when the original work is unidentifiable and unrestorable (at a reasonable price?), while modification is any other change.

But it should not be necessary to distinguish between modification and destruction. If the "reputation" and "stature" tests are roughly the same, and if the state of mind required are the same, there will be no reason to argue whether the action resulted in modification or destruction.

C. State of Mind—Intentional or Grossly Negligent

The other difference between the modification violation and the destruction violation consists in an apparently different wording for intent. The modification must be "intentional," but the destruction must be either "intentional or grossly negligent." However, when the modification results from attempts at conservation or public presentation, the statute says that the damage is not a "modification" or "destruction" unless it is caused by gross negligence. But surely an intentional modification during conservation or presentation would also be a modification. Summarizing, this means that there is no violation of the right of integrity if done negligently; there is a violation of the right of integrity if done intentionally; and there is a violation of the right of integrity if property is destroyed in a grossly negligent manner, or if property is modified as a result of conservation or presentation done in a grossly negligent manner.

It is unclear that there is any principled difference between negligence and gross negligence. My torts colleagues tell me such a distinction is doubtful. But legislatures continue to enact such statutes and courts continue to interpret them. "The behavior of a defendant must be flagrant, grossly deviating from the ordinary standard of care." *Hunter v. Squirrel Hill Assocs, L.P.*, 413 F.Supp.2d 517 (E.D.Pa. 2005) (dictum). It appears that one may be able to heighten the degree of negligence from ordinary to gross by notifying the owner of the potential damage and the means to prevent it. If the notified owner hired an independent contractor to remove the danger and the contractor's work was grossly negligent in failing to remove the danger and the art was modified as a result, the contractor would be liable; the owner would only be liable if he was grossly negligent in choosing the contractor or in supervising the repair, or if the work of the contractor were attributable to the owner under the doctrine of *respondeat superior*. The person held liable must be charged with gross negligence. Where the owner of a building died and the estate was put in the hands of an attorney who sold it to her brother who painted over plaintiff's mural on the building before receiving title, the court doubted the liability of the estate or the heirs. Neither the estate nor the heirs had painted over the mural, nor was the brother an agent of the estate or the heirs in painting it. *Roberto v. Est. of Hill*, 2007 U S Dist Lexis 28924 (S.D.Ca. 2007).

If there were no possible means of grossly negligent modifications other than those resulting from conservation or presentation, we might be able to state a unitary rule. But one might imagine a modification resulting from grossly negligent storage, such as storage near improperly contained acid or flammables. One might also imagine a grossly negligent modification resulting from the application of paint to some other item in such a careless way that it modified the work of art. One wonders why these actions should not result in a violation of the author's right of integrity, but they do not.

Thus, we have the bizarre situation that a grossly negligent modification not in the course of conservation or presentation would not incur liability, but liability would be incurred if the work is destroyed as a result of the same action.

D. The Fair Use Defense

VARA subjects both the right of attribution and the right of integrity to the fair use defense. It is hard to imagine how such a collision will arise.

The right of attribution only concerns association of the artist's name with the work. Fair use is the use of a work in a way unauthorized by copyright law, but permitted because a small part of the work is being used, it is being used in a noncommercial way, it is a parody, or it does not displace income that the copyright owner would normally receive. The number of cases where fair use can be a defense to failure to attach the artist's name to the work or attaching it to another work must be quite small. It might include attaching the artist's name to a work of art he did not create as a parody on the artist's work, but it might be difficult to establish the parody nature of it simply by misnaming the work's creator.

As to the right of integrity, Marcel Duchamp's L.H.O.O.Q., where he drew a moustache and beard on a reproduction of the Mona Lisa, would violate VARA if the Mona Lisa had been produced after VARA's effective date and if

Duchamp had used the original, or one of 200 numbered and signed copies of prints or photographs of it. Duchamp could claim a parody defense under the fair use doctrine. Again, a case most unlikely to arise in practice because of the cost of using a work of visual art, rather than a reproduction.

On the other hand, if someone really wants to make a point about a painting, nothing makes the point more strongly than destroying or modifying the painting. But whether a fair use defense could survive in light of the option of destroying or modifying a reproduction is questionable, because a fair use cannot take more of the original than is necessary to make the point. Where a reproduction is available, the amount of the original necessary to make the point is none of it.

E. Moral Rights with Special Rules: Works Attached to Buildings

Works attached to buildings are governed by two different rules. A line is drawn between works that cannot be removed from the building without destruction, distortion, mutilation or other modification of the work, and works that can. 17 U.S.C. § 113(d).

i. Work that Can Be Removed without Its Modification

If it is a work that can be removed from the building without its modification, the author loses his right of integrity if either the owner of the building has made an unsuccessful good faith attempt to notify the artist that the owner intends to remove the work, or the owner gives such notice and the author does not remove the work within 90 days. If the author does respond and removes the work at his own expense, the work now belongs to the author.

ii. Work that Cannot Be Removed without Its Modification

If it is a work that cannot be removed without modification, the author loses his right of integrity if he consented to the installation of the work in the building before the effective date of VARA, or the author and the building owner signed a written statement that specifies that the installation of the work may subject the work to destruction, distortion, mutilation, or other modification by reason of its removal. The statute says nothing further. By negative implication, if a work was installed after VARA and the requisite agreement was not signed by both parties, the work cannot be removed without violating VARA. But that seems illogical, as work that cannot be removed without its destruction is then treated more favorably than work that can be so removed. In *Board of Managers of Soho Int'l Arts Condominium v. New York*, 2003 U.S.

Dist. LEXIS 10221 (S.D.N.Y. 2003), the court assumed but did not discuss that the rule was that work that could not be removed without modification was not protected by VARA. What seems clear is that Congress did not intend to immobilize a building with an artwork. What is unclear is why the artist should not have the same right to salvage what he can of the work.

iii. The Building Owner's Conundrum

This provision is a trap for the unwary owner. Can the work be removed without being damaged? All work can be so removed if cost is no object and if one need not consider damage to the building. The owner is in a poor place to make this determination. In a recent San Diego case, a team of hired experts determined that the Encinitas Surfing Madonna could not be removed without damaging it. The until-then-anonymous artist removed it by taking out 18 screws. So a prudent owner will always give the 90-day notice, then proceed. If the artist has removed the work, it is gone, and belongs to the artist. If the artist does not remove the work, the owner of the building gets an expert's opinion that the work can be removed without destroying it, and may proceed to remove it without liability.

iv. Of Tenants and Trespassers

The statute assumes that every time an artwork is attached to a building, there is interaction between the owner and the artist. That may be true, but there are two other situations that should be considered.

An artist who wishes to paint a mural on a blank wall is likely to approach the person in possession of the property. That person will often be a tenant. Typically, an artist and a community organization will get together on a project to get neighborhood teens to do a mural under the direction of the artist. The organization raises the money and the artist donates his time. They jointly approach the proprietor of the business on the premises, often a tenant, offering to put the mural on his wall at no cost to him, pointing out the advantages of civic pride development and reduced juvenile delinquency. The tenant consents. When the lease terminates, the landlord retakes possession and wants to whitewash the mural. He argues that under property law, a tenant only has possession until the end of the tenancy, and cannot bind the landlord or the property after that. I believe that courts are more likely to hold landlords to comply with VARA in order to protect the artist who is unlikely to search title to discover whether he is dealing with an owner or a tenant.

A contrary result should obtain where the artist is a trespasser. In that case, there is no equity in favor of the artist, and neither the owner nor anyone holding under him has consented to having the work affixed to the property. But if the owner does any act that implies acceptance of the work, such as publicizing the artwork, VARA should apply.

F. Distinguishing Between the Right of Attribution and the Right of Integrity

These rights are fundamentally different. The right of attribution calls only for identification, confers great benefits on the artist and the public by requiring the truthful identification of the artist with the work or informing the public that the work has been modified, and imposes little cost to the owner.

In contrast, the violation of the right of integrity by modifying or destroying art is likely to result in a similar or greater reputational damage to the artist, but it may impose a serious cost on the custodian of the work who must pay for its storage when he no longer cares to display it.

Of course, nothing prevents the unwilling custodian from finding a willing buyer for the work, or donating it to a museum or university.

4. "Work of Visual Art"

Federal moral rights only protect the author of a "work of visual art." In Europe, where moral rights originated, protection is available to a much broader group of works. Definition of a "work of visual art" is crucial; unless that definition is met, the creator has no federal moral rights, and must rely solely on state law.

A "work of visual art" is defined both positively and negatively. Positively, it includes paintings, drawings, and certain prints, photographs and sculptures.

A. Work of Visual Art—Positive Requirements

i. Painting, Drawing, Print, Sculpture, and Photograph Defined

The type of work that is a "work of visual art" is intended to be broad. Statutory references to sculpture include, but are not limited to, castings, carvings, models and constructions. Painting "includes murals, works created on canvas, and the like." Prints may be "lithographs, serigraphs and etchings." Drawings include drawings made on computer (presumably with the aid of the computer's software) and printed out, though presumably only in a single copy. *NASCAR v. Scharle*, 184 Fed. Appx. 271, 2006 U.S. App. Lexis 15254 (3d Cir.) (dictum). Photographs are still photographs only. They do not include movies or videotapes, but can be either positives or negatives, prints, contact sheets or transparencies.

It is not immediately clear why an artwork on the medium of videotape or film is not protected. It may be that such works were thought to be too commercial to be considered fine art, but critical opinion in the art world is to the contrary. Or it is possible that the entertainment industry insisted that it be exempted from the problems of moral rights after losing French cases related to the colorization of old movies, and limiting photographs to still photographs is one way to do that. But the film industry is more than adequately protected by the exclusion from VARA of works made for hire.

The limits on protection of photographs to still photos excludes all manner of film and video art that are not produced by the entertainment industry, including the videos that appear daily on the internet. It is difficult to understand why the artists who produced these works should have no right to insist that their names be associated with their work, and no right to complain if someone modifies their work.

The broad types of work covered, and the fact that it need not be the final product, is illustrated by a case where a sculptor prepared a clay model to be used to create a bronze head for a sculpture of Queen Catherine Braganza, wife of King Charles II of England. The district court stated that a work is not disqualified "because it is part of a larger project," and noted (perhaps too facilely) that "in the artistic community, 'models' such as the clay sculpture are considered works of art in their own right." The court decided this despite the fact that VARA specifically excludes "model" from the definition of "work of visual art," presumably because the word "modelings" is included in the definition of "sculpture." *Flack v. Friends of Queen Catherine*, Inc., 139 F.Supp. 2d 526 (S.D.N.Y. 2001).

A useful way to proceed in the case of models is to ask whether the item to be protected is copyrightable. This effectively distinguishes between a small-scale version of a proposed work of art, which is protected by copyright once it is fixed, and a small-scale version of something already in existence, such as a model train engine, which would lack sufficient originality to qualify for copyright.

a. Materials Used

One might ask whether the material used constitutes a limitation. The statute contains no such limitation. Could a living plant be a sculpture and thus a "work of visual art"? Despite the creativity required of the landscape architect, it is unlikely the Congress intended the selection and combination of different plants to be a "sculpture." But a living plant that is pruned in a particular way to create a visual image other than its natural growth might well constitute "sculpture ... cast, carved or fabricated." *Kelley v. Chicago Park District*, 635 F.3d 290 (7th Cir. 2011).

Artists that are critically recognized have worked by building jetties, assembling works of rock or dirt, creating ice sculptures composed of frozen water transported from different countries of the world, assembling commercial boxes of pills on purchased, pre-made shelves, making words from neon tubing, making a 500-foot long fissure in a gallery floor, or creating environments by juxtaposing long lists of items including a burnt-out Boeing 747. Painters, in addition to oil, tempera, gouache, acrylic and watercolor, have used elephant dung. "Artists may work in a variety of media and use any number of materials in creating their works. Therefore, whether a particular work falls within the definition should not depend on the medium or materials used." "The courts should use common sense and generally accepted standards of the artistic community in determining whether a particular work falls within the scope of the definition." But in the midst of all this "feel-good" language in the legislative history, one must remember that there *is* a definition. A work, no matter how artistic, is not a "work of visual art" unless it is either a painting, drawing, sculpture, print or still photograph. Is one of Allan Kaprow's Happenings a "work of visual art"? Not unless it is a painting, sculpture, drawing, print or photograph, and it is hard to see how personal interaction, whether scripted or ad libbed, can be any of them. It also suffers the impediment of not being fixed, so not copyrightable. An installation or environment is not a painting, drawing or print, but it might certainly be classified as a sculpture, even though it is not cast, carved or modeled, but "constructed."

One might also wonder whether a tapestry is a "work of visual art." While one does not usually think of a tapestry as a painting, it is certainly a means of representation on a flat surface. Unlike rugs, tapestries have little practical use other than beautification.

Other unusual materials include works on glass. Dale Chihuly's pieces would have little trouble qualifying as sculptures, given their combination of color and form, even though they may be blown. Michael Arcega also works with glass, but his method is to attach vinyl to glass. He calls them sculptures but, as they are flat, they are more likely to qualify as paintings.

b. A Single Art Work

The artwork need not be confined to a single or contiguous space. A single artwork could be composed of various elements in different places in a hotel lobby. *Carter v. Helmsley-Spear, Inc.*, 71 F.3d 77 (2d Cir. 1995) (dictum). Four unconnected pieces of bronze sculpture could be a single work of art. *Pavia v. 1120 Ave. of the Americas Assocs.*, 901 F. Supp. 620 (S.D.N.Y. 1995). Park sculptures arrayed along a single axis in a park might be one integrated work of art, even though the entire park was not a "work of visual art" under VARA.

Phillips v. Pembroke Real Estate, Inc., 288 F.Supp. 2d 89 (D. Mass. 2003), *rev'd on other grounds* 459 F.3d 128 (1st Cir. 2006).

The fact that unconnected elements may or may not constitute a single work of visual art requires criteria for deciding whether a single work of art has been created, or whether it is several different works. If several different works, they can be rearranged without problem. If a single work, a rearrangement is a prohibited modification.

There is no size limitation on a work of visual art, and the definition's breadth with regard to both technique and material indicates no limitation based on method of creation or composition. One court toys with the idea of holding that a park cannot be a work of visual art, but concedes that "a sculptor could design a sculpture garden that includes multiple inter-related sculptural elements that form an integrated work of visual art." The court escapes deciding this by noting that not all elements of the park in the case before it were designed by the same artist, a spurious escape because the statute specifically contemplates joint authorship. The court's more serious decision suggested that the test was whether the various elements supposedly making up the work of art were integrated. Integration involved consideration of motifs and artistic design. In holding that the sculptures and stonework on a particular northeast to southwest axis are an integrated work of art, the court noted their integration both by their marine motifs and the use of either bronze sculptures, granite, or mosaics in spiral pattern. The court found that other bronze sculptures with marine motifs were works of art, but not part of this work of art, because they lacked both the granite and spiral patterns that visually tie the other works together. The court did not discuss whether the plantings along the axis were part of the integrated work of art. *Phillips v. Pembroke Real Estate, Inc.*, 288 F.Supp. 2d 89 (D. Mass. 2003), *rev'd on other grounds* 459 F.3d 128 (1st Cir. 2006).

One can think of other evidence suggesting that numerous pieces comprise a single work of art. The original contract commissioning the piece might so state; the artist may have made that statement before the litigation arose, or art critics might have called it an integrated work. The ability of the viewer to perceive the entire work simultaneously may be an important factor, but it is also possible that a key element of the work is the inability to perceive the entire work simultaneously, the integration of its various elements being realised only after the elements have been viewed individually.

Evidence to the contrary might show that the artist regarded the elements as separate works of art, or that critics discuss them individually rather than collectively. This would argue that each is an individual work and they are not integrated.

c. Site-Specific Work

Artists have had little success in arguing that because a work is site-specific, it cannot be moved, nor can items surrounding it be changed. *Phillips v. Pembroke Real Estate, Inc.*, 459 F.3d 128 (1st Cir. 2006). A good reason for this is the fact that VARA provides specific rules for works in buildings that differ in some respects from those for other works, and it is hard to imagine a more site-specific artwork than one on or in a building. More important, to let an artist who has prepared a work for a building or an open space commandeer the surrounding buildings or landscape as an element of her work that cannot be changed without violating VARA would extend its reach quite far.

ii. Multiples Other Than Photos

"Multiples" is a term used in the art world, but not in the statute. The statute refers to "a ... print, or sculpture, existing ... in a limited edition of 200 copies or fewer that are signed and consecutively numbered by the author...." The use of the word "copies" indicates that each of the copies must be identical to each other (except for the numbering and signature; the numbering will be different because it must be done consecutively, and the signature will be different because done by hand). Any "copy" that is not identical to the other copies will be a work "existing in a single copy," so will not be subject to the signing and numbering requirement.

Where a work exists in multiples, the statute seems to say that it may have no more than 200 copies. This is an attempt to separate individualized work from mass-produced work, but it is unclear how Congress seized on the number 200. It is certainly not unusual for artists to number 250 copies of a work, but it is more common to have significantly fewer copies than 200. This provision seems designed to pick a number that is neither unreasonably large nor unreasonably small as a dividing line between individualized work and mass-produced work.

Reading the language of the statute technically, no multiple is protected unless all comply. The language says that it is a "work of visual art" if existing "in a limited edition of 200 copies or fewer that are signed and consecutively numbered by the author...." Nonetheless, if the author makes five copies that are signed and consecutively numbered, then makes a sixth that is unsigned, is there any reason to deny VARA protection for the first five? This is like having an edition of five lithographs, then using one of them to create several thousand prints of it. The complying five would be works of visual art, while the non-complying thousand would not. This meaning can be derived from the words of the statute by stating that the limited edition is the signed and numbered pieces, which cannot exceed 200 and which is protected by VARA. The unsigned or unnumbered copies are not protected by VARA, but do not remove protection from the signed and numbered edition. Clearly, creating the 201st signed and numbered print destroys VARA protection for any of the first 200.

Regardless of how the "200 copies" language is interpreted, there may be protection for an original, even though multiples have been made. Printmakers frequently make prints of various "states" of a print called "proofs." Usually, a state would not be numbered, and sometimes would not be signed. It is still protected as a work of visual art because it is an original. But if that state is the last state and becomes indistinguishable from the remaining prints, it is part of the group that must be signed and numbered. The wording of the text suggests that it is the original, so need not be signed and numbered, but in fact it is one of the copies and should receive the first number.

There are additional requirements for multiples that differ depending on the kind of work.

iii. Photos

Photos must also be for exhibition purposes only. "Exhibition purposes" means that the print was not made for commercial purposes, so no actual exhibition of the print is necessary. The purpose for the photo is determined at the time the print is made. A later print of the same photo may be made for commercial purposes without terminating the status of the first print as a "work of visual art." It is unclear whether, once an image is used for commercial purposes, any subsequent prints of that image will qualify as a "work of visual art." Technically read, the legislative history might say that if the first print is not used for exhibition purposes, no subsequent print will be so classified. But since a later commercial usage does not disqualify an earlier exhibition print, the reverse should be true, so the question of whether the print is an exhibition print is not determined by the first image produced, but by the use contemplated when this particular print is first produced.

The purpose of the "exhibition purposes" clause is to assure that moral rights will not attach to work produced for commercial purposes, principally for advertising. Some of these works will be covered by the work made for hire doctrine because produced by an employee; others will be covered by the work made for hire doctrine because produced under contract with an independent contractor that specifically states that it is a work for hire and complies with the required conditions.

Photos must be signed and consecutively numbered by the author. The statute is clear that even the original photo must be signed by the author (though it apparently need not be numbered 1/1 if there is only one). The legislative history states two reasons for this that are actually only a single reason: to distinguish between photographs that are works of visual art and those that are not, and to give notice to subsequent transferees that this work is covered by VARA. This is certainly true of paintings and drawings which are always covered, but hardly true of prints or sculpture. How will the purchaser know whether the unsigned print or sculpture is an original, thereby covered, or one of multiples, an unsigned and unnumbered product of which there is at least one identical copy, thereby uncovered? Furthermore, the legislative history's presumption that works produced other than for exhibition are never signed is faulty. A work produced in response to a purchase demand will never be exhibited by the artist, but is very likely to be signed. Of course, that might be considered a work produced for exhibition if by that is meant a work that is not a work for hire and not a work produced for advertising purposes. A work produced for sale to a magazine, or for advertising, might well be signed. But no matter how faulty the rationale, the statute is abundantly clear.

iv. Numbered and Signed by the Author

The statute requires that the copies be numbered and signed "by the author," but the statute says nothing about whether the ordinary rule of agency law, that the actions of the agent become that of the principal, apply to the signing and numbering, which would not be part of the creative work of producing the work of art.

The same requirements apply to multiples of sculpture, but the artist can substitute a sculptor's mark for a signature. This raises an additional problem. If the author must personally sign and number, and the sculptor affixes his mark, must the sculptor retain evidence that he personally applied the mark, since a handwriting expert cannot provide that evidence?

To answer the question of whether the signing and numbering must be personally performed, one must ask what the purpose of signing and numbering the copies might be. The legislative history supplies three purposes. The primary purpose " … is to limit the works to which its protection extends." But "it is an additional advantage that numbering and marking also provides purchasers with notice of the work's protected status. It also implies, but does not explicitly state, that signing and numbering represents a warranty by the artist that the work is in the limited quantity indicated and that the work was produced by the artist."

As to the first reason, it is unclear that the requirement of numbering limits the number of works to which VARA applies. One could prove the number of copies produced by other means. Numbering and signing does provide the purchaser with notice that this is a work protected by VARA, but that notice is provided whether the numbering and signing is done by the author or by his agent, and few purchasers would be able to distinguish the signature of the creator from that of his agent. As to the third reason, if the numbering and signing of the work by the author provides a warranty of authenticity and of the limited number produced, then under normal agency law, the author would be equally liable for breach of that warranty if signed or numbered by his authorized agent.

A requirement that the author herself physically sign and number seems far too technical to be imposed. Support for that is found in the legislative history, which states: "[T]he Committee does not intend to create a rigid requirement akin to the copyright notice...." It also states: "Courts should be flexible in determining whether the placement of the numbering and marking is adequate to serve the purposes described above." Courts should likewise be flexible in determining whether the signing and numbering requirements are met.

There is no particular requirement for the placement of the numbering and signature. At least where numbering and signature on the front would deface the work, "[p]lacement on the back of the work or on the matting surrounding it would be sufficient." This statement from the legislative history is quite strange. Signing and numbering on the matt would disappear if the matt were replaced, and a purchaser of the re-matted print would never suspect that he was buying a "work of visual art." Likewise, if the signing and numbering were on the reverse of the print and the print were sold framed, the purchaser would be unaware of the status.

So one is tempted to conclude that the signing and numbering can be done either by the artists herself or by her authorized agent.

One might ask whether the requirements for signing and numbering comport with the Berne Convention. That treaty provides that the rights it provides should not be subjected to any formality. It appears that the requirement for signing and numbering is a prohibited formality. While that is interesting, it has no effect on United States law because the Berne Convention is a non-self-executing treaty that becomes part of United States law only to the extent that it is incorporated in federal legislation.

There is no additional requirement for an original work of art, such as a painting or drawing. It need not be signed or numbered or produced for any particular purpose.

B. Work of Visual Art—Negative Requirements

i. Work Made for Hire

VARA specifically excludes many items from the concept "work of visual art" even if they qualify as the paintings, drawings, sculpture, prints or photographs described above.

A work made for hire is not a work of visual art, so its creator has no moral rights.

As to the creation, the statute appears to be quite clear: a work made for hire is never a "work of visual art." This means that, consistent with the rules detailed in the Copyright chapter above, a work made for hire grants no moral rights to the employee who actually did the work and, contrary to the rule for copyrights, a work made for hire grants no moral rights to the employer either. The copyright rule is completely consistent with normal principles of agency, and gives a person who wishes to purchase the copyright a single individual to deal with; the VARA rule is not. Also inconsistent with copyright, if read strictly, the statute destroys all moral rights in a work if any part of the work is produced by employees.

But that raises a question not dealt with elsewhere in copyright law: when can we say that an entire work is a work made for hire? It is not dealt with in copyright law because the result of finding that something is a work made for hire is to vest the copyright in the employer. If there were several joint authors of a work, one of whom was an employee who produced his part of the work in the course of his employment, the result would be that the copyright interest the employee would otherwise have would be his employer's, and the employer would be a joint author with the others. With VARA, a vastly different consequence ensues. If a work is a work made for hire, it is not a "work of visual art," so no moral rights attach.

It is not unusual for a painter to hire someone to build his stretchers, stretch his canvas, and prime it. Nor is it unusual for a painter to have an assistant mix colors for his approval. The tradition where the master artist prepares a preliminary cartoon and his apprentices apply the preliminary coat and non-crucial items of the painting, which will be finished by the master artist, has been with us since the Renaissance.

What is true of painting is perhaps even more true of sculpture, especially sculpting in metals, and printmaking. A sculptor will prepare a model, but it would be unusual if the sculptor completes without paid assistance the various molds and castings that need to be made to produce a finished metal sculpture. Likewise, it is not at all unusual for a well-known artist to prepare the design for a print but to have the print made by workers who specialize in print-making.

Also, it is not uncommon for visual artists to be fulltime employees of a university. Their job is to teach students and produce scholarship which, in the case of visual artists, is usually a work of visual art. No university of which I am aware has a policy that vests the copyright in anyone but the visual artist, in effect operating as a transfer of the copyright from the employer to the employee if this is a work made for hire. But when the professor of visual arts has produced a "work made for hire," no one would own the moral rights to that work.

To further complicate the matter, one of the financial aid programs for college students developed by the federal government is the work-study program. Under this program, grants are made to universities where 80% of the student's compensation is provided by the federal government and 20% by the University. Students with need work at various places on campus, such as the library or department offices. They also work as research assistants for professors. If the professor is a professor of visual arts, that student is likely to be building stretchers, priming canvas, etc.

No guidance to the reasons for the strange VARA rule on work-made-for-hire is given. The economic explanation for the work made for hire doctrine of copyright law, that it eliminates transaction costs by giving the copyright to a single person who can economically transfer it does not work here, as the statute extinguishes the artist's rights, so there are none to transfer. Extinction may be appropriate in a major enterprise like Disney where many employees contribute to a single work because there is too little of the work of any one person to justify giving that person the artists' rights; in the typical fine arts case where one artist is assisted by one or two employees, it is hard to see any economic justification for extinguishing the right except a hostility to moral rights. The moral rights should go to the driving creative force behind the work. The employees who have a minor part of the creative work, by preparing stretchers and canvas, or signing and numbering prints for the artist, should have no moral rights; but the artist who hires them should have moral rights.

It seems unlikely that VARA was intended to remove all these instances where someone is paid to assist the artist from the definition of "work of visual art." It is also true that the "work made for hire" doctrine generally applies to the work of employees, but not the work of independent contractors. Nonetheless, it seems unlikely that Congress intended to remove moral rights from any artwork in which any employee was involved in any way. A more likely interpretation is that the "work made for hire" exclusion is intended to destroy the moral rights of the employees, but only destroys all moral rights in a work where employees had the preponderant role in the creative portion of the work.

ii. Copyrightable

A work that may not be copyrighted is also not a work of visual art. One theory might be that a work that lacks sufficient originality for copyright does not deserve the special protection of moral rights. But lack of originality is not the only reason for which things may be ineligible for copyright. A building may not be copyrighted, though the plans for it may be subject to copyright. *Pollara v. Seymour*, 344 F.3d 265 (2d Cir. 2003) (dictum). A person with unprotected national status may be disqualified from copyrighting.

More probably, both moral rights and copyright are instances of the separation of rights about an object from the physical object. The legislative history states that the requirement of copyrightability is intended to prevent interference with the public's right to exploit works that it is free to exploit under copyright law. This is an unpersuasive rationale, as the right to exploit a work that is in the public domain does not include the right to mis-label it, to modify it, or to destroy it. In addition, there is no obligation, with a copyrighted work, that the copyright and the moral right remain in the same hands. Copyrights are assignable; moral rights are not assignable, but are waivable if the waiver is sufficiently specific. So it is possible that neither the person who owns the work nor the person who owns the copyright can waive the moral rights.

One application of the copyright requirement is the "living" sculpture made of plant materials. Even if this is deemed to be a sculpture, it might be disqualified because not eligible for copyright, either because it is insufficiently "fixed" or because it is insufficiently original. *Kelley v. Chicago Park District*, 635 F.3d 290 (7th Cir. 2011). However, "fixed" does not mean permanent. Works in progress are sufficiently fixed to qualify for copyright, even though the artist plans to change them later. *Carter v. Helmsley-Spear* (dictum); *Mass. Museum of Contemp. Art Found. Inc. v. Büchel*, 593 F.3d 38 (1st Cir. 2010).

iii. Advertising

Merchandising items, advertising, and promotional works are excluded from "work of visual art." Each of these terms requires definition. It is unclear what "merchandising items" comprises. One might read it *in pari materia* with advertising and promotional material, in which case it would add nothing to the definition. On the other hand, one could read it as "merchandise," thereby excluding from "work of visual art" a limited edition, signed and numbered print, printed on a notecard. In light of the legislative history's broad interpretation of materials, the former interpretation should be preferred.

Given the opportunity to speak to this question, the Seventh Circuit instead stated that a print attached to a tile is not a "work of visual art" because it is not signed and numbered. The court could have used this occasion to declare that it is not a "work of visual art" because it is a merchandising item, but did not. *Lee v. A.R.T. Co.*, 125 F.3d 580, 583 (7th Cir. 1997) (dictum).

A work does not lose its status as a "work of visual art" because it is used in advertising. It is common to take a painting that will appear in a museum show and make it the centerpiece of posters advertising the show. The painting remains a "work of visual art"; the posters do not achieve that status for three reasons: there are too many of them, they are not signed and consecutively numbered, and they are advertising. But the original painting does not become advertising because its image is used in advertising.

The use of both "advertising" and promotional material assures that the material need not be used for products and services alone. It can be used to promote political candidates or ideas, or charitable events. *Pollara v. Seymour*, 344 F.3d 265 (2d Cir. 2003). It is still promotional and not a work of visual art.

The problem is that a work of visual art may look promotional, such as Andy Warhol's Campbell soup cans or shoes, and a promotional item may look like a work of fine art, especially since words are often used today in paintings. The intent of the author is important, and one might determine that intent from the initial use.

iv. Utilitarian Material

Descriptive, covering or packaging material or containers are also excluded from "work of visual art." Some of this material is utilitarian; all of it is commercial. In this case, it appears to be the intended use of the item, rather than its intrinsic quality, that predominates.

v. Utilitarian Objects

Also excluded are certain utilitarian items that are subject to copyright: poster, map, globe, chart, technical drawing, diagram, model, applied art, motion picture or other audio-visual work, data base, electronic information service, electronic publication. Books, magazines, newspapers and periodicals are also excluded. But one should be careful about taking these exclusions too far. There are artists who incorporate maps, globes and charts into their artwork. When these items appear by themselves for utilitarian purposes, they are not works of visual art; but when they are incorporated as design elements in artwork, this does not disqualify either the work or the portion occupied by the map, globe or chart as a work of visual art, because the globe is being used as artwork, rather than as a utilitarian object. It goes without saying that a representation of a globe or chart in a painting or sculpture is not disqualifying; it must be an actual globe or chart.

Nor should the inclusion of the word "books" in the list of items that are not works of visual art be read too literally. A recognized category of artwork is the artist's book. The artist's book is the creation of a book either by attaching various drawings and paintings to each other or by drawing or painting in a premade book. This is not a book in the ordinary sense of the word, but an original artwork, and should be a "work of visual art."

The legislative history makes it clear that these exclusions are not to be read too literally. "While subparagraph (A)(iii) also excludes any portions or parts of these types of works, a new and independent work created from snippets of these materials, such as a collage, is of course not excluded."

Still, one might ask what a poster, map, globe, chart, technical drawing, diagram, model etc. might be. One dictionary definition of poster is "a large printed placard, bill or announcement, often illustrated, posted to advertise or publicize some event." One might conclude that a poster must be printed, rather than created by hand, and that it must exist in multiple copies.

The definitional difficulty is particularly acute for models. Models are excluded from "work of visual art," while sculptures, according to the legislative history, includes, but is not limited to, "modelings and constructions." One way to distinguish "models" from "modelings" would be to construe "models" as intermediate steps in creation, but to see "modelings" as a method of creating the item, as it is often said that one models in clay. This distinction is unsatisfactory, as it is clear that both documents use the respective words as nouns. Also, the word model has many meanings. In addition to being an intermediate work in the creation of another work, a model can be a smaller representation of something. But neither size nor comparative size is a good measure of what is included in or excluded from the definition of "work of visual art." One way to reconcile the two definitions would be to hold that a "model" in the sense of the statute is a representation of an existing item, while a model made on the way to creating another artwork (whether of the same size or larger) is an artwork itself, just as a preliminary drawing is not removed from the definition of "work of art" when it is later used as a basis for a painting.

As if it were not clear enough that all of these items are excluded from the definition of a "work of visual art," there is also a specific provision that the right of attribution does not apply to any reproduction, depiction, portrayal or other use of a work of art "in, upon, or in connection with any item excluded from the definition of 'work of visual art,'" nor is "any such reproduction, depiction, portrayal or other use" a destruction, distortion, mutilation or other modification that would violate the right of integrity. It is unclear why this additional provision was thought necessary. The legislative history speaks of not protecting reproductions etc. embodied in non-qualified works such as books or movies, but those reproductions are already excluded: they are not works of visual art because they are not paintings, drawings, prints or sculptures. It is obvious either that the draftsmen did not understand the significance of the definition of "work of visual art," or they were at such pains to exempt the publishing and entertainment industries that they insisted on doing it twice— once in the definition of "work of visual art," and again in an exclusion from the substantive right.

However, this immunity may be misunderstood. For instance, if Audubon prepares a series of watercolor paintings of birds, each painting is a "work of visual art." If Audubon prepares up to 200 prints of each painting, each signed and numbered by Audubon personally, each of them is a "work of visual art." If Audubon decides to bind a set of the prints together into book form, each of the prints is still a "work of visual art," and the application of the rights of attribution and integrity are not prohibited because none of them is a "reproduction, depiction, portrayal, or other use of a work"—each is a work itself.

C. When Does a Work Become a Work of Visual Art?

For VARA to have any application, there must be a work of visual art. The legislative history provides no clue as to when something becomes a work of visual art. If VARA contained the right of divulgation—the right of an artist to determine whether the work is finished—the answer might be simpler. If there is a right of divulgation, it becomes a work of visual art when the artist says it is finished. Without a right of divulgation, the court must decide whether a work in progress has become a "work of visual art." That point is reached when there is sufficient creativity and sufficient fixation to qualify the work for copyright protection. *Mass. Museum of Contemp. Art Found. Inc. v. Büchel*, 593 F.3d 38 (1st Cir. 2010). Thus, as a work of art moves from inception toward completion, it is in fact many works of art, for each change in the work sufficient to be copyrighted makes it a new work of art. As long as those changes are made by the artist, there is no violation of the artist's moral rights.

5. Transfer, Duration, Waiver, Preemption

Moral rights are personal to the artist. They cannot be transferred. Federal moral rights terminate on the artist's death, though for a work produced before

1990 but sold thereafter, the moral rights extend for the full validity of the copyright, which is the life of the artist plus seventy years. State moral rights laws vary. In some states such as California, moral rights may be inherited by the artist's heirs and are valid for fifty years after the artist's death.

In theory, the artist may waive his moral rights in a written document. However, the document must be so specific that an effective waiver is unlikely. The waiver must "specifically identify the work, and uses of that work, to which the waiver applies...." It is unlikely that at the time of the initial sale of the artwork, the buyer will be able to identify the specific conditions under which he would want to modify or destroy the work.

Federal moral rights law provides that it pre-empts state law, but only in a limited manner. It does not pre-empt state law after the artist's death, and it does not pre-empt state law with respect to anything that is not a work of visual art. Consequently, the New York law would be pre-empted for prints of fewer than 200 copies, but would not be pre-empted for prints of between 201 and 300 copies, nor for prints that are either not signed by the artist or not numbered consecutively. Likewise, the New York law continues to protect reproductions. In dictum, *Board of Managers of Soho Int'l Arts Condominium v. New York*, 2003 U.S. Dist. LEXIS 10221 (S.D.N.Y. 2003) took a much stronger stance, suggesting that almost any provision that accorded moral rights before the artist's death for a work that is a work of visual art was pre-empted. California law is pre-empted during the life of the artist, but it is resurrected on the date of the artist's death.

6. Moral Rights and the First Amendment

None of the few cases on moral rights have discussed whether providing moral rights might in individual cases violate the First Amendment's protection of free speech. In most cases, no argument can be made that the work was modified or destroyed as an exercise of free speech. But consider the case where an organization devoted to decency made photocopies of sexual details of a large work, and mailed them to legislators and other persons they considered influential to attempt to build support for legislation and to cut off grants that aided this artist's work. The court held this a violation of the New York moral rights statute because the New York law covers reproductions and the excerpting of the work was a modification because it did not present the true character of the entire work. But the court did not consider that the violator was acting to petition the legislature, an activity that is surely protected by the First Amendment. *Wojnarowicz v. American Family Ass'n*, 745 F.Supp. 130 (S.D.N.Y. 1990).

Courts need to grapple specifically with whether such activities are largely protected by the U.S. constitution, unprotected like pornography, or partially protected like defamation.

7. Achieving Moral Rights By Other Means

It always remains open to an artist to secure moral rights by contract. Such a contract would not be limited by the VARA definition of "work of visual art," nor would it necessarily expire on the artist's death. But those contracts are difficult to negotiate, and it would be even more difficult to legally bind the purchaser's successors in interest.

More practically, some moral rights may be secured by the use of copyright. If the artist retains the copyright to her work, she also has the right to make derivative works. Any modification in the artist's work is likely to also be a derivative work, which the artist could prevent or seek redress for using his copyright. It seems unlikely that the destruction of the work would constitute a derivative work protectable by copyright.

8. The Rights of Divulgation and Repentance

While neither the right of divulgation nor the right of repentance exists today anywhere in the United States, art is quite portable. The prudent art lawyer recognizes that his client may move art to a foreign country where these rights exist, and must be able to advise his client about the dangers that await him.

The right of divulgation is the right to decide when a work is finished. To put it in the context in which it usually appears, it is the right to decide that the work remains unfinished. In the classic case on the subject, Lord Eden commissioned James McNeil Whistler to paint a portrait of Eden's wife, promising to pay between 100 and 150 guineas, depending on his degree of satisfaction. Eden saw the almost-complete painting and delivered a check for 100 guineas. Whistler was so insulted that he exhibited the painting, then refused to deliver it, painting out Lady Eden's face. The court refused to order Whistler to either complete the painting or to deliver it to Lord Eden, but ordered him to refund the purchase price and pay damages, and to refrain from making any use of the portrait. *Eden c. Whistler*, [1900] [D.P.] I, 497 [1900] Recueil Sirey [S. Jur.] I 490 (Cass. civ.).

The right to repent permits an artist who has disposed of a work to withdraw it from public view or to modify it if the work does not meet her current standards, on paying the owner for the property rights.

Checkpoints

- Moral rights are non-waivable rights artists have in the physicality and reputation of their works, while economic rights in those works such as property rights, re-sale rights and copyright involve only payments for use or ownership.
- Moral rights group together four distinct rights: the right of paternity or attribution, the right of integrity to prevent modification or destruction of the work, the right of divulgation to decide when the work is finished, and the right to repent or to retake the work.
- The right of divulgation and the right to repent are not protected in any U.S. jurisdiction.
- The right of paternity or attribution allows the artist to insist that his name be attached to works that he created, to remove his name from works he did not create, and to remove his name from works he created but that have been modified. It probably does not permit the artist to insist that the work be anonymous or pseudonymous.
- The right of integrity allows the artist to prevent the modification or destruction of his work.
- The terms "prejudicial to his or her honor or reputation" and "work of recognized stature" which are necessary to find violation of the right of integrity are easily satisfied, but do require that the work have some public recognition, though not necessarily praise from art professionals.
- A mental state is required for modification or destruction to be actionable. It must be intentional or, in the case of destruction, grossly negligent, or, in the case of modification during conservation, grossly negligent.
- Fair use is a defense to a moral rights action.
- A work that is attached to a building but can be removed without damaging the work is subject to a special rule. If the owner gives the artist 90 days notice to remove the work and the artist removes it, the work belongs to the artist. If the artist does not remove the work, the owner may destroy it.
- A single work is modified if its elements are placed in different relationships with each other, but whether a work with multiple pieces is a single work or many works is a question of fact. A site-specific work is not modified by being moved to another site or put in storage.
- Federal moral rights protect only "works of visual art," a limited class of artistic work that includes only paintings, drawings, and certain prints, sculptures and still photographs produced in limited quantities. Works of visual art must be copyrightable. Prints, sculptures and photos done in multiples must be signed and numbered by the artist, and photos must be produced for exhibition purposes.
- A work made for hire is not a "work of visual art," so it carries no moral rights.

- Useful items like advertising, containers, posters, maps, globes, charts or technical drawings are not works of visual art.
- Moral rights are personal to the artist. They cannot be transferred, and it is difficult to waive them.
- Federal law preempts state moral rights law during the lifetime of the artist for "works of visual art" only.
- The First Amendment guarantee of free speech may prohibit liability for moral rights where the work is modified or destroyed to communicate a message.

Chapter 8

Re-Sale Royalties

Roadmap

After reading this chapter, you should understand:

- Re-sale royalty mandates a seller of an art work to pay the artist a portion of the re-sale price. It is often considered a moral right but is more properly an economic right. It cannot be waived.
- Parameters: Re-sale royalties vary in different jurisdictions. Typically the seller must pay the artist a small percentage of the re-sale price. The royalty may pass to the artist's survivors after the artist's death.
- Application: Sales below a specified price usually do not carry a re-sale royalty. Some jurisdictions only apply the royalty when the sale price exceeds the purchase price; others apply regardless of the original purchase price. What is included in the sale price, such as seller expenses, differs greatly.
- Limits: A jurisdiction's re-sale royalty may apply to all sales or be limited to sales facilitated by art professionals.
- Enforcement: It may be difficult for an artist to determine when a sale has occurred (particularly private sales). Collecting the royalties can be difficult. Art professionals are required to withhold the royalty when a purchase occurs.
- Competition: If one jurisdiction has a re-sale royalty and another jurisdiction does not, art sales will likely be pushed to the latter.
- The starving artist: Advocates of the re-sale royalty argue artists often struggle financially and are taken advantage of by buyers who persuade them to sell their work below market value. The royalty redistributes part of the unjust profit to the artist. This argument assumes most artists sell their work below market value which is difficult to prove.
- Just compensation: An artist's later successes can increase the value of earlier works by that artist and the re-sale royalty compensates the artist for the increase. However, other factors not caused by the artist often influence a work's value.

1. What Is a Re-Sale Royalty?

Some economic rights of authors and artists are protected by copyright law. Their work cannot be reproduced without their permission. When their work is reproduced, the holder of the copyright usually demands a royalty in return for her consent to reproduce the work.

Many artists do not anticipate that their work will be reproduced, so no stream of income is generated from the copyright. Some of the value of this work is its rarity or, in the case of paintings and drawings, uniqueness. For those works, the copyright has little value. The value lies in the physical work itself. It is generally sold soon after it is created for a price that is not very elevated. It is then often resold by the initial buyer, often for a higher price. The increase in value of these works may be attributable to the increased fame of the artist and her work in the art market, yet the artist receives no share of that appreciation. The French developed the concept of the re-sale royalty (*droit de suite*, literally a right of following) to rectify this perceived inconsistency. A re-sale royalty obligates the re-seller of a work of art to pay the artist a portion of the price the re-seller receives. The fuller justification for the royalty is that the artist, who may have been paid little for the original sale of the work, is at least partly responsible, through his other works in the art market, for the increase in value that the owner of the art work receives. It can be analogized to the right a copyright author has to terminate transfers after 35 years.

Seventy-nine countries have adopted a form of re-sale royalty, and it has been included in article 4 of the Berne Convention, which theoretically requires all adherents to accord such a right. It is also the subject of a European Union directive, which obligates all member states to provide for re-sale royalties within the terms of the directive.

Some commentators consider re-sale rights to be moral rights because they belong only to the artist, and cannot be waived. It is preferable to regard re-sale royalties as economic rights because they are based on an economic transaction, the re-sale of a work; they entitle the artist only to a monetary payment, not an injunction; and they can be monetized in advance by assignment in some jurisdictions.

2. Parameters of the Re-Sale Royalty

The details of the re-sale royalty differ from jurisdiction to jurisdiction. The only state to enact a re-sale royalty was California, and that was declared unconstitutional in *Sam Francis Found. v. Christies, Inc.*, 784 F.3d 1320 (9th Cir. 2015) and *Close v. Sothebys, Inc.*, 894 F.3d 1061 (9th Cir. 2018).

A. Percentage of the Re-Sale Price

A re-sale royalty requires the seller of a work of art to pay the artist a fraction of the sales price. The amount varies, and in most cases is less than 5%. In some jurisdictions, the percentage declines as the sale price rises; a seller might pay 4% of the first $20,000, 3% of the next $30,000, etc. In one country, the royalty is based on the net profit, rather than the sales price, which adds additional administrative costs in verifying the original purchase price and any applicable expenses, but provides a fairer measure of the gain received by the re-seller.

B. Sales to Which the Re-Sale Royalty Applies

The re-sale royalty does not apply to all sales. There is often a minimum sales price below which the sale is exempt, around $1,000.

In some countries, the sale price must exceed the purchase price; not so in other jurisdictions, so there the seller might find his loss compounded by the re-sale royalty he must pay.

Laws do not define "sales price." Consider the case where a person purchases an art work at auction for $100,000. Add the 25% buyer's fee and the price becomes $125,000. The buyer may also pay V.A.T. or sales tax. The seller does not receive the buyer's fee or the tax, and pays a seller's fee (normally 20%) to the auction house. What is the sales price?

In some jurisdictions, the re-sale royalty applies to sales by anyone. In others, it applies only to sales at auction, or only on sales through art world professionals, such as dealers, galleries or auctions. Limiting its application to art world professionals makes its administration much more convenient, and probably captures the largest number of sales for sizeable amounts.

C. Who Benefits?

The artist who created the work receives the re-sale royalty.

After her death, the royalty may continue for various periods, and is paid to the artist's survivors. The artist might be able to freely devise it, or in other cases her testamentary power might be limited to natural persons or a collection society. In one country, the benefit of the re-sale royalty passes only to a surviving spouse.

The treatment of foreign artists is far from uniform. Countries may limit benefits to artists who are citizens or residents of that country, or of countries that provide reciprocity to its own citizens or residents.

One might wonder whether a portion of the re-sale royalty must be transfered from the artist to the agent who originally sold the work if the contract between the artist and the agent called for an agent's commission of a percentage of the sales price. The agent could argue that the re-sale royalty is a deferred payment of the sales price, so he is entitled to a commission on that. The artist will argue that the purpose of the law is to benefit the artist, not commercial agents. No statute mentions this problem, and there are no cases on it.

D. Methods of Enforcement

It may be difficult to enforce the re-sale royalty, for two reasons. One is the difficulty in discovering when a work of art has been sold. While this is not difficult if the work is sold at public auction, private sales would not easily come to the attention of the artist unless they were widely publicized. The seller has an incentive to publicize the availability of the work as widely as possible, but the art world tends to operate in a more discrete fashion, especially as the sales price creeps higher.

Art selling professionals, including auctioneers, are sometimes obligated to withhold re-sale royalties before turning the purchase price over to the seller. This not only gives the artist notice that the sale, whether by an auction house or a gallery, has taken place, it also provides for collection for the artist. This leaves only sales between private parties that have not gone through an art sale professional to be discovered by the artist.

The second enforcement problem is actually collecting the royalty. The above withholding requirement solves that problem for the sale through professionals, but private sales of an artist's work are not covered, and if the artist is not famous, the amounts may be relatively small. The right cannot be waived. Royalties collecting societies like A.S.C.A.P. collect re-sale royalties, and even in a jurisdiction where the right cannot be assigned, a "voluntary" agreement was concluded between such a society and an association of art dealers for collection of the royalty.

3. Should There Be Re-Sale Royalties?

The major arguments in favor of re-sale royalties might be termed the "starving artist" and the "just compensation" stories.

The starving artist argument is that artists in general are a group of people struggling to pay the rent and put food on the table. They are easily exploited, because of this desperation for cash, by gallery owners and buyers, so they often sell their works below a fair market price. When the buyer re-sells the work, some of that unjust profit should be shared with the artist.

The problem with the starving artist argument is that it rests on an initial premise, sale below market value, which is questionable as a matter of fact, and impossible to prove. Market value is normally defined as the price at which a willing buyer would purchase from a willing seller. The best evidence of that price is the price actually fixed in comparable transactions between unrelated parties. Since each work of art is unique, the best evidence of a fair market price for the work of a particular artist would be the price at which it was actually sold. To enact a re-sale royalty on the basis of the starving artist argument would be to assume that most artists sell their work at a price below fair market value, a proposition that would be difficult to establish.

A variant on the starving artist argument suggests that visual artists, unlike recording artists, do not receive copyright royalties every time their work is displayed. They lack the bargaining power to insert provisions for exhibition and re-sale royalties in their sales contracts, so the law must mandate it. But visual artists, like recording artists, can demand a royalty whenever their work is reproduced. The difference is that the work of recording artists is always reproduced to be enjoyed, while many people can visit a museum to see the original of an artwork. Also, since 1978, there is no presumption that the copyright in an artwork is transferred with the physical work, and there is no evidence that buyers make it a practice to demand the copyright.

The just compensation argument is on sounder grounds. Just compensation starts with the fact that the value of an artist's work is often influenced by the artist. If the artist's later work is well-reviewed and in demand, that will have a spillover effect to increase the value of the artist's earlier sold work. If that is true, the artist should be compensated for his part in raising the value of his work.

The problem with the just compensation argument is that it is the art market that determines the fair market value of the work. While it is true that the artist's subsequent artwork and promotional efforts can favorably influence the art market, many other factors can also cause an increase in the sale price of a work. These might include the promotional activities of the artist's gallery, the fact that the artist's work is bought by famous (or notorious) people, favorable reviews by important art critics, decisions by galleries or museums to mount a retrospective show of the artist's work or to purchase the artist's work, a trend for the market to favor a style of art to which the artist adheres, or generalized inflation in the art market. Trying to determine what portion of the value increase resulted from the artist's efforts and what resulted from other players seems an impossible task. It is perhaps for this reason that in the jurisdictions that have re-sale royalties, the percentage of the sales price that is exacted is relatively modest. (Another reason for the modest amount is that the percentage is not of the net profit, but of the sales price.)

One might also question whether the light is worth the candle. It has been suggested that the number of artists whose work significantly appreciates in value during their lives or soon thereafter is small, and most of those had significant financial success in their initial sales. If true, a re-sale royalty would primarily benefit artists who are already wealthy. For most artists, whose works sell in the $1,000 to $10,000 range, the royalty is not worth the trouble of trying to collect it. A cooperative society would reduce the cost of collection, as would the cooperation of professional art sellers.

For further guidance see SIMON STOKES, ARTIST'S RESALE RIGHT (*Droit de Suite*): UK LAW & PRACTICE (2d ed. 2012); Herbert I. Lazerow, *Art Resale Royalty Options*, 63 J. COPYRIGHT SOC. U.S.A. 201 (2016).

Checkpoints

You should have learned that:

- Artists whose artwork is not reproduced do not receive a stream of copyright royalties. A re-sale royalty entitles an artist to a portion of the re-sale price.
- No United States jurisdiction has a re-sale royalty.
- Where there are re-sale royalties, artists are usually given a percentage of the re-sale price of an art work or a portion of the net profit of the re-sale. After an artist's death, the re-sale royalty may extend to the artist's survivors for a period of time. Foreign artists may not be entitled to re-sale royalties or there may be certain residency requirements to be entitled to receive the royalty.
- Re-sale royalties do not always apply; a sale under a set minimum price may be exempt. Some jurisdictions require the sale price to exceed the purchase price while others do not, thereby increasing the seller's loss. Likewise some jurisdictions calculate the seller's expenses in determining what percentage artists receive while other jurisdictions do not.
- The royalty may apply to all sales or be limited to sale through art professionals like auctions, dealers and galleries.
- Re-sale royalties can be hard to enforce. It may be difficult to determine when a sale has occurred, and its price, and it may be hard to actually collect the

royalties, particularly in private sales. Art professionals are required to withhold re-sale royalties before giving the seller the purchase price which alleviates some enforcement issues.

- There are two justifications for the re-sale royalty. Artists struggle to make money and are easily exploited by buyers to sell their work below fair market value; the royalty gives the artists a portion of the seller's later profit. Also, the value of art work is influenced by the artist's behavior and later work, so the artist should share any increase in value.

Chapter 9

Taxes and the Art World

Roadmap

After reading this chapter, you should understand:

- Profit-seeking motive: A taxpayer who engages in profit-seeking activity is eligible for income tax deductions for the expenses of those activities.
- An artist can establish that he has profit-seeking motive by behaving as an artist in the business behaves.
- Collectors may establish they have profit-seeking motive for itemized deductions by making regular sales, but those deductions may not be taken 2018–2025.
- Home studio deductions: A person in the trade or business of being an artist can often deduct the cost of maintaining a studio in the artist's home. Generally only rooms used exclusively for the trade are deductible, and studios must be the principal place of business, a place where the artist meets frequently with clients, or a separate structure.
- Inventory expenses: Most businesses cannot deduct the cost of inventory, but artists and photographers may do so.
- Traveling expenses: Artists are permitted to deduct expenses related to their trade while traveling for business.
- Passive activity loss: Taxpayers cannot offset losses from passive business against income from other business activities. Passive activities are activities in which the taxpayer does not regularly, continuously, or substantially participate.
- Ordinary income: Artists who sell their work are taxed at ordinary income rates.
- Capital gains: Artwork or copyrights purchased as investments are taxed as capital gains.
- Gift: If a taxpayer gives property to charity and meets the ordinary requirements of a gift, the taxpayer may deduct from his income tax the fair market value of the given property.
- A gift requires donative intent, delivery, and acceptance.
- If a taxpayer intends to transfer property upon death, he should follow the requirements of a will or revocable trust closely.
- Valuation: The value of an artwork is the fair market value and may be influenced by defects later discovered.

- Comparable sales: In evaluating the value of artwork, look to comparable sales of similar artwork.
- Discounts: When a number of works by the same artist come on the market at the same time, the value of each is normally discounted because of the excess supply.
- Expert appraisals: Experts are usually crucial in valuing art. An expert's relationship to an artwork's owner goes to the credibility and persuasiveness of the appraisal.
- Penalties: IRS assesses penalties for a taxpayer who enters a valuation misstatement on his tax return; the appraiser of an inaccurate valuation may be liable to the taxpayer.

1. Introduction

Participants in the art world, like all of the populace, are subject to various taxes. " ... [T]here went out a decree from Caesar Augustus, that all the world should be taxed." Luke 2:1. This chapter details tax issues that are most likely to arise in the art world or call for special approaches because they exist in the art world. We will not discuss personal property taxes on art, except to note that even artists and collectors must pay personal property taxes if applicable. For those taxes, there is nothing special about their application in the art world except the devilish difficulty of valuation, discussed below. Likewise, the responsibilities of museums and art galleries to withhold income taxes on their employees do not differ from the liabilities of other employers, and are therefore omitted.

2. Income Tax

A. Profit-Seeking Motive

Art is viewed by the general populace as an activity that many people engage in for their pleasure. Since persons are allowed income tax deductions for expenses of a business or investment activity in excess of the income from that activity, some means must be found for distinguishing the artist or collector who is trying to make a profit from the hobbyist. While the hobbyist would like to deduct the costs of his hobby against his other income, the tax law accords deductions only for the expenses of a profit-seeking activity.

The question is usually whether the person is in the trade or business of being an artist. That in turn depends on whether the person is engaged in a profit-seeking activity. Different circuits formulate the test slightly differently. Some ask whether taxpayer has objectively manifested activities indicating that he is engaged in art for a profit. Others ask about the state of mind of the individual. In all circuits, those case by case approaches seemed wastefully litigious to Congress, which enacted a presumption that a person who made a profit on an activity in two of the previous five years had a profit-seeking motive. INT. REV. CODE OF 1986, §183(d). While that presumption is rebuttable, the Internal Revenue Service has treated it as a safe harbor, and not tried to rebut the presumption.

However, many artists and collectors who have not made a profit in two of the previous five years still wish to take deductions. They are permitted to do so if they can establish that they intended to make a profit. In determining whether there was a profit-seeking motive, different criteria are likely to be important, depending on whether the taxpayer asserts that he is in a trade or business, or whether the taxpayer seeks to assert a profit-seeking investment. While all factors are to be considered, the regulations suggest that the following factors point toward taxpayer being engaged in the activity for profit: (1) taxpayer carries on the activity in a business-like manner; (2) taxpayer or his advisors have expertise in the matter; (3) taxpayer spends most of his time on the enterprise; (4) assets used in the activity can be expected to appreciate; (5) taxpayer has been successful in similar or dissimilar activities; (6) taxpayer has turned a profit in this business; (7) taxpayer's profits over the life of the business have outweighed his losses; (8) taxpayer does not have significant income from other sources; and (9) there are no elements of personal pleasure in the activity. No one factor or group of factors is dispositive, so the results can be unpredictable.

i. Artists

An artist who contends she is in the trade or business of being an artist must be regularly engaged in that activity for profit. While it would be helpful if the artist drew up a business plan before becoming an artist that showed how she intended to make a profit, artists with pre-entry business plans are rare. More likely, the person will be considered to be in the trade or business of being an artist if she is trained as an artist and behaves the way an artist in the business behaves. The fun part of being an artist is creating the artwork; the part that creates the profit is selling it. So the court's inquiry is likely to focus on the artist's marketing activities, such as entering juried shows, seeking gallery representation, advertising, and holding public sales. Factors such as past sales, articles in the public or art press, substantial inventory and a substantial mailing list may indicate a profit-seeking motive. Changing the kind of work produced when it does not sell is another favorable factor, as is the amount of time spent on art related activities, whether creating it, selling it, teaching about it, or even running an art gallery for another person. While only the numbers for the taxable years in question can be considered in determining the amount of income, activities from other years can be considered in determining whether taxpayer had a profit-seeking motive in the years in question. *C. West Churchman*, 68 T.C. 696 (1977).

One of the greatest factors indicating that the individual is not an artist with a profit-seeking motive is possessing another trade or business generating substantial income. *Richard A. Stasewich*, 72 TCM-CCH 1 (#302) (1996), 81 TCM-CCH 1122 (#30) (2001). Successful lawyers and physicians have great difficulty in establishing that they are also in the trade or business of being artists. There is no good reason for this; a person can be engaged in multiple trades or businesses simultaneously. It is also unfair, as a person who has a substantial income from a working spouse or from investments does not suffer the same detriment. Persons who do not keep good financial records are less likely to be found to be in a trade or business, as are people who do not change their practices when they are inadequate to produce a profit year after year.

ii. Collectors/Investors

While artists are more likely to be in a trade or business, collectors are more likely to claim that they are collecting art as an investment. Deductions for investors are only available as itemized deductions, rather than as the trade or business deductions available to persons engaged in a trade or business. This means that the collector's deductions do not reduce his adjusted gross income, and are deductible only to the extent that they (along with other expenses) exceed two percent of the individual's adjusted gross income. These deductions are not available at all 2018-2025. Int. Rev. Code of 1986, §§ 67(g), 212.

The distinction between an investor in art and a hobbyist often lies in the occasional sale. Even a collector with great expertise is unlikely to be considered profit-seeking if he has never sold a piece, or has seldom done so. This is especially true if the collection is kept in the taxpayer's private residence. *Wrightsman v. U.S.*, 428 F.2d 1316, 70-2 USTC ¶9519 (Ct.Cl. 1970). This was so despite the taxpayer's extensive recordkeeping and expertise, such that taxpayer was frequently consulted by museums.

B. Deductions Available

i. Home Studio

A person who establishes that he is in the trade or business of being an artist can deduct all his ordinary and necessary expenses of carrying on that trade or business. For many artists, the principal such expense is the cost of maintaining a studio in the home.

Generally, expenses of maintaining personal living space are not deductible. However, deductions are permitted for rooms used exclusively for business if the room is either the principal place of business, a place where the artist meets clients or customers, or located in a separate structure from the living space. Most artists have no difficulty meeting the "principal place of business" requirement, because they have no other place of business. An artist with a studio away from his home is usually unable to meet the "principal place of business" requirement to deduct an in-home studio.

Where the artist has a gallery it may be a different story. Even with gallery representation, most artists spend considerably more time in their studios than at their galleries. Also, the gallery is usually not a physical place of business for the artist, but a place to which the artist consigns his work. It is only a place of business of the artist by the operation of agency law, which turns the gallery owner into the artist's agent.

Most artists cannot satisfy the alternate requirement of a place where they meet regularly with clients because most artists do not meet regularly enough with clients to have such a place. INT. REV. CODE OF 1986 §280A.

Whether the artist succeeds by establishing that the home studio is his principal place of business, a place where he regularly meets with clients, or a separate structure, the amount of his home studio deduction plus his other artistic deductible expenses cannot exceed his artistic income, except that deductions that would be available in the absence of the business use, such as real estate taxes, remain available. In other words, the home studio deduction cannot create a loss that will offset other income of the artist or his spouse. That loss can, however, be carried over to a subsequent year when the artist has sufficient income from his loss to absorb it.

ii. Inventory

A second item that artists frequently wish to deduct is their cost of preparing the artwork. Normally, this cost is nondeductible; the cost of inventory must normally be capitalized and recovered as the inventory is sold, whether the inventory is purchased or self-created. *Comm'r v. Idaho Power Co.*, 418 U.S. 1 (1974). However, Congress added an exception to this rule for artists and photographers, permitting them to deduct currently their inventory costs. INT. REV. CODE OF 1986 §263A(h).

iii. Traveling Expenses

Like other businesspeople, artists may deduct their traveling expenses. Usually, expenses of occurrences while traveling are also deductible. It is clear that a person may deduct the cost of accidents that happen while traveling on business. One case, wrongly decided in my opinion, refused to allow a deduction where an artist, traveling on business, had a mental breakdown and attacked another passenger. He sought to deduct his legal defense fees and the cost of settlement. The court held the expenses nondeductible, but was unable to satisfactorily distinguish previous cases where a person was able to deduct the costs of an auto accident or where a person was allowed to deduct legal expenses of defending an accusation of rape during a job interview. *Sam Gilliam, Jr.*, T.C. Memo 1986–81, 51 T.C.M. CCH 515 (1986).

iv. Passive Activity Losses

Many artists have more deductions in a year from their art than income, so they would like to offset the loss from their artistic endeavors against their other income or the income of their spouses. The passive activity loss rules prevent the offset of losses from passive businesses against income from other activities. A passive activity is one in which the taxpayer does not materially participate. Material participation involves activity which is regular, continuous and substantial. There is a safe harbor if the taxpayer spends more than 500 hours a year on the activity, and another where the taxpayer's activity constitutes substantially all the activity, and a third where the taxpayer spends at least 100 hours on the activity during the taxable year but spends no less time on it than does any other individual. It is thus not difficult for most artists to establish that their activities are not passive activities because most spend more than 500 hours (13 weeks fulltime) on the activity, and there are no other participants in this activity. Int. Rev. Code of 1986 §469; Temp. Treas. Reg. §1.469-5T.

C. Ordinary Income or Capital Gains?

i. Artist

The artist who sells her work is taxed on it at ordinary income rates, rather than at the more favorable rates reserved for long term capital gains. There are two reasons for this. The exclusion from the definition of capital assets of property held primarily for sale to customers in the ordinary course of a trade or business is one reason. The other reason is the exclusion of copyrights and artistic works produced by the seller. So neither the sale of the physical work, nor the sale of the copyright in it, receives long term capital gain treatment. INT. REV. CODE OF 1986 §1221(1), (3). Neither of those exclusions apply to the artist's widow or widower, assuming the widow or widower is not in the business of selling art, and was not a co-creator of the work with the artist.

ii. Collector

Neither a collector who buys the work nor the purchaser of the copyright is hobbled by either exception to the definition of property that is a capital asset. A collector does not hold work for sale to customers and is not in the trade or business of selling art; the copyright assignee is not holding a copyright he himself produced. If he holds the artwork or the copyright for at least a year, he is entitled to treat it as a longterm capital gain. However, the artwork is not taxed at the most advantageous capital gains rate (20% in 2020), but at 28% because it qualifies as a collectible, along with antiques, stamps and coins. INT. REV. CODE OF 1986 §§1(h), 408(m)(2).

iii. Feet in Both Camps

It is sometimes not clear whether an individual is engaged in a trade or business, in which case the artwork is property held primarily for sale to customers in the ordinary course of his trade or business and therefore taxed at ordinary income rates, or whether the individual is holding the artwork as an investment. It is normally an investment when a group of individuals decides to invest in art with the purpose of eventually selling it at a profit. But where the sales occur quickly and in great numbers, and the person managing the operation spends substantially his full time on it, it appears to be less an investment than a trade or business. *Hollis v. United States*, 121 F.Supp. 191 (N.D. Ohio 1954).

Whether a person, such as a gallery owner or artist, who is engaged in the trade or business of selling art, can also be a collector, or a person who invests in art, and how he distinguishes his business inventory from his investments, is an important question.

Some of these decisions may depend on how broadly one defines the person's trade or business. In *Churchman*, the court seemed to define Gloria Churchman's trade or business as anything having to do with art—making it, teaching about it, selling it, or running a gallery. By contrast, in *Est. of Douglas Chandor*, 28 T.C. 721 (1957), Chandor exclusively painted portraits on commission. His only deviation from that was a decision to paint a triple portrait of Roosevelt, Stalin and Churchill on speculation. He completed the portrait of Churchill, but was never able to portray all three. When he sold the portrait of Churchill, he claimed capital gains treatment on the grounds that his trade or business was not the broad one of being an artist, but the much narrower one of being an artist who paints portraits on commission. For that reason, the Churchill portrait was not held primarily for sale in the ordinary course of his trade or business because it was not held in his trade or business at all.

D. Exchanges of Like Kind Property

When artwork is sold, there is a taxable event. When artwork is exchanged, the seller was able to avoid income taxes. No gain or loss was recognized on the exchange of property held for productive use in a trade or business or for investment if it was exchanged before 2018 solely for property of like kind held for one of those purposes. INT. REV. CODE OF 1986, §1031. Justifications for this provision are that the taxpayer has not significantly changed his investment, and he has received no money with which to pay the tax. Now this provision is limited to realty.

E. Charitable Deductions

i. Requirements for a Gift

A person who gives property to charity is entitled to a deduction from his income tax for the fair market value of the item given. To make that deduction effective, the giver must meet the ordinary requirements of a gift, just as a person who bequeaths property to charity must meet the ordinary requirements of a will.

Both a gift and will require that the person executing it be competent and not be acting under duress. *Stephens County Museum, Inc. v. Swenson*, 517 S.W.2d 257 (Tex. 1974) is a cautionary tale. Two sisters made four gifts to a museum run by their brother. After the brother's death, they sought to invalidate the gifts on grounds that the brother exercised undue influence over them, and on grounds that there was not adequate delivery. The court affirmed one gift, revoked a second, and remanded for a trial as to whether undue influence was in fact exercised with respect to the other two gifts. The importance of complying with formalities is clear here. Substantial assets were expended to litigate this case all the way to the Texas Supreme Court that might have been used either by the museum or the donors and, if the donors took an income tax deduction for the gift that was invalidated, they must now include that amount in their income for the current year under the tax benefit rule.

A valid gift requires donative intent, delivery and acceptance. Acceptance is seldom a problem because acceptance is presumed in the absence of evidence to the contrary. There is usually abundant evidence of donative intent from statements made by the donor, and it is helpful where the owner has made a pattern of gifts and the gift in question fits into the pattern. But the owners of art are often loath to part with possession of their art, so there is often a question raised as to whether the owner has delivered the artwork to the donee, be the donee another individual or a charity. Aside from love of the art, owners often delay physical delivery of it because moving art can damage it; moving art is an occupation best left to professional art movers. Delivery of a document of gift is a valid substitute for actual delivery of the item at common law if the item is impossible (or sometimes difficult) to deliver. Delivery of a 1,100-pound bronze sculpture that was in storage was successfully effected by the donor's writing a memo of gift on the back of a photo of the work. *Mirvish v. Mott*, 18 N.Y.3d 510, 968 N.E.2d 906, 942 N.Y.S.2d 404 (2012).

Some jurisdictions have dispensed with the requirement that delivery be impossible. Delivery of a deed of gift, sometimes called either symbolic or constructive delivery, satisfies both the evidentiary reason for requiring delivery, to protect against the fraudulent assertion of a gift, and the function of delivery in impressing on the donor's mind that he is giving up the property. *Est. of Genecin v. Genecin,* 363 F.Supp.2d 306 (D. Conn. 2005). A gift of a Klimt was held validly delivered despite the fact that delivery was by letter, rather than a formal deed, the donor retained possession and the right to possession for his life. *Gruen v. Gruen*, 68 N.Y.2d 48, 496 N.E.2d 869, 505 N.Y.S.2d 849 (1986). Occasionally, a gift is found without actual or constructive delivery, such as when a donor has marked the donated property with the donee's name and has made statements under oath that the gift had been given, even though the donor retained practical control of the property. *Edinburgh v. Edinburg*, 492 N.E.2d 1164 (Mass. App. 1986). Such cases are not to be relied upon by the careful attorney. Nor does the fact that both donor and donee have access to the artwork, or co-own the property in which it is located, establish proper delivery.

On the other hand, sometimes what appears to be a valid delivery is not a valid delivery. In *Stephens County Museum, Inc. v. Swenson*, 517 S.W.2d 257 (Tex. 1974), the sisters delivered a deed of gift to the museum that was proper on its face, but the court held that evidence that the museum needed title to the property in order to secure a loan from a third party and that the sisters continued to treat the property as theirs was sufficient to support a finding that the delivery of the deed was not intended to transfer title.

ii. Amount of the Charitable Deduction

For an income tax charitable deduction, the artwork must be successfully given to the charity. In that case, the donor may deduct (subject to applicable limits) the fair market value of the property at the time and place given (see below for valuation). The donor pays no income tax on any increase in value that has occurred between his acquisition of the property and its donation. That increase in value entirely escapes income tax.

However, there are some exceptions. The person's deduction is reduced by the amount of accrued gain that would not have been long-term capital gain. Since an artwork is not a capital asset in the hands of its creator, the artist's deduction is reduced to his basis. Likewise, the donation of a work by a dealer that is part of the dealer's inventory is not a capital asset, so the dealer's deduction is reduced to his basis. The collector suffers no such reduction. The artwork in his hands is a capital asset—it is just a capital asset taxed at a higher rate than most capital assets.

A collector may suffer yet another significant reduction in her charitable deduction. Because artwork is tangible personal property and not a normal investment vehicle, the donor of that property must reduce her charitable deduction by the amount of the gain that would have been capital gains unless the charitable recipient uses the property in its exempt function. It is relatively easy for a museum or university to use donated artwork in its exempt educational function; it is more difficult for a church unless the artwork donated is a religious work. It may be still more difficult for a charitable organization like a hospital or a soup kitchen to do so. The period of use must be for at least three years. INT. REV. CODE OF 1986 §170(e).

3. Estate, Gift and Generation-Skipping Tax

A gift or bequest to a charity entitles one to a deduction from the estate, gift or generation-skipping tax. A person who intends to transfer property on death should strictly follow all the requirements for a will or a revocable trust, even though courts have occasionally stretched those requirements to accommodate the demonstrated intent of the testator. In *In re Estate of Greenfield*, 457 Pa. 114, 321 A.2d 922 (1974), testator left "my art" to the Philadelphia Museum, but most of the art in question was technically owned by a corporation which testator controlled. The Museum was not the residuary beneficiary. The court held that testator meant not only the art that he technically owned, but also the art that he controlled. *Clark v. Greenhalge*,

411 Mass. 410, 582 N.E.2d 949 (1991) awarded a painting to a neighbor that was listed among intended bequests in her notebook that never were placed in testator's will.

One cannot count on that stretching. In *Phipps v. Barbera*, 498 N.E.2d 411 (Mass. App. 1986), testator left three paintings to her half-sister for life, then to the NY Museum of Art that had a collection of the artist's paintings, but if that museum refuses them, to her cousin Barbera. There is no New York Museum of Art. There is one New York museum that has one of the artist's paintings in its collection, and the Boston Museum of Fine Arts has several. The trial court held that Boston Museum had not convinced him beyond a reasonable doubt that it was the intended beneficiary. Since beyond a reasonable doubt is the standard in a criminal case, the museum would have another opportunity to prove its case by a preponderance of the evidence.

4. Valuation

A universally important question is the valuation of the artwork. If the work is given or bequeathed to a charity, it must be valued to determine the amount of the charitable deduction. If it is given or bequeathed to a person that is not a charity, it must be valued to determine the amount that is subject to gift tax and perhaps how much of the individual's lifetime exemption the gift may have used; or how much is included in decedent's gross estate (and possibly subject to the generation-skipping tax).

The value of the work is its fair market value, the price at which a hypothetical willing seller would sell and a hypothetical willing buyer would purchase at the time and place of the transfer. However, all is not fixed at the time of transfer. Existing visible defects that are not noticed until a later time, but that were present in the work when donated, can be considered. *Doherty v. Comm'r*, 16 F.3d 338 (9th Cir. 1994). It is doubtful that scientific methods that were unavailable at the time of the gift could be introduced at the time of litigation to affect the value.

The assumption is that the sale takes place at retail, rather than at wholesale.

It is unclear whether the selection of an appropriate valuation methodology is a question of fact or a question of law. The fair market value of a work of art is a question of fact. Usually, the testimony of expert witnesses helps establish the value.

There are a number of different methods for valuing works, such as comparable sales, capitalized income, etc. In each case, there is heavy reliance on expert testimony.

A. Comparable Sales

An approach to valuing any asset would be to look for comparable sales. For most fungible goods, comparable sales exist. Since each work of art is unique, prices will be available for works that might only be roughly comparable. Adjustments need to be made for differences in size, subject matter, condition, rarity, quality of the works, and known provenance. The value of a work of questioned authenticity will be less than a work whose authorship is generally agreed upon. *Doherty v. Comm'r*, 16 F.3d 338 (9th Cir. 1994). Also, the most comparable sales may have occurred some distance in the past, and adjustments must be made for changes in the market for this artist or type of work.

Sales at auction are likely to be the most public sales, but are not always useful for several reasons. Many dealers buy at auction, making it more akin to wholesale than to retail. Auctions are unlikely to offer items that are not highly priced. While the prices at auction are public, it is not always clear that the price represents a genuine sale. Items are frequently sent to auction with a guarantee by the auction house or a third party that it will buy at a certain price if the bidding does not reach that level. A purchase under a guarantee would not be publicly identified, but it should not be counted as a comparable sale. Even absent a guarantee agreement, the auction house might choose to "buy-in" to maintain goodwill with a repeat customer. Also, an auction house might offer a good customer secret financing which would reduce the value of the listed sale price.

For those reasons, gallery sales are sometimes a better measure of fair retail prices than are auction sales. *Raymond Biagiotti*, T.C.Memo 1986-460, 52 T.C.M. CCH 588 (1986). But gallery sales have their own problems. Gallery asking prices are generally known, but there is no obligation to make public the actual sales prices on gallery sales. Knowledge of the sales prices is likely to be confined to the gallery that sold the work, thereby sharply limiting the number of persons who could be credible expert witnesses about gallery sales prices.

Factors that will reduce the fair market value and also require a change in the market are that the owner lacks good title, or that the work was illegally exported from a country. When the evidence of either is sufficiently strong, the work would not be salable through an auction house or a commercial gallery. In that case, the best evidence of its value would be on the illegal market. Tech. Adv. Mem. 91-52-005, PLR 9152005 (Dec. 27, 1991). But if it is difficult to learn of comparable sales in auction houses and commercial galleries, it is even more difficult to establish a value on the illegal market. Also, the illicit market that operated rather freely two decades ago is now considerably more constrained and secretive as a result of the UNESCO Convention, discussed below under Art Crossing Borders.

B. Capitalized Income

An approach to valuing art that generates income, such as a copyright or art that is commonly rented out, is to capitalize the annual income earned by the work. Such a valuation approach is complicated. While the owner will know both the gross and net rental amounts, the rate at which the income should be capitalized is a big question mark.

C. Discounts from Fair Market Value

Fair market value assumes a willing buyer and a willing seller. It also assumes a supply and demand curve that sets the value. When an artist or a gallery owner dies, the decedent usually has a considerable inventory of unsold work. If all that work were sold in the existing market on the date of death, the supply of works by that artist would be considerably expanded, while the demand for that artist's work would remain the same, or perhaps decline because people who wish to have a personal relationship with the artist can no longer do so. This would be a very different situation from any prior sales, so those sales would not be as comparable as they would otherwise be. In most cases, there is little proof of fair market value other than comparable sales. In order to adjust fair market value from a normal supply to a greatly increased supply, the fair market value of the individual pieces are discounted. This is called "blockage" because a block of the artwork is (theoretically) going on the market simultaneously.

For example, where the artist left 425 pieces but had sold fewer than100 pieces in the previous twenty-five years, unless the artist's death changes the market for his work, it might take more than a century to dispose of the estate. *Est. of David Smith*, 57 T.C. 650 (1972), *aff'd* 510 F.2d 479 (2d Cir. 1975). The problem usually lies in determining the appropriate percentage discount. One assumption commonly mentioned is that one person will buy the work in bulk, demanding a quantity discount. That person will normally be a dealer, who will buy in order to re-sell the work to his customers over a period of time. But the value such a person would pay should not be considered because the assumption of the tax law is that the work is to be valued at the retail level, and the dealer is only willing to pay a wholesale price for the block of work.

It is simply unrealistic to expect that an executor will be able to market the decedent's work directly to collectors himself, without using a dealer or, if it is high end work, an auction house. Thus the estate is unlikely to realize a retail price for the goods, and will instead derive either a wholesale price by selling the works to the dealer, or a retail price less the dealer's commission by selling the works through the dealer.

Another consideration is that the work will require considerable time to be disposed of without disturbing the functioning of the market. Whatever the reason for a blockage discount, a satisfying way of determining the amount of the blockage discount has not been devised. Sometimes the court will determine that some works, by their individual characteristics, are subject to a steep blockage discount (75% in the case) because of the time and effort required to dispose of them, while others receive a more moderate discount (25% in the case) because they will be more quickly sold without significant effort. But that does not provide any principle to help determine the blockage discount percentage. *Est. of Georgia T. O'Keeffe*, T.C.Memo 1992-210, 63 T.C.M. (CCH) 2699 (1992).

One case took the present value of the art and used the likely rate of disposition in an orderly market to determine when the proceeds of the sale of all of the works would be available, then treated those proceeds as though they were annuity payments and discounted them back to the present. *Louisa J. Calder*, 85 T.C. 713 (1985). The case has not been much followed. While the amount of a blockage discount is a fact question like the fair market value of the work, it seems like a hypothetical fact question because there is seldom evidence showing how much putting a large body of work on the market reduces the sales price. Art dealers simply do not suddenly increase the quantity of an artist's work in the market, so there is no such evidence to introduce.

Taxpayers have also sought a discount where they own a fractional interest in the artwork, or there are other impediments to the use or sale of the art. The discount for a fractional interest was imported from corporate stock, where owning less than half the stock of a company means that the shareholder does not have corporate control. Whether owning a fractional share in an artwork deserves such a discount may be disputed. Most restrictions on use or sale are disregarded by statute in computing fair market value. Taxpayers have won some discounts for fractional interests in art, but those discounts had been no more than 10% because proof of the discount percentage had been minimal. *Est. of Robert C. Scull*, T.C.Memo 1994-211, 67 T.C.M. CCH 2953 (1994.) In *Est. of Elkins, v. Comm'r*, 767 F.3d 443, 2014-2 U.S. Tax Cas. (CCH) ¶60,683 (5th Cir.), the court presents a template for successfully planning these transactions that resulted in a 45% discount. What is problematic about these fractional interests is that their sole effect seems to be to reduce the estate tax, and those fractional interests are usually left to the owners of the remaining interest in the art, giving the heir its undiscounted value while the estate has suffered an estate tax on a lesser amount. That is a problem that only legislation can fix.

D. Burden of Proof

As a presumption of correctness attaches to the I.R.S. Commissioner's determination, taxpayers often lose valuation suits because they fail to carry their burden of proving the actual value. Both taxpayer and I.R.S. are likely to rely on expert testimony.

E. Appraisals and Expert Testimony

Increasingly, experts who testify are people with expertise about the relevant art market, rather than art history expertise.

Not all appraisals are persuasive. An appraisal with no comparables to support it, where the appraiser appears to know little about the painter or the work, is likely to be completely disregarded. The result of that may be that if the person presenting the appraisal has the burden of proof (as the taxpayer usually does) and presents no other evidence, that person will lose the case because he will not carry his burden of proof. *Charles A. Weil*, T.C.Memo 1967-78, 26 T.C.M. CCH 388 (1967).

Since *Daubert v. Merrell Dow Pharmaceuticals*, 509 U.S. 579 (1993), expert testimony must relate to an issue in the case, which is usually not a problem. It must come from someone qualified to testify "by knowledge, skill, experience, training, or education," which does not normally pose problems either. The problem is that the proposed testimony must be supported by appropriate validation: evidence must be introduced of reliability. That reliability can be provided by the methods used being testable, by a demonstration that the expert has a low error rate, by the method being subject to peer review, and by general acceptance in the profession. Testing and peer review are more compatible with scientific evidence than with value evidence. Unless a person has frequently testified about value, he is unlikely to have a significant enough track record to establish an error rate. That leaves his qualification to testify based solely on general acceptance in the field of valuation.

Doubts about the value of an artwork may be amplified if the owners of the work do not insure it or do not treat it as though it were valuable. *Dennis M. Vander Hook*, T.C.Memo 1977-347, 36 T.C.M. CCH 1394 (1977).

Judges are likely to be suspicious of expert testimony by persons on the I.R.S. Art Advisory Panel, a voluntary group of art experts who advise IRS on the value of paintings without compensation, as being too favorable to I.R.S. *Heriberto A. Ferrari*, T.C.Memo 1989-521, 58 T.C.M. CCH 221 (1989), *aff'd* 931 F.2d 54 (4th Cir. 1991). But one court held that expert witnesses are not only not disqualified because they participate on the Internal Revenue Service's Art Advisory Panel, but gave that expert's opinion substantial weight even when the person helped the Art Advisory Panel evaluate the painting in question. On the other hand, the fact that the expert is also a friend and longtime business associate of taxpayer may entitle his opinion to minimal weight. *Furstenberg v. United States*, 595 F.2d 603 (Ct. Cl. 1979).

While a major focus on the value of art may be taxes, counsel should not forget that art may need to be valued for pre-nuptial agreements, insurance, in case of divorce, if the collection needs to be divided on the death of the owner because it is in the residuary estate that is left to several persons and, in some states that determine the executor's compensation based on the value of decedent's estate, the value of art will be included in that calculus.

F. What Is at Stake—Interest and Penalties

Filing a tax return with valuation errors can be costly. If the errors are not too great, one needs to pay interest on the underpayment at the official rate. If there is a substantial valuation misstatement, which means a value which is 200% or more, or 50% or less, than the true value, the penalty is 20% of the tax due. If there is a gross valuation misstatement, meaning a value which is 400% or more, or 25% or less, than the true value, then the penalty doubles to 40% of the tax due. Int. Rev. Code of 1986 §6662. The penalty for fraud is 75% of the tax due. Int. Rev. Code of 1986 §6663. This can have serious consequences for the taxpayer. It can also have serious liability consequences for the appraiser who might have provided the inaccurate value. See the chapter on Authentication below.

G. The Art Advisory Panel's Process

The Panel consists of twenty-five experts. They need not be certified experts. In theory, no return information that is identifiable is disclosed to them. The disclosing IRS employee would be guilty of a felony. But the unique artwork in question is disclosed to them, and art experts often know who the owner of a unique artwork is.

In the course of litigating a dispute with IRS, taxpayers often want to know more about the discussions in the Art Advisory Panel. Generally, an expert witness' notes about his research are discoverable. IRS has resisted discovery of Art Advisory Panel work on the grounds that it falls within the executive privilege exception, but courts have held that executive privilege is designed to protect the candor of intragovernmental communications. The meetings of the Art Advisory Panel are closed to protect the confidentiality of information provided by taxpayers, so there is no reason to refuse to provide information about the deliberations of the panel to taxpayer. Such disclosure is limited to matters related to this particular determination, and will not permit disclosure of discussions about the value of other artworks, even if they are comparable. *Bradford C. Bernardo*, 104 T.C. 677 (1995); *Proctor & Gamble Co. v. United States*, 2010-1 U.S. Tax Cas. (CCH) ¶50146 (S.D. Ohio 2009).

5. Tax Shelters

A generation ago, a series of tax shelters emerged attempting to reduce the income taxes of the wealthy. The pressure to do this has been reduced by both a reduction in the maximum rate of tax and efforts by Congress and IRS to reduce shelter opportunities. Art was not neglected in these tax shelters.

One significant shelter involved the sale of art masters. A master is a silkscreen or lithograph plate. The buying taxpayer received the right to make copies of those masters at his own expense, as well as the appropriate copyrights. The rights cost around $550,000. The buyer received two appraisals stating that the masters were worth at least what the buyers were paying, and opinions from two large law firms that the investment would qualify for the investment credit of 10% of the full purchase price in the first year, plus accelerated depreciation. The opinion states that an accrual basis taxpayer could deduct the anticipated future interest costs in the first year, and a cash basis taxpayer could deduct the interest as paid. The tax benefits are dependent on the buyer's intent to engage in the business of exploiting the art master, and also on the fair market value of the master being at least as great as the purchase price. In one case, about 18% of the purchase price of $550,000 was paid periodically over the first 14 months; the balance was due twelve years later on a nonrecourse note.

The court found as a fact that the masters had negligible value compared to the purchase price. It found the appraisals unpersuasive, as they seemed to be stock appraisals applied to all the masters sold by the firm that employed the appraisers. The appraisals cited no persuasive comparables, nor did they discuss how much the market might be depressed if large numbers of prints came on the market at the same time. It further found that taxpayer was motivated primarily, if not exclusively, by tax considerations. The court held that there was no economic substance to the transaction, and denied deductions for the investment credit and depreciation. It allowed the deduction for interest actually paid because there were genuine loans, but a deduction for interest accrued but unpaid was denied. Additional interest was assessed for the valuation misstatement. *James L. Rose*, 88 T.C. 386 (1987).

It will not surprise you to learn that the Roses sued the seller and both appraisers. The lawyers had sufficiently covered their backsides by conditioning their opinion on the proposition that the tax benefits depended on the masters being worth at least the purchase price.

Other disappointed investors have sued their sellers on a number of theories. Federal securities law charges have generally been dismissed on the grounds that, under the circumstances, art was not a security. A security is an investment of money in a common enterprise with profits to come solely from the efforts of others. *SEC v. W.J. Howey Co.*, 328 U.S. 293 (1946). In certain circumstances, art could be a security under federal law. Several state courts have supported state securities fraud actions. There was one recovery under a state RICO law with securities fraud as the predicate offense. It awarded the buyer of an art master triple damages on grounds that what was sold was a security. It was a common enterprise because both seller and buyer depended on the outcome of the enterprise, the buyer for his profit and the seller for payment of a nonrecourse note. *Daggett v. Jackie Fine Arts, Inc.*, 733 P.2d 1142 (Ariz. App. 1986).

6. Sales and Use Taxes

You would think that nothing could be simpler than the imposition of sales or use taxes on the sale of art. That would be true but for the peculiarity of the sales and use tax laws of some states. Normally, a sales tax is imposed on the seller of merchandise at retail within the state. Each state determines the amount of the sales tax. The highest rate I have found is 10%. To assure that residents of a state do not go to another state to make major purchases, states with sales taxes also impose use taxes. Use taxes are normally at the same rate as sales taxes, but apply to items bought out of state but used within the state.

So assume that your client is a resident of California who buys a painting at auction in New York. You would think that he would pay New York sales tax, but he does not. The New York sales tax contains a rule that if something is bought in New York and immediately exported, there is no New York sales tax. You would then think your client should pay California use tax. And he might. But California has a rule that if the property is used for at least ninety days outside California, no use tax is due because the property is not coming new to California. But where can the property be used for ninety days outside New York and outside California? There are five states that do not impose use taxes: Oregon, New Hampshire, Delaware, Montana and Alaska. So your client loans the painting for four months to a museum located in one of those states with the condition that it be continuously displayed. At the end of that time, the painting is sent to the owner in California. No sales tax need be paid; no use tax need be paid. If the painting was purchased for $1 million, that is a savings of $100,000.

Checkpoints

You should have learned that:

- Income tax deductions are only available for taxpayers with profit-seeking motivation. A taxpayer best demonstrates that motivation who has objectively manifested activities that show he is engaged in the world of art for profit, or by showing a profit in 2 of the previous 5 years.
- To be engaged in a trade or business, an artist must be engaged in regular activity for profit. Factors such as an artist's marketing activity, past sales, and time spent on art help determine if an artist has a profit-seeking motive.
- Only itemized deductions are available for investors or collectors who claim their activity as an investment, rather than a trade or business, and they are not available 2018–2026. A lack of sales or a collection kept in a private residence may distinguish an investor from a hobbyist.
- When a taxpayer exchanges like kind property with another, he can defer income tax because there is no money received to tax, no substantial change in taxpayer's investment and no currently recognized loss or gain.
- If an artist has a home studio where a room is used exclusively as the principal place of business, to meet clients, or is located in a separate structure, the expense of maintaining this studio may be deductible.
- Congress has made an exception for artists to the rule that inventory is non-deductible, allowing them to deduct current cost of preparing artwork.
- Expenses incurred on business travels related to an artist's business are deductible.
- The passive activity loss rules prevent offsetting passive business losses against income generated from other activities. There are safe harbors available for taxpayers meeting certain requirements concerning the taxpayer's time spent on such activities which most active artists can satisfy.
- Quick and frequent sales indicate a taxpayer is engaged in a trade or business, subjecting art sales to ordinary income rates. One who buys art or a copyright as an investment is taxed at capital gains rates for collectibles.
- The fair market value of property gifted to charity may be deducted from most taxpayers' income tax.
- Fair market value of property is a question of fact that is usually established by testimony of expert witnesses. There may be discounts from fair market value when a supply of an artist's work greatly increases.
- When comparing sales of artwork to determine an artwork's price, size, condition and changes in the market may alter its value. If a work is illegally exported or lacks good title, the artwork's fair market value may be lowered.
- Comparable sales that support an appraised price and the expert's knowledge of the artist or work may increase the persuasiveness of the appraisal. Not all appraisals are credible, particularly when the expert is a friend or business associate of the artwork's owner.

- Fraud and valuation errors on tax returns subject a taxpayer to penalties.
- Notes from the I.R.S. Art Advisory Panel about an expert witness' views are generally discoverable, but any disclosure is limited to matters related to the determination of the value of that specific artwork.
- Tax shelters to reduce the income taxes of wealthy taxpayers include the sale of art masters such as silkscreens or lithograph plates. Courts have limited and denied these types of deductions and Congress has made an effort to reduce these opportunities.

Chapter 10

Authenticity

Roadmap

After reading this chapter, you should understand:

- Authenticity of an art work may relate to the period in which it was produced, its condition, its state of restoration, and whether it was created by the named artist.
- Scientific evidence based on the materials used cannot presently prove which artist made a work but can conclusively establish that the work was not made by an artist if the materials were not used until after the artist's death.
- Provenance helps prove authenticity by showing the whereabouts of a work over time. It can be difficult to establish because records may be lost, never made, or fraudulent, and copies of the work may be made by the owner himself.
- Connoisseurship: The evaluation of a work by experts who compare its similarities or differences to other works reliably attributed to an artist.
- Recovery for misattribution: Buyers may recover damages from their sellers if purchasing a misattributed work through common law recoveries and sales law statutes.
- Common law tort recovery: To recover under fraud, a buyer must prove the seller made a representation he knew was untrue, the seller knew a reasonable buyer would rely on that representation, and that the buyer actually relied on it. A negligent misrepresentation action has the same requirements except the buyer only needs to prove the seller was negligent in making the representation, not that the seller knew it was untrue. The buyer must also prove the seller owed the buyer a duty which does not typically exist between seller and buyer.
- Common law contract recovery: If a seller promises to deliver a work and then delivers something else and the buyer reasonably relies on the seller's representation, the seller is liable. It is reasonable for a buyer to rely on a representation of fact but it is unreasonable to rely on an opinion. Courts may distinguish between representations made before and after a purchase.
- Sales law statutes: Both the Uniform Sales Act and the Uniform Commercial Code hold sellers liable for breach of warranty for misattribution if buyer reasonably relied on the attribution.
- Express reliance: Buyers may include clauses in bills of sale expressly stating buyer reliance on seller's representations. If buyer had an expert examine the

work before sale, buyer is precluded from claiming reliance if the defect is one such an expert should have noticed.

- Statute of limitations: For breach of present warranty under the UCC expires four years from the time of delivery.
- Future promise: A promise of future action is not breached and the statute of limitations does not begin to run until the future performance is due and not performed.
- Fraudulent concealment: The statute of limitations does not run if defendant fraudulently conceals the defect.
- Continuing conduct: When a seller is involved in a continuing course of action, the statute of limitations does not begin to run until the last action occurs.
- Inherently unknowable injury: The doctrine of inherently unknowable injury, which extends the running of the statute of limitations until a plaintiff discovers or should have discovered an injury, has been applied to the recovery of property. Cases conflict on whether this applies to buyers who purchase misattributed works.
- United Nations Convention on Contracts for the International Sale of Goods (CISG) is the governing law for sales between residents of different countries that participate in the treaty. Auction sales are exempt, as are sales for personal, family, or household uses unless seller is unaware the buyer purchased the work for those reasons.
- CISG does not require reliance or being part of the bargain. It has no statute of limitation though the buyer must notify the seller of the specific lack of conformity to the contract within a reasonable time of when the buyer should have discovered it but in all cases within two years after delivery in order to contest the quality of the goods and recover.
- Art legislation: Many states have enacted laws specifically for the sale of art. They generally do not require plaintiff to show that the attribution was part of the basis of the bargain, but may limit liability to situations where seller's representations were without a reasonable basis in fact at the time they were made.
- Contract adjustments: Auction houses often include provisions in contracts that allow an auctioneer to rescind a sale if it determines it might be subject to liability from the sale, even without establishing lack of authenticity.
- Federal Trade Commission (FTC): The FTC can sue to stop unfair and deceptive trade practices, even if the practices are truthful but deceptive to reasonable consumers. Past violations justify a preliminary injunction to prevent fraud before the trial ends.
- Criminal liability: A seller who knowingly sells inauthentic artwork may violate state and federal criminal offenses including mail fraud, wire fraud, and obtaining money by false pretenses.

- Authenticators: Scholars and appraisers are often used to prove or disprove authenticity. They may be liable for misattribution and subject to actions for malpractice, defamation, or product disparagement.
- Malpractice: Authenticators are liable to their clients for failure to use the special knowledge or skills they advertise. Appraisers are only liable to third parties if a duty of care to that party exists. Some states find a duty to anyone that appraiser can reasonably foresee would be given the appraiser's appraisal.
- Defamation liability to third party: For an appraiser to be liable to a third party for defamation, the third party must prove an appraiser's attribution is false, was reasonably understood by the public, and damaged the reputation of the third party. The appraiser may defend himself on freedom of speech grounds.
- Product disparagement liability to third party: For an appraiser to be liable to a third party for product disparagement, the third party must prove the appraiser's speech or conduct was false, the appraiser acted with malice, the appraiser communicated the falsity to another party, and it reduced the value of plaintiff's property.
- Malicious prosecution: Courts have held owners of misattributed work and their lawyers liable for compensatory and punitive damages for abuse of process and malicious prosecution when they unreasonably sue an appraiser and the suit is dismissed but the appraiser incurred substantial legal costs.
- Refusing to authenticate and exculpatory clauses: Many experts create exculpatory or indemnity clauses to shield themselves from lawsuits. These are usually ineffective against gross negligence and wilful misconduct allegations. There is no obligation to authenticate unless there is a contractual obligation.
- Destroying forgeries: An artist's moral rights may be violated if anyone destroys or defaces a forgery.
- Antitrust laws: To succeed in an antitrust action, an owner must prove the work of the artist is the relevant market, that the defendant attempted to monopolize the market or there was an agreement among defendants to restrain trade in the market, and that the monopolization attempt or agreement caused damages.
- Trademark: The Lanham Act protects the goodwill of sellers. A plaintiff suing under the Lanham Act must prove a false designation of origin or false description or advertisement of fact, and must show public confusion is likely.

1. What Is the Quality of the Work?

The law normally requires that the quality of the work be as represented. The quality of a work of art might go to its functionality. A statue designed to be part of a support system for a building must in fact support the building. In this, the legal problems of selling art are indistinguishable from the legal problems of selling other useful objects. What distinguishes art from other goods is that the price does not usually depend on function. Rather it often refers to the artist to whom it is attributed, to the period in which it was produced, to its condition, or to the rarity of the piece. For example, a painting sold as a Rubens will attract a higher price than the same painting attributed to one of his former apprentices who is a lesser name in the art world.

Representations that have been litigated include:

attribution to a particular artist
attribution to a particular period
whether the artwork was made for a particular patron
in whose collection the artwork has resided
the condition of the work
the value of the work.

The most frequently litigated question involves attribution of the work to a particular artist or period.

One must first decide what constitutes a work by the artist. In the Renaissance, an artist had a studio to help him produce his work and to train upcoming artists. Some of the work would be done by apprentices; other parts would be done by assistants. Ghiberti reported that twenty-one artists, including such household names as Donatello and Michelozzo, worked on the Baptistery doors that Michaelangelo later named "The Gates of Paradise." Yet it is considered a work by Ghiberti because he oversaw the endeavor. Likewise, it is common for modern prints to be printed by professional printers like Gemini G.E.L., but that printing is done under the supervision of the artist who created the plate from which the print was made. And few modern metal sculptures are cast by the sculptor; commercial foundries are used instead, under the supervision of the sculptor.

Less artist supervision occured with the 80 Goya prints, "Disasters of War," all printed from plates etched by the Spanish master between 1810 and 1820. But the etchings were so disturbing that they were not printed until 1863, 35 years after Goya's death; obviously, they were printed by someone else, and without Goya's supervision. These too are considered authentic Goyas. The circumstances that prevented the artist from supervising the printing are known, and no one who knows anything about Goya prints is deceived.

There is precedent for this view that artist supervision is key. New York art legislation defines "artist" as the person who "conceives or creates the image." *Wesselman v. International Images, Inc.*, 645 N.Y.S.2d 263 (Sup. 1996) held that the person who creates the image need not be the person who prints it in order to be the artist, though this was not an authentication case.

Then there are the works that have suffered damage. The damaged works are by the named artist, and the damage is readily visible. When the damage is repaired by a restorer, at some point the restoration may be so great that the work of the original artist largely disappears. A judgment must be made of whether the restored work is that of the original artist or that of the restorer.

Determining whether the work is really by that artist or from that period is likely to depend on three types of evidence: scientific evidence, provenance, and connoisseurship.

A. Scientific Evidence

Today, scientific evidence can only conclusively establish that the work was not made by a particular artist by showing that it was not made during the time in which (s)he lived. One can sometimes establish with rough accuracy the date at which the wood used to make the panel on which the painting rests was cut. In one case, the high carbon 14 content of the canvas showed that the cotton and flax used to make it was grown after 1959, four years after the artist's death. Or the paint used might not have been manufactured during the artist's lifetime.

More positively, scientific evidence can establish that the paint or canvas or wood used in the disputed painting is of the same age and type that the artist used in other paintings, but that does not prove that the artist actually made the painting. Some scientists are attempting to program computers to recognize brush strokes of individual painters. Success in that endeavor would positively identify the work of those painters, but successful matching of brush strokes has thus far eluded the scientists.

B. Provenance

Evidence of provenance, the whereabouts of the work over time, can be persuasive. The gold standard would be the ability to trace the whereabouts of the work from the artist's easel to the present day. The gold standard is seldom met, even for modern artists. Records are lost, destroyed or never made. Even if the gold standard is met, that does not guarantee that some owner (or his trusted servant) has not had a copy made and substituted it for the original. See *Wildenstein & Co. v. Wallis*, 756 F.Supp. 158 (S.D.N.Y. 1991), where Mrs. Wallis, who did not want her husband to know that she was borrowing on the security of paintings, had copies made to deceive her husband into thinking that the originals were still hanging on the walls.

Also, the records that constitute the provenance may be fraudulent, purporting to show the work in non-existent collections or in collections the work never entered, as in *United States v. Schultz*, 333 F.3d 393 (2d Cir. 2003).

Cooking up a fraudulent provenance is possible even when those records lie in the archives of a world-renowned museum– or two or three of them. LANEY SALISBURY & ALY SUJO, PROVENANCE: HOW A CON MAN AND FORGER REWROTE THE HISTORY OF MODERN ART 73–79, 83–84, 95–97, 105–113, 115–119, 199–207 (2009) details how a con man hired a forger to create paintings in the style of dead artists, then smuggled fake documents and catalogues into the archives to prove their provenance. Despite these potential defects of provenance, a good provenance will often win the day when the opinions of connoisseurs are divided, as was the case with a damaged Calder mobile. *Greenberg Gallery, Inc. v. Bauman*, 817 F.Supp. 167 (D.D.C. 1993) *aff'd mem.* 36 F.3d 127 (D.C.Cir. 1994).

C. Connoisseurship

Connoisseurship is the evaluation of the work and the appraisal of its similarities to and differences from other works reliably attributable to artists. This often involves matters of opinion as to whether the similarities or differences are real, and their significance.

What was said about the opinions of experts in the chapter on taxes above applies with equal force here. The process of weighing conflicting expert testimony is dissected at *Greenberg Gallery, Inc. v. Bauman*, 817 F.Supp. 167 (D.D.C. 1993) *aff'd mem.* 36 F.3d 127 (D.C.Cir. 1994).

Attributions of works are always shifting. In 2019, there were new paintings by, or reattributions involving, El Greco, Alonzo Sanchez Coello, Artemesia Gentileschi, Cimabue, Leonardo da Vinci, Eugene Delacroix, Caravaggio, and Diego Velazquez. And the painting attributed to Renoir belonging to Donald Trump is "fake news". Many more reattributions may have occurred, but did not make news because they did not involve artists of the first rank.

A work that was actually done by the named artist may fail to be authenticated either because critical opinion is that too little of the work was done by that named artist compared to work done by other artists in his studio, or because a restoration of the work has been so energetic as to erase too many traces of the named artist's hand. *Kirby v. Wildenstein*, 784 F.Supp. 1112 (S.D.N.Y. 1992).

2. Recovery by Buyer for Misattribution

Suppose that a painting is sold as a Rubens. Later, scholarly opinion believes that it was not by Rubens. May the buyer recover?

A. Common Law Tort Recovery

At common law, the deceived buyer could sue in tort for fraud. Fraud is difficult to prove. It requires that plaintiff prove that the seller made a representation that he knew was untrue; that the seller knew that a reasonable buyer would rely on that representation; and that this buyer did in fact rely on it. It is usually easy to prove that the seller represented that the painting was a Rubens, but much more difficult to prove that the seller knew that it was not a Rubens; that the seller knew that a reasonable person would rely on the representation; or that this buyer did in fact rely on it. Without scienter, an allegation of fraud fails. *Krahmer v. Christie's Inc.*, 911 A.2d 399 (Del. Ch. 2006). There is likewise no fraud where there is no reliance. For example, where a buyer bought five statues using an experienced agent who had reasonable time to examine the statues before the purchase, the court found that the purchaser did not reasonably rely on the seller's representation, but instead on the skill of his agent. *Levin v. Gallery 63 Antiques Corp.*, 2006 U.S. Dist. Lexis 70184 (S.D.N.Y. 2006). A good example of the problems of proving fraud is *Foxley v. Sotheby's Inc*, 893 F.Supp. 1224 (S.D.N.Y. 1995), where plaintiff alleged fraud in a promise that an authenticator's letter would be delivered with the painting, that the letter would be based on the authenticator viewing the painting, that it would in fact authenticate the painting, and that the auction house fraudulently failed to inform plaintiff that the authenticator was a person whose authentications were known to be erratic. The court dismissed all the fraud counts, the first because there was no allegation of intent to defraud, the second and third because the statements were never made, the third also because the letter not having been delivered, it could not have been relied on by purchaser, and the last because the name of the authenticator had been disclosed and her authentication record was public knowledge, as easily accessible to plaintiff as to defendant.

An action for negligent misrepresentation is somewhat different. All the above requirements must be met except plaintiff need not prove that seller knew that his representation was untrue; he need only prove that seller was negligent in making the representation. In order to recover, the buyer must prove that the seller owed the buyer a duty resulting from a special relationship between the two. There is normally no fiduciary duty in the buyer-seller relationship (and the auction house is the agent of the seller, not the buyer), and the court did not seem disposed to deviate from that rule even where the buyer had purchased a number of items from the auction house over a long period of time. *Krahmer v. Christie's Inc.*, 903 A.2d 773 (Del. Ch. 2006). Normally, when an owner hires an appraiser, that would establish a special relationship, but the court was unwilling to so hold where the appraisal is provided by the auction house without charge.

B. Common Law Contract Recovery

Contract law came to the rescue. Where a seller promises to deliver something but delivers something else, the seller is liable to the buyer if the buyer reasonably relies on the seller's representation. The focus of the question then becomes reasonable reliance.

i. Fact or Opinion?

A distinction is drawn between a representation of fact, upon which it is reasonable to rely, and an opinion, upon which it is not reasonable to rely. In a case where the art was produced by artists dead for more than a century, the judge ruled that the seller as a matter of law was not liable because no one could reasonably think after such a long period of time that the seller could accurately identify the painter. *Jendwine v. Slade*, 2 Esp. N. P. C. 572, 170 Eng. Rep. 459 (N.P. 1797). But in a later case, where the attributed artist had been dead for 35 fewer years, the judge left to the jury the question of whether the seller had made a statement of fact or a statement of his opinion that the paintings were by Canaletto, and the jury found that it was a statement of fact. *Power v. Barham*, 111 Eng. Rep. 865 (K.B. 1836).

ii. Reasonable Reliance

There is another difference between the two cases. In *Jendwine*, the attribution to Lorraine and Teniers was in the auction catalogue, delivered to the buyer before he made his purchase. In *Power*, the attribution to Canaletto was made in the bill of sale, delivered to the buyer after he had made his purchase. In the first case, buyer could have relied on the representation in making his purchase; in the second, he could not have relied because the representation was made after the purchase. One might suppose that in *Power* the written representation was a confirmation of previous oral representations, but the case report is silent on this point.

C. Sales Law Statutes

i. Uniform Sales Act

The twentieth century saw the enactment of statutory provisions on sales, such as the Uniform Sales Act, which seemed to give buyers added protection, but courts were more disposed to adhere to the status quo. In *Weisz v. Parke-Bernet Galleries, Inc.*, 351 N.Y.S.2d 911 (Sup. Ct. App. Term 1974), it is unclear whether the court held for seller because seller's disclaimer of a warranty was prominently displayed in the auction catalogue, or because the inherent nature of an auction calls for the bidder to rely on his own judgment rather than the auctioneer's representations, so there should have been no reliance by the buyer. The trial court had held for the purchaser of the supposed Dufy, *Weisz v. Parke-Bernet Galleries, Inc.*, 67 Misc.2d 1077, 325 N.Y.S.2d 576 (Civ. Ct. 1971), because the buyer denied having noticed the conditions of sale and lay people would not ordinarily notice a page and a half of conditions for sale in a catalogue eighty pages long. The trial judge thought more was required of the auction house to draw everyone's attention to the content of the conditions of sale. He thought that Parke-Bernet expected people to rely on their assertions of authorship. It was clear that neither party had any reason to know of the forgery, but the auction house had superior expertise to the buyer. The buyer had never before purchased a work of art, and the auction house was in a position to spread the loss from forgeries among its many clients by a slight increase in the prices it charged.

ii. Uniform Commercial Code

The Uniform Sales Act was followed by the Uniform Commercial Code, and by the United Nations Convention on Contracts for the International Sale of Goods for sales between merchants resident in different countries that have ratified that treaty. These new rules displaced the common law, but only where the new rules were inconsistent with common law. UCC § 1-103(b).

a. Substantive Warranty Law

UCC § 2-313(1)(a) provides "Any affirmation of fact or promise made by the seller to the buyer which relates to the goods and becomes part of the basis of the bargain creates an express warranty that the goods shall conform to the affirmation or promise." The following subsection specifies that this applies to "any description of the goods." Here again, the buyer sometimes had difficulty in establishing that the representation was part of the basis of the bargain, even where that was interpreted liberally to mean that it was part of the deal. Buyers began inserting clauses in bills of sale like "In order to induce [buyer] to make the purchase, Seller ... makes the following warranties. ..." *Rogath v. Siebenmann*, 129 F.2d 261 (2d Cir. 1997). Courts then drew a distinction between defects disclosed by the seller before the contract was signed, which were not part of the warranty unless specifically called out, and defects learned by the buyer from other sources before the contract was signed, which were always covered by the warranty. *Id.* Buyers do not rely on a seller's statement about the work when they have an independent expert examine the goods except to the extent that such an expert is unlikely to detect the deviation from seller's statement. UCC § 2-316 comment 8. No case has decided whether the buyer relies on seller's representations when the buyer is an independent expert, but the same rule should apply. Buyer's remedies differ depending on whether she has rejected the work. A buyer who rejects the artwork must give timely notice of the rejection, but she need not specify the reason for the rejection unless the seller might correct the defect. UCC §§ 2-602, 2-605. She is entitled to recover any monies paid plus damages. UCC § 2-711(1). However, it is unusual that the buyer discovers the defect and rejects the work. The buyer is much more likely to accept the work and discover its nonconformity at a much later time, when buyer tries to sell it. In that case, a successful plaintiff should be entitled to damages measured by the difference between the fair market value of the work actually delivered at the time and place of acceptance and what its fair market value would have been had it conformed to the warranty, unless special circumstances show different damages. UCC § 2-714.

The UCC also provides for an implied warranty of merchantability. Some controversy has arisen over whether an artist must inform a potential buyer if a painting is a copy of another painting. A court stated that the artist has that obligation, but found that the existence of the similar painting did not cause any damage in this case. *Factor v. Stella*, No. C 58832 (Super. Los Angeles Cnty Calif. unpublished 1978). The judge's unexpressed reasoning must have been that everyone assumes that a painting is unique, so the fact that this painting is a copy of another painting would make this painting unmarketable.

b. Statute of Limitations

1. *Cause of Action Usually Accrues on Delivery*

Under the UCC, the statute of limitations for breach of warranty is generally four years from the time of the sale:

> [A] cause of action accrues when the breach occurs, regardless of the aggrieved party's lack of knowledge of the breach. A breach of warranty occurs when tender of delivery is made [except where the warranty] explicitly extends to future performance of the goods and discovery of the breach must await the time of such performance. UCC § 2-725(2).

Plaintiffs try to avoid the four-year statute and the time it begins running by various arguments. One claimed that it was an ordinary contract action claiming rescission for mutual mistake of fact, on which the statute was six years. The court held that the UCC statute of limitations applied, in part because plaintiff was seeking damages for lost profits rather than rescission. *Firestone & Parsons v. Union League of Philadelphia*, 672 F.Supp. 819 (E.D. Pa. 1987). Another argued that the cause of action did not accrue until plaintiff's possession was disturbed or, alternatively, that the New York demand-and-refusal rule to start the statute of limitations for replevin should apply. The first claim was unsupported by authority, and the second was rejected because plaintiff was suing to rescind his purchase, not for replevin. *Doss v. Christie's*, 2009 U.S.Dist. LEXIS 88882 (S.D.N.Y.) In both cases, the court characterized the underlying transaction as a sale of goods to which the UCC applies.

2. *Escape from Cause of Action Accruing on Delivery: Future Promise*

One must determine whether the seller's statement is a representation of existing fact or a promise to do something in the future. In most cases, a statement of authorship appears to be only a statement of existing fact. "This painting is by Canaletto" appears to be only an express statement of fact. It may also be construed as an implied promise by the seller to use his best efforts to support that attribution if it is challenged, or to indemnify the purchaser if the Canaletto attribution cannot be sustained. An implied promise of future performance is not enough under the UCC. An explicit promise of future performance is required.

The difference is important, because most buyers do not closely examine their art purchases soon after buying. The most common time that trouble arises is when the buyer decides to sell the work, and an appraiser or potential agent questions its attribution. This is often likely to be more than four years after purchase.

Thus, the distinction between a representation of fact and a future promise may be crucial. The representation of fact is breached, if it is ever breached, at the moment it is made. Either the painting is by Canaletto, or it is not. If the representation includes a promise to take future action, that promise is not breached until the painting's attribution is called into question and the seller fails to take the promised action. In the case of a promise of future action, the statute of limitations begins to run when the future performance is due and the seller fails to make good on his promise. No court has dealt with whether a promise to pay the buyer the then fair market value of the paintings is a promise calling for future performance.

While most courts have not considered this possibility or rejected it out of hand, one court has opined that when a dealer attributes a work of art to a specific artist, that is both a statement of fact that the work is now by that artist, and a future promise that the work will continue to be regarded by the art community as a work by that artist. *Balog v. Center Art Gallery-Hawaii, Inc.*, 745 F. Supp. 1556 (D. Haw. 1990). It distinguished the sale of ordinary goods, where it is easy to determine whether they work or not, from art, which does not "perform."

3. *Escape from Cause of Action Accruing on Delivery: Fraudulent Concealment*

A second possible escape from the statute of limitations lies in the doctrine of fraudulent concealment. The statute of limitations for the recovery of property does not run while the defendant fraudulently conceals the property. In *Balog*, the property was in the hands of the plaintiff, so was not concealed by the defendant. But defendant periodically sent appraisals to plaintiff indicating that the work was increasing in value, which the court found to be a type of fraudulent concealment of the fact that the work was not genuine. The court did not mention this, but it was probably influenced by the defendant's long history of selling fake artwork and its criminal conviction.

By contrast, in *Krahmer v. Christie's Inc.*, 911 A.2d 399 (Del. Ch. 2006), plaintiff bought a work sold by a third party at a Christie's auction in 1986. Plaintiff had purchased other works through Christie's. In 1990, a Christie's employee came to plaintiff's house and gratuitously appraised all of plaintiff's art, providing an estimate double what plaintiff had paid for the Benson work four years earlier. This was a tort case alleging fraud, but the court still had to deal with the statute of limitations. The court found that Christie's had not engaged in fraudulent concealment. There was no evidence that defendant knew the work was not genuine in 1990. The court considered the appraisal to be simply good customer relations, not an intent to deceive.

4. *Escape from Cause of Action Accruing on Delivery: Continuing Course of Conduct*

A third possible escape from the statute of limitations comes when defendant is involved in a continuing course of action. In that case, the statute begins to run when the last action in the continuing course of conduct occurs. In *Balog*, that last act was the last mailing of the updating appraisals, which occurred within four years of the date on which suit was filed. But in *Firestone & Parsons v. Union League of Philadelphia*, 672 F.Supp. 819 (E.D.Pa. 1987), insisting that a challenged Key painting was in fact by Bierstadt was not a continuing course of conduct.

Neither the fraudulent concealment by appraisal argument nor the continuing course of conduct by appraisal was pursued in *Foxley v. Sotheby's Inc,* 893 F.Supp. 1224 (S.D.N.Y. 1995), where the court threw out plaintiff's allegation of fraud because it was brought neither within the New York statutory period of six years nor within two years of the time that plaintiff should have discovered the fraud.

5. Escape from Cause of Action Accruing on Delivery: Inherently Unknowable Injury

Many jurisdictions have adopted rules for tort cases delaying the running of the statute of limitations where the injury was inherently unknowable and the plaintiff had no reason to know of the injury. Most commonly, these begin with cases where a surgeon leaves something inside the plaintiff while he is under anesthesia. In that case, the statute of limitations begins to run when the plaintiff discovers, or should have discovered, the injury. Such cases have been extended to other torts and often to the recovery of property. For further discussion, see the Discovery Rule in the chapter on Title below. While the court seemed willing to discuss whether the inherently unknowable injury rule might apply to the sale of a misattributed painting, it held that plaintiff was not entitled to that doctrine because plaintiff could have hired an authenticator before buying, so he had reason to know of the injury. *Krahmer v. Christie's, Inc.*, 903 A.2d 773 (Del. Ch. 2006).

There is a serious contradiction between the two *Krahmer* opinions. On the one hand, the court absolves Christie's, a multi-million dollar corporation, of any obligation to take further steps to assure that the painting it is selling is genuine because " … no efficient avenue was available by which to unequivocally verify the authenticity…." On the other, it refuses to categorize plaintiff as a person who had no reason to know of the misattribution of the painting because " … a prudent buyer of artwork, as in other commercial transactions of similar value, can safeguard his or her investment by verifying its authenticity with an independent third party appraisal." You cannot have it both ways. If there is no efficient way for an art professional to discover the misattribution, *a fortiori* there is no efficient way for a consumer, even one who is an amateur art collector, to discover it. Though such considerations are inappropriate in determining whether the statute of limitations has expired, one wonders if the *Krahmer* court held the view attributed above to the *Weisz* court, that regardless of statute, a person who buys at auction should rely only on his own resources. The view that the purchaser should protect himself by hiring an expert before buying has been rejected in New York. *De Sole v. Knoedler Gallery, LLC,* 974 F.Supp.2d 274 (S.D.N.Y. 2013).

6. *Escape from the UCC statute of limitations by pleading fraud or RICO*

It may be possible to escape the strict UCC statute of limitations if the facts permit plaintiff to plead fraud or RICO. In both cases, the statute of limitations does not begin to run until plaintiff discovers, or should have discovered, the injury. In *De Sole v. Knoedler Gallery, LLC*, 974 F.Supp.2d 274 (S.D.N.Y. 2013), some of the plaintiffs were able to allege facts that supported a fraud or RICO recovery, while others were not. For RICO, see below.

7. *Problems with the Cause of Action Accruing on Delivery*

The difficulties that occur because the cause of action accrues on delivery can be seriously unfair. Imagine a case where A sells a painting warranted to be a Canaletto to B in 2008. B sells it to C in 2012, warranting that it is a Canaletto. In 2014, C discovers that it is not a Canaletto. C can recover from B, but B cannot recover from A because more than four years have elapsed since the painting was delivered to B.

The same problem can occur with a warranty of title. As discussed more fully in the chapter on Title below, many courts have adopted the discovery rule to determine when the statute of limitations begins to run for purposes of recovering stolen artwork, but do not adopt the discovery rule for breach of warranty. The result is that a purchaser of art may lose the work because the owner of the art was able to assert his rights a generation after it was stolen, but the purchaser cannot recover from his seller because of the expiration of the statute of limitations for the warranty.

iii. Convention on Contracts for the International Sale of Goods (CISG)

Since 1990, the United Nations Convention on Contracts for the International Sale of Goods is the applicable United States law for contracts between persons resident in different countries that have signed the Treaty. It does not apply to auction sales, or to sales for the personal, family or household use of the buyer unless the seller did not know, and had no reason to know, that the artwork was purchased for those purposes.

If CISG applies, seller must deliver goods which are of the quality and description required by the contract, unless buyer knew or should have known that they were not. If the goods are described as being by a specific artist, they must have been produced by that artist. Art. 35(1).

CISG has no requirement of reliance, or being part of the bargain. But article 35(3) adds: "The seller is not liable ... for any lack of conformity of the goods if at the time of the conclusion of the contract the buyer knew or could not have been unaware of such lack of conformity." This is a considerably different standard than "basis of the bargain," and the burden of proof rests with the seller to demonstrate that the buyer "could not have been unaware."

The buyer must examine the goods within as short a period of time as possible, art. 38(1), and will lose the right to contest conformity of the goods if she does not notify the seller specifying the nature of the lack of conformity within a reasonable time after she has discovered it or ought to have discovered it, but in no case longer than two years after delivery. Art. 39. Buyers' remedies include rescission and damages. CISG leaves the statute of limitations to domestic law except where covered by the UN (New York) Convention on the Limitation Period in the International Sale of Goods, 60 Fed. Reg. 3484 (1995).

iv. Art Legislation

The reader has probably noticed that none of the above provisions are specific to the sale of art. Many states, including those which had the most active art markets, then enacted laws that specifically targeted art sales. § 13.01 of the New York Arts and Cultural Affairs Law provides:

> "Notwithstanding any provision of any other law to the contrary:
>
> "1. Whenever an art merchant, in selling or exchanging a work of fine art, furnishes to a buyer of such work who is not an art merchant a certificate of authenticity or any similar written instrument it:
>
> (a) Shall be presumed to be part of the basis of the bargain; and
>
> (b) Shall create an express warranty for the material facts stated as of the date of such sale or exchange."

This would seem to create a fully binding warranty, but subsection 2 provides:

> "2.... in construing the degree of warranty, due regard shall be given the terminology used and the meaning accorded such terminology by the customs and usage of the trade at the time and in the locality where the sale or exchange took place."

One would have thought that enactment of this legislation would have made a seller absolutely liable when the artwork was not created by the artist indicated, but that was not the case. The standard that emerged asked whether the buyer has established by a preponderance of the evidence that seller's representations were without a reasonable basis in fact at the time the representations were made. *Dawson v. Molina, Inc.*, 463 F.Supp. 461 (S.D.N.Y. 1978). So a sales contract, even with an express warranty, is not an insurance policy.

How does the purchaser prove that the seller's representation was without a reasonable basis in fact? With some representations, this is easy. Where the representation was that the vase had been exhibited at the Metropolitan Museum of Art in 1916 and no effort was made to ask whether that vase was still in the Met's collection, which it was, the court held that the representation was without a reasonable basis in fact. *Dawson v. Molina, Inc.*, 463 F.Supp. 461 (S.D.N.Y. 1978).

Whether a representation about authorship has a reasonable basis in fact is more difficult, in part because it usually depends on connoisseurship. Presumably one gathers all the opinions about the work at the time of the sale and tries to evaluate whether a seller in possession of all that information would have been reasonable in his representation. Each case decided has relied on expert testimony about the artwork in question. They have not always been precise in distinguishing what was known in the art world at the time of the sale from what was known at the time of trial, which is always some years later. Where the experts agree on the attribution, the judge is likely to adopt their opinion. When faced with a conflict between a positive attribution and a qualified one, such as a statement that the expert believes the work was made in the Chien Lung period, but might have been in the Tao Kuang reign, the unqualified opinion will be given more weight. The court should also take into consideration the number of experts expressing their opinions on each side, the reputations of the experts, and the persuasiveness of their explanations of why they make their attributions.

Most specialized art legislation contains stricter standards for merchants of multiples than for merchants selling paintings or drawings.

Specialized art legislation usually does not contain a separate statute of limitations.

Where specialized art legislation is designed to apply to artworks with modest pricetags, care needs to be exercised to assure that there can be economical enforcement. The California legislation became largely precatory for inexpensive works when a court denied class certification for a suit, denied attorneys' fees and required a successful plaintiff to return the work for recovery, in a situation where the framing probably cost more than the artwork. *Grogan-Beall v. Ferdinand Roten Galleries, Inc.*, 133 Cal. App. 3d 969, 184 Cal. Rptr. 411 (1982).

v. Contractually Authorized Adjustments

Sometimes consequences follow even if lack of authenticity is not established. It is common for auction houses to provide in their contracts that the auctioneer has the right to rescind the sale when it determines "in its sole judgment" that it might be subject to liability as a result of the sale. This has the effect of appointing the auctioneer as an arbitrator. Had the clause stated that the contract could be rescinded if the auctioneer would be subject to liability, that would be an objective standard, so the inauthenticity must be established. In the clause quoted above, considerable, but not unlimited, discretion is given to the auctioneer, who must make a good faith determination that he "might" be subject to liability. Any serious controversy about authentication should be sufficient, such as a situation where the normal authenticator of the artist's works refuses to provide authentication. Such a provision will override both a warranty and the normal fiduciary liability of an agent. *Greenwood v. Koven*, 880 F. Supp. 186 (S.D.N.Y. 1995). For more discussion, see the chapter on Commercial Relations below.

D. RICO

The federal Racketeer Influenced and Corrupt Organizations Act (RICO), 18 U.S.C. §§ 1961-1968 provides both criminal penalties, forfeiture, and the civil recovery of triple damages plus costs and attorneys fees, for violation. A RICO violation requires that the defendant through two or more acts constituting a pattern of racketeering activity injures plaintiff's business or property by activities affecting interstate or foreign commerce. Normally, the commerce requirement is satisfied through using the mail, phone or the internet. The RICO violation is an agreement to sell forged paintings, thereby depriving plaintiffs of money. There is normally more than one person involved in perpetrating the fraud.

3. Administrative Enforcement

The Balogs (see 2.C.ii.b.2 above) were not alone in being defrauded by their sellers, Center Art Gallery. The sellers' depradations were sufficiently widespread to attract the attention of the Federal Trade Commission, who sued to halt unfair and deceptive trade practices.

Practices may be unfair and deceptive even if technically truthful. Defendant in *Federal Trade Comm'n v. Magui Publishers, Inc.*, 1993 U.S. App. LEXIS 28684

(9th Cir.) published prints on blank paper signed by Dali imitating Dali designs with an attribution that it was by Dali, engraved by atelier Spalaikovitch, printed by Giraudon and published by Magui. Technically, all that was stated was true, but the court held that "by Dali" implied to the reasonable consumer that Dali was involved in the operation when he was not.

The FTC has a weapon most buyers lack: it can request a preliminary injunction to prevent fraud during the pendency of the trial. Regulatory agencies are not bound by the usual rules of equity in seeking a preliminary injunction. Having proven past violations, it need only show the likelihood of future violations. The court will then issue a preliminary injunction if it is appropriate considering the totality of the circumstances. In *Federal Trade Commission v. Austin Galleries of Illinois, Inc.*, 1988-2 Trade Cas. (CCH) ¶ 68,340 (N.D.Ill. 1988), the court had issued a preliminary injunction preventing defendant from selling lithographs purported to be by Picasso, Dali, Chagall or Miro without giving 20 days' notice to the FTC and allowing an FTC expert to examine the works. Defendants proposed to sell 122 lithographs, of which the FTC's expert determined that 120 of them were fakes. He also examined 253 supposed Picassos and determined that they were all fakes. This testimony was corroborated by others. The FTC requested a blanket injunction on selling works by those artists, because it was too burdensome to examine each print to determine whether it was genuine. The court enjoined the sale of any lithograph by those artists, but permitted the defendant to submit other works, such as aquatints and linocuts, for FTC approval because defendant had few of them in inventory and the evidence of fakes among them was less overwhelming than for the lithographs. In essence, the court disabled defendant from selling most of its inventory before the trial was concluded.

It is occasionally alleged that the sale of art is the sale of a security. It is likely that the sale of a mutual fund where the underlying assets are artwork would be the sale of a security, but then it would be the interest in the mutual fund that is the security. A security is an investment in a common enterprise, with the expectation of profits solely from the efforts of others. Buying an artwork is certainly an investment, and usually profits occur only from the increase in value of the work, which is not something that the owner's personal efforts usually cause (though one can think of exceptions). The problem usually lies in finding that the investment is in a common enterprise. In a case where plaintiff bought twelve paintings with a right to exchange them at fair market value for other paintings, it was held that these were not securities because there was no common enterprise. Plaintiff was the sole owner of the paintings and, if they were exchanged for other paintings, he would be the sole owner of the other paintings. He would not share any gain from any painting that occurred while he did not own it. *Stenger v. R.H. Love Galleries, Inc.*, 741 F.2d 144 (7th Cir. 1984).

4. Criminal Liability

Persons who knowingly sell inauthentic art may be subject to criminal liability at both state and federal levels. The company that sold to the Balogs and its officers were convicted on numerous counts of the federal offenses of mail and wire fraud. *United States v. Center Art Galleries-Hawaii, Inc.*, 991 F.2d 804 (9th Cir. 1993). Obtaining money by false pretenses is a crime in all states.

5. Liability of Authenticators

Key players on questions of authenticity are scholars and appraisers. Scholars and appraisers can be liable for misattribution in common law actions for malpractice, defamation, or product disparagement. Disappointed owners might also resort to federal statutory actions, such as antitrust, trademark, and RICO. The likelihood of the owner prevailing is small, but the suits are brought nonetheless. Owners of art as a class are not usually impoverished. This is a problem for appraisers and foundations, as their resources usually do not approach those of art owners, and the cost of defending even a frivolous suit can be great. They have responded with some defensive tools of their own.

A. Malpractice

i. Liability to Clients

The usual liability of authenticators to their clients is an allegation of professional malpractice. A potential buyer might hire an appraiser to provide an opinion about the authorship of a work and its current value. Relying on the appraisal, the buyer purchases. Later, critical opinion believes that the work was created by a different artist. The appraiser's liability to his client is the same as that of any other professional. A person with special knowledge or skill who performs services for others must do so with reasonable care consistent with those special skills. The question is whether the appraiser exercised the reasonable care that a professional appraiser would exercise. Determining the level of care that is reasonable for a professional appraiser is a question of fact; determining whether this appraiser failed to meet that level of care is also a question of fact. The profession of art appraiser is unregulated. There is no hard law on how an appraiser appraises. Attempts to prove professional standards may include soft law codes of professional practice by voluntary associations, such as the College Art Association Code of Ethics for Art Historians and Guidelines for the Professional Practice of Art History (1995), IRS guidelines for appraisers (especially when the appraiser is told that the appraisal is sought for tax purposes), and evidence of common practice in the industry. *Est. of Querbach v. A & B Appraisal Service*, Civ. No. L-089362-85 (N.J. Super. Ct. 1987).

ii. Liability to Third Parties

The person who commissions the appraisal is not the only potential plaintiff. In many situations, an appraiser can reasonably expect that the appraisal will be relied upon by others. For instance, where the owner of a painting commissions an appraisal and notifies the appraiser that he is planning to either sell or insure the painting, the appraiser can reasonably anticipate that the appraisal will be shown to and relied on by potential buyers in the first case and by an insurance company in the second.

The appraiser would only be liable to a third party if the appraiser had a duty to that third party. The scope of a professional's duty is a question of law. In most states, an appraiser has no duty to unspecified persons. A minority of states hold that an appraiser has a duty of care to anyone, whether specified or not, who is within a group that the appraiser can reasonably foresee would be supplied with the information the appraiser provides.

A lesser duty is likely to be imposed if the party seeking the appraisal has no long-term relationship to the appraiser, and if the appraisal is casual, and gratuitously given.

B. Third Party Liability: Defamation or Disparagement

An appraiser can be liable to a third party on grounds of defamation or disparagement.

Defamation requires a false statement damaging to the reputation of a person. In the context of an appraiser attributing a work to one artist, this will normally constitute an (implied) criticism of anyone who attributes the work to any other artist. The criticism might be that the attributor is incompetent, or that he is venal. The plaintiff bears the burden of proving that the appraiser's attribution is false. He also bears the burden of proving that the alleged defamation of plaintiff was reasonably understood by the public. His cause of action is subject to defenses based on freedom of speech.

Product disparagement requires words or conduct reflecting negatively on property. To state that a painting is not by Leonardo when the owner of the painting maintains that Leonardo painted it would reflect negatively on the painting's value. To succeed, plaintiff must establish that defendant's speech reduced the value of his property; that defendant's speech was false; that defendant communicated the falsity to a third person (publication); and that defendant acted with malice. Malice can be proven, or malice can be presumed when defendant unnecessarily interferes in the affairs of others with which he is not concerned. *Travis v. Sotheby Parke Bernet, Inc.*, Index No. 4290179 (Sup. Ct. Nassau Cnty Spec Term part V-D 11 November 1982).

The most famous of such cases is *Hahn v. Duveen*, 130 Misc. 871, 234 N.Y.S. 185 (Sup. 1929), where the renowned British art dealer, Joseph Duveen, awakened in the middle of the night by a telephone call from a Kansas City reporter, responded to the reporter that Mr. Hahn's painting of *La Belle Ferronière* could not possibly be by Leonardo because the Leonardo version of that work was hanging in the Louvre. In a later letter based on examination of a photograph, Duveen confirmed his view that the Hahn painting was not a Leonardo, and added that he believed along with most experts that the Louvre painting was likewise not by Leonardo. The court refused Duveen's motion for a directed verdict, holding that there was enough evidence to support a verdict for plaintiff had one been reached. Rather than retry the case, the parties settled, with a rumored substantial payment from Duveen to Hahn. In the 1990s, the Hahn painting was again not authenticated by the leading Leonardo scholar. It was sold in 2010 for a substantial sum as "not a Leonardo." A third version of the painting has now surfaced, which no one claims was by Leonardo.

C. Defensive Clawback: Abuse of Process or Malicious Prosecution

In short, it is not unusual for a person disappointed by a failure to authenticate, or a person who has relied on an authentication that later turns out to be questionable, to sue the appraiser. Most such suits have lost, and that is the end of it. But sometimes the mouse devours the hawk. In a case where an auction house asked an appraiser to authenticate a Charles Russell watercolor and the appraiser instead identified the artist as his own grandfather, Olaf Seltzer, the owner sued to force the appraiser to change his appraisal. That suit was dismissed, but Seltzer the appraiser incurred $45,000 in legal costs. The appraiser in turn sued the owner and his lawyers, including a large Los Angeles law firm, for abuse of process and malicious prosecution. Abuse of process occurs when one individual sues another to coerce the other to change his behavior from a behavior he has a right to enjoy. A trial award of

$1 million in compensatory damages, and punitive damages of $100,000 against the owner, $150,000 against his individual lawyer, and $10 million against the law firm, was upheld. *Seltzer v. Morton*, 336 Mont. 225, 154 P.3d 561 (2007).

D. Defense: Refusal to Authenticate or Contractual Protection

Because of the propensity to sue, some experts and foundations no longer offer authentication services. Others offer authentication services, but impose onerous contractual conditions on persons submitting work for authentication, such as promises by the owner not to sue or to indemnify the authenticator for any litigation expense, or requiring advanced approval of the owner to the authenticator marking the artwork inauthentic.

By law in France, one person is the recognized authenticator of an artist's work, subject to being overruled by a court, usually after a recommendation by a court-appointed master. In the U.S., there is no such law, but a small number of individuals hold enormous power over authenticating works. They are either the foremost scholars on the artist, usually the authors of the artist's *catalogue raisonné,* or a foundation established by the artist late in life or in his will.

While the failure of the foremost experts to authenticate has no legal significance, it may have enormous practical significance. Major auction houses may refuse to sell the work as by the listed author without an authentication by an expert. If the auction house does sell the work, the market will surely depress the price without authentication. In one case of disagreement among scholars, the failure of one scholar to include the work in the *catalogue raisonné* was estimated to have reduced the likely auction sale price to 25% of what it would have been had the author included it.

Authenticators' attempts to shield themselves from liability by exculpatory or indemnity clauses, or to permit them to mark the artwork, have been only partly successful. Those clauses may shield the authenticator from liability for negligence, but they are strictly construed to their precise terms. In *Foxley v. Sotheby's Inc,* 893 F.Supp. 1224 (S.D.N.Y. 1995), an exculpatory clause that did not cover gross negligence or bad faith did not exclude an action for gross negligence. In fact, exculpatory clauses are generally held ineffective where plaintiff alleges gross negligence or wilful misconduct. *Simon-Whelan v. Andy Warhol Foundation for the Visual Arts, Inc.*, 2009-1 Trade Cases ¶76,657, 2009 WL 1457177, 2009 US Dist LEXIS 44242 (S.D.N.Y. 2009). Though the liability is private, there is a public interest in keeping the potential liability as a way of policing extreme misconduct.

Even if such a clause is held valid, if an authenticator stamps a work "FORGERY," the authenticator may expose himself to liability to the artist for violating the artist's moral rights by modifying the work if the artwork is sufficiently recent to be subject to moral rights. See the Moral Rights chapter above.

Ironically, the authenticator who finds his imprimatur indispensable because the market demands it has no obligation to respond to a request to authenticate any work. In the absence of a contractual obligation, the authenticator has no obligation to make a decision—even in a world where the art market will take indecision as an indication of likely inauthenticity. *Thome v. Alexander & Louisa Calder Foundation*, 70 A.D.3d 88, 890 N.Y.S.2d 16 (2009).

6. Destroying a Forgery

At the end of the day, may a forgery be destroyed in order to prevent others from being defrauded by it in the future? If the owner of the work were willing to destroy it, that might seem like an ideal solution. But the owner of the work may be unwilling to destroy his own property. Even if the owner is willing to destroy the work, he might face liability for doing so if the forgery were created after 1990 (or earlier under some state statutes), as he violates the moral rights of whoever created the artwork under the Visual Artists Rights Act, 17 U.S.C. § 106A, or comparable state law.

Furthermore, the fact that the authenticator believes the work to be a forgery does not mean that a court will agree.

Perhaps the police power might be used to permit the state to destroy the work. There is no exception in VARA for action of the state, and there are no laws specifically permitting the government to destroy forgeries. There are statutes permitting the state to abate public nuisances. In one case, the New York Attorney General failed to convince a court that canvases in the style of famous painters like Picasso but signed with the forger's name that could be easily removed constituted a public nuisance. *State of New York v. Wright Hepburn Webster Gallery, Ltd.*, 314 N.Y.S.2d 661 (Sup. Ct. 1970), *aff'd* 323 N.Y.S.2d 389 (App. Div. 1971).

7. Antitrust and Trademark Actions

Disappointed owners often believe that there is some conspiracy afoot that violates the antitrust laws, the Lanham Act or other federal laws, and join those causes of action to common law and state statutory claims. Thus far, few plaintiffs have succeeded in proving those allegations, but the number of complaints alleging federal counts is increasing.

A. Antitrust

The first problem confronted under antitrust laws is defining the relevant product market. When alleging that actions with respect to the work of one artist violate the law, plaintiff must prove that the work of that artist is the relevant market. If the market includes several artists with similar styles and the defendant authenticates only one of those artists, there is unlikely to be an antitrust violation. Even less so if the market is defined as work by all abstract expressionists, and even less so if it is work by all artists working during the period. The relevant market may be determined by how sales are advertised, or whether alternate works would satisfy the same taste. *Vitale v. Marlborough Gallery*, 1994 Trade Cas. ¶70,654, 1994 U.S. Dist Lexis 9006 (S.D.N.Y. 1994). However, the opinions have been largely conclusory on this point, and do not seem to have required plaintiff to prove that potential buyers collect only the artist in question, or that if works by that artist are unavailable, they do not purchase works by other artists.

Next, plaintiff must prove either an attempt to monopolize by defendant, or an agreement among defendants to restrain trade in that market.

Finally, plaintiff must prove damages resulting from the agreement or monopolization attempt. Where plaintiff alleged that a conspiracy existed between the only two recognized authenticators of Andy Warhol's work to raise prices and to eliminate competing artworks by stamping them "Denied," plaintiff could not succeed on the price inflation count because he did not buy from one of the defendants and bought before the conspiracy began, but he did suffer damage due to marking his work "Denied." *Simon-Whelan v. Andy Warhol Foundation for the Visual Arts, Inc.*, 2009 WL 1457177, 2009-1 Trade Cas. (CCH) ¶76,657 (S.D.N.Y. 2009).

B. Trademark

In order to succeed under section 43(a) of the Lanham Act, plaintiff must prove a false designation of origin or a false description or advertisement of fact. Publishing a statement that a painting was not created by the person who in fact created it would qualify if it is stated as a fact, but not if it is stated as an opinion. The Lanham Act is designed to protect both the goodwill of the seller of goods and the ability of the consumer to distinguish between producers, but it gives no remedy to the consumer who is deceived. It is clear that the artist is protected by the Lanham Act, and so is his gallery. Courts have stated that a collector who holds a number of works by the artist and who attempts to sell some of them has a sufficient interest to invoke section 43(a). *Boule v. Hutton*, 70 F.Supp. 2d 378 (S.D.N.Y. 1999) *aff'd and vacated on other grounds*

328 F.3d 84 (2d Cir. 2003). Plaintiff must also show that public confusion is likely, which should be easy when a work by one artist is attributed to another.

Usually, plaintiff's Lanham Act problem is in finding that the false statement was used in connection with commercial advertising. Few authenticators actually sell goods, and in order to constitute commercial advertising, the statements must be disseminated to the purchasing public. That would be the case if the false authentication certificate were included in a gallery catalogue where the gallery held the work for sale, but not in a museum catalogue where the work is not for sale. Publication of a *catalogue raisonné* is unlikely to be sufficient for liability if the publisher does not also offer works for sale.

One attraction of a Lanham Act case is that attorneys fees can be awarded to the prevailing party "in exceptional cases," though exceptional cases are rare. 15 U.S.C. § 1117.

For further discussion of the use of trademark law, see the chapter on Trademarks above.

Checkpoints

- Authenticity of an art work may relate to the period in which it was produced, its condition, its state of restoration, and whether it was created by the named artist.
- Scientific evidence based on the materials used presently cannot prove which artist made a work but can conclusively establish that the work was not made by an artist if the materials were not used until after the artist's death.
- Provenance helps prove authenticity by showing the whereabouts of a work over time. It can be difficult to establish because records may be lost, never made, or fraudulent, and copies of the work may be made by the owner himself.
- Connoisseurship is the evaluation of a work by experts who compare its similarities or differences to other works reliably attributed to an artist.
- Buyers may recover damages from their sellers if purchasing a misattributed work through common law tort or contract recoveries and sales law statutes.
- To recover under fraud, a buyer must prove the seller made a representation he knew was untrue, the seller knew that a reasonable buyer would rely on that representation, and that the buyer actually relied on it. A negligent misrepresentation action has the same requirements except the buyer only needs to prove the seller was negligent in making the representation, not that the seller knew it was untrue. The buyer must also prove the seller owed the buyer a duty which does not typically exist between seller and buyer.
- If a seller promises to deliver a work and then delivers something else and the buyer reasonably relies on the seller's representation, the seller is liable. It is reasonable for a buyer to rely on a representation of fact but it is unreasonable

to rely on an opinion. Courts may distinguish between representations made before and after a purchase.

- Both the Uniform Sales Act and the Uniform Commercial Code hold sellers liable for breach of warranty for misattribution if buyer reasonably relied on the attribution.
- Buyers may include clauses in bills of sale expressly stating buyer reliance on seller's representations to assure that they have valid warranties. If buyer had an expert examine the work before sale, buyer is precluded from claiming reliance on an express warranty if the defect is one such an expert should have noticed.
- The statute of limitations to sue for breach of present warranty is four years from the time of delivery.
- A promise of future action is not breached and the statute of limitations does not begin to run until the future performance is due and not performed.
- The statute of limitations does not run if defendant fraudulently conceals the defect.
- When a seller is involved in a continuing course of action, the statute of limitations does not begin to run until the last action occurs.
- The doctrine of inherently unknowable injury, which extends the running of the statute of limitations until a plaintiff discovers or should have discovered an injury, has been extended to the recovery of property. Cases conflict on whether the discovery rule applies to buyers who purchase misattributed works.
- United Nations Convention on Contracts for the International Sale of Goods (CISG) is governing law for sales between residents of different countries that participate in the treaty. Auction sales are exempt, as are sales for personal, family, or household uses unless seller is unaware the buyer purchased the work for those reasons.
- CISG does not require reliance or being part of the bargain. It has no statute of limitation though the buyer must notify the seller of the specific lack of conformity to the contract within a reasonable amount of time of when buyer should have discovered it but in all cases within two years after delivery in order to contest the quality of the goods and recover.
- Many states have enacted art legislation to protect consumers. They generally do not require plaintiff to show that the attribution was part of the basis of the bargain, but may limit liability to situations where seller's representations were without a reasonable basis in fact at the time they were made.
- Auction houses often include provisions in their contracts that allow an auctioneer to rescind a sale if it determines it might be subject to liability from the sale, even without establishing lack of authenticity.
- The Federal Trade Commission (FTC) can sue to stop unfair and deceptive trade practices, even if the practices are truthful but deceptive to reasonable consumers. Past violations justify a preliminary injunction to prevent fraud before the trial ends.

- A person who knowingly sells inauthentic artwork may commit state or federal criminal offenses including mail fraud, wire fraud, and obtaining money by false pretenses.
- Scholars and appraisers are often used to prove or disprove authenticity. They may be liable for misattribution and subject to actions for malpractice, defamation, or product disparagement.
- Authenticators are liable to their clients for malpractice if they fail to use the special knowledge or skills they advertise. Appraisers are only liable to third parties if a duty of care to that party exists. Some states find a duty to anyone that the appraiser can reasonably foresee would be given the appraiser's appraisal.
- For an appraiser to be liable to a third party for defamation, the third party must prove an appraiser's attribution is false and was reasonably understood by the public, causing damage to the reputation of the third party. The appraiser may defend himself on freedom of speech grounds.
- For an appraiser to be liable to a third party for product disparagement, the third party must prove the appraiser's speech or conduct was false, the appraiser acted with malice, the appraiser communicated the falsity to another party, and it reduced the value of his property.
- Courts have held owners of misattributed work and their lawyers liable for compensatory and punitive damages for abuse of process and malicious prosecution when they unreasonably sue an appraiser and the suit is dismissed but the appraiser incurred substantial legal costs.
- Risk of suit has caused many experts to create exculpatory or indemnity clauses to shield themselves from lawsuits. These are usually ineffective against gross negligence and wilful misconduct allegations. There is no obligation to authenticate unless there is a contractual obligation.
- An artist's moral rights may be violated if anyone destroys or defaces a forgery.
- To succeed in an antitrust action against an authenticator, an owner must prove the work of the artist is the relevant market, that the defendant attempted to monopolize the market or there was an agreement among defendants to restrain trade in the market, and that the monopolization attempt or agreement caused damages.
- Trademark protects the goodwill of sellers. A plaintiff suing under the Lanham Act must prove a false designation of origin or false description or advertisement of fact, and must show that public confusion is likely.

Chapter 11

Title

Roadmap

After reading this chapter, you should understand:

- Warranty of title: A sale of art carries with it a warranty of title unless it is disclaimed.
- Voidable title or entrusted art: A buyer receives good title even though his seller had a voidable title, or if he buys in the ordinary course of business from a merchant who deals in goods of the same kind to whom the owner entrusted possession.
- Stolen art: A buyer does not receive good title to stolen art in the U.S. In some countries, a buyer receives good title to stolen art if he is a good faith purchaser or if he buys at a government sponsored auction.
- Not stolen art: Art is not stolen if it has been abandoned, gifted, willed or sold.
- Adverse possession: The possessor of stolen art can sometimes prevail using the doctrine of adverse possession, which requires open and continuous possession as owner for the period of the statute of limitations.
- When does the cause of action accrue? On the crucial question of when the cause of action accrues for stolen art, one jurisdiction holds that it is when the owner demands its return and is refused; others use the discovery rule which provides that the cause of action accrues when the owner discovers or should have discovered the facts necessary to sue if the owner has exercised due diligence; still others when the art is stolen.
- Despite the expiration of the applicable statute of limitations, through the end of 2026 the owner may sue within six years of actually discovering the facts needed to sue.
- Tolling of the statute: The statute of limitations does not run when the artwork is out of the jurisdiction or when it is being fraudulently concealed.
- Laches: The owner may be barred by laches if he delays bringing suit and the defendant is disadvantaged by that delay, such as by the death of witnesses.
- Civil Law prescription: Civil law jurisdictions have acquisitive prescription statutes giving a long-time possessor title, and a shorter period for a good faith purchaser to acquire title by prescription.

1. Seller's Obligation to Deliver Good Title

A seller of art, like a seller of other things, warrants that he is conveying good title to the art he sells, and that the purchaser is taking the artwork free of any unknown encumbrances, such as security interests. That warranty can only be negated if the buyer knew or should have known that the seller was transferring a more limited interest, such as only the interest the seller had. The rules for recovery generally follow the rules for recovery under warranty set forth in the chapter on Authenticity above with respect to the Uniform Sales Act, the Uniform Commercial Code, and the United Nations Convention on Contracts for the International Sale of Goods. If the sale is subject to the UN Convention, the buyer must give notice of the claim against the property within a reasonable time after he learns of it. UCC § 2-312; UN Convention on Contracts for the International Sale of Goods arts. 41, 43.

A. Remedies

While remedies for the breach of such a warranty on real estate are limited to the amount of the purchase price, a buyer who does not receive good title to artwork is entitled to the fair market value of the artwork at the time and place at which he must give it up, because that is the damage he suffers. With objects such as art that may substantially appreciate between the date of the sale and the date of the loss, the amount of the likely loss is difficult to predict and impossible to insure. *Menzel v. List*, 198 N.Y.S.2d 979 (N.Y. 1969). The seller's only protection would be to insert a clause in the contract that the seller is not warranting that he is conveying good title, or that the damages will be limited to the purchase price.

B. Voidable Title

Normally, in order to convey good title, the seller must have good title. But there are some cases where a seller can convey good title even when he does not have good title. A seller who has voidable title can convey good title to a good faith purchaser. A person has voidable title if he buys on credit and does not pay, or pays by a check that is later dishonored. UCC § 2-403(1). A good faith purchaser used to be a person who did know about the defect in the title and who made the inquiries appropriate to his status. A consumer needed to make no special inquiries, while a person who is an art dealer may be held to a higher standard, required to make the inquiries customary in the trade. *Porter v. Wertz*, 416 N.Y.S.2d 254 (Sup Ct App 1979).

The obligation to make customary inquiries sometimes applies where the custom in the trade is so slipshod as to be ludicrous. It makes little sense to talk about making customary inquiries when in the trade it is customary to make none. In a case where the purchaser (who was not an art merchant) knew who the owner of the painting was and bought from another who had acted as the owner's agent in the past but was not acting as the owner's agent in making the sale, the purchaser was protected because it was unusual in that art market to verify the agent's authority to sell. *Lindholm v. Brant*, 283 Conn. 65, 925 A.2d 1048 (2007). This was true despite the fact that the purchaser had asked for certain assurances that were not forthcoming, and bought despite lacking those assurances. Today, whether a consumer or a merchant, good faith requires honesty in fact, and the observance of reasonable commercial standards of fair dealing. UCC § 1-201(b)(20). It is unclear whether the latter phrase obliges the person to exercise reasonable commercial precautions, or whether it is limited to fair dealing in his decision making. The cases involving art merchants have interpreted it as requiring extra self-protective diligence. But this revision of the UCC has been adopted in only half the states that have considered it.

C. Owner Entrusts Artwork to Merchant Who Deals in Goods of That Kind

Another exception to the rule that the purchaser only receives the title his seller had is where the owner entrusts his artwork to a person who deals in goods of that kind and that person sells the artwork to a person buying in the ordinary course of the seller's trade or business. UCC § 2-403(2). This rule has been strictly applied. Where the owner entrusted his art to a person that he thought was an art dealer but was in fact a con man who had taken the name of a delicatessen employee, the owner had not entrusted his art to a dealer. Though the case did not specifically discuss it, it appears that the important question is not what is in the owner's mind, but to whom the goods are actually entrusted. *Porter v. Wertz*, 416 N.Y.S.2d 254 (Sup Ct App 1979).

The other part of the rule requires that the purchaser buy in the ordinary course of the seller's business. One only buys in the ordinary course if one is in good faith which, as indicated in the previous section, may depend on the jurisdiction. In *Porter*, it is doubtful if a sale by the con man to a person who was not a good faith purchaser who then resold the work to a good faith purchaser would result in the ultimate purchaser receiving good title.

2. Stolen Art

None of the above cases involved stolen art. The law in the United States on that point is clear and uniform. A purchaser from a thief gets no title, no matter how bona fide that purchaser may be. Likewise, the interposition of a long chain of bona fide purchasers between the thief and the current bona fide purchaser confers no title. The rule is otherwise in some countries whose legal systems are based on Roman law. Those countries choose to provide more protection to the security of commerce than to the security of title. They mostly have higher standards of diligence to qualify as a bona fide purchaser, but in those countries a bona fide purchaser from a thief will acquire title. *Bakalar v. Vavra*, 619 F.3d 136 (2d Cir. 2010).

Since the American rule on stolen art is clear and has no exceptions, one might wonder why there is so much litigation necessary to recover stolen art. The possessors of claimed stolen art usually respond with two kinds of defenses. One group of defenses constitute civil procedure defenses such as choice of law, lack of jurisdiction, and *forum non conveniens*, that are discussed in the chapter on International Litigation for Art Lawyers below. The other group of defenses are property law defenses. They contend either that the artwork was not stolen, or that the possessor has acquired title by adverse possession, or that laches applies.

A. Not Stolen but Abandoned

It may be contended that the property was not stolen. Instead, it was abandoned by its owner, with the result that the first person to reduce it to possession becomes the owner. Any property except a fee simple in land can be abandoned. Abandonment requires failure to use the property for a significant period of time and an intent to abandon. Failure to use is easy to prove; intent to abandon is not. Intent to abandon must be voluntary. Where the owner left his artwork in his apartment in Brussels while fleeing the advancing German army at the beginning of World War II, the court had no difficulty in finding that there was no intent to abandon the art. *Menzel v. List*, 267 N.Y.S.2d 804 (Sup. Ct. 1966). Likewise, where an Eastern European artist and his heirs left artwork with his gallery in Chicago for half a century through the depression, World War II and the Cold War, inquiring about it only at intervals of many years, the court held that the work had not been abandoned. *Mucha v. King*, 792 F.2d 602 (7th Cir. 1986).

A second, but undiscussed, aspect of these cases is that the property, while unused for a long period of time by the owner, was not put in a place where it was accessible to the public, which is the usual situation where abandonment is found.

Where property is put in a trashcan or left where it is accessible to the public, such as on the city-owned strip between the sidewalk and the street, a further question arises. Did the owner put it there? Artwork may be discarded by workmen hired to do a construction job, but they may not have been authorized by the owner of the work to abandon it. This is clearest when the art is owned by a public agency that takes decisions by votes.

B. Not Stolen but Bequested

In one case, it was alleged that the artwork was not stolen, but was left to the possessor by will. This defense was unsuccessful in part because the testator did not own the artwork at her death, and in part because the will purported to leave the artwork to her husband with a simple request that he leave it to the museum. Even had she owned the art, a request is not an effective testamentary disposition that would have conveyed a future interest to the museum. *Altmann v. Republic of Austria*, 317 F.3d 954 (9th Cir. 2002), aff'd 541 U.S. 677 (2004). But it is certainly possible to dispose of art either by will or by intestate succession.

C. Not Stolen but Gifted

I have not found a case that alleged that artwork was not stolen because the owner had given it to the possessor or his predecessor, but it is certainly possible. The possessor would need to prove the three elements of a gift—donative intent, delivery and acceptance, the most difficult of which is usually delivery. For more discussion about gift requirements, see the chapter on Taxes above.

One case in which this argument might have been raised, but was not, was *United States v. Portrait of Wally*, 2002 U.S. Dist. LEXIS 6445 (S.D. N.Y. 2002). In 1938, Ms. Bondi sold her Vienna art gallery to Mr. Welz as part of the Aryanization process. In 1949, the Austrian Restoration Commission restored the gallery to her, but *Portrait of Wally* was in the Belvedere Museum, and Ms. Bondi knew it. She explained that she did not sue the Belvedere, deeming any quarrel with the Belvedere "not possible" because the Belvedere is the museum of modern art in Vienna and she had just been reinstated as the proprietor of her modern art gallery in Vienna. While it might have been alleged that Ms. Bondi made a gift of Portrait of Wally, or more precisely of her cause of action to recover *Wally*, to the Belvedere, one might question whether there was donative intent or a realization of reality; there was certainly no delivery, either of the artwork or of a document conveying her cause of action.

D. Not Stolen but Sold

The most common allegation is that the work was not stolen, it was sold to a predecessor of the possessor. In the Holocaust years 1933–1945, a number of restrictions were placed on portions of the population subject to Axis control, notably Jews. Most specifically, many Jewish collectors and gallery owners were forced to sell their art under a policy of Aryanization to specific Nazis, usually at a fraction of its then fair market value. While all the forms of a sale were followed, no genuine sale took place because the arrangement was under duress. Just as a burglar who takes art from your house is no less a burglar if he leaves you $5 for it, these sales demonstrated the same lack of consent on the part of the sellers as the burglary. *United States v. Portrait of Wally, A Painting by Egon Schiele*, 2002 U.S. Dist. LEXIS 6445 (S.D.N.Y. 2002).

More difficult are the cases where an individual was so impoverished that his only resort was to sell his art. For instance, a manufacturer whose sole source of livelihood, his manufacturing plant, was confiscated in 1933, sold art at auction in Amsterdam to raise living expenses. While the Allied Military Command issued a presumption that any transfer of art by persons in persecuted groups in Axis-controlled territory 1933–1945 was involuntary, this sale did not occur in Axis-controlled territory, and it is likely that the presumption could be rebutted. The art was not taken by a government. Though the seller was under duress, it was not duress supplied by the ultimate buyer or persons with whom the buyer colluded.

One element tending to indicate duress is if the work is sold for substantially below its market value. That is difficult to prove unless the work is resold in the same market soon thereafter. A sale by a dealer would be expected to command a higher price than a sale by an individual, if only because the expected value of the warranty of title would be greater. A sale to a dealer is likely to be at a lower price than a re-sale by that dealer because of the dealer's expected profit margin. A sale in a local market is likely to be at a lower price than a sale in an international market because of the latter's larger number of potential buyers.

E. Proving that Art Has Been Stolen

Normally, the plaintiff bears the burden of proof, which means that in most cases, the owner or his descendant must prove that the art has been stolen.

New York has a different rule. Once the plaintiff makes a threshold case showing that he has an arguable claim that art has been stolen, the burden of proof shifts to the possessor to prove that the art was not stolen. It is impossible to prove a negative. The only way to prove that the art was not stolen is to prove that it was acquired by abandonment, gift, bequest, or sale. *Bakalar v. Vavra*, 619 F.3d 136 (2d Cir. 2010) is a good example of the results of that presumption. The owner of the drawing, who was imprisoned at Dachau, executed a power of attorney authorizing his wife to execute an inventory of his art work. She did so. A few days later, a Nazi estimator filed an identical inventory. The court held that this raised a presumption that the work had been stolen. There was further evidence that four hundred pieces of art were shipped out of Austria soon thereafter, but there was no inventory identifying those pieces. The work in question surfaced a dozen years after the war in the possession of the owner's wife's sister in Brussels. The current possessor, a remote grantee from the sister, could not prove that the work had not been stolen, so it was considered stolen as a matter of law. Had the question gone to the jury, there was enough evidence to find that this work was one of the four hundred shipped out of Austria, or that it passed from the owner to his wife when he died, then to her sister when she died.

Sometimes, proof that a work has not been stolen is found by the court in the subsequent action of the owner. An attempt by the owner to buy back the work that has allegedly been stolen may be seen as acknowledging the correctness of the possessor's title, rather than a desperate attempt to re-acquire a painting with sentimental as well as monetary value. This is especially true when no theft was reported. *In re Peters*, 821 N.Y.S.2d 61 (App. 2006). While this might be a logical inference in the United States in 2006, the court completely ignores the reality of life in Nazi Germany after 1933, where such a complaint would have been useless, especially for someone who had fled the country.

There is no such evidentiary presumption in most states.

The Federal Rules of Civil Procedure require more. In *U.S. v. Mask of Ka-Nefer-Nefer*, 2012 U.S. Dist. LEXIS 47012 (E.D. Mo.), the U.S. brought a forfeiture action under the National Stolen Property Act against the St. Louis Museum of Art. The court dismissed the action, holding that the government must file enough facts to enable the claimant to understand the theory of forfeiture, file a responsive pleading, and undertake an adequate investigation. The complaint only states that the mask was found missing in 1973. There was no evidence that it was either stolen or smuggled out of the country. The complaint does not state that the mask was stolen, when, where or why it was stolen, who stole it, or identify the law under which the mask was either stolen or illegally exported.

F. Adverse Possession

The most consistently asserted property law defense is that of adverse possession.

Adverse possession of personal property is adapted from the doctrine of adverse possession of real property. Back in medieval days in England, real property was transferred by the owner going on the land and handing the grantee a twig or a clod of dirt and mumbling some magic words in front of witnesses. But witnesses died, and before too many years, it was impossible for most people to prove that they owned land unless they were the descendants of the persons described as owners in Doomsday Book. So English statutes were passed providing that if a person had been in peaceful possession of land as owner for a period of time that finally settled at 21 years, that person would be considered the owner of the property from the time his possession began. Peaceful possession required that the person's possession be open, rather than hidden; continuous, rather than occasional; and not with the permission of the true owner, as would be the case for a tenant or a licensee.

This rule was imported into personal property. Little difficulty was found with its application to wagons or livestock, as their use would naturally be open. Applied to art, furniture, jewels or wine, whose use is normally private, problems were perceived, because the true owner would have no opportunity to discover who had his property. Also, the statutes of limitation for recovery of personal property were much shorter than those for recovery of realty, typically between two and six years.

The purposes of adverse possession are these. It bars litigation of claims so old that proof may be difficult because of fading memories or death of witnesses. It quiets title in the person who appears to the community to be the owner. It often protects good faith purchasers, as they have no reason to use the property other than openly (though good faith is not required in most states). Finally, it permits the termination of litigation at the pleading stage, before the large costs of discovery and trial are expended. An incidental result, though not a purpose, is that it deprives both the true owner and the false claimant of the opportunity to prove their cases if they have been insufficiently diligent.

The key to all the cases is that the statute of limitations does not begin to run until the cause of action accrues. With real property, the cause of action accrues when the person possesses the property. Previous serial trespasses do not count.

For personal property, different states apply different rules. The rule for realty might be applied; one state applies the demand and refusal rule; and some states apply the discovery rule.

i. When Does the Cause of Action Accrue?

a. Fraudulent Concealment and Property Outside the Jurisdiction

The statute of limitations does not run during periods of fraudulent concealment. It is difficult, if not impossible, to conceal land. It is quite easy to conceal personal property. In the simplest case, where an art thief places the art work in a safe deposit box, the statute does not begin to run until the thief is no longer concealing it. Likewise, the statute does not run while the stolen property is outside the jurisdiction.

ii. Demand and Refusal Rule

New York, the most important United States jurisdiction for art law because of the volume and prices of art sales there, follows the demand and refusal rule. That is, a cause of action does not accrue and the statute of limitations does not begin to run until the true owner demands the return of his property from the possessor and the possessor refuses to return it. This is a rule that is very favorable to the true owner, though it has its origin in a desire to protect the good faith purchaser. Originally, an action of replevin or trover would lie when the owner alleged a right to the chattel, followed by its loss through conversion, and the fact that it was in the possession of defendant. This was deemed sufficient for a defendant who knew he did not own the chattel, but to protect a good faith purchaser from unsuspected liability, a New York court in the 19th century required that the owner apprise the possessor of his right to the item and demand its return. The wrongful act was the refusal to return the item.

Taken to its logical conclusion, this means that the owner may not sue before making a demand and seeing it refused, and the statute of limitations only begins to run at that time. This has the curious result that the statute of limitations begins to run in favor of a thief much earlier than it runs for a good faith purchaser. *Menzel v. List*, 267 N.Y.S.2d 804 (Sup. Ct. 1966). There is no place in the statute of limitations defense to discuss whether plaintiff unduly delayed bringing suit. *Republic of Turkey v. Metropolitan Museum of Art*, 762 F.Supp. 44 (S.D.N.Y. 1990). But that fact is relevant to the laches defense discussed below.

iii. Discovery Rule (Discovered, or Should Have Discovered)

A number of jurisdictions, including most of those that have recently pronounced on the question, have adopted the discovery rule for determining when the cause of action accrues. The discovery rule provides that a cause of action accrues when the owner discovers or should have discovered all the information necessary to bring his cause of action, provided that the owner has been duly diligent in trying to locate his possession. The discovery rule has been widely adopted in tort cases, especially those involving medical malpractice where the plaintiff was unconscious (usually due to anaesthesia) when the negligence occurred, and makes perfect sense in that context. Its application to the recovery of stolen property is more problematic.

a. The Due Diligence Requirement

The first problem is that an owner is not entitled to the discovery rule unless he can prove that he was duly diligent in attempting to locate his property. How much diligence is due is essentially a fact question that results in an inability of lawyers to predict the likely result.

Situations that might show diligence include reporting the loss to partners, police, insurance companies, art loss registries, organizations of art dealers and major auction houses; hiring private investigators to search for the missing art; posting notices on the internet; advertising in art publications. More dubiously, courts have stated that advertising in international publications and pursuing claims for compensation from governments constitute due diligence. *Dunbar v. Seger-Thomschitz*, 638 F.Supp.2d 659 (E.D. La. 2009), incorrectly characterizing *Vineberg v. Bissonnette*, 548 F.3d 50 (1st Cir. 2008), where the court actually held that Bissonnette had abandoned the statute of limitations argument.

On the other hand, a person may make a perfectly rational decision to keep the loss private. He may fear that publicizing the loss will push the artwork even further underground. A museum may not wish to alarm potential contributors or attract undue attention from the state attorney general, who might wonder if the museum's trustees are exercising their required duty of care. *Solomon R. Guggenheim Foundation v. Lubell*, 77 N.Y. 2d 311, 569 N.E.2d 426, 567 N.Y.S.2d 623 (1991).

In weighing the steps necessary to find due diligence, courts have not always required plaintiffs to exhaust all possible avenues, and may be influenced by defendant's lack of diligence. *Autocephalous Greek-Orthodox Church of Cyprus v. Goldberg & Feldman Fine Arts, Inc.*, 717 F. Supp. 1374 (S.D. Ind. 1989), *aff'd* 917 F.2d 278 (7th Cir. 1990). Nor is it always clear whether the court is holding that the owner did not use due diligence, or that he should have discovered the whereabouts of the work at an earlier time. *Dunbar v. Seger-Thomschitz*, 638 F.Supp.2d 659 (E.D. La. 2009) *aff'd* 615 F.3d 574 (5th Cir. 2010).

Due diligence is required even when that diligence would not have discovered anything, *Erisoty v. Rizik*, 1995 U.S. Dist. LEXIS 2096 (E.D. Pa. 1995), though it is hard to understand why. If due diligence would have discovered something, the statute of limitations begins to run from the time it should have been discovered. If it would not have discovered anything, no one is prejudiced by allowing plaintiff the benefit of the discovery rule. The only sensible explanation for the requirement of due diligence is that a plaintiff who does not use due diligence has effectively abandoned his rights in the artwork. One court has suggested that the reason for requiring due diligence is to establish that the plaintiff's lack of knowledge was objectively reasonable. *Museum of Fine Arts v. Seger-Thomschitz*, 623 F.3d 1 (1st Cir. 2010). But the plaintiff's lack of due diligence is irrelevant if due diligence would have discovered nothing.

The most pernicious aspect of requiring due diligence is that it postpones a decision on whether the statute of limitations has expired. One of the reasons for the statute of limitations is to dispose of the case before both parties spend large sums of money preparing for trial. The decision of whether the owner has exercised due diligence can come only after extensive discovery, probably all the discovery that will occur in the case, and after a mini-trial on the question of due diligence. Under those circumstances, little expense is saved if the judge decides that the owner did not exercise due diligence and is therefore not entitled to the discovery rule.

b. Determining When the Owner Should Have Discovered

The second problem with the discovery rule is, assuming that the owner satisfies the due diligence test, the difficulty of determining when the true owner should have discovered all the necessary facts to sue. In theory, if the owner has exercised due diligence he will discover all the necessary facts when he in fact discovers them. But proof of that time lies peculiarly within the control of the owner, so there is likely to be substantial argument about the conclusions to be derived from knowing particular facts, when they should have been known, etc. However, any appearance of the artwork on the internet that identifies its location, at least today when the use of the internet is ubiquitous and "google" has become a verb as well as a noun, is the moment from which the owner should have known all he needs to know to institute suit. *Museum of Fine Arts v. Seger-Thomschitz*, 623 F.3d 1 (1st Cir. 2010).

In short, the discovery rule substantially prolongs the running of the statute of limitations, resulting in increased uncertainty and destroying one of the advantages of statutes of limitations, the disposal of lawsuits before discovery and trial make them really expensive.

What the discovery rule has animating it is that it appeals to a sense of fairness, in that an owner's rights are not foreclosed before he could reasonably have been expected to discover what he needs to know in order to sue.

c. Application of the Discovery Rule: O'Keeffe

A paradigm was the case that first brought the discovery rule to art law, *O'Keeffe v. Snyder*, 416 A.2d 862 (N.J. 1980). Georgia O'Keeffe, 92 years old at the time of the appeal, alleged that three of her paintings were stolen in 1946 from An American Place, the gallery run by her husband, the photographer Alfred Stieglitz. She never told Stieglitz about two of the three missing paintings. There was no police report, and the works were uninsured. While she discussed the loss with acquaintances in the art world, there was no general publicity until 1972, when O'Keeffe reported the theft to the Art Dealers Association of America. In 1975, O'Keeffe discovered that the paintings were in a New York gallery and, a few months later, that they had been sold to a New Jersey gallery.

The New Jersey gallery purchased the paintings from an Ulrich Frank, whose father, Dr. Frank, gave him the paintings in 1965. He exhibited two of them anonymously in a one-day show at the Jewish Community Center in Trenton in 1968. Frank does not know how his father acquired the paintings, but he recalls seeing them in his father's apartment in New Hampshire as early as 1941–1943. He claims that his father was distantly related to Stieglitz, which O'Keeffe denies.

Stieglitz died in the summer of 1946; Dr. Frank died in 1968.

The court held that the discovery rule applied, and remanded the case to determine whether Georgia O'Keeffe had used due diligence and when she should have discovered who had the paintings. The parties settled.

If the case were ever tried, its substantive issue was whether the paintings were stolen, or whether they were acquired by Dr. Frank by gift or sale. Two persons were in a position to give evidence on this point, Alfred Stieglitz and Dr. Frank, but both of them were dead. Their evidence was unavailable. That is one important reason to have a statute of limitations. One problem with the discovery rule is that it may delay the running of the statute of limitations so long that one party or both are deprived by death of vital witnesses in trying to prove the case.

iv. Absolute Discovery Rule

It had been suggested that California had an absolute discovery rule so that the statute of limitations did not begin to run in California until the owner discovered the facts necessary on the basis of *Naftzger v. American Numismatic Society*, 49 Cal. Rptr. 2d 784 (App 1996). In that case the court did not discuss when the plaintiff should have discovered the loss, only when the plaintiff did discover it. But in a later case applying California law, the Ninth Circuit did not even entertain that possibility. Elizabeth Taylor, the noted actress, purchased the painting involved at auction, and there was an article about the purchase in the newspaper. She also lent the painting to the Metropolitan Museum in New York for a four-month show where the painting was on display with an attribution of ownership to her. The court stated that either of those public appearances was enough that the plaintiff should have discovered all he needed to know. *Orkin v. Taylor*, 487 F.3d 734 (9th Cir. 2007). At that point there appeared to be no absolute discovery rule.

In 2002, the Holocaust Art Recovery Statute of Limitations allowed suit for the recovery of art stolen during the Holocaust against art professionals (museums, dealers, galleries or auction houses) through the end of 2010. That law was declared unconstitutional in *von Saher v. Norton Simon Museum of Art at Pasadena*, 592 F.3d 954 (9th Cir. 2010) because the federal pre-emption of state powers in the Holocaust art area under the foreign affairs power deprived the state of power to enact this law.

During the same year, California responded with a new law providing a 6-year limitation period for "specific recovery" from an art professional of fine art stolen from the owner by fraud or duress during the last century. The cause of action accrues when the owner actually discovers the whereabouts of the work and the fact that the owner has a right to it. CALIF. CODE CIV PROC. § 338 (c)(3). The new statute, which expired in 2018, was held constitutional because not directly targeted on foreign affairs in *Cassirer v. Thyssen-Bornemisza Collection Found.*, 737 F.3d 613 (9th Cir. 2013), so there was one absolute discovery statute of limitations.

v. The Traditional Rule: Cause of Action Accrues When Possession Begins

The rule for realty, and the traditional rule for personalty, was that the cause of action accrued when one person was in possession of the property of another, and the statute of limitations began to run at that time. No recent judgment has adopted that rule. Most jurisdictions have not had a recent case.

vi. HEAR Act through the End of 2026

In 2016, Congress passed the Holocaust Expropriated Art Recovery Act. This act did not repeal existing statutes of limitations, but provided that through the end of 2026, actions to recover art stolen 1933–1945 as a result of Nazi persecution may be brought either under the otherwise applicable statute of limitations, or six years after plaintiff actually discovers what (s)he needs to know in order to sue, whichever is longer. However, the takings clause of the constitution prevents the extension of a statute of limitations from taking a person's property, so the HEAR Act will have no effect if the defendant acquired the art by adverse possession or prescription prior to the end of 2016. It is likely to have little effect in New York, because most plaintiffs will file suit soon after their demand is refused. It may have significant effect in a discovery jurisdiction. See Herbert I. Lazerow, *Holocaust Art Disputes: The Holocaust Expropriated Art Recovery Act of 2016*, 51 INT'L LAWY. 195 (2018).

vii. Possession that Begins Permissive

Many possessions begin with the consent of the owner. They include leases, joint ownerships, and bailments. To start the running of the statute of limitations, something must occur to turn a permissive possession into a hostile one. For example, co-tenants are each entitled to occupy the land, so occupancy by one co-tenant does not begin the statute of limitations. The statute begins when the co-tenant in possession excludes from the property the co-tenant out of possession. In the case of a bailment, the statute of limitations is not set in motion until the return of the property has been demanded by the bailor and refused by the bailee. Alternately, the statute starts when the possessor's repudiation of the owner's title is clearly brought to an owner's attention. In *Bufano v. San Francisco*, 233 Cal. App. 2d 61, 43 Cal. Rptr. 223 (1965), the city or its predecessor retained possession of one of plaintiff's sculptures lent originally for a show. The court declined to find that the statute of limitations had begun to run when the artist was locked out of a studio where the work was stored, when the sculpture was lent by the city to the housing authority, moved to the dump, or moved to a sewage treatment plant, over the course of more than twenty years. One might also regard old loan laws, discussed below, as an exception to the rule requiring exclusion.

viii. Adverse Possession of Personal Property

The *O'Keeffe* court also decided that adverse possession should not apply to personal property. It did not nullify the application of statutes of limitation to actions for recovery of personal property. If the lower court had decided that Georgia O'Keeffe was barred from suing because she was insufficiently diligent, because of the doctrine of laches, or because she should have discovered all she needed to know more than six years before bringing her action, Snyder would retain possession of the paintings, but would not have title. Nor could he ever obtain title in New Jersey. Snyder could transfer his right to possession to anyone, but he could not convey title, as is required on a sale unless specifically disclaimed. Uniform Commercial Code § 2-312; CISG art. 41. Georgia O'Keeffe and her heirs would retain title forever, but have no right to reclaim the property. No jurisdiction has followed that part of the decision.

ix. Elements of Adverse Possession

Adverse possession requires that the adverse possessor must possess the property the way an owner would possess the property: it would be open, rather than hidden; continuous, rather than occasional; and not with the permission of the true owner, as would be the case for a tenant or a licensee. The sticky point for art is that a true owner would not normally possess art in a way that the public would know about. Indeed, one of the features of the art world is secrecy. Purchases at auction are more often than not made by agents who do not identify their principals.

It is unclear what possession is sufficiently open to satisfy the requirement. Ulrich's one-day exhibition at a venue not normally part of the art world was clearly not enough. Where a painting was purchased by a famous person, Elizabeth Taylor, so that the purchase was covered by the news media, and she was listed in the *catalogue raisonée* as owner, and the painting was included in a show at the Metropolitan Museum of Art for four months, and she unsuccessfully offered the work for sale at auction, for which auction there was a published provenance that listed her as the owner, it was held that her possession was sufficiently open to support her acquisition of title by adverse possession. *Orkin v. Taylor*, 487 F.3d 734 (9th Cir. 2007).

No cases have discussed the requirement that possession of artwork be continuous.

As to the third requirement commonly called hostility, it is clear that permissive possession does not lead to adverse possession, no matter how long it may last. In one case a painting by Gilbert Stuart was loaned to a museum for more than half a century. Since the museum's possession was with the consent of the painting's owner, the museum was unable to establish title by adverse possession. *Redmond v. New Jersey Historical Society*, 132 N.J.Eq. 464, 28 A.2d 189 (N.J. 1942). The same result occurred where the loan lasted sixty-four years. The statute did not begin to run until the executor demanded that the museum return the paintings. *In re Estate of McCagg*, 450 A.2d 414 (D.C. App. 1982). Also see *Houser v. Ohio Historical Society*, 62 Ohio St. 77, 403 N.E.2d 965 (1980).

However, some states have enacted old loan laws, providing that if there has been no contact between the lender and the museum for a set period (of between seven and twenty-five years), the museum may give the owner notice and, if the owner does not respond within a fixed period of time, the owner can no longer recover the artwork, and the museum obtains title because "[a] lender shall be deemed to have donated loaned property to a museum if the lender fails to file an action to recover the property on loan to the museum within the periods specified...." CALIF. CIV. CODE §§ 1899–1899.11.

Where there is no old loan law, state unclaimed property laws may result in the escheat of the work to the state.

x. Laches

The doctrine of laches has assumed great importance in New York because of the practical unavailability of the statute of limitations due to the demand and refusal rule. In *Solomon R. Guggenheim Foundation v. Lubell*, 77 N.Y.2d 311, 569 N.E.2d 426, 567 N.Y.S.2d 623 (1991), the Lubell's bought a painting from a reputable gallery twenty years before. That painting had been stolen from storage at the Guggenheim Museum. The court placed the burden of proving that the work was not stolen on Lubell, rejected an adverse possession defense based on the statute of limitations because of the demand and refusal rule, but remanded for a determination of whether the suit was barred by laches.

Laches is the equitable version of the statute of limitations. A person cannot bring suit if he was aware of his claim, he inexcusably delayed taking action, and the other party was prejudiced as a result. The parties settled in *Lubell*, so there was no determination of whether or how laches applied. In *Bakalar v. Vavra*, 819 F.Supp.2d 293 (S.D.N.Y. 2011), *aff'd per curiam* 500 Fed. Appx. 6 (2d Cir. 2012), the court found that the ancestors of the parties claiming to be the heirs of Fritz Grunbaum knew about their relationship and Fritz' death and did not proceed to assert their rights. This might have prejudiced the good faith purchaser of the property, because the person through whom he traced his title was alive at that time and could have provided testimony about how she acquired the drawing. In response to the claimants' argument that they should not be bound by their ancestors' actions, the court noted that otherwise the lawsuit would be re-set every generation. One might have added that they were bound by their ancestors' actions because they derived their rights in this case from their ancestors. In response to the argument that their ancestors could not have sued because they did not know who had the drawing and therefore did not know whom to sue, this went to the question of whether they unreasonably delayed. To determine that, the heirs must prove that their ancestors were reasonably diligent in searching for the painting.

Other courts are not so quick to credit lost testimony, and the trial judge has wide discretion in deciding whether to apply laches. In *Brady v. Garrett*, 66 S.W.2d 502 (Tex. Civ. App. 1933), the court refused to find laches when plaintiff, widow of Pat Garrett, waited more than twenty-eight years after the bailment was made to recover from the bailee the gun that killed Billy the Kid, during which period both the bailor and bailee had died. The purpose of the bailment, display of the gun in bailee's saloon, terminated fourteen years before suit was filed. Because the court found that plaintiff owned the gun, the fact that neither Garrett nor the bailee was alive to testify if there was any change in the bailment relationship was irrelevant because Garrett had no authority to sell or give the gun.

The net result of New York's combining the demand and refusal rule with laches is to come out relatively close to New Jersey's rule in *O'Keeffe*: all the facts and circumstances of the case must be examined, including the diligence of the owner and the good faith of the purchaser, before the substance of the case can move forward. That is expensive. At the end, if the purchaser prevails on grounds of laches, he does not have good title, just as in New Jersey. But as long as he maintains possession, no one can take the property from him.

xi. Epilogue on Adverse Possession: Who Wins?

In many cases involving attempted recovery of Holocaust art, plaintiff heirs are often peculiarly disconnected from the owners from whom the art was confiscated. Instead of being direct descendants, they are often quite collaterally related, or not related at all. Most of them never knew the original owner, and that is likely to be the case more frequently as time passes. Furthermore, they achieve their status as heirs in *ex parte* proceedings in which the person from whom they are claiming the art cannot participate. Fritz Grunbaum had different heirs in two different litigations. Cf. *Bakalar* with *In the Matter of the Grand Jury Subpoena Duces Tecum Served on the Museum of Modern Art*, 719 N.E.2d 897 (N.Y. 1999). While these matters should have no bearing on the outcomes of the cases, one might note that close relatives who personally knew the original owner from whom the art was confiscated have generally fared well. On the possessor's side, United States museums have had more success at retaining art than have foreign museums, with private individuals in between.

xii. Prescription in Civil Law Countries

There are similar rules in countries whose legal systems are based on Roman law that terminate litigation (extinctive prescription) or award title (acquisitive prescription) after a specified period of time. While the rules vary from country to country, they can be grouped into several classes.

In all cases, there is an absolute period of time beyond which the owner cannot sue to recover the property. In France, this used to be thirty years under former article 2262 of the French Civil Code; it has been reduced to 20 years in 2008 by article 2232. In Germany, it is thirty years. BGB § 197(1)2. In some countries a good faith purchaser acquires title in a shorter period than one who knows about the theft. BGB § 937. A palimpsest, a Greek manuscript overwritten with medieval liturgical texts, disappeared from a library in Constantinople after 1906 and turned up in the collection of a French civil servant in the 1920s. It was sent to auction at Christie's in New York in the 1990s. The court ruled that New York choice-of-law doctrine would have chosen French law, whose prescriptive provisions confirmed the French civil servant's title. If New York law had been selected, the court said in dictum that laches would bar the original owner's suit because the delay in suing encompassed the death of the civil servant, who was the only possible witness to his original acquisition of the palimpsest. *Greek Orthodox Patriarchate of Jerusalem v. Christie's*, Inc., 1999 U.S. Dist. LEXIS 13257, 1999 WL 673347 (S.D.N.Y. 1999).

In some countries, a good faith purchaser, even from a thief, acquires title immediately. BGB § 932. In some countries any purchaser at a government-run sale acquires good title.

The definition of a good faith purchaser varies from country to country, but in general, it requires both that the person not know of the theft, and that the person exercised the sort of diligence in his purchase that a reasonable buyer would exercise.

Checkpoints

- Sale of an artwork carries with it a warranty of title unless title is disclaimed.
- A buyer receives good title if his seller had good title, or if he is a good faith purchaser and seller either had voidable title, or is a merchant who deals in goods of the same kind who was entrusted possession by the true owner and the buyer buys in the ordinary course of his seller's business.
- A buyer of stolen art does not receive good title in the U.S. In some civil law countries, a buyer receives good title to stolen art if he buys in good faith or if he buys at a government-sponsored auction.
- Art is not stolen if it has been abandoned, gifted, willed or sold. Each of those transfers must be voluntary.
- A person who is in open and continuous possession as owner of artwork for the period of the statute of limitations is the owner of it.
- The cause of action for recovery of artwork accrues in one jurisdiction when the owner demands its return and is refused; others use the discovery rule which provides that the cause of action accrues when the owner discovers or should have discovered the facts necessary to sue if the owner has exercised due diligence; still others when the art is stolen.
- Despite the expiration of the applicable statute of limitations, through the end of 2026 the owner may sue within six years of actually discovering the facts needed to sue.

- The statute of limitations is tolled when the artwork is out of the jurisdiction or when it is being fraudulently concealed.
- If the statute of limitations has not expired, the owner may be barred by laches if he delays bringing suit and the defendant is disadvantaged by that delay, such as by the death of witnesses.
- Civil Law jurisdictions have acquisitive prescription statutes giving a long-time possessor title, and some have a shorter period for a good faith purchaser to acquire title by prescription.

Chapter 12

Commercial Art Relationships

Roadmap

After reading this chapter, you should understand:

- Contracts commissioning art should be in writing to fix what is to be produced, define the warranty, provide security for performance, specify a time of completion, and provide for dispute resolution.
- Buying existing art: A sale of goods requires compliance with the statute of frauds.
- Agency relationships are established when an artist sells through a dealer. Those relationships require the dealer to observe a duty of loyalty to the artist that forbids conflicts of interest.
- Art consignments at common law are bailments imposing different duties on the agent depending on whether the bailment is for the benefit of one of the parties or for mutual benefit.
- Art consignment damage liability: Special art legislation often provides that consignee is absolutely liable for loss or damage.
- Art consignments payment to consignee at common law leaves the consignor as a general creditor, but special art legislation often gives consignor priority by establishing a trust relationship.
- Creditors of consignee prevail over consignor under the UCC unless consignor takes special steps. Recent UCC amendments exempt consumer goods from this rule. Special art legislation often gives consignor priority.
- Agency agreements are normally construed according to the contract. Default rules require that the agent exercise a duty of loyalty and a duty of care to the principal.
- Other duties: Friends and business acquaintances of artists may be asked to undertake other duties, such as executors of wills or trustees of foundations. The standards applicable to them will be different than if they were just friends or business acquaintances, as they will be judged by the standards of executors or trustees.
- Auctions create agency relationships that are usually successfully modified by the specific terms of the auction house's contract.

1. General Overview

This chapter deals with the commercial relationships involved in the purchase, sale and financing of art. More specifically, each player in the art world—the artist, the collector, the gallery owner, the dealer, the auctioneer, and the bank that uses artwork as security for a loan—may form relationships with any of the other players. The law will establish the default rules for those relationships, which are often modified by contract. The initial default rules are often the law of agency, sometimes modified by specific art-related legislation.

2. Purchasing Art Directly from the Artist

A. Commissioned Work

The main legal aspects of a contract to commission work from an artist were in place as early as 1466 when Sr. Bernardo de Lazzaro (no relation that I can establish) employed Master Pietro Calzetta (1435?–1500?) to paint the chapel of the Eucharist in the church of St. Anthony in Padua.

i. Contract in Writing

The contract is in writing and signed by all the parties to be charged, thus satisfying the requirements of most states' statutes of frauds, and the work was to be completed in less than one year (in fact, less than six months, by Easter 1467, which was March 31). In some jurisdictions, there may be doubt about whether a commission to deliver a painting (or in this case to decorate a chapel) is a contract for the sale of goods or a contract to provide personal services. Usually they will be classified as service contracts because the principal value is the skill and expertise of the individual, but one should not forget that in addition to painting, there are goods provided in the construction of the altarpiece and the curtain covering it. A case in which the contract was held to not violate the statute of frauds because it could be performed within one year without discussion of whether it was provision of services or a sale of goods was *Foxley v. Sotheby's Inc,* 893 F.Supp. 1224 (S.D.N.Y. 1995). Plaintiff alleged an oral contract whereby if he withdrew a Cassatt from defendant's auction but left his other consignments, defendant would reimburse him for what he paid for the Cassatt. The court obviously assumed that it was a service contract because it used the statute of frauds for services.

A prudential reason to have a written contract, even where one is not required by law, is that disputes might arise about the terms of the contract. In *Brockhurst v. Ryan*, 2 Misc.2d 747, 146 N.Y.S.2d 386 (Sup. 1955), the client contended that the oral contract was for portraits of his wife and two of his three children, but the court found that the contract was for all five members of the client's immediate family. That dispute could have been avoided by a written contract.

ii. What Is to Be Produced

The obligations of the painter are set forth in some detail in the 1466 contract. He is to fresco the ceiling with four prophets on a blue background with stars in fine gold. The marble and Sr. Bernardo's heraldry is to be in blue and gold. (Blue and gold were the most expensive colors, as gold was made from real gold, and blue was made by crushing imported ultramarines.) Some things are to be done to a standard of "fine," others to a standard of "good." The altarpiece is to rise all the way to the vault, and to contain a design which is attached to the contract, made by Niccolo Pizzolo (1420?–1453) owned by Francesco Squarcione (1395?–1468?). (Both Calzetta and Pizzolo were apprentices of Squarcione. Pizzolo was killed in a street brawl. There is no mention in this contract of a payment to Squarcione by either de Lazzaro or Calzetta for the use of the design. That may have been a professional courtesy, or it may be in a separate contract that has been lost.) There is no statement in the contract about what part of the work must be done by Calzetta himself, but he is responsible for the quality of all of the work.

iii. Warranty

Calzetta gives a twenty-five-year warranty on the work. The remedy is specified as damages and interest.

iv. Security for Performance

Calzetta also provides a performance bond in the form of the promise of Galeazza Musatto, presumably a person of means, to make it good if Calzetta defaults. The contract does not reveal if Calzetta paid Musatto for the guarantee.

v. Time for Completion

The contract provides for completion by Easter 1467. The wise commissioner will provide a completion date. In default of anything specific, the parties may argue about what a reasonable time for completion might be. If there is no time for completion in one contract, but a deadline set in another, the artist is likely to devote his time to the work with the specific deadline.

vi. Price and Payment Methods

De Lazzaro, for his part, agrees to a price of 40 ducats, with an advance deposit of 10 ducats to allow Calzetta to purchase materials and start the work, and a periodic payment of another 10 ducats when Calzetta completes the altarpiece. The bigger the job, the more likely the artist will demand a deposit and periodic payments. In neither *Wolff* nor *Brockhurst* below was there an initial deposit, but *Brockhurst* provided for payment when each of the portraits was delivered. The better practice is to require both a deposit and periodic payments, especially where, as in a portrait of a person who is not famous, the work would be unsalable if the commissioner breaches the contract or goes bankrupt.

vii. Implied Terms

Terms may be implied in an artist's contract. Where activities are necessary to permit the contract to be performed, a court will read promises about those activities into the contract. For instance, it is common to do portraits from life. The subject of the portrait spends time modeling for the artist. Where there is a contract to paint someone's portrait, the court will imply a promise that the commissioner will produce the subject for a reasonable number of sittings when that is within the commissioner's power, as it would be if the subject were the person who commissioned the portrait or a close family member. Brockhurst was held in breach for failure to sit and to produce his son for sitting.

One could imagine a similar result had de Lazzaro taken away Calzetta's keys to the chapel, thereby preventing Calzetta from completing his promised performance.

viii. Dispute Resolution

One item that is missing from the contract is a dispute resolution clause. In case of disagreement, who will determine whether the work is "good" or "fine" as promised, or whether it complies with the other requirements of the contract? No such clause was necessary because it was understood that such a dispute would be settled by a jury of masters of the guild (*arte* in Italian) to which Calzetta belonged.

In commissions of artwork, it is not uncommon to provide that the work will be satisfactory to the client. This raises the question of whether the client's judgment can be absolutely subjective, as implied by the words, or whether the client is limited by some objective standard. In *Wolff v. Smith*, 303 Ill.App. 413, 25 N.E.2d 399 (1940), the court divided the world of contracts into those producing functional items, where an objective standard would prevail, and those involving taste, where the client's decision was not subject to external review.

There are other cases providing that similar language appoints the client as an arbitrator. An arbitrator must make his decision in good faith. The court does not discuss this, but it appears that the client in *Wolff* might have met this standard, because he assigned a number of reasons why the portrait of his deceased father did not please him, including differences from a previous portrait the artist had made of his father.

The completely subjective standard may result in there being no contract. In general, when one party has the ability to avoid a contract at his discretion, it is implied that the other party has a like ability. However, that will not help the artist who has already completed the portrait. No contract means no payment.

Where no standard is expressed for a commissioned portrait, the question is whether the portrait shows a reasonable likeness to the sitter. In *McCrady v. Roy*, 85 So. 2d 527 (La. App. 1956), the court said: "[T]he portrait fails to depict a reasonable likeness of Mrs. Roy. She is an attractive woman of refined and relatively youthful appearance, possessed of fine regular features, good coloring and of a slight trim figure, whereas the portrait reveals a buxom, unattractive middleaged woman, lacking in refinement of appearance and possessed of coarse features." The artist argued that this was his interpretation of Mrs. Roy. This reminds one of the (perhaps apocryphal) delivery by Picasso of his portrait of Gertrude Stein. She exclaimed, "But it does not look like me!", to which Picasso responded, "It will."

ix. Sales, Use and Value Added Taxes

One matter not dealt with in the 1466 contract is taxes. In Europe, there is likely to be a value added tax, which is normally included in the final price. In the United States, there will be a sales or a use tax if it is a contract for the sale of goods, and that tax may apply to the provision of services in some states. Normally, the sales or use tax is added to the contract price. It is good practice to specify in the contract whether the price includes taxes, or whether they will be assessed additionally.

x. Copyright

In the absence of a specific promise that the artist will assign the copyright in writing, the copyright for the work remains with the artist. If the person commissioning the work can conceive of a circumstance under which he would want to display the work without the artist's name, or to modify or destroy the work, permission to do the act contemplated should be incorporated in the commissioning contract with sufficient specificity to meet the requirements of VARA. See the chapter above on Moral Rights.

xi. *Choice of Law*

If there is any hint that the transaction has contacts with more than one jurisdiction, it would be prudent to insert a choice of law clause in the contract so that the parties do not at a later date argue about what law should apply. This would be useful if the parties are residents of different states, or if the work is to be made or installed in a state other than the common residence of the parties, or is to be financed by an entity from another state.

xii. *Public Commissions, or Commissions Under Percentage for Art Rules*

The most common public commissions are to decorate government buildings. One might also receive a commission under a percentage for art rule, that requires that a certain percentage of the cost of a building, sometimes a public building, sometimes a privately-owned building, be devoted to the purchase of artwork for the building. Most of the rules discussed above will be the same. There are several differences. A public commission may pose a problem of enforcement unless the public entity has waived its sovereign immunity. There are some special rules when dealing with government contracts that are beyond the scope of this work. There may be special requirements to invoke a statute of limitations against the government.

B. Buying Already Completed Works from the Artist

When buying completed work from an artist, it is clear that there is a sale of goods that is likely to be governed by the Uniform Commercial Code or the Convention on Contracts for the International Sale of Goods (CISG), depending on the circumstances.

i. *Statute of Frauds*

The Statute of Frauds will apply if the contract is governed by the Uniform Commercial Code (but not if governed by CISG; see art. 11) requiring a writing signed by the party to be charged if the sale price exceeds $500, and it is unwise to rely on being able to invoke an exception, such as judicial admission or promissory estoppel. *Hoffman v. Boone*, 708 F.Supp. 78 (S.D.N.Y. 1989); *Marvin Inc. v. Albstein*, 386 F.Supp.2d 247 (S.D.N.Y. 2005). Promissory estoppel is difficult to prove as it requires an unambiguous promise, foreseeable reliance on that promise, and an unconscionable injury. It is unclear what might qualify as an unconscionable injury, but courts have refused to place travel expenses, embarrassment, disappointment, or foregoing other business opportunities in that category. If you cannot get past the Statute of Frauds defense, you cannot present your case to the trier of fact.

Sometimes, the Statute of Frauds can be navigated by putting together different documents to prove that there is a contract, but that technique requires the right circumstances. In *Phoenix Ancient Art, S.A. v. Kimbell Art Foundation*, 2003 WL 227905119 (S.D.N.Y. 2003), plaintiff alleged a sufficient writing based on a receipt, a repurchase agreement, minutes of the defendant's board, and a draft contract. Several of those documents were signed by Kimbell, but neither individually nor collectively did they purport to be a contract. The board resolution authorized the staff to make the purchase, but the resolution itself did not constitute an acceptance of the offer.

One other escape from the UCC Statute of Frauds is available where there is a deal between merchants evidenced by a writing that is not objected to within ten days by the party to be charged. UCC § 2-201(2). In *Phoenix*, Kimbell objected within ten days.

ii. Valid Contract

There must also be a valid contract. Whether there is a contract depends on whether the parties objectively intended to be bound. To determine this, the court considers whether the parties have expressly reserved the right not to be bound absent a written contract, whether there has been partial performance, whether the parties have agreed to all the terms, and whether the agreement is of a type that is usually in writing. In finding that there was no contract, *Phoenix Ancient Art, S.A. v. Kimbell Art Foundation*, 2003 WL 227905119 (S.D.N.Y. 2003) said that the Kimbell had declined to be bound before receiving both a bill of sale and warranty form as "condition of purchase"; that there was no part performance, as the sculpture in question had been shipped to Kimbell as security for another agreement; that the parties had not agreed to all terms, as there were still blank spaces in the documents to be completed; and that not only was it common for an art purchase for $4 million to be in writing, but the parties' course of dealing had been to reduce everything to writing, and that had been plaintiff's uniform custom for all sales in excess of $1 million.

iii. Performance

The warranties set forth in the previous chapters are applicable, and the artist is a merchant who regularly sells goods of that kind. The terms of the contract may be supplied by course of performance, course of dealing or usage of trade. UCC § 1-303; CISG art. 9.

iv. Licensing Requirements

The artist who sells his own work may require a license from the local authorities. For discussion of the constitutional right to sell art in public, see the Freedom of Expression chapter above.

3. Artists or Collectors Who Sell Through Galleries or Dealers

A. Sale to a Gallery or Dealer

It is not unusual for a gallery or a dealer (collectively a dealer) to buy a significant number of works of the artist for re-sale, though this is much more common in Europe than in the United States. No special relationship between the artist and the dealer arises. The dealer owns the work and has no obligation to the artist other than to pay the artist the price for the work.

As a variation on outright sale, a dealer may agree to buy all of an artist's work for a specified period. A century ago, such a purchase usually involved periodic payments that enabled the artist to pay the rent and eat while he produced the work.

The artist might give the dealer an option to buy a specific work at a specific price, or a right of first refusal to acquire any of his works at the price offered by a third party. In none of these cases is the relationship between the artist and the dealer anything other than seller and buyer.

This sort of arrangement is not currently common in the United States, so it is unlikely that there would be any trade usages applicable. But there might be a course of performance or course of dealing that would supply the terms of such a contract.

B. Agency Relationships

An artist and a dealer may enter into an agency relationship where the dealer will represent the artist. While the nature of the relationship depends on the agreement, the agent generally has both a duty of loyalty and a duty to exercise due care in executing his responsibilities to his principal. An agent entrusted with art with authority to sell it cannot buy it for his own account, even for more than the requested sales price, without informing the artist that he is the buyer. An agent's duty of loyalty to his principal includes avoiding conflicts of interest. *Est. of Franz Kline*, N.Y.L.J. March 31, 1964 (N.Y. Sup. 1964), at 14, held that no sale could have taken place between the artist and his agent because the later-deceased artist was never notified of the agent's desire to purchase.

i. Consignment

a. As Bailment

A consignment is an agreement where the owner of property entrusts the property to an agent with authority to sell the property. The owner retains title to the property until it is sold to the purchaser. In the United States, consignments are the typical way in which art is sold. In more than half the states, there is specialized art legislation, designed to protect both the consumer and the artist. Those laws differ from state to state, but they generally provide that where an artist puts his artwork in the hands of a person who is an art merchant for purposes of sale, there is a consignment unless the artist has actually been paid for the work. CALIF. CIV. CODE § 1738–1738.8. In some states, the statute also benefits the artist's heirs if the artist is deceased.

In consignments, as well as in other relationships where an artist or collector entrusts artwork to an agent, the agent's technical status is a bailee of the art for mutual benefit. That is also true when an artist or collector lends art to a museum for a temporary show. Such a bailee is generally liable if his negligence results in damage to the artwork, and is absolutely liable for misdelivery. In *Tytla v. Shortell*, No. CV 9103977318 (Conn. Super. 1993), plaintiff exhibited at defendant's gallery. There was no alarm system. Three of plaintiff's paintings were stolen in a burglary. The court refused summary judgment, commenting that failure to redeliver property in the same condition in which it was received raises a presumption of bailee's negligence. Whether defendant bailee breached his duty of due care by not having an alarm system, whether plaintiff artist's failure to request security discharges defendant's duty, and whether not having an alarm system was the proximate cause of the loss, are all questions of fact for the jury.

Two cases with similar facts reached different results, perhaps based on classification of the bailment. Both involved jewelers who lent their jewelry to museums for exhibition. Both had their jewelry placed in locked display cases, and it was stolen. In *Colburn v. Washington State Art Ass'n*, 141 Pac. 1153 (Wash. 1914), the court held this a bailment for mutual benefit, though it did not specify why. Perhaps it thought that the jeweler's chance of selling this or similar jewelry would be enhanced by exhibition. As such, plaintiff needed to prove negligence, and the court held as a matter of law that there was no negligence where the jewelry was placed in a locked showcase. In *Gardini v. Museum of the*

City of New York, 19 N.Y.S.2d 96 (N.Y. City Ct. 1940), the court characterized the bailment as gratuitous, and said the failure to deliver the diamond brooch at the end of the bailment raised a presumption of negligence, which defendant had not overcome by proving that the display case was locked, where the key was kept in the manager's office desk which was locked except when it was broken open and not repaired for some time. The court disregarded a statement in the receipt that the Museum would not be responsible for taking more means to safeguard items entrusted to it than it took to safeguard its own items.

In most states with art legislation, the consignee is absolutely liable for damage or loss of the artwork, without the artist having to prove any fault on the part of the consignee. The important question is the measure of damages. In *Pelletier v. Eisenberg*, 177 Cal. App. 3d 558, 223 Cal. Rptr. 84 (1986), nine of the ten paintings that the artist consigned to the gallery were destroyed or damaged in a fire. The gallery argued that its liability should be limited to the amount it would have paid the artist had each work been sold: the agreed-upon purchase price less the agreed-upon commission. The court held that the artist was entitled to the fair market value of the works without diminution for commissions because the work was not sold. Had the work been sold, the artist would have reaped reputational benefits of being an artist that people wanted to buy, and his works would appear in public in the future if sold or lent by the purchaser. Where the work is destroyed, the artist does not reap those benefits. On the other side, the court pointed out that the gallery was only entitled to a commission if it sold the work; the gallery has not earned a commission where the work is destroyed, rather than sold. This is consistent with the measure of damages in the law of bailments. If the bailee is liable, it is for the undiminished fair market value of the bailed property.

b. Construction of Art Legislation

Courts have tended to construe art legislation in ways favorable to the artist, in accord with the purpose of the legislation, and to be liberal in granting preliminary relief. In *Wesselman v. International Images, Inc.*, 645 N.Y.S.2d 263 (Sup. 1996), the court held that a corporation could be an artist if it was the corporation that was producing the work, and that a dealer included people who published or sold art prints, even if the actual printing was done by employees or subcontractors. It was not necessary for the artist to deliver print masters directly to the dealer; the statute was invoked even if they were indirectly delivered. Most important for the artist trying to recover the prints, the court issued a preliminary injunction ordering the dealer to deliver the prints to a neutral third party pending the litigation because the artist had demonstrated a likelihood of success on the merits. It was uncontested that the dealer was selling work and not remitting the proceeds, and the possibility of irreparable injury existed because the prints had been moved to Florida so possibly beyond the effective jurisdiction of the court, and the proceeds from sale of the prints might not be recoverable because the dealers were divorcing and in a questionable financial situation.

Some (but not all) preliminary relief was provided in *Nabor v. Steinitz*, N.Y.L.J., Jan. 27, 1992, at 24 (Sup. 1992). Defendant gallery agreed to give plaintiff artist a show and spend $27,300 to produce art for the show in return for two paintings plus ten percent of the value of any sculpture produced during the show. Plaintiff, who had provided twenty-four of fifty works for the show before the agreement was made, sought return of all fifty pieces of artwork. The court issued a preliminary injunction for return of the twenty-four works delivered which were a consignment and a trust about which the court found that plaintiff was likely to succeed, but not for the twenty-six later works the ownership of which is disputed in the suit. There is always irreparable harm because artwork is unique. Balancing the equities, the court found none for the gallery, and thought that the artist needed to have some work he could sell during the pendency of the litigation because a person should not be deprived of his livelihood.

c. Determining if the Arrangement Is a Sale or a Consignment

When an arrangement between an artist and a dealer is called either a sale or a consignment, that is not determinative. It depends on the substance of the arrangement. In *Matter of Friedman*, 64 A.D.2d 70, 407 N.Y.S.2d 999 (1978), the artist's widow entered into an agreement with a gallery in which she transferred ownership to the gallery. The gallery owner promised to put the work in condition for sale, use his best efforts to sell the work, and remit half the amount collected from the sale of the work. The gallery owner held the works for fourteen years before suit was brought. An exhibition of Friedman's works from which nothing was sold had been held, and the gallery owner sold one picture five years later at a much lower price than had been asked at the exhibition. The ambiguous terms of the agreement were clarified by the fact that normally an outright sale is for a sum certain, that later-enacted art legislation "clarifying" previous law defined this as a consignment, and that the gallery owner had made certain statements inconsistent with full ownership. It being a consignment, that relationship was terminated by the consignor's death. The paintings were ordered returned to the heirs after discussion in dicta of both substantive and procedural unconscionability in setting up a relationship the full nature of which was unexplained and put the gallery owner in a position of conflict of interest.

d. Sale of the Artwork

On sale of the artwork, the purchaser receives good title. If the agent has sold following the owner's instructions, the owner's title is conveyed to the purchaser. If the agent has violated the owner's instructions in selling for too little, the purchaser, if buying in the ordinary course of the agent's business, receives good title under UCC § 2-403, as discussed in the chapter on Title above.

When the agent receives full payment from the purchaser, that extinguishes any liability the purchaser might have to the owner. The agent now owes the owner the purchaser price less the agreed-upon commission. *Graffman v. Espel*, 1998 U.S. Dist. LEXIS 1339 (S.D.N.Y. 1998). That places the artist in no better position than any other general creditor. It was not uncommon for artists not to be paid by their agents. Art legislation usually provides that the proceeds of sales are trust property held for the benefit of the artist. The result of that is that the artist is entitled to payment from the gallery, and is entitled to trace the funds and receive payment from whomever has received those funds from the agent. CALIF. CIV. CODE §§ 1738–1738.8.

e. Security Interests

It is not usual for galleries to borrow money. Borrowers frequently take security interests in property owned by the gallery. Usually, a gallery has very little that can be used as security for the repayment of a loan other than its inventory. With inventory financing, it is common to give a security interest that includes after-acquired inventory, which was the case in *Rayfield Investment Co. v. Kreps*, 35 S.3d 63 (Fla.App. 2010). Kreps, a collector, had consigned his painting to a gallery for sale that had previously given a security interest in its inventory. When the gallery did not repay the loan, the lender foreclosed. The court held that Kreps' painting was an asset on which the lender could foreclose. UCC § 2-236 classifies a consignment as a security interest. A perfected security interest has priority over a subsequent unperfected security interest. The lender had filed a financing statement, thereby perfecting his security interest.

The court stated that Kreps could only prevail on one of three conditions. He could have prevailed had he tagged his painting as being his and with the gallery on consignment; the gallery could have posted a notice that some of its goods were there on consignment; or the consignor could have perfected his interest with a UCC filing. It apparently does not matter that the consignee could remove the tag or the sign that consignor posted when consignor brought his painting. Alternatively, the court states that the consignor would win if the consignee was generally known to creditors as selling the goods of others. The trial court had found that this lender not only knew that the consignee sold the goods of others, his agreement called for participation in the profits of those sales. On appeal, the court stated that the consignor must prove the number of creditors of the consignee at the time of consignment, their identity, and which ones knew that the consignee sold the goods of others. Given that most sales by galleries are on consignment, one would think that a creditor either knew or should have known that a gallery art inventory was likely to be on consignment. The Mark Murray Gallery in New York states on its website that it both buys art and accepts it on consignment. One wonders whether that statement is sufficient to establish that the consignee was generally known to creditors as selling the goods of others.

In 1999, the Uniform Commercial Code was amended to exclude from the definition of "consignment" goods that are consumer goods, defined as those "used or bought for use primarily for personal, family, or household purposes." UCC § 9-102(23), but that amendment had not yet been enacted in Florida when *Rayfield* arose. It had been enacted in Massachusetts. *In the Matter of Haley & Steele, Inc.*, 20 Mass. L. Rep. 204 (Super. 2005), the court assumed that consumer consignors were excluded from the definition of consignment without providing any facts about why it believed that these people held the artwork primarily for personal, family, or household purposes on the one hand, or for investment purposes on the other, or whether the court thought that investment purposes were personal, family or household purposes. The court also thought that the artwork was not on a sale or return basis, so not covered at all under the UCC. It held that the law of bailments applied, and since the owner of the artwork retained title to the bailed item, he prevailed over the art gallery's creditors.

In response to cases like *Rayfield*, most art legislation provides that paintings consigned by an artist are held in trust for the artist. This is strange phraseology. In a consignment, the consignor continues to hold title; a trust is characterized by the separation of title, which lies with the trustee, from the beneficial owner. It is probably the intent of these laws that the consigned artwork cannot be reached by creditors of the consignee, and some of them so state. This would not have helped Kreps, as he was a collector, not an artist (though at least one state's legislation has been amended to include collectors in this benefit). This art legislation can occasionally have curious consequences. In *Zucker v. Hirschl & Adler Galleries, Inc.*, 648 N.Y.S.2d 521 (Sup. 1996), the gallery alleged that it loaned money to the artist on the oral security of the work, while the artist claimed that the loan was only to be repaid from the artist's share of the proceeds of sale. Pending trial, the court ordered the work returned to the artist because of the trust relationship established by New York art legislation.

f. Types of Agencies: Exclusive or Non-Exclusive, or Geographic

The agency may be either exclusive or non-exclusive, or may be limited to a geographic area. In general, UCC § 2-306 requires an exclusive agent to use its best efforts to promote the artist's work and requires that the artist use her best efforts to supply the agreed-upon work.

Questions may arise about the agent's authority. An agent who is required to use her best efforts to promote the artist's work may allege that this grants the agent all the rights that the artist had that might be useful in promoting the work. He might argue that he can make copies of the work to promote its sale, despite the fact that the artist retains the copyright in the work. In *Basquiat v. Baghoomian*, 1992 Copyright L. Dec. ¶ 26,824 (S.D.N.Y. 1991), the executor of the artist's estate alleged copyright infringement in the production of a catalogue for an exhibition of the artist's works, and the gallery owner defended on grounds of fair use. The court properly denied summary judgment for both parties. While only hinted at by the court and apparently not argued by the parties, a prior question is whether the gallery was the artist's agent, whether that agency was exclusive, whether that agency impliedly authorized the agent to exercise the artist's rights under the copyright law, and whether the acts alleged were indeed in furtherance of the purpose of the agency, the sale of the artist's work.

In a case where the principals authorized their agent to sell their work, the court ruled as a matter of law that the authority to sell included the authority to give a warranty, but left to the jury the question of whether the authority to sell included the authority to provide an estimate of the value of the works, even if clearly marked "for insurance purposes." *Goldman v. Barnett*, 793 F.Supp. 28 (D. Mass. 1992).

The meaning of the terms of the agency will often need to be construed, even when the words used seem to express a plain meaning. In *Nakian v. Di-Laurenti* 673 F. Supp. 699 (S.D.N.Y. 1987), the agreement provided that "The Agent shall have the right to select and retain possession of the Artist's works for exhibition, display and consignment to various galleries, art dealers, museums and exhibitions." This seems to give the agent the absolute right to select and keep works, regardless of number or quantity, even if the artist objected. The gallery held three hundred of Nakian's sculptures, of which it exhibited a dozen at a time that it rotated each month. Did that mean that the agent had the right to withhold the sixty-five pieces of the artist's works chosen for a major museum show, and refuse to cooperate when the museum asked for access to other work to photograph it for a catalogue? The court thought not, and issued a preliminary injunction even though there were substantial factual issues in dispute about whether the agency relationship had been breached. The court had no trouble finding that irreparable injury would result if the artist's work were not displayed in this museum show that had been four years in the planning. The court framed the other requirements as either likelihood of success on the merits, or a situation where the merits are in serious litigation and the balance of hardships tips decisively for plaintiff. Picking the second test, it pointed out that serious controversy had been raised about both law and facts, and plaintiff had shown considerable hardship if an injunction did not issue ordering the works released, while defendant had offered no evidence of the hardship it would experience if the works were not released. The court then ordered many more works released than were covered either by the proof of irreparable harm or by the balance of hardships.

An agent may violate his authority. The agent will be liable to his principal, but that will be little comfort if the agent is insolvent. As we saw in the chapter on Title, if the principal entrusts possession of the work for sale to an agent who deals in goods of that kind, the agent can pass good title to a buyer in the ordinary course of his business, regardless of the fact that the agent sold for less than authorized or on terms that offered more credit than allowed or the agent failed to remit the purchase price to his principal. *Graffman v. Espel*, 1998 U.S. Dist. LEXIS 1339 (S.D.N.Y. 1998). One possibility for protection is an all risk insurance policy that covers all risk of physical loss. Insurance companies argue that agent malfeasance is not a risk of physical loss. *Frigon v. Pacific Indemnity Co.*, 2007 WL 756384 (N.D.Ill. 2007), held that when the consignee sold the paintings and failed to turn over the proceedings, that became as much of a conversion as if the consignee had destroyed the paintings.

g. Termination by Death

An agency normally terminates on the death of the principal. It can also normally be revoked at will. These two doctrines can be problematic, particularly with an exclusive agency, where the agent may make a substantial investment to try to promote the artist's work. Where the agency is not intended to be revocable either at will or by death, it is good practice to state that in a written agency agreement and to specify that there is consideration on both sides of the agreement. In *Est. of Franz Kline*, N.Y.L.J. March 31, 1964 (N.Y. Sup. 1964), the sale of a painting to the Art Institute of Chicago was nullified because the artist's death revoked the agency. As in *Phoenix*, the court noted that the resolution by the Art Institute Board did not complete the sale; it only authorized the Institute to buy the work. In *O'Keeffe v. Bry*, 456 F Supp 822 (S.D.N.Y. 1978), Ms. Bry claimed that she had an oral appointment as Georgia O'Keeffe's agent for life and to handle the art sales of the estate, but the court held the contract not binding under the statute of frauds because it could not be performed within a year and it was not in writing. Like Phoenix, Ms. Bry tried to prove a writing by a combination of documents and was equally unsuccessful because, among other things, the language in the documents was precatory rather than directive.

h. Secrecy, Undisclosed Principals and the Agent's Commission

A factor to be taken into consideration is the secrecy sought by many participants in the art world. Secrecy is sought for a number of good reasons. If it is known that a work has been offered for sale and not sold, that tends to depress the price of that work in the future. If it is known that a person owns valuable paintings, that may make that person a target for burglars. A public sale might raise questions about the financial state of the seller, implying that he needs to sell the work to support his lifestyle. Knowledge that a person owns a valuable artwork might cause a revenue agent to carefully examine the person's income tax returns to see whether the reported income is commensurate with the amount spent on the art. For whatever reason, sellers often do not wish to be identified, nor do they want their work identified. In *Marvin Inc. v. Albstein*, 386 F.Supp.2d 247 (S.D.N.Y. 2005), neither the work, nor the artist, nor the seller is mentioned; it is simply a superior work from a highly desired period of a well-known artist.

This secrecy may impact the agent's commission. In *Faggionato v. Lerner*, 500 F.Supp.2d 237 (S.D.N.Y. 2007), the agent thought she had brokered a deal for the sale of a Monet by her undisclosed principal for $13 million. Apparently, the seller was unwilling to either sue or have his name revealed. To proceed with the suit, the agent needed to prove that she was an agent; otherwise she had no interest in the suit and no standing. Under French law, which was applicable to this contract, she could neither prove her agency, nor that she was a third party beneficiary of the contract, so she had no standing.

It appeared that a break in this secrecy was imminent because New York law permits the finding of a writing that satisfies the Statute of Frauds in auctions where the writing includes "the name of the person on whose account the sale was made". This seemed to call for revealing the identity of the seller, but the court held that revealing the identity of the auction house acting as agent for the seller satisfied the statute, thus making the requirement meaningless. William J. Jenack Estate Appraisers & Auctioneers, Inc. v. Rabizadeh, 22 N.Y. 3d 470, 5 N.E. 3d 976, 982 N.Y.S.2d 813 (2013).

In *Weil v. Murray*, 161 F.Supp.2d 250 (S.D.N.Y. 2001), Murray made a contract for his undisclosed principal, Peck. The principal denied that he had authorized the relationship. The court denied summary judgment for Peck because there were genuine issues of fact as to whether he and Murray had entered into an agency relationship. Parties may create an agency relationship whenever written or spoken words or conduct of the principal reasonably cause the agent to believe that the agent is authorized to act for the principal. The principal is liable for the acts of his agent within his actual authority, and also for acts within his apparent authority.

ii. Shifting Relationships

Some situations begin as consignments, then change. In *Weil,* the Weils consigned their Degas to Murray, thereby establishing a relationship of principal and agent. When Murray notifies the Weils that he has sold the painting to an undisclosed principal, he is the agent of both the seller and the buyer, thereby raising a conflict of interest to which the buyer has presumably already consented, and the seller consents by not objecting. But a buyer for an undisclosed principal is also a party to the contract, which would have violated his agency relationship with seller had the agent not disclosed it. The court grants summary judgment to the Weils because it finds that Murray had a contract to buy the Degas, did not pay for it, and accepted the painting by receiving and retaining it for a period longer than required for a reasonable opportunity to inspect it. In addition, Murray exercised dominion over the Degas by sending it to a conservator for cleaning and restoration. That judgment is for the purchase price, which is equivalent to granting specific performance to the buyer. The normal buyer's remedy for breach of a contract of sale is for the seller to mitigate damages by reselling the item, then claim damages as the difference between the two sales prices plus any additional expenses incurred. The full purchase price remedy is authorized by UCC § 2-709(1)(a) in only two limited cases: where the property cannot reasonably be resold, and where the buyer has accepted the property, so the seller cannot safely re-sell it because he no longer possesses it.

4. Death of an Artist

Most artists leave unsold artwork when they die. The executor or administrator of the artist's estate has more duties than one who administers a normal estate. A normal estate may consist of investment assets and the family home, and may entail standard responsibilities of paying debts and federal and state taxes. In settling the artist's estate, the executor must oversee the sale or donation of the unsold artwork, and often run the artist's business.

Administration of the estate is complicated by additional scrutiny. Before death, the artist ran his own affairs and formed the relationships he wanted over his lifetime. On death, four new players mount the stage: the administrator or executor, usually a close relative; the attorney for the estate; the probate judge; and representatives of federal and state taxing authorities. When one of the beneficiaries is a charitable foundation, a fifth player enters: the state attorney general in her role as supervisor of the state's charities. Each is likely to question the sometimes-informal relationships established by the artist. The value of the artwork is subject to scrutiny, as detailed in the chapter on Taxes above. Exclusive dealerships that are not in writing or that are carelessly drafted can be avoided. Settlement of the estate is likely to be carefully scrutinized.

The executor or other fiduciary is not permitted to act in a situation where he has a conflict of interest that would prevent him from devoting his loyalty to the estate. Before Mark Rothko's suicide, he had established a foundation with three friends as co-directors—the accountant Reis, the painter Stamos and the anthropology professor Levine. The three were also named executors of Rothko's will. There were three other directors of the foundation. Rothko left eight hundred paintings, one hundred of which were quickly sold to the Marlborough Gallery, Rothko's dealer at his death, and the rest were consigned equally quickly to the gallery for twelve years at a 50% commission, continuing an eight-year exclusive representation that called for the gallery to earn only a 10% commission.

Reis was elected a director of the Marlborough Gallery a month before Rothko's death. He received a salary for the part-time position. This constituted a conflict of interest because as executor, he should dispose of the paintings as profitably as possible, while it was in Marlborough's interest to obtain them as inexpensively as possible. Reis informed his fellow executors of the conflict and abstained from formal decision-making about disposition of the paintings, but did not resign either position.

Some months after the Rothkos were consigned to Marlborough, Stamos entered into a similar consignment arrangement for his own paintings, though one more favorable to Stamos than the Rothko consignment. Stamos' percentage of the sale price was higher, the duration of the arrangement shorter, and Stamos could set and change minimum prices, whereas minimum prices for the Rothkos were forever fixed at the date of death valuation. Also, Marlborough purchased a Stamos painting at auction while the executors were contemplating the arrangement with Marlborough. This too constituted a conflict of interest.

The third director, Levine, realized that Reis had a conflict of interest and warned Reis about it, but did nothing to assure that Reis' conflict did not influence the decisions of the executors.

The court does not find that the executors were self-dealing. Self-dealing would only have occurred if they had bought from or sold to the estate, and would have been a prohibited action. The court does find a breach of the duty of loyalty on the part of Reis and Stamos, and a breach of the duty of care on the part of all three executors.

For this, the executors were removed without commission for their past services.

The contracts with the Marlborough Gallery were set aside, the court declaring that they were voidable because the gallery knowingly induced the executors to enter into them. As a result the roughly 650 unsold paintings were returned to the estate.

Damages were assessed for the 140 paintings already sold by Marlborough against Levine for their fair market value when transferred to Marlborough of roughly $6.5 million, against Reis and Stamos for the current fair market value of the paintings of roughly $15.7 million, with Marlborough jointly and severally liable for both amounts, subject to the limit that the estate could not collect a total of more than $15.7 million.

While we speak here of Marlborough as being a single entity, it formally consisted of twenty-one separate legal entities, all controlled by Frank Lloyd. Since Lloyd and the various Marlborough entities did not clearly distinguish between themselves, the court pierced the corporate veil and held them jointly and severally liable.

It is unclear why the measure of damages should be different for Levine than for Reis and Stamos. Normally, when trustees breach their duty by selling at too low a price, the measure of damages is the difference between the price obtained and the fair market value of the property at the time and place of sale, the damages obtained from Levine. The court points out that where the trustees sell when they had a duty to retain property, the measure of damages is the current fair market value of the property, but that measure was inapplicable here because the trustees were not obligated to retain the property. The court partly justifies application of the current fair market value rule by distinguishing selling too low as negligence from selling much too low when there is an obvious conflict of interest, which is a breach of trust. This suggests that the real difference is between negligence and breach of trust, whether that breach results from selling when the trust instrument directs you to hold or from selling to someone that constitutes a conflict of interest. The court also tries to justify the damages by citing *Menzel v. List*, 267 N.Y.S. 2d 804 (Sup. Ct. NY County 1966), discussed in the chapter on Title above, where current fair market value damages were assessed in order to make the parties whole. In *Menzel* the defendant had the option to either return the artwork or pay damages equal to its fair market value, whereas here the defendants could not return the artwork because it had been sold to a bona fide purchaser. Citing *Menzel* does not explain why Levine was assessed a lesser level of damages. Then the court clarifies that it is only awarding compensatory damages, not punitive damages, but comments that awarding present fair market value should deter fiduciaries from future similar violations. But if compensatory damages are current fair market value, that still does not explain why Levine was assessed a lower amount. It cannot be explained on the grounds that he was merely negligent, because his knowledge of Reis' conflict of interest and failure to do anything about it was clearly an intentional breach of his responsibilities as executor.

The court did not mention that there was another potential conflict of interest in this case. As trustees of the foundation, the three executors had an obligation to try to maximize the amount received by the foundation, which might conflict with the executors' duties to treat all the beneficiaries under the will fairly. There was no need to mention this as the executors treated both the foundation and the other will beneficiaries equally unfairly.

The court also does not mention that Rothko, when he drew his will, might have been aware of the possibility of conflicts of interest for Reis and Stamos, and named them as executors nonetheless. The conflicts when the will was drawn were only potential, rather than real, as the close relationship with Marlborough developed after the will was signed. Reis, who drafted Rothko's will, might have inserted a clause stating that Rothko realized that conflicts of interest were possible, but wanted the three persons to serve as executor anyhow, and that he waived any liability that might have attached to them because of those conflicts. An express statement in the will might have been sufficient to permit them to serve as executors, but it is doubtful if it would excuse a breach of fiduciary duty of this magnitude because the court may disregard even an express waiver of an executor's duty as interfering with the proper administration of decedents' estates. *Matter of Estate of Rothko*, 84 Misc.2d 830, 379 N.Y.S.2d 923 (Surr. Ct. 1975), *aff'd* 43 N.Y.2d 305, 372 N.E.2d 291, 401 N.Y.S.2d 449 (1977).

Agents of the Internal Revenue Service read the newspapers. The result in this case induced them to assess \$18.5 million in self-dealing excise taxes plus \$2.5 million in penalties against Reis under INT. REV. CODE OF 1954 § 4941, which has a different definition of self-dealing than common law, and that assessment survived taxpayer's motion for summary judgment. *Est. of Reis*, 87 T.C. 1016 (1986). The Rothko Foundation, like most artists' foundations, is considered a private foundation under the tax law and subject to some very specific rules. See the chapter on Museums below.

There is little that is specific to art about *Rothko*. The same result would have occurred had the content of the estate been real property. Two things make the case particularly instructive for the art world. One is the tendency to establish a foundation as part of the artist's estate plan which adds both an extra player and an extra potential conflict of interest to the non-art estate.

The second is that the common tendency of people to name friends as executors means that the artist's friends named executors will often be other artists who, like Stamos here, desperate for recognition, are easily placed in a position of conflict of interest.

We are reminded of two other facts of life by *Rothko* and *In the Matter of the Estate of Andy Warhol*, 629 N.Y.S. 2d 621 (Surr. Ct. 1995). One is that complex estates involving art can take an immense amount of work, expertise and responsibilities for executors and lawyers who are overseeing the distribution of unsold artwork. Provisions to assure that they will be adequately compensated are indispensable, but a straight percentage fee may turn out to be unconscionable in an estate that turns out to be worth much more than originally anticipated. Failing to include appropriate provisions in a retainer agreement can make that contract unenforceable. The second practical lesson is that the probate court is always watching for unreasonable fees, so the wise executor or attorney should keep careful track of time devoted and responsibilities undertaken.

5. Auctions

Alternatively, a seller may decide to sell at auction. Traditionally, most of the buyers at auctions were re-sellers, so an auction price was regarded as the wholesale price. More recently, the number of collectors at art auctions has increased, especially at very high end auctions.

A. How Auctions Work

The seller negotiates a consignment agreement with the auction house. The consignment agreement creates a contractual relationship and the auctioneer becomes the consignor's agent, assuming fiduciary responsibilities to the consignor. Auction houses publish their standard commission rates. The consignment contract, which is not made public, will normally set the commission rate and, in the case of exceptionally desirable work, may even provide for no commission payable by the seller, and divide the buyer's premium between the auction house and the consignor. A reserve price may be agreed upon. A reserve is a minimum price at which the artwork will be sold. Reserve prices are so common that UCC § 2-328(3) states that auctions are "with reserve" unless explicitly stated to be without reserve. To attract business, auction houses often offer the seller a guarantee. A guarantee is a promise that if the work does not attract high enough bids to reach a specified amount, the auction house or a third party will buy it for that amount.

For some items, the seller may actually be the auction house. In that case the auction house is selling as a principal, not as an agent. There is no requirement that an auctioneer reveal which lots are on consignment and which lots belong to the auction house.

Potential buyers usually inspect an artwork and review the conditions of sale of an auction house prior to the opening of an auction. Bidders register in advance with the auction house, and receive a bidding number.

In a typical auction, the auctioneer asks for bids. Potential buyers bid in person, by an agent, on the phone, or in advance by a written bid. Some auctions allow online bidding as well.

The buyer is the person who places the highest bid before the gavel falls ending the sale on that item.

B. Bidding

Special arrangements for secret bidding signals can be agreed upon in advance between a potential buyer and the auctioneer. Buyers often wish to remain anonymous. As the names of successful bidders are not announced, only their bidding numbers, not being perceived as making a bid may preserve that anonymity.

There are restrictions on who may bid at an auction. A seller of a specific artwork cannot bid on his own property during the auction. The practice of using someone who bids just to raise the price is fraudulent. Both English and United States courts regard that as fraudulent because it makes it appear to a prospective buyer that there is a bona fide competitor when there is not. *Bexwell v. Christie*, 1 Cowp. 395 (1776); *Veazie v. Williams*, 49 U.S. 134 (1850). For the same reason, bidding by the owner's agent is prohibited.

Discouraged but difficult to stamp out is collusive bidding. Collusive bidding may involve a group of bidders interested in purchasing the same art. They may agree on which member of the group will bid for which piece, then have an agreement as to how the pieces, whose price has been restrained by their agreement, will be divided among them, sometimes by the winning bidder holding a private auction composed solely of the conspirators.

C. Sale

Each lot is sold to the high bidder accepted by the auctioneer before the hammer falls. The UCC states that the auctioneer has discretion to reopen the bidding if another bid is made while the hammer is falling. That discretion is often reinforced in the conditions of sale. Auctioneers usually exercise that discretion both because of their duty to their principals,, which require them to seek the highest price possible, and because the auction house's revenue usually increases with the sale price. The auctioneer can rely on spotters; he does not actually have to see the bid himself. In *Callimanopulos v. Christie's Inc.*, 621 F. Supp. 2d 127 (S.D.N.Y. 2009), a bidder who thought his bid was the last before the hammer sounded sued for the goods after the auctioneer had exercised his discretion to continue the bidding. The court noted that plaintiff's agent was positioned where she did not have a clear view of the subsequent bidder and reviewed the videotape of the auction, determining that there was in fact another bid as the hammer was descending that would permit the auctioneer to re-open the bidding.

D. Jurisdiction over the Successful Bidder

The understanding is that the successful bidder will pay for the item, either in cash or by some means that has previously been arranged with the auction house. Bidders may win the bidding but have no immediate cash to pay for the artwork. As an agent for the seller, the auction house must make satisfactory arrangements for payment before releasing the goods. Other successful bidders suffer from a disease called buyer's remorse. They decide not to pay. Such a buyer can expect a suit by the auction house. Nonresidents of the state in which the auction is held may try to assert a lack of personal jurisdiction to avoid paying, especially if the bidder was a phone or e-mail bidder. Even such a bidder resident in California, as long as he makes repeated bids, is held to have actively participated in the auction and transacted business in the state within the meaning of the New York long arm statute when the auction house tries to enforce the successful bid. *Parke-Bernet v. Franklyn,* 26 N.Y.2d 13, 256 N.E.2d 506, 308 N.Y.S.2d 337 (1970). Further, where the California bidder has on his own initiative requested an open telephone line for the auction and an auctioneer's employee's only function is to assist the bidder by carrying out the bidder's instruction during an auction, the bidder has transacted business through an agent in the state and is subject to jurisdiction of the state courts where the auction was held.

E. Responsibility of Auction House to Buyer and Seller

The law provides that when a seller consigns his goods to the auction house, the auction house becomes his agent. Likewise, when the buyer enters a successful bid, the auction house becomes his agent. But those general rules are almost entirely worthless.

The real document that governs the relationships of the auction house is the part of the auction catalogue that contains the conditions of sale. The seller's signature on the consignment agreement incorporates the conditions of sale, as does the buyer's registration as a buyer. The conditions of sale waive many rules of law designed to protect buyer and seller, and courts have upheld most of those waivers. It is clear that the terms of an agency can be modified by a contract, though it is unclear if there are limits on what terms can be modified and to what extent.

It is common that the conditions of sale give the auction house sole discretion to rescind a sale. In *Kohler v. Leslie Hindman, Inc.*, 80 F.3d 1181 (7th Cir. 1996), that discretion was given if the sale was likely to subject the seller or the auction house to liability under a warranty of authenticity. The conditions of sale also specified that all sales were "as is." A potential buyer expressed doubt about whether the Kohler's painting was done by Rousseau and asked for a pre-sale authentication. As that was not possible, the auctioneer, without consulting the owner, orally promised the inquirer that if he were the successful bidder, he could return the painting within roughly thirty days if an expert determined that Rousseau did not paint it. The inquirer was the winning bidder and sent the picture to France for authentication. The expert authenticator's opinion was that the painting was not by Rousseau. The purchaser returned the painting to the auction house five months after the auction. The court first construed the conditions of sale as giving the auction house the ability to rescind the sale if the seller or the auction house might be threatened with suit. It believed that the standard was not an objective standard of whether such a suit was reasonably likely to succeed. Because of the words "in our sole discretion," the court held this to be a subjective standard. As long as the auction house acts in good faith, a rescinded sale does not constitute a breach of the auction house's fiduciary duty. The court does not consider the validity of the oral contract, or the fact that the painting was returned considerably after the deadline in the oral agreement. It focuses instead on whether any of the actions of the auction house might indicate bad faith, and finds none. It states that the oral agreement, even though not communicated to seller, was a necessary inducement to get the prospective purchaser to bid.

In a similar case, *Greenwood v. Koven*, 880 F.Supp. 186 (S.D.N.Y. 1995), the discretion of Christie's auction house was phrased more broadly. It was authorized to rescind the sale if in its sole judgment the sale may subject Christie's or seller to any liability. Under New York law, the auction house and the seller could not sell the Braque pastel as is because the law imposed a non-waivable warranty if the seller identified the work as by Braque. The buyer expressed doubts about the authenticity; Christie's experts re-examined the work and assured the buyer of authenticity; the buyer was unsatisfied and asked for an outside expert's opinion; Christie's sent the work to the person who under French law held Braque's moral rights and the right to authenticate; that person believed that the work was not by Braque; Christie's rescinded the sale. The court found that Christie's made the decision in good faith, and that none of the steps it undertook violated its fiduciary relationship to the seller as modified by the conditions of sale. Investigating the authenticity of a painting when liability may result if it is not authentic is within that duty.

Conditions of sale do not always save the auction house, especially when the house violates its own rules. In one case, the auction house persuaded the owner that he would obtain higher prices at auction than at a private sale. It gave the owner optimistic estimates of what the work would likely fetch, then did not communicate doubts its staff expressed to the owner. It persuaded the owner to set a reserve price higher than the high estimates it publicized for the auction, with the result that several paintings did not sell, thereby further depressing their value for future sales. The court held that the agent's fiduciary duty includes communicating to the principal any concerns about the likelihood that the paintings will sell at auction at their set reserves. The auctioneer does not have to guarantee a successful auction, but the auctioneer must provide important and relevant information in a timely manner to its principal concerning the auction. It should not allow reserves to be set in violation of its own policy. It reversed the trial court's dismissal of the case, and commented that the measure of damages should be the difference between the value of the paintings before the auction and their value after the auction. Four of the paintings were subsequently sold at reduced prices after plaintiff gave defendant the opportunity to buy them. The court did not discount the possibility of punitive damages, since plaintiff alleged that defendant had acted recklessly. *Cristallina S.A. v. Christie, Manson & Woods Intern., Inc.*, 117 A.D.2d 284, 502 N.Y.S.2d 165 (1986). One might add that the measure of damages puts the auction house in a bind. It would like to have as low a fair market value before the auction as possible, but as a practical matter, defendant would have difficulty contesting the estimates it had given plaintiff as the fair market value before the auction, because doing so would help prove plaintiff's case of violation of defendant's fiduciary duty.

F. Regulating Auctions

Art is not the only subject matter of auctions. Auction houses are subject to licensing and regulation, but those matters usually do not differentiate art auctions from other auctions, and do not deal with specific art problems like authentication.

Specialized art legislation does not usually deal separately with auctions, but will sometimes include auctions as art merchants subject to certain duties. " 'Art merchant' means a person who is in the business of dealing, exclusively or non-exclusively, in works of fine art or multiples, or a person who by his occupation holds himself out as having knowledge or skill peculiar to such works.... The term 'art merchant' includes an auctioneer who sells such works at public auction...." New York Arts & Cultultural Affairs Law § 11.01.2.

On the other hand, each individual statute must be examined. For instance, CALIF. CIV. CODE § 1812.601(d) defines an auctioneer as an individual, thereby excluding corporations from being auctioneers for purposes of that statute. As a result, e-Bay is not subject to that statute. *Ewert v. eBay, Inc.*, 2008 WL 906162 (N.D. Cal. 2008).

Auctions are subject to the antitrust laws. At the top of the auction ladder, there is fierce competition between auction houses to secure the best artwork for sale. That has permitted owners with especially desirable art to negotiate deals not available to everyone. To end this competition, Sotheby's and Christie's agreed to not give discounts from their published sales prices or to extend extraordinary financing to sellers. The two auction houses were convicted of violating the Sherman Act, and several of their officers and employees were also convicted. *United States v. Taubman*, 2002 WL 54873 (S.D.N.Y. 2002), *aff'd* 297 F.3d 161 (2d Cir. 2002).

Checkpoints

- Contracts commissioning art should be in writing to fix what is to be produced, define the warranty, provide security for performance, specify a time of completion, and provide for dispute resolution.
- Buying existing art is a sale of goods requiring compliance with the statute of frauds for sales.
- Agency relationships are established when an artist sells through a dealer. The dealer must observe a duty of loyalty to the artist that forbids conflicts of interest.
- Art consignments are bailments at common law imposing different duties of care on the agent depending on whether the bailment is for the benefit of one of the parties or for mutual benefit.
- Special art legislation often provides that consignee is absolutely liable for loss or damage to the consigned goods.

- When a buyer pays the consignee the buyer has no further obligation at common law, leaving the consignor as a general creditor. Special art legislation often gives consignor priority by establishing a trust relationship.
- Creditors of consignee prevail over consignor under the UCC unless consignor takes special steps to label his goods. Recent UCC amendments exempt consumer goods from this rule. Special art legislation often gives consignor priority.
- Agency agreements are normally construed according to the contract. Default rules require that the agent exercise a duty of loyalty and a duty of care to the principal.
- Friends and business acquaintances of artists may be asked to undertake other duties, such as executors of wills or trustees of foundations. The standards applicable to them will be different than if they were just friends or business acquaintances, as they will be judged by the standards of executors or trustees.
- Auctions create agency relationships that are usually successfully modified by the specific terms of the auction house's contract.

Chapter 13

Museum Law

Roadmap

After reading this chapter, you should understand:

- Form of organization: Museums may be organized as any business form, but they are most commonly organized under state nonprofit corporation laws for educational purposes. They usually qualify as § 501(c)(3) organizations for tax purposes. They are not permitted to distribute profit to any individual.
- Supervision by Attorney General: Museums are subject to supervision by the state attorney general, which may include requiring the submission of periodic reports.
- Tax benefits: Museums usually do not pay income or property taxes, and contributions to museums are usually deductible from income, gift or estate tax liability. Obtaining property tax exemption is usually the most difficult.
- Unrelated business income: A museum is taxed on its unrelated business income, defined as income from operating a business that is not related to its exempt purpose. A restaurant and a bookstore are both businesses, but they are related to a museum's exempt purpose if the restaurant is primarily for employees and guests, and if the bookstore sells only books about artwork.
- Private foundations are a special class of museum supported by a few individuals to which special rules apply evidencing more supervision and a shorter life span.
- Museum governance: A board chooses the major officers and sets general policy. Members of the board owe a duty of loyalty and a duty of care to the museum.
- Duty of loyalty is defined by the purposes of the museum, and requires that the board members not engage in self-dealing or take advantage of any conflict of interest they may have. Purposes may be determined from the museum's charter or from the requirements the law imposes on charitable organizations.
- *Cy pres* and deviation: When changes have occurred since the museum was established that make the achievement of its purposes impractical, a court may order a change in museum purposes to the nearest practical charitable use if the person who established the museum had a general charitable intent. Likewise, the court can order a deviation from mandated administrative matters for impracticability.
- Duty of care requires reasonable care and diligence in the management of the museum's assets. Trustees are judged under the business judgment rule which provides no liability if the trustee exercises reasonable business judgment.

- Enforcing trustee duties is left largely to the state attorney general. A taker in default of a gift may have enforcement powers, as may the donor of a gift under some circumstances.
- Museum acquisitions should be the subject of a policy according to museum association guidelines so that museums acquire ownership of authentic works. Acquisition guidelines generally do not distinguish between purchases, gifts and loans, though there are obvious practical differences.
- Restoration of works in the collection is a duty of the museum. In unusual cases, a restorer may have a claim for unjust enrichment against the owner of the artwork.
- Museum de-accessions: There is little hard law other than the general duties of loyalty and care. Most museum organizations have accreditation standards that limit de-accession to generating funds for future purchases, but prohibit it for operating expenses or building improvement.
- Museum labor law contains no special rules because the employer is a museum. It is subject to normal rules about union bargaining, specific contracts and at will employment.
- Termination of employees covered by union contracts, civil service or individual contracts will be governed by the terms of the contracts. At will employees can be terminated for any reason, but cannot be terminated for a prohibited reason such as race, sex, national origin, disability, age, or in retaliation for the exercise of some protected right, such as refusal to violate the law, the exercise of a government duty like jury service, whistle-blowing, or the exercise of a right in connection with employment, such as filing a worker's compensation claim.
- Discrimination: Federal and state laws frequently prohibit employment discrimination, including discrimination in pay, on grounds of race, sex, national origin, disability, or age.

1. Introduction: Of Hard Law and Soft Law

Museums are central to the education and culture of America. Not only are they central to educational, artistic and scientific discovery, they also are big business. Museums in America attract 850 million people annually, more than five times the number of people who attend major-league baseball, basketball, football and hockey games combined. Since museums are big business, in many ways they operate as corporations, but in others they are more like charities or trusts. This chapter will discuss museum structure and operation.

Museums are governed by a combination of hard law and soft law.

Hard law is the law with which we are all familiar. It consists of statutes, regulations and caselaw. Its binding nature on museums, their officers and directors, is the same as any other law. Violation can result in damages or an injunction, and occasionally criminal prosecution.

More than any other subject in art law, museums are also governed by soft law. Most museums belong to one or more associations of museums. Those associations either accredit museums or admit museum directors to membership based on their museums' compliance with a set of accrediting rules. If the privileges of membership are desired, the museum must adhere to those accrediting rules. It is true that the sanctions are less draconian, and the process is controlled by fellow museum directors who probably have both great sympathy for others who run museums and great knowledge of the shortfall when comparing this person's operation of the museum to normal practice. Nonetheless, both because museum directors wish to maintain their reputations with their peers (to say nothing of becoming the director of a more important museum) and because the periodic reinspections constitute continuing surveillance, compliance with museum organizations' standards is pretty good. Another reason soft law tends to be effective with museums is that they are constantly soliciting contributions from the public, so their standing with the public is important. Also, when courts try to articulate appropriate conduct for museums, they are likely to turn to accreditation standards, thus converting soft law into hard law.

2. Structuring the Museum

A museum can be structured as a trust or a corporation. Most museums are incorporated as non-profit organizations under state statutes for nonprofit corporations. A museum need not be incorporated, but there are many benefits to incorporation, such as ease of ownership of assets, perpetual existence, and limited liability. Nonprofit corporations also receive additional benefits such as exemption from a variety of regulations, taxes and common law rules, such as the rule against perpetuities. Many organizations that give grants will only consider non-profit organizations as potential recipients, and museums often seek grants to support some of their activities.

A. Corporation

i. Purposes

A nonprofit corporation can have only limited purposes under state law. The corporation must be organized under one of the enumerated purposes. These purposes often include relief of poverty, promotion of education or religion, or mutual benefit (a form of insurance). Museums usually choose education. Likewise, a corporation's purposes are limited under federal tax law. While all § 501(c) organizations are exempt from federal income tax, contributions to only a limited set of those organizations are deductible. Contributions to chambers of commerce, business leagues, sports organizations or mutual benefit societies do not give the contributors tax deductions. Again, education is a permitted purpose in achieving both tax exemption for the organization and a tax deduction for contributions to it. INT. REV. CODE OF 1986 § 501(c)(3).

ii. Limits on Distributing Profits

A second requirement for a nonprofit corporation is the non-distributional constraint. A nonprofit corporation may not distribute a dividend, income, or profit to a member, director or officer of the non-profit corporation. This does not mean that a non-profit cannot be profitable. If it is profitable, the profits must be devoted to the purpose for which the non-profit is organized. Reasonable salaries to employees are allowed.

iii. Supervision by Attorneys General

Since non-profit corporations are spared the watchful eyes of stockholders or beneficiaries, the state oversees the management of the nonprofit corporation by its trustees, officers and directors. That responsibility is lodged in the state's Attorney General. But state Attorneys General have many responsibilities and a limited budget. While the New York and Pennsylvania Attorneys General have a reputation for vigilance in overseeing their charitable organizations, most states have quite limited staffs devoted to this function.

The supervision of the Attorney General may be based on common law, or it may be enshrined in statute. If statutory, it will be subject both to construction and constitutional challenge. In *The People ex rel. William J. Scott, Attorney General v. George F. Harding Museum,* 374 N.E.2d 756 (Ill. App. 1978), the Attorney General brought suit under the Illinois Charitable Trust Act, which by its terms also covered charitable corporations, to require the museum to file informational returns required of charitable trusts, and to not dissipate the assets of the museum. The museum contended that it was not covered by the statute because it was educational, rather than charitable, in nature. The court found that the word charitable in the statute was a broad term that included educational. Charitable was defined as promoting the well being of social man in numerous ways, not just alms-giving. There was a constitutional challenge to the statute on equal protection grounds because the statute required less extensive reporting for schools than for other organizations. The court rejected this challenge because the different reporting requirements were rational. It pointed out that schools have identified students, any one of whom might complain to the Attorney General about mismanagement, but few people were likely to be aware of or complain of museum mismanagement.

B. Trust

Sometimes a museum is operated as a trust. Sometimes a museum that is a corporation receives property as a trustee.

A trust is a fiduciary relationship where a party, known as a trustee, holds property that is administered for the benefit of others, known as the beneficiaries. In the case of a museum, the beneficiaries are usually the general public, but they might be a more limited class, such as the students at an art school. It is also possible that the instrument establishing the trust might accord some benefits to a limited class, and other benefits to the general public. If a trust is established to benefit a single individual, or a small group of individuals, it will not qualify as charitable for federal tax purposes because the group of potential beneficiaries is too limited.

3. Tax Considerations

Museums are aided in acquiring valuable art and land to house the art, as well as accumulating an endowment, through tax breaks directly related to art collecting and the non-profit nature of a museum.

A. Property Tax

Real property is generally subject to a state *ad valorem* tax assessed annually. Most states accord exemptions from the property tax for property devoted to charitable purposes, including museums.

State property tax exemptions are normally subject to strict criteria. In Pennsylvania, for example, the institution must prove that it is a purely public charity. A purely public charity must prove that it (1) advances a charitable purpose, (2) donates or renders gratuitously a substantial portion of its services, (3) benefits a substantial and indefinite class of persons who are legitimate subjects of charity, (4) relieves the government of some of its burden, and (5) operates entirely free from private profit motive. It is normally the last of these requirements that is most difficult to meet. Excessive salaries of officers can be a problem. In one case, the fact that employees could be rewarded based on productivity was enough to doom the exemption, regardless of the fact that there was no evidence that anyone ever received productivity payments. *Guthrie Clinic, Ltd. v. Sullivan County Bd of Assessment Appeals*, 898 A.2d 1194 (Pa. Comm. Ct. 2006). The fact that the Guthrie Clinic operated much like a normal, for-profit medical office did not help its case.

A different problem was exposed in *Georgia O'Keeffe Museum v. County of Santa Fe*, 133 N.M. 297, 62 P.3d 754 (App. 2002). The appropriate administrator had denied the museum's application for property tax exemption under the New Mexico constitution, which provided an exemption for property used for educational or charitable purposes, having found that the primary uses of the property were to operate a museum where admission was charged and to operate a museum gift shop. In reversing the administrator, the court implied that charging a reasonable admission fee did not disqualify a museum from being educational. It specifically said that a museum need not operate regular classes to be educational; it is enough if the museum preserves and shows exhibit-worthy items, carries on appropriate educational programs and is a public benefit. The court remanded the case for further evidence.

State tax exemptions come under scrutiny in hard economic times. States forced to find more money in their budget often consider revoking property tax exemptions of charities. Those exemption qualifications are much more closely scrutinized then. Sometimes the action is indirect, as in Hawaii's failed proposal to tax the income of nonprofits at 1%.

Nonprofits in some states make payments in lieu of property taxes, or PILOTs. These payments are "voluntarily" made by charities to the state. While they are not mandatory, many charities find them useful in helping to secure property tax exemptions, clear zoning hurdles for ambitious building projects, and similar government approvals. In Boston, a substantial amount of the city's land (almost half by some estimates) is exempt from property taxes because used as churches, museums, educational institutions, or other charities; the city has urged charities to pay a fourth of what they would actually pay in property taxes.

B. Tariffs

The property tax exemption is not the only tax incentive museums are offered. The tariff exemption has been instrumental in lowering the cost of acquiring foreign art. The Payne-Aldrich Tariff of 1909 added the importation of original works of art more than twenty years old to the duty-free list.

The tariff rule was directly related to one man, J. Pierpont Morgan. Morgan had an extensive collection of art outside the United States. He planned to give many photographs to the Metropolitan Museum of Art, but under then-current tariff law, importing the photos would cost $1.5 million. Congress was moved by this potential gift to put free admission of fine art into the tariff law if the art was at least 20 years old. This art age limit was removed four years later. Incidentally, only a small portion of Morgan's photos were given to the museum. Most were sold at auction.

C. Estate and Gift Tax Deductions

Art museums also benefit from charitable deductions from the gift and estate taxes. These taxes are assessed on the fair market value of any gift or bequest. Since 1917 Congress has allowed a deduction from taxable income for contributions to American organizations that are operated exclusively for religious, charitable, scientific, literary, or educational purposes.

The gift and estate tax deductions provide a great monetary incentive for persons to donate to museums. A gift or bequest of artwork is included as potentially taxable under the gift or estate tax. A gift of a work of art is deductible in the amount of the fair market value of the property at the time of the gift, regardless of how much the donor may have paid for the art. The increase in the value of donated art while the donor holds it is never taxed under the income tax.

The generosity of the gift tax has allowed great works of art to make their way to American museums. Few other countries provide similar tax incentives. However many other countries fund museums, whereas in America museums are largely privately funded.

D. Income Tax Exemption and Deductions

i. General Rules

Non-profit corporations can gain tax-exempt status. This tax-exemption means the organization does not pay federal income tax on any profit related to its exempt functions that it realizes. The exemption is secured by filing an application for an advanced ruling with the Internal Revenue Service (IRS). There are many different kinds of organizations that qualify for nonprofit organization status. The most valuable status is that of a § 501(c)(3) organization, because contributions to it are deductible for purposes of the income, gift and estate tax. Those non-profits must claim non-profit status as either a charitable, religious, scientific or educational organization. Museums are generally educational. No substantial part of the organization's activities can be propaganda or attempting to influence legislation (with certain exceptions). It cannot support or oppose candidates for political office. Nor can any part of its net earnings inure to the benefit of any private shareholder or individual.

ii. Charitable Purposes

An organization does not cease operating for charitable purposes because it is successful, or because it grows significantly. *Presbyterian and Reformed Pub. Co. v. Comm'r*, 743 F.2d 148 (3d Cir. 1984) involved a corporation formed to disseminate the system of belief of the Presbyterian Church of the United States, primarily by publishing books. When it notified IRS that it was accumulating money to buy land between the religious organization whose views it espoused and its printer, IRS revoked its exemption. The court indicated that the act of accumulating revenues may call into question a tax exempt purpose, but did not explain why. Perhaps its view is that the revenues should be currently devoted to the tax exempt purpose. But no one has ever suggested that a church could not accumulate money to build its own church building and move from rented quarters, or that a university could not accumulate money to build a classroom building.

iii. Private Inurement

The main thrust of IRS action in *Presbyterian* was that the earnings inured to a private person. The organization had an increase in commercial activity, it accumulated capital, and its income exceeded its expenses, largely as the result of publishing an author whose books became very successful. It also changed from a volunteer staff to a professional staff. The court was not troubled by the level of commercial activity or the fact that income exceeded expenses, as that is the goal of most non-profit organizations. There was no evidence that any person in a controlling position at the organization profited from the accumulation of capital. While the salaries increased greatly with the replacement of volunteers by professional staff, there is no evidence that the staff was paid more than fair compensation for their services, so the court reversed the revocation of the organization's non-profit status.

The United Cancer Council, a breakaway from the American Cancer Society, did not fare as well. In desperate straights, it contracted with a professional fundraiser for an exclusive five-year period at a high cost, and also gave the fundraiser unusual rights related to its mailing lists, as well as some control over any funds it raised. The court questioned whether the fundraiser had become the person in control of UCC. If so, and if the payments to the fundraiser were more than the fair market value of the services provided, this would be private inurement. As it happened, the fundraiser was enormously successful, but at enormous costs. The net that UCC received of $2.3 million was only ten percent of the total amount raised. They did not renew the contract with that fundraiser, and the fundraiser's successor was unsuccessful, sending the organization into bankruptcy. Alternatively, the court thought there might have been a breach of the trustees' duty of care that resulted in a contract that was not at arm's length. That would constitute a gift of organization property to the fundraiser that would constitute a prohibited private inurement. *United Cancer Council, Inc. v. Comm'r*, 165 F.3d 1173 (7th Cir. 1999).

iv. Unrelated Business Income

Income that relates to the non-profit organization's purpose is tax exempt. A non-profit organization's investment income is also tax exempt. If the organization has unrelated business income (UBI), that income is taxed. That is because Congress did not want to give a tax-exempt organization an unfair advantage when competing with a taxable business. An unrelated business is any business or trade unrelated to the charitable purpose for the organization's tax exemption. There are exceptions to UBI: if the business done is performed by the organization without compensation, for the convenience of the organization's members at their usual place of employment, the selling of gifts or contributions, or for advertising purposes, it is not UBI.

For example, if a museum has a gift shop selling postcards with a picture of the artwork from the exhibit and the museum's name on the postcard, income from that merchandise is not UBI because it furthers the museum's message and acts as an advertisement for the museum. The same is true of reproductions of works in the museum, copies of folk art from the collections of other museums, and instructional literature about art. If however, the museum also sold scientific books or magnets with the cityscape on them and no mention of the museum, that would be UBI and the profit from that merchandise would be taxed. Rev. Rul. 73-104, 1973-1 Cum. Bull. 263; Rev. Rul. 73-105, 1973-1 Cum. Bull. 264.

Museum restaurants and snack bars allow visitors to devote more of their time to the collection, so their profits are not UBI, at least where the museum does not advertise to the general public and where access to the venue is only through the museum. Rev. Rul. 74-399, 1974-2 Cum. Bull. 172. Where one can access the eating facilities without patronizing the museum, as in most California museums, the result is unclear. The income could either be entirely related, entirely unrelated, or could be allocated based on a study of typical patronage.

Investment income is not UBI because it is not business income. The line between certain types of investment income and business income is not always clear, but the latter often involves the provision of some active service. In *Sierra Club Inc. v. Comm'r*, 86 F.3d 1526 (9th Cir. 1996), the club rented out its mailing lists, and the court held that to be investment income because the club did not maintain the lists itself. It hired a subcontractor. This seems a distinction without a difference. If maintaining the lists itself would have been a business, the fact that it is subcontracted makes it no less a business. The club also entered into an agreement with a bank for solicitation of credit card business by the bank in exchange for royalties based on member sign-up and charges. The court denied summary judgment because there were disputed issues of fact, and on remand, it was held that the fact that the Club retained the right to approve mailings in order to control the Club's image did not make this the provision of services.

v. Private Foundation Rules

Most small museums are supported by a sole donor. Any museum that does not enjoy widespread public support is likely to be a private foundation. INT. REV. CODE OF 1986 § 509. The legal requirements of private foundations are many and quite technical, and violations can incur substantial penalties. In *Gladney v. Comm'r*, 745 F.2d 955 (5th Cir. 1984), the tax consequences ended up being 105% of the prohibited activity. For other private foundation problems, see *Greenacre Foundation v. United States*, 762 F.2d 965 (Fed. Cir. 1985) and *Est. of Reis*, 87 T.C. 1016 (1986).

vi. Income Tax Deductions for Contributions

For discussion of rules on income tax deductions for contributions to museums, see the chapter on Taxes above.

4. Management of Museums

Museums are usually managed by collective bodies, whether they are organized as trusts or corporations. They may be called a board of trustees or a board of directors. They are usually unpaid volunteers, often selected for their ability to give money or art, their ability to raise money from others or persuade others to give art, or their political and community connections. They are expected to exercise their responsibilities in a timely, competent, and faithful manner. The board members are bound by fiduciary obligations that are mostly the product of common law. These fiduciary duties are divided into the duty of loyalty and the duty of care.

The board is responsible for setting the general policies by which the museum is operated. It is also responsible for choosing the major officers of the museum, who are charged with its daily management. Boards are often required to authorize all purchases, and sometimes all acquistions, even donations.

There is some disagreement about the nature of the fiduciary standard. Is it the standard of business corporation directors, the standard of trustees of a private trust, or an intermediate standard?

Business corporation standards are judged by the business judgment rule. This rule requires that corporate directors act in good faith. There is a presumption that the directors of a corporation make business decisions on an informed basis with the honest belief that the course taken was in the best interests of the corporation. There is no prohibition on corporate directors doing business with their corporation as long as they disclose the relationship. Trustees of private trusts are held to a higher fiduciary standard. Private trust trustees must act with undivided loyalty to the trust and for the benefit of the trust beneficiaries. They may not engage in transactions with the trust unless this is specifically authorized in the trust instrument. The current trend is to hold museum trustees to the business judgment standard when dealing with the museum's finances, and to the private trust standard when evaluating their fulfillment of the duty of loyalty.

A. Duty of Loyalty

The duty of loyalty entails the obligation to remain loyal to the purposes for which the non-profit corporation was created, and to follow any dictates set forth in the organizing instruments, be they a trust, articles of incorporation, bylaws, or mission statement. Directors should not vote on any matter in which they have a conflict of interest, and might be obligated to do more to isolate that conflict.

i. A Matter of Construction

The trustees' obligations of loyalty are frequently defined by the construction of the gift instrument. In *Commonwealth v. Barnes Foundation*, 398 Pa. 458, 159 A.2d 500 (1960), the Barnes Foundation had closed its museum to the general public, reserving it entirely for students and faculty. The court construed the words "the advancement of education and the appreciation of the fine arts" as requiring the admission of the general public to the museum. It was aided in this by another clause of the document saying "the plain people ... shall have free access to the art gallery ... whenever it is open to the public," implying an intent by Dr. Barnes that it be open to the public sometimes. The court was also aided by the fact that the corporation had applied for and received tax exempt status, which would only be available if it were an institution providing public benefits. Closing the museum to the public might put that tax exemption in jeopardy. The same court a few years earlier had dismissed a case seeking to open the collection to the public brought by a newspaper reporter on grounds that he lacked standing. *Wiegand v. Barnes Foundation*, 374 Pa. 149, 97 A.2d 81 (1953). There was no doubt about the Attorney General's standing to enforce charitable restrictions.

In the absence of specific language, it may be necessary for a museum to be open to the public as a matter of state law in order to qualify as a charitable organization. *People ex rel. Scott v. Silverstein*, 86 Ill. App.3d 605, 408 N.E.2d 243 (1980) made a blanket statement that museums must be open to the public, but one can envision museums maintained for training conservationists that would be educational but would not need to be open to the public.

A donor who wishes his museum to be closed to the public should not only state that specifically, but should add a reason why being closed to the public does not destroy the educational or charitable nature of the gift.

The prohibition of using museum property for "social functions" was held not to apply to fundraisers for the museum itself. *In re Barnes Foundation*, 453 Pa. Super. 243, 683 A.2d 894 (1996).

The scope of the gift may also be a matter of construction. Louise Murdock left funds to a trustee to establish an art collection for the city of Wichita if Wichita provided suitable space for it. The trustee wanted to hire a conservator to inspect and conserve the paintings bought for the collection, and to publish a catalogue of the collection. There was no specific authorization to do either in the trust document, but the court held that those two activities were implied as activities necessary to have a proper collection. *Parkinson v. Murdock*, 183 Kan. 706, 332 P.2d 273 (1958).

ii. Loyalty as a Matter of Law

The principal law-imposed duties of loyalty, other than following the terms of the governing instrument, are to avoid self-dealing and conflicts of interest.

A museum trustee should not buy from or sell to the museum. There may be a way for a trustee to deal with the museum, even though it is not good practice. In *Attorney General v. Olson*, 346 Mass. 190, 191 N.E.2d 132 (1963), there was a proposal that the museum buy realty from one of the trustees to construct a museum building. The court stated that this was improper even though the deal was fully disclosed, an independent appraisal valued the property at 140% of the proposed purchase price, the seller did not dominate the board, and the seller did not vote on whether or not to buy. The trust did not in fact buy the property, so suffered no damage, and the trustee was not surcharged. The implication of this case is that a museum that wants to enter into a transaction with one of its trustees should seek court approval, but this will usually be so costly as to be impractical.

There were two allegations of violation of the duty of loyalty in *People ex rel. Scott v. Silverstein*, 86 Ill. App.3d 605, 408 N.E.2d 243 (1980). One was that the directors conspired to vote each other excessive salaries. The other was that the museum borrowed money from a bank in which one of the trustees held 35% of the voting stock. The case settled without going to trial.

Normally, it is a violation of the duty of loyalty to give away museum property. This became problematic for many artworks stolen during the Holocaust that ended up in museums and were not claimed until after the statute of limitations expired. AAM Guidelines on Holocaust Art provide that "museums may elect to waive certain available defenses." This is an attempt to assure museum directors that they did not violate the duty of loyalty by refusing to assert the statute of limitations. One could always argue that it is not a violation of the duty of loyalty to give back property that has been stolen because of the loss of goodwill and potential loss of donors that retaining the property would entail, but specific endorsement by a museum association's guidelines provides more comfort.

It is a violation of the duty of loyalty for a trustee to take advantage of a business opportunity that properly belongs to the museum. As many museum trustees are avid art collectors, this usually occurs when a trustee buys a work of art that has been offered to the museum.

iii. Cy Pres *and Deviation*

The duty of the board is to pursue the purposes of the non-profit corporation.

Suppose circumstances have changed so that fulfilling that purpose is no longer feasible, or the administrative procedure set forth in the chartering doctrine is no longer possible? In that instance, the board may invoke the doctrines of *cy pres* and equitable deviation.

Both doctrines require that changes in circumstances since the effective date of the gift have rendered the provisions of the charitable disposition impractical. There is a difference between *cy pres* and deviation. *Cy pres* is used when the purpose of the charity becomes impractical; deviation is used when the administrative provisions set forth become impractical. It is easier to allow deviation than *cy pres*, so some courts state that they are dealing with a mere administrative provision, and use the doctrine of deviation. The question of how many trustees the Barnes Foundation would have and how they were to be selected is clearly an administrative provision, and the court easily ordered deviation because a larger board would have the resources to raise (and give) more money and more expertise (and contacts) to properly discharge its function. *The Barnes Foundation, a Corporation*, 2004 WL 1960204 (Pa. Com. Pleas). In a more questionable decision, the court found that where the museum was located was also an administrative provision without discussing whether it might have more appropriately been characterized as a purpose. The court permitted a move from Lower Merion to downtown Philadelphia despite language in the instrument stating that the works were not to be moved. *In re Barnes Foundation*, 2004 WL 2903655 (Pa. Com. Pleas).

While the doctrines of cy pres and deviation originated with trusts, they will apply to any gift for charitable purposes, whether in the form of a trust, or a gift or bequest to a corporation or other entity.

If the court finds that changes in circumstances render the purposes impractical, to proceed with cy pres, it must then find whether the grantor (or testator) would have wanted the trust terminated, or whether the grantor would have wanted the closest practicable charitable solution. In order to find the latter and invoke cy pres, the court looks for a general charitable intent in the donor, rather than an intent limited to the specific gift. To permit a change either in the purposes of the gift or in the administrative provisions established by grantor, the court must find that the requested changes are as close as practical to the grantor's intent.

a. Impracticality

Whether the purposes of a gift have become impractical depends in part on what one considers the purposes of the gift from examining the original grant.

In the Matter of the Application of Lewis Nixon, Sr., 248 A.D. 373, 288 N.Y.Supp. 382 (App. 1936), Emma Gary bequeathed to the Metropolitan Museum of Art her Sèvres china dinner service, jewels, laces and embroideries, and paintings, on condition that the articles be placed on exhibition together in that museum in the name of the testatrix in a place approved by her executors, that the articles should be exhibited perpetually and should not be sold. The will provided alternative museum beneficiaries if the conditions were breached. It also left the residue of the estate to the museum to provide funds to do all this, but by the time Emma died in 1934, the depression had wiped out the residue. The court interpreted the purpose of the gift as the exhibition together of all Emma's possessions, and had no difficulty in finding that purpose impractical. None of the museums that were alternative takers were willing to accept the gift on its terms without a substantial endowment to support the exhibition requirements.

By contrast, in *Board of Trustees of The Museum of the American Indian, Heye Foundation v. Board of Trustees of The Huntington Free Library and Reading*

Room, 197 A.D.2d 64, 610 N.Y.S.2d 488 (1994), one charitable trust, the Heye Foundation, gave a gift of books to another charitable trust to be held for the use of the staff of the first trust, as well as the general public. When the first trust was absorbed into the Smithsonian Institution and the staff moved from New York to Washington, the court held that the use by the staff might be more difficult, but it was not impractical, given the use the staff had previously made of the books and the modern technology now available, and that there would be no change in the use made by the general public. This ruling had the added benefit of allowing the court to avoid deciding the question of whether the supposed gift was actually a gift or a contractual arrangement, as the Huntington undertook building and collection improvements in reliance on it.

In most decided cases, impracticality is found either because the number of potential beneficiaries has become trivial due to changes in society, such as retirement homes for vocations dwindling in size, or because the restrictions on the gift are so tight that it is impossible to raise enough money to comply with those restrictions. A strange case is *In re Fisk Univ.* 392 S.W.2d 582 (Tenn. App. 2011). There the impracticality bore no relationship to the gift. Georgia O'Keeffe had given a number of her paintings and Steiglitz photographs to a southern university. That university was experiencing financial problems of a severe nature and could not devote its resources to the upkeep and display of these artworks. Whether that is the sort of impracticality that the doctrine requires is questionable.

Generally, courts do not properly consider the requirement that there be a change in circumstance since the establishment of the gift. In *Lewis Nixon*, there was a change in circumstance after the execution of the will, but not after the effective date of the bequest, the death of Mrs. Gary. The same was true in *Harris v. Attorney General*, 31 Conn. Super. 93, 324 A.2d 279 (1974), where Theodate Riddle left a 150 acre estate with a main house and outbuildings as a museum for the art work "in the main house." Trustees wanted to sell one outbuilding, the Gundy, on grounds that it was not appropriate for museum use because of steep stairs and significant repairs needed, and because sale would reduce the annual deficit by removing repair costs and adding money. In holding that the trustees could sell the Gundy, the court mentioned that approximation, which seems to be the Connecticut word for deviation, does not require change in circumstances since the creation of the trust, as the Gundy was just as unsuitable for museum use when Mrs. Riddle died as when the case was decided. This was not a holding, as the court found that testator's intent was not to have the Gundy used as a museum.

The requirement of a change in circumstances does not exist in a state that has adopted the Uniform Trust Code § 413.

b. General Charitable Intent

The question is usually phrased whether the grantor had a general charitable intent, and courts discuss the question as though the only choices are whether the property would stay with the designated charity and be put to a different use, or whether the property would be returned to the grantor or the grantor's heirs. There is a third possibility, that the property should be shifted to a different charity that can make a use of it closer to the purposes of the original charitable grant. Most often courts have found that the grantor did have a general charitable intent and would have wanted the closest possible charitable use by this charity. One reason for this is that returning the property to the donor or his heirs often results in inclusion in gross income under the tax benefit rule.

This seems reasonable in some cases, questionable in others.

In *Georgia O'Keeffe Foundation v. Fisk University*, 312 S.W.3d 1 (Tenn. App. 2009), the court found general charitable intent from the fact that Ms. O'Keeffe had made similar gifts to other institutions, and because the donation contained no termination language or gift to an alternate beneficiary. It stated that the fact that there was no gift over for breach of condition was a strong factor in finding a general charitable intent. But a gift over can either be to a charity or to an individual, and there is no reason for a draftsman who knows property law to insert a specific gift over if he wants the gift to return to the estate; the estate would have a reversionary interest. In *Phipps v. Barbera*, 498 N.E.2d 411 (Mass. App. 1986), the fact that there was a gift over to a noncharitable beneficiary convinced the court that there was no general charitable intent.

In the Matter of the Application of Lewis Nixon, Sr., 248 A.D. 373, 288 N.Y.Supp. 382 (App. 1936), was a very different case. There was no trust in this case, but an outright gift. The court found, over a strong dissent, a general charitable intent despite the very specific instructions, the fact that the items were personal to Ms. Gary and the fact that other museums were named as alternate takers. It probably helped that all the museums named as alternate takers declined to take under Ms. Gary's restrictions.

§413 of the Uniform Trust Code, which is in effect in about half the states, provides a simplified form of cy pres and deviation, which operates whenever the purpose of the trust is illegal, impractical, impossible or wasteful. There is no need to find a change in circumstances or a general charitable intent. The donor can stay the court's ability to apply cy pres by specifying a gift to a person who is not a charity provided that twenty-one years have not expired from the establishment of the trust, or if the donor has a reversion and the donor is still alive at the time of the action. This provision does not affect the ability of a donor to provide that the property will pass to another charity if a condition on a grant is broken.

c. As Close as Practical

In *Nixon*, the court approved a plan whereby all Ms. Gary's jewels would be sold to provide an endowment so the remainder of her property could be displayed in accord with the gift. While there was evidence that the jewelry was not of museum quality, the jewelry constituted 90% of the value of the gift. The implication is that the sale would generate considerably more than would be required to display the other items. The court's opinion does not even discuss whether the sale of less than all of her jewelry would have been both practical and closer to her intention.

In *Re Barnes Foundation,* 2004 WL 2903655 (Pa. Com. Pleas), the Barnes Foundation asked the court to allow a change in the location of the gallery from Merion, Pennsylvania to Philadelphia. The court found the changes were reasonable. The court looked at Barnes' intent when donating the gallery and determined he intended that the gallery would have a much larger audience than a gallery in Merion would provide, given changes in land use regulations in Merion. This allowed the court to enable the trustees to move the gallery despite the clear prohibition in the trust instrument on moving any art work, since the donor's intent was also to display the art to a wide public audience. Though the courts did not rely on it, it is interesting to note that the initial document, drawn by future Supreme Court Justice Owen Roberts, contains in paragraph 11 a cy pres clause stating that if it is impossible to administer, the property and funds "shall be applied to an object as nearly within the scope herein indicated and laid down as shall be possible" in connection with an existing and organized institution then in being in Philadelphia or its suburbs.

B. Duty of Care

A trustee has an obligation of reasonable care and diligence in the management of the museum's assets. If a trustee does not use reasonable care, he or she is liable to the museum. The duty of care encompasses many aspects of managing a museum. The duty of care includes the duty to take possession of and to protect the museum property; the duty to make the museum property productive through prudent investment; and the duty to sell museum assets to render the trust more profitable or its investments more diverse.

A California court has explicitly laid out what comprises the duty of care. The court determined that members of the board of directors or trustees are required to act in the highest good faith toward the beneficiary, i.e. the public.

However, trustees for museums are granted broad discretion in managing the affairs of the museum. The trustees have discretion about what art to display, where to display it, what art to purchase and what art to sell. Unless it is proven they have abused their discretion the court will not interfere with their management of the museum. A good example is *Owens v. Magill*, 308 S.C.556, 419 S.E.2d 786 (1992), where the purchaser of paintings from a third party in a contract providing that the paintings would be temporarily housed at the museum revoked his loan of them to the museum in order to sell them. The museum might have asserted its rights as a third party beneficiary to the original purchase contract, but decided not to do so as the lenders were the museum's major benefactors and had a number of works on loan to the museum for which the museum could not claim third party beneficiary rights. The court commented that the museum trustees did not abuse their discretion in deciding not to assert the museum's argument. In short, the statement of the standard is very high at a general level, but its specific application defers to the business judgment of the trustees.

In order to show the trustees have not abused their discretion, many museums follow the guidelines of museum organizations, especially as they relate to selling and purchasing art.

Allegations of breach of the duty of care that have surfaced in the cases have mostly involved mismanagement or condoning mismanagement. They have included failure to properly care for museum property, failure to diligently analyze prospective museum investments, or disposing of museum property for less than its value. *People ex rel. Scott v. Silverstein*, 86 Ill. App.3d 605, 408 N.E.2d 243 (1980). The case settled, so we have no concrete facts telling us what is mismanagement or condoning mismanagement.

Other allegations of violation of the duty of care have not been upheld, usually because the choice made by the trustees was within their discretion. This conclusion was sometimes bolstered by the trustees seeking expert advice and following it. It was not a violation of the duty of care to diversify investments on the advice of an investment counselor, even if the diversification resulted in a significant loss. Following police advice on security precautions was endorsed. The museum collection could either be insured or not. *Harris v. Attorney General*, 31 Conn. Super. 93, 324 A.3d 279 (1974).

A trustee can no longer be a passive trustee. In earlier times, a person might be appointed trustee for his contributions, his contacts or his political influence, and told that he need not attend meetings or read voluminous correspondence. Today a trustee who never attends meetings or participates in governance decisions is likely to find that he is liable for violating the duty of care he owes to the museum.

C. Enforcing Museum Duties

The state Attorney General has standing to enforce the duty of care and the duty of loyalty. Doctrine denies standing to newspaper reporters, *Wiegand v. Barnes Foundation*, 374 Pa. 149, 97 A.2d 81 (1953), citizens, *Owens v. Magill*, 308 S.C.556, 419 S.E.2d 786 (1992), and taxpayers in a state that permits them to sue for waste of public moneys, *Hardman v. Feinstein*, 195 Cal. App.3d 157, 240 Cal. Rptr. 483 (1987), and even a foundation that was the successor of the donor. *Georgia O'Keeffe Foundation (Museum) v. Fisk U*, 312 S.W.3d 1 (Tenn. App. 2009). Standing should be available for a taker in default when the question is whether the museum has or is about to violate a conditional gift that would result in an interest vesting in the taker. A person who gives money to a museum on condition that it name its building after the giver should certainly have standing to sue for the return of the money if the building is not named for him within a reasonable time, though sometimes the suit needs to be brought as a breach of contract action to ensure standing.

Limiting standing in most cases to the state Attorney General has consequences. Those offices have limited budgets. They can undertake a limited number of investigations and lawsuits. Attorneys General are most likely to become active when there is a proposal to move charitable assets out of the state, where there is a credible allegation of criminal activity such as fraud or embezzlement, or when extensive publicity has made the question a matter of public controversy.

D. Museum Acquisitions

The first job of museum acquisitions is to assure that the museum is actually acquiring what it thinks it is getting. The formalities of gifts, wills and purchases discussed in the chapters on Taxes and Commericial Art Relationships above should be reviewed.

Museum guidelines require that museums have a written policy on acquisitions. They further specify that museums should be satisfied that they are getting good title and that the work has not been illegally exported. For art that was in Europe 1933–1945, the American Association of Museum Directors guidelines are more specific. If there is evidence of unlawful confiscation, the museum should not acquire the work unless it finds evidence of restitution.

i. Purchases

Museums purchase artwork from all over the world. They need to assure that the art they are purchasing is authentic. The museum also needs assurances that the art has not been stolen and that the museum is not violating any laws or ethics by completing the transaction. These purchases are governed by applicable commercial law, as discussed above in the chapters on Authenticity and Title.

AAMD Guidelines suggest that museums purchasing items that were in Europe 1933–1945 seek assurances that the seller has title and that the work is free of claims. Phrased broadly, this does not require that the seller formally warrant the title, but that would be a good result if attainable.

ii. Gifts

Museums often receive collections and funding in the form of gifts. As discussed in the chapter on Taxes above, the museum needs to assure that the gift is effective.

Museum guidelines do not generally distinguish between acquisition by gift and acquisition by purchase, but this is deceptive. A museum is unlikely to purchase artwork that it does not wish to add to its collection. The same is not true of a gift. Museums may accept unrestricted gifts for a number of reasons. Pieces that are not museum quality or that do not fit into the collection can be sold, providing funds to buy art that does fit the collection. Sometimes museums accept gifts from people they wish to cultivate because the people are potential future donors of art or funds. While there is no less reason in these circumstances to verify title and authenticity, these acquisitions will not jump through the same hoops in the acquisition policy as will acquiring a work by purchase.

One problem with a gift is that it may limit a museum's remedies. The Bloedels bought a Matisse from Knoedler Gallery in 1954, and gave it to the Seattle Art Museum in 1991. The Matisse had been stolen by the Nazis during World War II from Paris dealer Paul Rosenberg. The Museum returned the painting to Rosenberg's heirs and sued Knoedler for fraud. The court granted summary judgment for Knoedler because there was no evidence that Knoedler defrauded the museum, or that the Bloedels had assigned their claims to the Museum. *Rosenberg v. Seattle Art Museum*, 124 F.Supp.2d 1207 (W.D.Wash 2000). It does not appear that Knoedler raised the issue of expiration of the statute of limitations.

iii. Loans

Often a museum or art institute receives items on loan from a private citizen or another museum. These loans are subject to the law of bailments, discussed in the Commercial Art Relationships chapter above. Museum guidelines on acquisition of potential Holocaust property, even for short-term loans, are the same as for purchase.

E. Caring for the Collection

Museum pieces require care. In addition to the need to keep them clean and in an appropriately climate-controlled environment, artwork can be damaged by flood, storm or fire, and are subject to looting and vandalism. Assuring appropriate care is part of both the duty of loyalty and the duty of care imposed on the directors.

In addition to routine care, many works of art require restoration. Museums generally either have their own conservation studios, or contract out restoration work.

Restoration can be more problematic when the work does not belong to the museum.

Such situations arise in two contexts.

Under NAGPRA, discussed below in the Native American artifacts chapter, a museum may be obligated by statute to repatriate artifacts to a tribe. The statute is silent on the museum's right to demand costs of conservation or restoration.

The other common situation is where items are on loan to a museum. It is unlikely that there would be serious costs incurred for restoration of a short-term loan, though it is clear that in the absence of a specific contract provision to the contrary, the museum must return the loaned item to the owner in the same condition in which it was received.

More problematic is the long-term loan. In a perfect world, the loan agreement would have a specific provision on conservation and restoration, or when the need arose, the museum would contact the owner to arrange for the necessary work. We do not live in a perfect world. What sometimes occurs is that the museum does the conservation it considers necessary, often overlooking the fact that the work is only in its possession on loan. When the owner terminates the loan, the museum might look for compensation. This invokes the doctrines of *quantum meruit* and accession. In order to recover, the restorer must act in good faith. This requires either a belief that the work belongs to the restorer, or a situation where the work must be done to avoid loss to the artwork and it is not possible to contact the owner. In most cases, a museum will be able to establish neither because its own records will reveal that it is not the owner and will also reveal the address of the lender. But it is possible that the lender might have moved or died, or the museum's records might have been destroyed. If the restorer can establish good faith, he is entitled to fair compensation for the work done, but not in excess of the benefit conferred thereby on the owner.

An unusual situation occurred in *Hoelzer v. City of Stamford*, 972 F.2d 495 (2d Cir. 1992). In 1934, James Dougherty painted six huge murals commissioned by the United States Works Progress Administration for Stamford High School. A generation later during reconstruction, workmen removed the murals and placed them with other construction debris. They were rescued by a student, who turned them over to a United States General Services Administration representative, who in turn brought them to plaintiff Hoelzer, a restorer. Hoelzer wrote the GSA representative several times explaining the damage and the work proposed, but received no response. He began the necessary work in the early 1970s. By 1980, the city knew about his work and its representatives visited Hoelzer to observe the progress. In the late 1980s, the city claimed the murals and the GSA disclaimed them. Hoelzer claimed them as abandoned property. The court held that the city never abandoned its ownership interest because there was no evidence of intent to abandon. It did not decide whether Hoelzer acted in good faith because it found that the city was estopped from raising that question by its continuing knowledge that Hoelzer was doing the restoration in expectation of being paid. The bill came to $557,200, which the court held to be reasonable, but an amount considerably in excess of what the city might have expected to pay. Unusually, the court gave the city the option of paying that amount or abandoning its title to the murals by delivering them to Hoelzer, which it did.

F. Museum De-Accessioning

i. Hard Law

Technically, de-accession is the removal of a work from the museum's collection, and disposal is the sale or gift of the work. Usually, the term de-accession is used for both because the most common means of de-accessioning is to sell the work.

There is no hard law restricting de-accessioning except the application of the duties of loyalty and care. One illustration of this hard law, decided on the basis of the duty of loyalty, concerns the Wilstach estate, which established a trust of Wilstach's artworks and a fund to augment them. Sixty years after it was established, the paintings were administered by the Philadelphia Museum of Art. The document provided "the collection will be kept together." There is no prohibition on sales. Mrs. Wilstach gave broad discretion to her trustees "to make such rules and regulations in regard to the use and enjoyment of said collection as will best conduce to the end intended." The trustees' request for permission to de-accession certain work, presenting a fifteen-year study of the collection, was granted. The works selected for sale fell into eight categories:

1. 19th-century paintings by artists of minor importance whose reputations had not risen.
2. 19th-century paintings by major artists whose reputations had fallen.

3. Older paintings of little artistic merit by unidentified artists, or which are attributed to a particular school.
4. Minor works by important artists.
5. Paintings below museum quality erroneously attributed to specific artists.
6. Fakes or forgeries.
7. Practice pieces or student works by well-known artists.
8. Paintings too small to adequately illustrate the artist's work for museum purposes, or so large that they take up too much space relative to their artistic importance.

Wilstach Estate, 1 Pa. D. & C.2d 197 (Orph. Ct. 1954).

ii. Soft Law

However, there is significant soft law. Museum associations have had much to say about selling off parts of the collection.

The problem is that many items enter the collection that the museum staff does not believe are truly museum quality. They may be received as part of a larger bequest or donation to induce a collector to give works more central to the museum's collection. For that reason, laws that are frequently proposed prohibiting museums from selling any object from their collection are routinely opposed by the museum community and routinely defeated.

Problems usually arise in difficult economic times when museums have trouble supporting their operating budgets. There is a great temptation to sell valuable works in order to cover the bills.

The Association of Art Museum Directors has promulgated standards. They prohibit the museum from taking loans on the security of works in the collection. They require that the museum develop standards for acquisition related to the purpose of the collection. They enjoin museums to carefully consider whether to accept donations. They require that funds from the de-accessioning of work, and earnings on those funds, be used only for the purchase of other works for the collection. Those funds cannot be used for operating expenses or for capital improvements. De-accession decisions should be recommended by professional staff and approved by the trustees, and priority should be given to disposition to another public entity that will keep the work before the public, or exchange of a work by a living artist for another work. They set forth eight good reasons for de-accessioning:

1. The work is of poor quality and lacks value for exhibition or study.
2. The work is a duplicate that has no value as part of a series.
3. The work has been stolen, illegally imported or subject to other legal claims.

4. The work is fraudulent or forged and lacks either aesthetic merit or historical importance.
5. Its physical condition is so poor that restoration is not practical.
6. It is no longer consistent with the mission or collecting goals of the museum.
7. Disposal is part of the museum's effort to improve its collections.
8. The museum is unable to care adequately for the work because of its particular requirements.

The polar positions are the sale of a work to raise money, and the disposition of a work for good artistic reasons related to the collection. The best way to assure that courts and the general public believe that the action falls into the second category is to engage in the sort of rigorous study that was present in *Wilstach.*

Sanctions for violation of AAMD Guidelines are not trivial. The National Academy Museum in NY sold two important Hudson River School paintings in 2008 to pay its bills. The Association of Art Museum Directors imposed sanctions. It banned loans and program collaborations between the Academy and AAMD members. Potential donors refused to contribute to the Academy. The director was replaced by a new director. The governance structure changed. The Academy promised to expand its fund-raising capacity. AAMD sanctions were lifted after 20 months, but the Academy remained on probation for five years.

AAMD sanctions may be less effective with university art galleries. While the reputational loss for the gallery director is the same, university art galleries are less likely to mount shows where they borrow from other museums and more likely to display the work of their own faculty and students. Further, it is usually the president of the university who is deciding to sell a work to fund the university. In one recent case, the president of Brandeis lost his job after proposing to liquidate the university's art collection to make up an operating deficit, and his successor announced that the liquidation would not take place. In another, the court approved the sale of a half-interest in the work, which would take it away from study at the university for half the year. *In re Fisk Univ.* 392 S.W.2d 582 (Tenn. App. 2011).

G. Special Powers

Occasionally, state law confers special powers on museums. A New York law allowing certain museums to condemn property to help finance the museum was held not to be prohibited special legislation. *Hotel Dorset Co. v. Trust for Cultural Resources of City of New York*, 46 N.Y.2d 358, 385 N.E.2d 1284, 413 N.Y.S.2d 357 (1978).

5. Museum Labor Law

A. Employment Law Generally

Museums are normally corporations. They may be established as ordinary business corporations, or they may be set up under special nonprofit corporation statutes. Occasionally they are trusts. Regardless of form, they operate under the general labor laws. There are no special labor laws applicable to museums. While special laws do not apply, museum counsel probably spend more time on labor relations than on any other single subject.

A museum's employees may be represented by labor unions. In that case, the rights of employees will be governed by the contracts negotiated between the museum and the unions. The relationship between the museum and the unions will be governed by federal labor law. The museum's principal obligations are to recognize a union supported by a majority of the work group, and to bargain with it in good faith over wages, hours and working conditions.

A museum that is part of a state or city may instead be governed by public employee labor relations law. That will regulate the relations between the museum and the unions representing its employees, while the negotiated contracts and whatever civil service rules apply will govern the relationship between the museum and the employees subject to those contracts.

In the absence of union contracts, the ordinary law of employment contracts applies to the employment relationship between a museum and its employees. This is true whether the contract is to employ the museum director, its curators, its conservation staff, its administrative staff, its guards or its maintenance workers. Some of these workers will have written contracts setting forth the terms of their employment in some detail. Most will not. They will be people hired for an indefinite period to do a particular job at a specific compensation, but there will be no detailed contract. These employees are called "at will" employees. While it is frequently stated that an employee without a contract is an at will employee, that is not true. All employees have contracts, either express or implied. An at will employee is an employee that is not covered by a collective bargaining agreement between the museum and an appropriate union and is employed for an indefinite period. A person who is employed for a fixed period of time, such as six months, or who is employed to perform a specific task, such as to research the provenance of a particular artwork, is not employed for an indefinite period, so is not an at will employee.

It is not unusual for a museum to have some employees subject to union contracts, some employees subject to individual, detailed contracts, and some at will employees. However, it is somewhat artificial to distinguish between these three types of employees. The relationship between each type of employee and the museum is governed by contract. In one case, it is a union contract; in a second, it is an individually negotiated contract; in the third, the parties have agreed to minimal terms of the contract such as hours and pay, and the law supplies all the other terms.

B. Terminating Employees

i. General Rule

The most serious action an employer can take against an employee is to terminate the employment. Most union contracts and civil service rules provide that an employee may be terminated only for good cause. They define "good cause" in relatively general terms. They establish a dispute resolution procedure, usually involving arbitration, for determining whether good cause exists to terminate the employee.

The rules for at will employees are different. The classic statement is that an employer can terminate an at will employee for good reason, bad reason or for no reason at all without any liability. This is not true. An at will employee cannot be terminated for a prohibited reason, which is a more accurate way of stating a bad reason. Prohibited reasons may be erected by the U.S. or state constitutions, federal or state law, or judicial decision. Examples of prohibited reasons include discrimination on grounds of race, sex, national origin, disability, or age.

It is also commonly stated that there are three common exceptions to the ability of an employer to discharge an at will employee: implied contract, public policy and implied covenant of good faith and fair dealing. As we will see, public policy is another prohibited reason for discharge, while implied contract and implied covenant of good faith and fair dealing are both questions of contract interpretation that may result in the employment relationship not being an at will employment.

Whether these exceptions should exist is a threshold question that each jurisdiction must confront. They are supported by considerations of basic fairness, implementing the intentions of the parties, and furthering important government policies. On the other hand, they can result in considerable expense for an employer, both in litigation costs and in establishing and maintaining a system of record-keeping to present evidence in areas where groundless claims seem particularly numerous.

ii. Public Policy Exception

The public policy exception has had a growing reception, and is now in effect in most United States jurisdictions. That exception holds that an employer may be liable for damages for discharging an employee if the discharge undermines an important public policy. For example, in *Phillips v. Goodyear Tire & Rubber Co.*, 651 F.2d 1051 (5th Cir. 1981), the employee alleged that he was fired for testifying truthfully about the employer's conduct. The Fifth Circuit refused to create a public policy exception in a diversity case, where it was applying the law of Georgia or Texas, neither of whose courts had announced a public policy exception.

While most jurisdictions (but not Georgia yet) have a public policy exception, the unanimity disappears when we ask what the content of that exception might be. The public policy exception generally applies when permitting the employee to be discharged would frustrate an important goal of government. These situations can be grouped into four classes of cases. Not all jurisdictions subscribe to all four classes, nor is the content of each class the same in all jurisdictions.

One class of cases that violates public policy is when an employee is fired for refusal to violate the law in connection with his job. An example might be refusing to drive the museum truck when the employee did not have the required commercial driver's license, or refusal to participate in the theft by the museum of a lender's artwork.

A second class of cases that violates public policy is when an employee is fired for performing public duties. That is the heading that Phillips alleged in the case above, because it is a public duty to respond to a subpoena. In many states, there are statutes that prevent discharge for missing work to perform a public duty, such as jury duty. If there is no specific statute, jury duty is likely to be included as performing a public duty.

A third class of cases refers to whistle-blowing: informing a government agency or your employer about the employer's violation of the criminal law, or a violation by another employee. This might include information that money received as a grant from the National Endowment for the Arts was spent by the museum director to refurbish his own house, or a complaint that a museum supervisor was engaging in sexual harassment.

The fourth class is the exercise of a legal right related to the job, such as filing a workman's compensation claim for on-the-job injuries or litigation against the museum for back pay.

One factor in determining whether the public policy exception should apply is whether employees are likely to be the principal source of information for the government agency about law violations. This will frequently be the case, as employees are the people best situated to know what the museum is doing. Where the violations involve relations between the museum and its employees, such as violations of labor laws, failure to properly withhold taxes, or the like, it would be unusual if anyone other than an employee would know enough facts to effectively complain. If employees could be fired for providing this information, it is unlikely to ever come to the attention of the government because the penalty for witnesses bringing it forward would be loss of a job, a penalty too severe for most people to risk.

Another factor may be whether failure to provide a remedy would frustrate a law. Worker's compensation is meant to replace the torts system as a remedy for work injuries. If an employer could fire a worker who used worker's compensation, the legislature's intent in setting up the worker's compensation system would be frustrated.

A significant question is whether the public policy exception applies if the employee's action is not related to work. Suppose an employee reports to the police that the museum director has been selling drugs on his own time at a place removed from work. The report certainly aids in enforcement of the drug laws, but it is unclear that the employee has a better position than any other citizen to detect the violation.

iii. Implied Contract

The implied contract exception is not truly an exception to the rules for at will termination. If there is proof of an implied contract, the employee is not an at will employee if the implied contract contains a termination procedure or implies long-term employment. Like other contracts, the implied contract must be supported by consideration, and contain an offer and an acceptance. One analysis is that writing a provision into an employee manual is an offer, which is accepted by the employee continuing to work for the employer after being notified of the change. Continuing to work also provides the consideration for the promise.

But what is the promise? Usually, the implied contract provides either that employees are only terminated for good cause, or that employees will be terminated in reverse order of seniority. There may be many other things contained in an employment policy, but if they do not pertain to method of discharge or length of employment, they are not relevant to the question of whether the person is an at will employee.

The easiest way to prove an implied contract is by a written statement because of the certainty that the statement was made and because it permits the court to know the statement's content with assurance. Such statements are usually contained in employee handbooks or employment policy statements. The larger the employer, the more likely there will be such written evidence. The form of a promise is not required. Statements in the documents that employees are only discharged for cause are likely to create implied contracts. A statement of a list of reasons for discharge of an employee may be argued to exclude other reasons for discharge. One might also argue that contributions to a pension plan that remains unvested is an implied promise that the employee will not be discharged before the pension vests except for good cause.

Because of the frequency with which these documents are found to create rights in employees, it has become common for employers to insert language in handbooks providing that they confer no additional rights on employees. While some courts have enforced those disclaimers, there is a tendency to refuse to enforce them unless they are unambiguous and clearly brought to the attention of the employee.

Implied contracts are often established by oral representations or by a course of dealing. It is often the case that the oral representations are congruent with employment manuals, so it is unclear whether it is the statement, the manual or the combination that forms the implied contract. Course of dealing involves the practice of the employer. If the employer has never discharged an employee except for good cause, this course of dealing may become part of every employment contract.

iv. Duty of Good Faith and Fair Dealing

The duty of good faith and fair dealing is likewise not really an exception to the ability to terminate an at will employment; it is a doctrine that prevents the employment from being at will. In some states, relational contracts are interpreted to impose an implied duty of good faith and fair dealing on the parties in their performance of their obligations. Such a duty would require good cause for terminating the employment relationship. Fewer states impose the good faith exception than either the public policy or the implied contract exception.

v. Federal and State Statutes on Employment

State and federal statutes limit the "at will" employment doctrine in many ways. Most of them are protection against discrimination, or protection from retaliation for claiming some benefit. Employers cannot discriminate against employees on the basis of race, gender, age, or disability. The relevant federal statutes are the Civil Rights Act of 1964 (commonly referred to as Title VII), the Equal Pay Act, the Age Discrimination in Employment Act and the Americans with Disabilities Act. Museums, like all other businesses, must be mindful of these acts when making employment decisions. In addition, there are many prohibitions that apply only to people who contract with the federal government, or who receive federal funds. It is not unusual for a museum to receive a grant from the National Endowment for the Arts to partially support a specific exhibition, subjecting the museum to these laws. Many states have similar, but not identical, laws, and some municipalities have followed suit.

Procedures for recovery may vary. Sometimes recovery is by direct suit. In other cases, an administrative regime has been established to try to mediate the claim, or to signal that plaintiff can at least prove a *prima facie* case before the employer can be put to the expense of litigating. If there is such an administrative proceeding, a potential plaintiff must exhaust that administrative remedy before filing suit. Suit on any grounds that he did not raise before the agency will be barred. *Kelly v. American Museum of Natural History*, 1999 U.S. Dist. Lexis 15363, 1999 WL 782475 (S.D.N.Y. 1999).

a. Discrimination on Grounds of Race

Discrimination on grounds of race may be prohibited by 42 U.S.C. § 1981. A successful § 1981 plaintiff may demonstrate that he is a member of a racial or ethnic minority, that the museum intended to discriminate on grounds of race or ethnicity, and that the discrimination interfered with a contract right protected by § 1981. Alternatively, he can prove that he is being punished for efforts to secure rights for racial or ethnic minorities regardless of his race, and that the punishment interfered with his § 1981 rights.

b. Civil Rights Act

The Civil Rights Act of 1964 (Title VII), 42 U.S.C §§ 2000e to 2000e-17, provides in part that "it shall be unlawful employment practice for an employer ... to discharge any individual, or otherwise to discriminate against any individual with respect to his compensation, terms, conditions, or privileges of employment, because of such individual's race, color, religion, or sex or national origin." To be successful in a Title VII action plaintiff must prove discrimination. While years ago, discrimination was usually overt and there was plenty of evidence of discriminatory intent, today it is much less common to talk about discrimination. Discrimination can be proven in one of two ways: a pretext analysis and a mixed motive analysis.

Under the pretext analysis, plaintiff must prove that (1) he is a member of a protected class; (2) he was qualified for his position; (3) he suffered an adverse employment action; and (4) the adverse employment action took place under circumstances that give rise to an inference of unlawful discrimination. Once the plaintiff has proved these four elements, the burden then shifts to the defendant to show a legitimate, non-discriminatory reason for the employment action taken. If the defendant satisfies his burden, the burden shifts back to the plaintiff to prove that the employer was actually motivated by illegal discrimination.

In many cases, the employment action will result from a mixture of motives. The museum may claim that it discharged the curator because her last show was not well attended and was criticized in the local papers. The curator may allege that the discharge decision was made by a new young museum director who does not believe that older people project the hip image that the museum wants to convey. In addition, the curator may allege that the new director is leery of the extra costs that older employees add to the museum's health insurance premiums. Under a mixed motive analysis the plaintiff must submit direct evidence of the defendant's discriminatory animus. The plaintiff must show that the discriminating and illegitimate factor, in this case age, played a substantial role in the employment decision. The evidence produced for this mixed motive analysis might include policy documents, or statements and other behavior by decision-makers. If the plaintiff can prove discrimination then the burden shifts to the defendant to prove that the decision would have been the same in the absence of discriminatory intent. *Kelly v. American Museum of Natural History*, 1999 U.S. Dist. Lexis 15363, 1999 WL 782475 (S.D.N.Y. 1999).

Recent legislation grants more limited recovery where discrimination has been a motivating factor in the action.

Even where there has been some evidence of discrimination by museum employees, an employee may have difficulty in prevailing where there are valid reasons for denying employment, such as failure to disclose honesty-related discharges on the job application. *Piascik v. Cleveland Museum of Art*, 426 F. Supp. 779 (N.D. Ohio 1976).

c. Equal Pay Act

The Equal Pay Act, 29 U.S.C. §206(d), is designed to assure that men and women performing the same work receive the same compensation. Plaintiffs in Equal Pay Act cases often join a count for recovery under Title VII. Plaintiff's initial burden of proof is satisfied by showing that she performed work equal to a man's, and that he was better compensated than she was. Actual proof of motive is not an element of a *prima facie* case. While this is not a comparable pay provision that would look only at the comparative education levels required for the jobs, the work need not be identical. The work must be reasonably similar, as do the amount of skill required, effort, responsibilities and similar working conditions. Factors that are considered in an EPA action include quantity and quality of production, education, work experience, conduct and skill. If the jobs are similar enough in the aggregate the jobs should be considered equal even if there are slight variations. The burden then shifts to the defendant to show that the unequal compensation is justified.

At least in theory, defendant now has different defenses open to it, depending on whether this is an EPA claim or a Title VII claim.

To rebut an EPA claim, a defendant must prove by a preponderance of the evidence one of four affirmative defenses. It must prove the difference in pay is the result of (1) a seniority system, (2) a merit system, (3) a system which measures earnings by quantity or quality of production, or (4) a differential based on any factor other than sex.

To rebut a Title VII claim, the defendant is not limited to these four defenses. The defendant need only provide a legitimate reason for the apparent discrimination that negates the inference of gender discrimination. It is not immediately apparent what reason that negates sex discrimination might be that would not fall within one of the four defenses to the Equal Pay Act. *Grigoletti v. Ortho Pharmaceutical Corp.*, 570 A.2d 903 (N.J. 1990).

d. Age Discrimination in Employment Act

The Age Discrimination in Employment Act, 29 U.S.C. §§621–634, prevents discrimination against workers over forty on grounds of age. The ADEA requires that a plaintiff must prove (1) he was in the age group protected by the ADEA; (2) he was discharged or demoted; (3) at the time of his discharge or demotion he was performing his job at a level that met his employer's legitimate expectations. The discharged employee does not have to be replaced with someone outside the protected class; the employee must only prove he lost his job because of his age. Substantially younger is enough. *O'Connor v. Consolidated Coin Caterers Corp.*, 517 U.S. 308 (1996). However, it will be difficult to prove age discrimination discharge if the employee is replaced by someone who is older than he is unless there is a change in management between the two acts or unless there is clear evidence of discrimination.

e. Disability Discrimination

The federal Americans With Disabilities Act (ADA), 42 U.S.C. §§12101-12213, The Rehabilitation Act, 29 U.S.C. §§701-796*l*, and many state statutes prohibit discrimination in employment against persons with disabilities. Each statute has its own peculiarities. As a general rule, not all employers are subject to each act, but most museums are likely to be covered employers. One act requires that the employer have fifteen employees for at least twenty weeks in the year. That would include most, but not all, museums.

To establish a *prima facie* case of wrongful termination based on a disability under the ADA, a plaintiff must prove (1) his employer is subject to the ADA; (2) he suffers from a disability within the meaning of the ADA; (3) he could perform the essential functions of his job with or without reasonable accommodation; and (4) he was fired because of his disability. *Zuppardo v. Suffolk County Vanderbilt Museum*, 19 F. Supp. 2d 52 (E.D.N.Y. 1998), *aff'd mem.* 173 F.3d 848 (2d Cir. 1999).

A disability under the ADA is defined as a physical or mental impairment that substantially limits one or more major life activities of such individual. A major life activity is one that is an activity that the average person in the general population can perform, such as walking, and it must be substantially limited so the person with the disability cannot perform the life activity or can only perform the activity for a very short period of time. To determine if it is a substantial limitation the court will look at the duration and severity of the impairment, and will not consider ameliorative steps the employee could take such as medication or prosthetics.

Alternatively, a person is disabled under the Act if there is a record of his disability, or if the employer believes that the individual suffers from the disability, even if he does not. Thus, if the employer discriminates against the employee as though the employee were disabled but the employee is not disabled, that discrimination remains actionable.

An employee is not qualified for a job if its performance would pose a direct threat to the employee's health while on the job.

If an employee or applicant is disabled, the employer is obligated to provide reasonable accommodation so that the person can do the job. What accommodations are reasonable has been a fertile source of litigation. Generally, employees have succeeded in getting one-time accommodations from large employers, and less well with ongoing changes from small employers, especially when those changes involve considerable expense.

Perhaps more significant than employee relations is the obligation of a museum to accommodate patrons with disabilities. This includes access problems such as elevators, ramps, handrails, doors and restrooms. It is unclear whether a museum must make its exhibits intelligible to the blind and deaf.

C. Defamation

Another important aspect of the employment relationship is the possibility that a museum will become involved in a defamation lawsuit with an employee, a former employee, or a job applicant. That question is dealt with in the Defamation chapter above.

For further guidance, see Mark A. Rothstein, Charles B. Craver, Elinor P. Schroeder & Elaine W. Sholen, Employment Law (6th ed. 2019).

Checkpoints

- Museums may be organized as any business form, but they are most commonly organized under state nonprofit corporation laws for educational purposes. They usually qualify as § 501(c)(3) organizations for tax purposes. They are not permitted to distribute profit to any individual.
- Museums are subject to supervision by the state attorney general, which may include requiring the submission of periodic reports.
- Museums usually do not pay income or property taxes, and contributions to museums are usually deductible from income, gift or estate tax liability. Obtaining property tax exemption is usually the most difficult.
- A museum is taxed on its unrelated business income, defined as income from operating a business that is not related to its exempt purpose. A restaurant and a bookstore are both businesses, but they are related to a museum's exempt purpose if the restaurant is primarily for employees and guests, and if the bookstore sells only books about artwork.
- If a museum is a private foundation because supported by a few individuals, special rules apply evidencing more supervision and a shorter life span.
- Museums are governed by a board that chooses the major officers and sets general policy. Members of the board owe a duty of loyalty and a duty of care to the museum.
- The duty of loyalty is defined by the purposes of the museum, and requires that the board members not engage in self-dealing or take advantage of any conflict of interest they may have. Purposes may be determined from the museum's charter or from the requirements the law imposes on charitable organizations.
- When changes have occurred since the museum was established that make the achievement of its purposes impractical, a court may order a change in museum purposes to the nearest practical charitable use if the person who established the museum had a general charitable intent. Likewise, the court can order a deviation from mandated administrative matters for impracticability.
- The duty of care requires reasonable care and diligence in the management of the museum's assets. Trustees are judged under the business judgment rule which provides no liability if the trustee exercises reasonable business judgment.
- Enforcing trustee duties is left largely to the state attorney general. A taker in default of a gift may have enforcement powers, as may the donor of a gift under some circumstances.
- Museum acquisitions should be the subject of a policy according to museum association guidelines so that museums acquire ownership of authentic works. Acquisition guidelines generally do not distinguish between purchases, gifts and loans, though there are obvious practical differences.

- Restoration of works in the collection is a duty of the museum. In unusual cases, a restorer may have a claim for unjust enrichment against the owner of the artwork.
- Museum de-accessions are limited by the general duties of loyalty and care. Most museum organizations have accreditation standards that limit de-accession to generating funds for future purchases, but prohibit it for operating expenses or building improvement.
- Museum labor law contains no special rules because the employer is a museum. It is subject to normal rules about union bargaining, specific contracts and at will employment.
- Termination of employees covered by union contracts, civil service or individual contracts will be governed by the terms of the contracts. At will employees can be terminated for any reason, but cannot be terminated for a prohibited reason such as race, sex, national origin, disability, age, or in retaliation for the exercise of some protected right, such as refusal to violate the law, the exercise of a government duty like jury service, whistle-blowing, or the exercise of a right in connection with employment, such as filing a worker's compensation claim.
- Federal and state laws frequently prohibit employment discrimination, including discrimination in pay, on grounds of race, sex, national origin, disability, or age.

Chapter 14

Art in War

Roadmap

After reading this chapter, you should understand:

- Sources of law on the treatment of art in war are mainly the Hague Convention, its Second Protocol, and national regulations or training manuals.
- Distinguishing the Hague Convention from its Second Protocol is important because twice as many countries have adhered to the Convention as have joined the Second Protocol, and the U.S. is not a member of the Second Protocol.
- Peacetime activities: The Hague Convention calls on nations during peacetime to plan to protect art in case of hostilities. The Second Protocol is more specific, calling for a national inventory, appointment of an official in charge, protection of art from fire or collapse in the event of war, and locating cultural items away from military targets.
- Wartime activities: The Hague Convention prohibits reprisals against cultural property, or targeting cultural property except when waived for military necessity. The Second Protocol specifies that waiver can only be by a person of high rank, and places additional conditions on the waiver.
- Vandalism: The Hague Convention requires a country to prevent or put a stop to vandalism against cultural property.
- Booty and pillage: A country can take booty, items useful in prosecution of the war, and use it for its own purposes. Other items would be pillage if taken, and they cannot be taken.
- Occupation: The Second Protocol prohibits illegal export or transfer of ownership of art. It severely restricts archaeology.
- Seizure of enemy property: There is no prohibition on seizure of enemy-owned property without compensation that is located within the territory of the seizing state.

1. Introduction

Nowhere in Art Law is the ever-present gap between law as aspiration (law on the books) and law in operation (what actually happens) as great as in the area of legal obligations related to art in war. By art in war I mean four interrelated activities: activities during peacetime that might be said to be in contemplation of potential war; activities during hostilities; activities during occupation; and activities once full peace is re-established. The reason for this gap lies in some combination of the nature of the norms being either international or military law, and the natural proclivities of the persons charged with enforcing them.

Commands to destroy religious artwork in war date to biblical times. "You must destroy all the sites at which the nations you are to dispossess worshiped their gods, whether on lofty mountains and on hills or under any luxuriant tree. Tear down the images of their gods, obliterating their names from that site." Deut. 12:2–3. The world has seen periods of wholesale destruction of art in both civil and international wars, especially in the French revolution, World War I and World War II.

Appropriating art in wartime stands on a different historical footing. As long ago as the Roman republic, a distinction was made between things that could be taken in war, classified as booty, and the taking of things that were impermissible, called pillage. Nonetheless, large amounts of art flowed from the conquered nations to Rome, and the appropriation of art became a matter of policy for the Napoleonic empire around 1800 and the Nazi Third Reich from 1935–45.

On this subject, there was a period where only domestic rules applied. The turn of the twentieth century saw a treaty that had only modest adherents. Two world wars and their abuses led to the Hague Convention on the Protection of Cultural Property in the Event of Armed Conflict (1954), 249 U.N.T.S. 240, and a tightening of its standards in a Second Protocol in 1999, 2253 U.N.T.S. 212, that constitute the principal international law standards today.

2. Reasons for the Rules

Rules on the treatment of art in wartime seem to result from two impulses: efficient administration and substantive policy.

In every organization of even moderate size, be it a government, an army, or a business, there is a desire at the top to speak with a single voice and to control the activities of everyone within the organization to advance the organization's goals and to minimize the opportunity for its agents to indulge their individual proclivities at the expense of either the organization or its clientele. In business organizations, this usually results in codes of conduct and form contracts. In government administration, including the military, it usually takes the form of rules, education, and procedures for determining when those rules have been violated, and a system or redress and sanctions.

One goal of promulgating rules is to inform people in the field of expectations about their behavior.

That goal explains the need for rules. It says little about the content of those rules. For example, at one point, it was common to compensate soldiers minimally, but to permit them to supplement the meager compensation provided by their employers by permitting them to pillage the possessions of a conquered city. This was a policy decision.

As an example of a policy decision, a group of French intellectuals in 1796 petitioned the French government to bring the world's greatest art to Paris for three reasons. First, the French people's exquisite sensitivity will allow the art world to progress more rapidly than if great art is dispersed among less talented peoples. Second, France is the country best equipped to assure the safety of great works of art, an ironic declaration coming less than a decade after the French Revolution resulted in probably the greatest destruction of its own art by its own people that any country has ever endured. Third, the economic element, people will come from all over the world to see great art and to learn to produce it.

In contrast to this nationalistic approach, the second and third clauses of the preamble to the Hague Convention stress the internationality of art. According to the treaty, art is the heritage of the peoples of the world, not the nations. Destruction of art reduces the cultural heritage of all mankind, not just the heritage of the country that owned the art. We will see in a moment that making cultural property the heritage of all peoples, rather than the heritage of a particular nation, creates both philosophical contradictions within this treaty, and philosophical conflicts with other important treaties.

Article 7 of the Hague Convention requires that each nation adhering to it insert into military instructions provisions to help implement the treaty; undertake appropriate education; and establish specialists in cultural property. The Second Protocol goes further, requiring contracting states to establish administrative machinery and to make effective provision for criminal prosecution of serious violators. 2d Prot. Arts. 15–21. Throughout this discussion, one must distinguish between the Convention and the First Protocol, and the more specific Second Protocol, which has only half the number of countries as adherents as the Convention does. The United States has not ratified the Second Protocol.

3. Destruction

A. Activities During Peacetime in Contemplation of War

Domestic law says nothing about what a country should do about art in peacetime in contemplation of war. The United States maintains a National Registry of Historic sites, and many countries designate artworks as vital to the national patrimony, but neither of those activities is primarily in contemplation of war.

In the Hague Convention, the parties promise to prepare during peacetime to safeguard cultural property within their own territory against the foreseeable consequences of armed conflict. This provision is entirely precatory because the countries are to do so "by taking such measures as they consider appropriate." Article 3. The Second Protocol adds that such measures of preparation include the preparation of inventories of cultural property, planning emergency measures to protect against fire or collapse, plans for removal of property or its protection on site, and the designation of a government official responsible for safeguarding, but only "as appropriate." 2d Prot. art. 5. The countries also agree to refrain from using cultural property in ways likely to expose it to damage, which means that likely military targets should not be located in the vicinity of art. Art. 4(1).

Countries where most museums are run by the government under the supervision of the Ministry of Culture may have comprehensive inventories of the cultural treasures in their museums, but it is doubtful that much effort has been expended to inventory the cultural treasures in private hands or standing independently in public spaces. In a country like the United States where museums are mostly private, and government-supported museums are mostly supported by city, rather than the national government, a national inventory is even less likely.

As to emergency measures to protect art from fire or collapse, the safety of all buildings in the United States and many other countries is regulated by local law. It is unclear that art is a significant item in the enunciation of these rules, or that the response of the building to typical war damage is a consideration.

There is no national U.S. official responsible for safeguarding art or for supervising plans for its removal or protection in time of war.

Article 1 of the Second Protocol defines a military objective as "an object which ... makes an effective contribution to military action and whose ... neutralization ... offers a definite military advantage." One might note that this definition in the U.S. would include the White House, where most major military decisions would be finalized. Less than a mile from the White House lie more than a dozen federal and at least two private museums, as well as monuments commemorating a like number of national figures and wars, including the Washington Monument and the Jefferson and Lincoln Memorials. The White House itself contains fine art.

These may be among the reasons that the United States has not ratified the Second Protocol.

While the inventory and other planning suggestions are all good ideas, and it is especially important to have one national official with responsibility for getting it done, it is hard to see any significant enforcement that is likely. The purpose of the rules seems to be for use in internal budget discussions to try to secure more funds for these purposes.

These rules appear to be written with the developed world in mind; most developing countries lack the resources to inventory their cultural property, much less the technical personnel or government resources to employ them to effectively plan for the removal or protection of it. It seems unlikely that any country, contemplating military action against another, would point out through diplomatic communication that the other country had located a military target near cultural property. If it did, the response is more likely to be rude than diplomatic.

B. Activities During Hostilities

During hostilities, cultural property faces two kinds of threats. It can be intentionally destroyed, usually justified as a way to weaken the enemy's will to fight on seeing its artwork destroyed. There is no evidence that destruction of a country's cultural treasures induces the country to yield, but that does not seem to deter the destruction. The second danger is incidental damage. The artwork is destroyed because the intention is to gain some military advantage, and that military advantage either requires the destruction of the artwork or the destruction is caused accidentally. Both United States practice and the Hague Convention try to prevent both forms of damage.

The first comprehensive United States statement on the subject of art in time of war, the Lieber Code, Instructions for the Government of Armies of the United States in the Field (1863), says little about destruction. It only states that cultural properties "must be secured against all avoidable injury, even when they are contained in fortified places whilst besieged or bombarded." Art. 35. It is unclear whether this obligation falls on the besieged or the besieger or both and, more important, what injury is avoidable. Presumably all injury is avoidable if the army will take its operations elsewhere, but that does not seem to be the sense of the clause. It also comments that "in no case shall [cultural property ever be] wantonly destroyed or injured." Art. 36. Wanton destruction means that the destruction is without any planned benefit to the destroyer, so this provision probably adds nothing to the previous prohibition.

The Hague Convention flatly prohibits reprisals against cultural property. Art. 4(4). It also prohibits acts of hostility toward cultural property except in cases where military necessity imperatively requires waiver. Art. 4 (1) & (2). Because it appeared that anyone in command of as small a group as a squad of a dozen soldiers might issue a waiver, the Second Protocol adds that such a waiver will usually require action by a person who commands a battalion or a larger group of soldiers (usually at least 300). This would normally be a senior officer like a lieutenant colonel, though precise requirements differ from country to country and from time to time. A waiver may only be granted if the cultural property has been turned into a military objective, such as by troops being quartered in the building, and only when there is no way to achieve the same military objective without damaging the cultural property. Even if all the above apply, the commander should weigh the importance of the military objective against the likely damage to the cultural property, and he is obliged to try to avoid incidental damage, as well as direct damage. 2d Prot. art. 5.

These provisions raise an interesting conflict with the preamble. If cultural property is the heritage of "all peoples," by what authority can an official of one state (and an unelected official of that state) "waive" the rights of all peoples that the Convention has set in place?

Most of the Hague Convention consists of negative commands. The treaty also imposes the positive obligation to prevent or put a stop to vandalism against cultural property. Art. 4(3). It is not clear that the drafters of the Convention ever considered the military or fiscal impact of this rule. One commentator estimates that there are more than 10,000 archaeological sites in Iraq. Assuming that guards work an 8-hour shift 7 days a week, and that one guard on duty is enough for each site, guarding those sites to prevent or stop vandalism would require 30,000 troops. It is unlikely that any invading or occupying nation would assign such a large contingent to the task.

The United States, in its military action in Iraq, did not protect the national museum from looters. It is unclear whether a country, in the initial stages of an invasion, can do so, at least without significant advanced planning and the assignment of extra resources. The first task of the military commander is to eliminate opposition to the invasion, both by the organized military, and by irregular resistants. It is only when some order is achieved that one can expect the suppression of looting and vandalism. Further, it can be argued that the duty to protect against pillage and vandalism is a negative duty that only applies to those acts done by soldiers of the invading army, but the phraseology of the Hague Convention fits better with a positive duty to prevent pillage or vandalism from all sources, and also fits better with the policy of imposing a duty on a country that has at least a share of governing power to use that power to protect art.

There is no "military necessity" exception to the prevention of pillage or vandalism, or to the prohibition on damaging cultural goods as reprisal.

The Hague Convention also attempts to bind as broad a swath of combatants as possible. The Convention tries to bind rebel forces that have not signed it, and specifies that in a three-cornered conflict where one of the combatants has not signed but the other two are parties to the Convention, the parties must observe the Convention with respect to each other. Arts. 18–19.

C. During Occupation

The rules of the Lieber Code do not distinguish between active hostilities and occupation, so all the rules set forth above for destruction should apply during occupation.

The Hague Convention assumes that during an occupation, the legitimate former government continues to function. It calls on the occupying power to back up that former government in safeguarding and preserving cultural property where the former government is unable to do so. Art. 5.

A question may be raised whether the obligations of an invading army also apply during that army's occupation. One might note that the duty to prevent looting and vandalism is contained in Article 4, relating to active hostilities, and not repeated in Article 5, on occupation. Dispensing with this duty during occupation makes little sense, especially since the occupier has more ability to prevent pillage and vandalism than does the invading army.

4. Looting

A. During Hostilities

Generally, taking the artwork of another by a private party is prohibited by local law. The Lieber Code contains a blanket prohibition on private appropriation. Art. 36.

Whether a belligerent government may appropriate publicly-owned artwork is another question. If the item is booty, one government can acquire it by capture. The definition of booty varies from time to time and from country to country. Under the Lieber Code, one government can seize "all public movable property" of the other government. Art. 31. Property of churches, hospitals, schools or museums is not to be considered public property. Art. 34. The conquering country may remove artwork for its own benefit if it can be removed without being injured, with ultimate disposition to be decided in the peace treaty. Art. 36. It is unclear whether this last provision applies only to public property or to all art works.

More recent definitions of booty show some variety. In World War II, both Germany and the United States held that booty includes warfare items, such as arms, uniforms, ships, horses and other means of transportation or communication. Less obviously, it is sometimes defined to include food and materials used to make clothing in excess of normal household supplies, perhaps on the grounds that foodstuffs and clothes are required to support an army. *Menzel v. List*, 267 N.Y.S. 2d 804 notes 1 and 2 (Sup. Ct. NY County 1966).

Thinking of booty in its broadest sense, it can be conceptualized in two ways. It is legitimate to deprive the enemy of resources it can use to make war, and it is equally beneficial to increase the supply of those resources for your own military so it can make war more efficiently. Confiscating property from the enemy is doubly beneficial, as it both deprives the enemy of the use of that property and increases your army's own resources.

But what resources? In a real sense, the most important resource for making war is money because it permits the purchase of all other resources. But it presses the argument too far to argue that any property that can be turned into money is booty. If that were the case, there would be no reason to distinguish booty from pillage. The line may more appropriately be drawn between items that directly affect the war effort, which are booty, and things that can only affect the war effort by being converted into money, which are not. Booty seldom includes art, even if the artwork is owned by the other belligerent state. If the item is not booty, its acquisition by the state is unlawful and will not support title in someone who is a transferee of the state. *The Marquis de Somereules*, Nova Scotia Stewart's Vice Admiralty Rep. 482 (Halifax 1813); *Menzel v. List*, 267 N.Y.S. 2d 804 (Sup. Ct. NY County 1966). One situation in which a work of visual art could be considered booty would be if it were painted on the side of an operable or reparable tank, but here it is the tank that is the booty, and the art is also classified as booty unless it can be separated from the tank. Another situation might be where the art could become a rallying point for the enemy, as the U.S. apparently considered Hitler's art might have become at the end of World War II, as reported in *Price v. U.S.*, 69 F.3d 46 (5th Cir. 1995) *modified* 81 F.3d 520 (5th Cir. 1995).

International law is to the same effect, whether the cultural property is privately or publicly owned. The Hague Convention places restraints on warring armies. States "shall refrain from requisitioning movable cultural property..." in the other state. Art. 4(3).

In the First Protocol, each state promises to prevent exportation of cultural property, and to return cultural property illegally exported into its territory. This is also true of cultural property deposited in another country for safekeeping. 1st Prot. art. 1.

Even if the definition of booty is extensive enough to include particular pieces of art, it remains within the discretion of the capturing government to return the art to its previous owner as a matter of comity. Comity is likely to be exercised based on equitable considerations, such as the likelihood that the recipient will safeguard the art, and in contemplation of future reciprocity. *The Marquis de Somereules*, Nova Scotia Stewart's Vice Admiralty Rep. 482 (Halifax 1813).

B. During Occupation

It appears that the prohibition on requisitioning movable cultural property in the Hague Convention applies during occupation also. In addition, the Second Protocol prohibits "illicit export, other removal or transfer of ownership." It also prohibits archaeological excavations except those "strictly required" to safeguard, record or preserve cultural property. 2d Prot. art. 9. As all archaeological excavations have in part the aims of safeguarding, recording and preserving cultural property, the work here is done by the words "strictly required." If a potential site is being looted, one can argue that its safeguarding by excavation is strictly required, but a better reading would be that the posting of guards would be adequate to deter the looting, so the excavation is not strictly required.

C. On the Eventual Peace

Under the Lieber Code, when cultural property has been removed from one country to another, the fate of the artwork is to be resolved by the peace negotiations. By contrast, the Hague Convention provides that the art will be returned. 1st Prot. art. I(3).

5. Seizing Property of Enemy Civilians

In addition, a country may seize property within its borders. For example, it is common for a country at war to seize all the property of whatever kind belonging to citizens of the opposing state. This includes artwork. *Case Concerning Certain Property (Liechtenstein v. Germany)*, 2005 I.C.J. 6. Remedies for persons affected may be quite limited. In the United States, the appropriate statute is the Trading With the Enemy Act, 50 App. U.S.C. §§ 1–44.

6. Cultural Property Defined

The Hague Convention only applies to cultural property, so it is important to define the term. Cultural property is defined very broadly to include both movable and immovable property. Specifically mentioned are monuments of architecture, art or history, whether religious or secular; works of art; manuscripts, books or other objects of artistic, historical or archaeological interest; groups of buildings of historical or artistic interest, such as historical districts; scientific collections; books or archives containing reproductions of the above; and the buildings used principally to preserve or exhibit any of the above, such as museums, libraries, archives, or shelters. Art. 1.

One can argue that cultural property covered by the Hague Convention is only that property that is recognized by all peoples because the definition is limited to property "of great importance to the cultural heritage of every people...." This might be read as requiring a designation from some international body, such as UNESCO. That would limit the scope of the Hague Convention much more than was intended, in part because when the convention was negotiated there was no international body certifying sites, and in part because the types of items specifically covered, like books and scientific equipment, are unlikely to be so widely recognized.

7. Enforcement

To the extent that these rules are part of domestic law, they will normally be contained in military training manuals, and enforced as part of the country's system of military justice. In most countries, military punishments receive less publicity than civilian punishments, so one is less likely to learn about discipline for injuring art. Military justice systems tend to be quasi-criminal in nature, so require a relatively high standard of proof of facts. Also, the persons administering the military justice system are likely to be soldiers who, in deciding whether to recommend punishment, are likely to look at the actions from a military point of view, and to allow a broad scope for discretion, on analogy to the business judgment rule.

Imposing rules by treaty may be a way to have them incorporated into domestic law. While these measures may in practice be precatory, they sometimes may induce countries to comply.

The first problem with enforcement of treaties is that treaties are contracts between the countries that sign them. Enforcement in the traditional sense is by suit instituted by one country against another in the International Court of Justice.

As to the direct enforcement of the Hague Convention, that seems unlikely. At Nuremburg Alfred Rosenberg, who was responsible for enormous looting and destruction of art, was also responsible for far more serious crimes for which he was tried and hanged. It is unlikely that one country that has been at war with another country will bring suit for destruction of art when it has been the victim of aggressive war because it suffers so much other damage from the war. Further, bringing suit against another country is not something a country does lightly because there are always diplomatic repercussions. For that reason, some treaties have established internal dispute resolution mechanisms, but this has not occurred with the Hague Convention.

When violations of these rules are committed by states, other rules may prevent enforcement by private parties, such as the doctrine of sovereign immunity, the Act of State doctrine, or post-war treaties that may waive the rights of citizens of the contracting states.

But the dictum in *Matter of Flamenbaum*, 22 N.Y.3d 962, 1 N.E.3d 782, 978 N.Y.S.2d 708 (2013), is instructive: "The 'spoils of war' theory proffered by the Estate—that the Russian government, when it invaded Germany, gained title to the Museum's property as a spoil of war, and then transferred that title to the decedent—is rejected. The Estate's theory rests entirely on conjecture, as the record is bereft of any proof that the Russian government ever had possession of the tablet. Even if there were such proof, we decline to adopt any doctrine that would establish good title based upon the looting and removal of cultural objects during wartime by a conquering military force."

Checkpoints

- The sources of law on the treatment of art in war are mainly the Hague Convention, its Second Protocol, and national regulations or training manuals.
- Distinguishing the Hague Convention from its Second Protocol is important because twice as many countries have adhered to the Convention as have joined the Second Protocol, and the U.S. is not a member of the Second Protocol.
- The Hague Convention calls on nations during peacetime to plan to protect art in case of hostilities. The Second Protocol is more specific, calling for a

national inventory, appointment of an official in charge, protection of art from fire or collapse in the event of war, and locating cultural items away from military targets.

- The Hague Convention prohibits reprisals against cultural property, or targeting cultural property except when waived for military necessity. The Second Protocol specifies that waiver can only be by a person of high rank, and places additional conditions on the waiver.
- The Hague Convention requires a country to prevent or put a stop to vandalism against cultural property.
- A country can take booty, items useful in prosecution of the war, from private citizens in the other state, and use it for its own purposes. Other items would be pillage if taken, and they cannot be taken.
- The Second Protocol prohibits illegal export or transfer of ownership of art during occupation. It severely restricts archaeology.
- There is no prohibition on seizure of enemy-owned property without compensation that is located within the territory of the seizing state.

Chapter 15

Restricting the Movement of Art Across National Borders

Roadmap

After reading this chapter, you should understand:

- Drying up the market for stolen or illegally exported art is a significant argument for restricting the international movement of art. It applies more forcefully to artifacts than to fine art because artifacts are more likely to be unidentifiable and more likely to be damaged, and the loss of knowledge from removal from their find-spots more significant.
- Artifacts control differs from country to country. Most countries combine ownership restrictions with export restrictions. Three approaches involve private ownership, public ownership, and public ownership with a reward for the finder and the landowner.
- Fine arts control focuses on export restrictions. Some countries have none; in others an attempt to export results in confiscation of the art; in most there is an export license that must be obtained; in some, a purchase or a request to export triggers a right of first refusal in the government to purchase the artwork.
- Free trade treaties allow countries to impose export restrictions on art to protect national treasures. Export tariffs do not qualify because they do not protect.
- The European Convention on Human Rights contains provisions on rights to property, the right to leave a country, and the right to travel that might be used to permit an individual to export his art.
- National patrimony has no agreed-upon definition, nor is there any requirement that items be designated as part of the national patrimony in advance.
- Cultural heritage of a country is broadly defined by the 1970 UNESCO Convention as any work that has ever had any contact with a country.
- The 1970 UNESCO Convention seeks international cooperation for export control by requiring signatories to develop an export license, prevent their museums from acquiring illegally exported property and prevent the import of property stolen from museums and facilitate its return on payment of just compensation.

- The 1970 UNESCO Convention allows a country whose cultural heritage is endangered to seek and receive concerted international action to prohibit import of endangered property.
- United States implementation of the UNESCO Convention permits forfeiture of stolen property or property on which there has been a false customs declaration. Knowingly receiving stolen property is a crime in all states. The President is authorized to forbid imports as part of an international cooperation effort.
- Museum organization guidelines, international cooperation efforts, and self-help can aid in recovering stolen or illegally exported property.

1. Introduction: Fine Art Differs from Artifacts

To paraphrase Rousseau, "Art was born free, but is [almost] everywhere in chains." While free trade has become the post-World War II mantra, countries have tried to prevent the export of their art treasures by enacting different laws. The controversy between source states (the countries where art was produced) and market states (the countries where art is currently collected) is ongoing.

A distinction can be made between fine art and artifacts. The location and value of fine art is normally known. It is in the hands of persons who have incentives to safeguard it from damage by the elements or from other causes, or from theft. It tends to be unique or easily identifiable, either because it is the only example of its kind, or it is one of a numbered series of artworks.

By contrast, artifacts, the products of bygone civilizations, are often yet to be discovered. Many remain buried. Of those that have been discovered, not all have been catalogued and identified. While some are unique, others are examples of generic products. Both generic products and undiscovered artifacts are hard to identify if they are removed from their places of discovery before being thoroughly studied. They have value as collectors' pieces, but they also have value in educating us about life in earlier civilizations. The educational value of an artifact depends on the work of trained archaeologists, as well as properly dating the artifact, which sometimes requires its association with other artifacts of the same era found at the same site. A katsina found in a katsina-producing area tells a different story than a katsina found in an area where the native tribes produced no katsinas.

No country is willing to devote the resources required to protect its archaeological sites and its potential archaeological sites. This is even true of the United States. The western third of the country is filled with national parks, monuments and forests that contain many active and yet-to-be-discovered archaeological sites. That vast territory is protected by a modest number of park rangers for whom the protection of sites is only a small part of the job.

Both fine art and artifacts are subject to theft, but there is a difference. Since fine art is more easily identifiable, it is more easily recoverable. Nothing is lost by the temporary removal of fine art from where it is kept. Artifacts, on the other hand, are often not identifiable at all, so never recoverable. In addition, they are often found either buried or attached to larger properties such as temples. When they are removed from their sites, the educational value of the finds is often reduced. There is also frequently damage done to the artifact or to the item to which it was attached when they are removed, sometimes by bulldozing, sometimes with chainsaws.

In this factual situation, source countries argue that no part of their cultural heritage should leave the country. The display of these items within the country helps create a sense of national or local unity, exposes the younger generation to its artistic tradition so that it can be continued, and contributes to local scholarship. It increases tourism, as people must visit to see these items. It dries up the legitimate market for stolen art, thereby reducing the incentive to steal from museums, churches or archaeological sites, and reducing the likelihood that artifacts will be damaged or taken out of context. On the other hand, it creates a black market for those items whose export is banned unless the enforcement budget is set at a level adequate to prevent it, which is almost never the case. The last two observations are particularly true when the source country is relatively poor and market countries that are demanding these goods are relatively wealthy.

Market countries argue that retaining artwork in the source country impoverishes the world. Thousands of Native American arrowheads would be more usefully displayed a few at a time in museums in each major city around the world to introduce the populace to Native American culture rather than concentrating them all in the United States, where most would never be displayed because there are so many of them. Spreading the art of countries throughout the world would provide different models for artists to use as inspiration, and would foster a worldwide art scholarship. The geographic dispersal would also provide insurance against the massive destruction of a country's art production, whether from war, pollution, iconoclasm or industrial development.

For further discussion of the harmonies and conflicts between cultural nationalism and cultural internationalism, see John Henry Merryman, *Two Ways of Thinking About Cultural Property*, 80 Am. J. Int'l L. 831 (1986).

2. National Approaches to Preserving Patrimony

A. Approaches to Artifacts

i. Different Approaches

Countries have approached the preservation of their artifacts in a variety of ways. The principal ways are by restricting ownership and restricting export.

ii. U.S. Private Ownership

As further detailed in the chapter on U.S. preservation of cultural property, artifacts discovered on private land belong to the owner of the land; artifacts on government land belong likewise to the owner of the land; and artifacts on unowned land belong to the finder.

This approach has the advantage of providing maximum encouragement to land occupiers to explore what is hidden beneath their land; does not encourage trespass; and requires a minimum of government supervision.

iii. Public Ownership

In many countries, artifacts belong to the state. Whether compensation will be paid to the finder in some amount will depend on local law.

An example where artifacts belong to the state with no compensation is the Egyptian Law 117 (1983) discussed in *United States v. Schultz*, 333 F.3d 393 (2d Cir. 2003). Unless such laws also confiscate or buy back all artifacts in private hands, they are usually accompanied by requirements that anyone owning an artifact on the effective date of the law register it with the state. This is because it would be difficult at a later point to determine whether the artifact was discovered before or after the effective date of the law, as there is no central registry of artifacts in most states. Evidence of possession prior to the effective date might be available for some artifacts, but not for most.

This approach tries to minimize the private incentive to do amateur archaeology or worse, unscientific excavation, because no rewards are provided. It does nothing to encourage the report of accidental finds.

iv. Public Ownership Plus Reward

Another possibility is that artifacts belong to the state and the state will grant a reward or fee to persons responsible for their discovery. This is the approach adopted by Iran and England.

The English approach, embodied in England Treasure Act 1996, Ch. 24, is instructive. It is limited to three classes:

1. items that are at least 200 years old and belong to a class previously designated by the government,
2. is one of a number of coins found together that is at least 300 years old, or a similarly aged metal object containing at least 10 percent precious metal, or
3. treasure trove, which is gold or silver in any form without regard to age, where it appears that the owners have hidden it and the current owners cannot be discovered.

The finder of any such item must notify the coroner within 14 days of the find. The coroner holds an inquest to determine who owns the items found. If the original ownership can be determined, it belongs to that person or his heirs. If the item is discovered as part of a franchise granted, it will belong according to the franchise agreement. Otherwise, it belongs to the state. The coroner must also determine whether a reward is appropriate, how much it should be, and to whom it should be paid. Normally, the reward is equal to the fair market value of the items, and the reward is shared between the occupier of the land on which the find is made and the finder. Typically, the coroner's inquest launches a scientific archeological expedition to try to learn as much as possible about the circumstances of the find.

This approach tries to provide private individuals with some incentive to discover items, and great incentive to report any discoveries promptly so that scientific archaeology can be put in place. It encourages cooperation between seekers and occupiers of the land.

v. Export Restrictions

These approaches are sometimes combined with restrictions on export of artifacts. Those restrictions are described below.

B. Approaches to Fine Arts: Export Restrictions

Many countries have restrictions on the export of art and artifacts. Those restrictions may take a number of different forms.

i. Attempt to Export Results in Confiscation

One form of export control is a law prohibiting illegal export, with the consequence either that the property is confiscated by the state, or the consequence that the property may be confiscated by the state. An example is the New Zealand law discussed in *Attorney-General of New Zealand v. Ortiz*, [1982] 3 All E. R. 432 (C. A. Civil), where the court's first duty was to interpret the

New Zealand law. While it appeared that the better interpretation was that the exported chief's door would be automatically forfeited, Lord Denning was loath to adopt it. He said it would violate international law because it would permit New Zealand to prescribe legal consequences of actions outside its territory, as the door would not have been exported until it passed out of New Zealand territory.

Lord Denning's dictum allows for much to be criticized. First, there is nothing unclear about the statute, which states in § 12(2): "An historic article knowingly exported or attempted to be exported in breach of this Act shall be forfeited...." Second, the knowing export was preceded by a knowing attempt to export that took place within the territory of New Zealand. Third, Lord Denning is simply wrong about international law. There is in the United States an interpretative presumption that a law will only regulate acts outside its borders (unless committed by its own citizens or companies) if legislative intent for extraterritorial regulation is clear. Assertion of jurisdiction to prescribe "conduct outside its territory that has or is intended to have substantial effect within its territory" and "certain conduct outside its territory by persons not its nationals that is directed against the security of the state or against a limited class of other state interests" is permitted. The latter embodies the protective principle and includes espionage "... and conspiracy to violate the immigration or customs laws." RESTATEMENT THIRD, FOREIGN RELATIONS LAW OF THE UNITED STATES § 402-403.

ii. Attempt to Export Violates Law

In many of its provision, the New Zealand Historic Articles Act is typical of export restrictions. There is typically a definition of the item whose export is restricted, frequently requiring that it be at least a certain number of years old, or that it be produced before a certain year. There follows authorization for the government to acquire the item if it is of exceptional value. Permission must be received from the government to export the item, the granting of which is largely discretionary. Exporting the item without permission is a criminal offense. The maximum penalty, a fine of no more than 200 pounds, does not seem designed to deter anyone. The New Zealand statute is not typical in providing for a remedy of confiscation for violation. It is also not typical in authorizing a middle ground between granting permission and refusing permission. In New Zealand, the government may publish a notice inviting anyone to make an offer to purchase the item. If no offer is accepted by the owner, permission will be granted to export. Thus New Zealand seems to establish three categories of items, one of which cannot be exported, one of which can be freely exported, and the third of which contains items that the government would prefer not to have exported, but finds their retention in the country not crucial enough to justify spending government funds.

Other countries' laws vary in their details. In Italy, when the government has declared a work to be of "historic and artistic interest," the owner of the work must notify the government of any proposed sale, which gives the government the right to acquire the item at the purchase price within two months. If the government exercises that option, the work becomes the property of the government. If it fails to exercise the option, it becomes the property of the purchaser. But the purchaser must still obtain an export license if he wants to remove the work from Italy. *Beyeler v. Italy*, 33 Eur. Hum. Rts. Rep. 52 (2000).

French law permits the government to classify a work as an artistic treasure either before or after it is proposed to be exported, at which point the work cannot be exported. If it does this, the government must pay the owner the difference between the value of the work if exportable and its lesser value if it must remain in France. That difference can result in a substantial payment, and does not make the work accessible to the public by placing it in a museum. It simply restrains its export from France.

iii. Export Is Generally Authorized

Generally, the owner of art may export it from the United States without obtaining any permissions. The knowing export of stolen art is prohibited by the National Stolen Property Act. Certain property, such as some eagles or parts of certain eagles, cannot be sold or exported, even if incorporated into artwork. P.L. 87-884, 76 Stat. 1246 (1962).

3. International Law of Restrictions on Art Movement

A. Free Trade Except to Protect National Treasures

Since World War II, there has been a wholesale shift, from the pre-war international trade restriction and customs duties, to freer trade postwar. The General Agreement on Tariffs and Trade (GATT) (1947), to which most of the world adheres, provides for elimination of quotas and export license requirements, and requires that a country reduce its tariffs for all signatories to the lowest levels that country accords to any other country: most-favored-nation treatment. (Arts. I, III, XI) Likewise, the Treaty of Rome Establishing the European Community (1956) requires the elimination of quotas and customs duties on trade between the Member States. (Arts. 12, 30, 34, now arts. 25, 28 and 29).

Each treaty contains an important exception for art. GATT will not prohibit measures "imposed for the protection of national treasures of artistic, historic, or archaeological value" [Art. XX(f)], and the European Union shall not prohibit restrictions justified by "the protection of national treasures possessing artistic, historic or archaeological value" [originally art. 36, now art. 30]. As a result, neither the GATT (now administered by the World Trade Organization, 164 member countries) nor the European Union (27 member countries, all of whom are WTO members) treaties promoting free trade restrain those countries' discretion in managing art exports as long as the restriction is for "the protection of national treasures."

B. Taxing Export Is Not Protecting

There is one case interpreting this clause. The European Commission brought a declaratory judgment action in the European Court of Justice against the Italian Republic, which imposed a tax on the export of artwork to other Member States. The court held that artwork constitutes goods because they are products which can be valued in money and can be the subject of commercial transactions. It then held that the exception for protection of national treasures did not apply to tariffs because tariffs only made those treasures more expensive, but did not protect them by preventing their export. *Comm'n v. Italian Republic*, 1968 E.C.J. 423 (1968). While this case only applied to export from one Member State to another, it effectively nullified the tariff for all countries, as an artwork could be exported from one Member State to another without tariff, then re-exported from the destination Member State that lacks an export tariff to a state outside the European Union.

This case does not deal with quotas or export prohibitions, but it is clear that an export license to send artwork out of the European Union can be refused pursuant to national legislation if the art is covered by domestic legislation protecting national treasures. European Council Regulation (EEC) No. 3911/92 of 9 December 1992 on the Export of Cultural Goods, art. 2.

C. The European Convention on Human Rights

For the 47 states that are members of the Council of Europe and have signed the European Convention on Human Rights, the situation may be different.

Several provisions of that Convention may bear on the right of an individual to move art from one country to another.

Article 1 of Protocol No. 1 provides: "Every natural or legal person is entitled to the peaceful enjoyment of his possessions. No one shall be deprived of his possessions except in the public interest and subject to the conditions provided for by law and by the general principles of international law. The preceding provisions shall not, however, in any way impair the right of a State to enforce such laws as it deems necessary to control the use of property in accordance with the general interest...."

This provision guarantees a person the right to peacefully enjoy his possessions, with two exceptions. A state may deprive a person of his possessions in the public interest, in accordance with the law of that state and general principles of international law, which provide for prompt and fair compensation when a person's property is confiscated. The second exception allows a state to regulate the use of property in accordance with the law and the general interest. In construing that provision in a case where Italian law gave the state a right to purchase art at the price a buyer paid for it, the European Court of Human Rights stated that it is in the general interest for a state to control the market in works of art to protect its cultural and artistic heritage and to assure public access to the works. But this general interest must achieve a fair balance with the rights of the individual, and that balance requires proportionality between the means used and the ends to be achieved. However, none of that discussion can be treated as holding, as the Court found for the purchaser on grounds that Italian court construction permitting Italy to exercise its purchase rights more than four years after being notified created too much uncertainty and permitted the state to acquire the work at considerably less than its fair market value, which was not a fair balance and violated the applicant's rights under the Protocol. But because its decision was based on the vagaries of the particular case, the Court leaves us no idea whether such a pre-emption law exercised in a much shorter time would violate the Convention. *Beyeler v. Italy*, 33 Eur. Hum. Rts. Rep. 52 (2000).

Similar questions can be raised under the Fourth Protocol, which reads:

"Art. 2.2. Everyone shall be free to leave any country, including his own.

"Art. 2.3. No restrictions shall be placed on the exercise of these rights other than such as are in accordance with law and are necessary in a democratic society ... for the protection of rights and freedoms of others."

It can be argued that a country cannot prevent a longtime owner of art from leaving the country and taking his art with him. A law preventing export would need to be justified as protecting the rights of others, but it is difficult to see what rights others might have to art that need never be displayed to the public, unless the "other" is the state that might be thought to have a right to protect its artistic heritage.

D. Defining the National Patrimony

It thus becomes important to define what works a government can prevent from leaving the country. A government can clearly prevent stolen art from leaving the country. In terms of the European Convention, returning art to its owner would be "in the public interest," "subject to the conditions provided for by law," and consistent with general principles of international law. They are likewise "necessary in a democratic society ... for the protection of rights and freedoms of others," specifically the rights of the owners of the artwork that has been stolen. While neither the GATT nor the European Union Treaties have any specific exemption from free trade that might authorize restricting trade in stolen property, the assumption of those documents is that the person attempting to export the goods has a right to those goods. This would not be the case with stolen property.

More important is the case where the ownership is uncontested in the person who wishes to export the art. Here GATT and the European Union both require that the works be " ... national treasures of artistic, historic, or archaeological value." Under the European Convention of Human Rights, retaining national treasures in the country might qualify as protecting the rights and freedoms of others, though this is questionable if the works are in private hands and not subject to a requirement of public display for a reasonable period of time each year.

Judge Friendly properly asks what "national treasures" might mean when Italy tries to recover a painting by Henri Matisse, a Frenchman, produced in France, that had been acquired by an Italian and kept in Italy. *Jeanneret v. Vichey*, 693 F.2d 259 (2d Cir. 1982). In 1982, fewer than fifty states had ratified the new UNESCO Convention on the Means of Prohibiting and Preventing the Illicit Import, Export and Transfer of Ownership of Cultural Property (1970), and few of the ratifiers were major states. At the end of 2019, the convention had 140 member states, including most of the major countries in the world. The provisions of the treaty bind the member states as a matter of international law. Whether they become law within any of those states depends on domestic law. In some states, any ratified treaty becomes domestic law. In others, no provision of a ratified treaty is domestic law; it is only the enactment of a law internally that will do that. In the United States, a treaty intended to be self-executing, like all of our tax treaties, becomes domestic law, while a non-self-executing treaty like the Berne Copyright Convention only becomes domestic law to the extent that it is separately enacted. As to the impact of a widely enacted treaty on states that are not parties to it, that depends on whether its provisions have become an accepted part of the practice of most nations so as to become customary international law.

The UNESCO Treaty does not define "national treasures." It uses instead the term "cultural heritage." It can be argued that everything that is part of a state's cultural heritage is a national treasure. It can also be argued that there is a general category of cultural property, and within that group lies a smaller category of cultural heritage of a particular state, and within cultural heritage lies a smaller group of national treasures.

What is clear is that the cultural heritage of a state is very broad. Article 4 says it includes:

- a1. property created by the state's nationals;
- a2. property of importance created in the territory of the state by foreign nationals or stateless persons residing there;
- b. property found within the territory;
- c. property acquired by missions with the consent of the country of origin;
- d. property acquired by freely agreed exchange; and
- e. property received as a gift or purchased legally with the consent of the country of origin.

Like many definitions, this definition answers some questions and raises others.

Take, for instance, Doménikos Theotokópoulos (1541–1614), popularly known as "El Greco." He was born on Crete, then part of the Venetian Republic, which is now part of Italy. Crete is now part of Greece. He lived for a time in Rome, which was then under the control of the Pope and a small part of which is now the independent country called the Vatican City State. He spent the rest of his life in Toledo, Spain. His works are in collections all over Europe and in the United States.

It appears that all of his works can be claimed as cultural heritage of both Greece and Italy under a1 above, because the state of which he was a national, the Venetian Republic, is now Italy and the territory of which he was a national is now Greece. Spain can claim that the many works he created there are part of Spanish cultural heritage under a2.

There is some ambiguity about the scope of paragraph b above. The English-language version of the treaty could confine b to works excavated in the country, but the French version makes it clear that it applies to anything found on the territory. This would include works excavated there, but also any work that was ever located in the country (or in territory that later became part of the country). As an example, El Greco's Laocoön was in collections in Spain, France, Germany, Switzerland and Serbia, and is now at the National Gallery in Washington. So six countries can claim it as part of their cultural heritage because it was once found there.

E. UNESCO Convention Tries to Provide Effective Control

It had become clear that the laws providing for national ownership or restricting export were not having the desired effect of preventing theft of art objects or their export. Countries to which items were exported were often unwilling to enforce the laws of other states, which is further discussed in the chapter below on International Litigation for Art Lawyers.

The UNESCO Convention on the Means of Prohibiting and Preventing the Illicit Import, Export and Transfer of Ownership of Cultural Property was signed in 1970 to remedy this defect.

Article 1 defines the subject matter of the treaty very broadly, and does not require that any item be of a certain age.

While qualified by language giving the parties discretion such as "consistent with national legislation" and "as appropriate for each country," the parties should develop an export license that will identify items properly exported, (art. 6) prevent their museums from acquiring illegally exported property, and prevent the import of property stolen from museums or public monuments and facilitate its return on payment of just compensation. (Art. 7) The parties promise to impose penalties or administrative sanctions on persons importing stolen or illegally exported property, (art. 8) and to oblige dealers to keep appropriate records and warn buyers of export restrictions. (Art. 10) Where a government believes that its cultural patrimony is in danger and there is concerted international action to prevent this, a state should prohibit import of the endangered property. In addition, a state should assist another state in the recovery of property stolen from the first state. (Art. 9)

i. European Reaction

The European Union responded with a regulation and a directive.

The regulation provides for an export license for the export of artwork outside the European Union. The certificates are to be issued by the Member States. What is covered is more narrowly defined than the UNESCO Convention. Some types of work require a certain antiquity; others must be worth at least a certain amount of money before the export system applies. In all cases, an export license may be refused if the property is covered by a national system designating it a national treasure. European Council Regulation(EEC) No. 3911/92 of 9 December 1992 on the Export of Cultural Goods, O. J. L 395, 31/12/1992.

The European Union leaves the regulation of exports to countries that are not European Union members to the Union's individual Member States.

The European Union issued a directive on unlawful exports from the territory of a Member State. That directive calls on Member States to establish procedures for the return of artwork unlawfully exported from other Member States, and establishes strict time limits of one year from discovery, or a total of 30 years from illegal export, or 75 years from illegal export in the case of goods from a public or ecclesiastical site. (Art. 7) Council Dir 93/7/EEC of 15 March 1993 on the Return of Cultural Objects Unlawfully Removed from the Territory of a Member State, O.J. L 074, 27/03/1993.

In the United Kingdom, there is a general provision enabling the seizure and return of stolen items that are attempted to be imported. It is also a crime to knowingly handle stolen goods. Under the Dealing in Cultural Objects (Offences) Act 2003, it is a crime to dishonestly deal in a cultural object if it has been removed from a structure of historical, architectural or archaeological interest, knowing that the removal constitutes an offense under the applicable law. The requirement of scienter in this law and its criminal nature will make it an unwieldy instrument for recovering stolen property, and the law has no provisions to deal with illegally exported property from a country not a member of the European Union.

ii. United States Law

The United States has a number of laws that might meet its obligations under the UNESCO Convention. Like the United Kingdom, those laws are not collected in a single place, increasing the cost of their use.

Where a person importing an item makes a materially false statement to customs, the item may be civilly forfeited to the United States. 18 U.S.C. §§ 542, 545. It is clear that a statement of the value of an item is material if it would change the amount of the tariff due. The test of materiality is whether it would have a natural tendency to influence the customs officials. So the test is whether a reasonable customs official would alter his behavior depending on whether the statement made had been true. In *United States v. An Antique Platter known as a Gold Phiale Mesomphalos c. 400 B.C.*, 184 F.3d 131(2d Cir 1999), it was held that claiming an artwork originated in Switzerland when it actually originated in Italy was material because customs manuals alerted officials to

Italian laws that nationalized items found, whereas there were no such laws in Switzerland. An argument of harmless error because no reasonable person would have thought that such a classical item would have originated in Switzerland was brushed aside as frivolous. It is worthy of note that the underlying contract of sale for the item provided for refund of the purchase price if it was seized by customs, so the purchaser (or at least his lawyer) had anticipated the problem.

The phiale was excavated in Sicily and found to be of Sicilian origin, and was only in Switzerland for a short time. One might change the facts a bit to ask, if the item had been of Greek manufacture (as many items found in Italy were), excavated in Italy and had been in Switzerland for more than a generation, would it be a material mis-statement to name Greece, Italy or Switzerland as the country of origin? With commercial goods subject to tariff for which the question about origin is intended, the origin is clearly the place of manufacture. That is not so clear with antiquities, where the time of manufacture is so far in the past and the tariff structure does not turn on the place of origin. In the case imagined, Greece is the place of manufacture, but one can easily argue that 2,000 years of residence under Sicilian soil had made Italy the place of origin. While more difficult, one could also argue that the item's repose in Switzerland for more than a generation had made Switzerland the country of origin.

This provision is not limited to finding goods when they are crossing the border. The phiale in question was seized from Steinhardt's home. There is no geographic limit, and an action may be brought within five years of the time that customs discovers or should have discovered the mis-statement.

Attempting to import or transport in interstate commerce property worth at least $5,000 that you know is stolen is a criminal act under the National Stolen Property Act. Conviction can result in forfeiture to the United States. 19 U.S.C. § 1595a(c). When forfeiture occurs under either NSPA or customs law, the United States will commonly restore the property to its rightful owner. While there is no clear authority for that other than the generality of 19 U.S.C. § 1609(a), it has been stated in dictum that the United States may dispose of forfeited property "as it sees fit." *United States v. Various Ukrainian Artifacts*, 1997 U.S. Dist. LEXIS 19952 (E.D.N.Y.).

The *Phiale* case is not a typical fact situation. The most typical fact situation is one in which the artwork is imported to New York specifically for sale, usually at one of the large auction houses. The appearance of the artwork in the auction catalogue is what triggers protests by the true owner. In that situation, the consignor is outside the United States and not subject to criminal prosecution, so the consignor's risk is loss of the artwork and the legal fees of defending a civil forfeiture action. But the auction house is located in the United States and with proper facts might be charged either with conspiracy to import or being an accomplice. That might be enough to induce the auction house to pay its foreign client an amount sufficient to induce the client to not contest the forfeiture with the understanding that criminal charges will be dismissed against the cooperating auction house.

There is now an "innocent owner" defense to most federal civil forfeiture actions but that innocent owner defense does not apply to customs violations. The burden of proof is on the person asserting that he is an innocent owner. 18 U.S.C. § 983(d). An owner must be innocent, but also reasonably diligent; at least, he cannot be wilfully blind to obvious caution signs. One argument in *Phiale*, that an innocent owner defense was implied because it was constitutionally required to avoid a Fifth Amendment challenge on grounds of taking property without just compensation, was summarily rejected without serious discussion.

That stolen property includes property subject to a foreign law that nationalizes all artifacts was stated in *United States v. McClain*, 545 F.2d 988 (1977), 551 F.2d 52 (1977), 593 F.2d 658 (5th Cir. 1979), but the holding was that the Mexican law relied upon was too vague to support Mexican ownership. *United States v. Schultz*, 333 F.3d 393 (2d Cir. 2003) convicted defendants based on such an Egyptian law that was proven to have been enforced within Egypt, reaffirming the decision in *United States v. Hollinshead*, 495 F.2d 1154 (9th Cir. 1974), based on Guatemalan law. All of these were criminal prosecutions.

Plaintiffs have fared less well in civil actions based on government ownership statutes. In *Government of Peru v. Johnson*, 720 F.Supp. 810 (C.D. Cal. 1989), one of four grounds on which defendant prevailed was that there was no showing that the government ownership law was ever enforced within Peru. But the British courts do not seem to care whether the law is enforced within the country, as there was no finding on this point in *Government of the Islamic Republic of Iran v. The Barakat Galleries Ltd.*, [2007] EWCA Civ 1374, [2008] 1 All E.R. 1177 (App). Perhaps that reflects a quarter century of changing attitudes toward such laws.

It does not appear that illegally exporting artwork that has not been stolen will support a conviction or forfeiture under NSPA. However, 19 U.S.C. §§ 2091-2095 authorize the Secretary of the Treasury to keep a list, either general or specific, of stone carvings and wall art that are pre-Columbian monumental or architectural sculpture or murals subject to export control by the country of origin. Items on that list may not be imported into the United States and are subject to forfeiture.

All states of the United States criminalize stealing property and knowingly receiving stolen property. Now 18 U.S.C. § 668 makes it a federal crime to steal from or knowingly receive property stolen from a museum located in the United States if the property is more than 100 years old and worth at least $5,000, or if the property is worth at least $100,000 regardless of age.

The United States has also enacted the Convention on Cultural Property Implementation Act (1983) (CCPIA), 19 U.S.C. §§ 2601–2613. Under this law, a foreign country may ask the United States to ban or restrict imports of its cultural property, which is defined as important archaeological material at least 250 years old, and important ethnographic material produced by pre-industrial societies. If the President finds that the cultural property of the other state is menaced, that the other state has taken reasonable steps to defend its cultural property, that the application of import restrictions (along with similar restrictions by other states) would substantially deter the pillage of the other state's cultural property and there is no less drastic remedy available, the President may enter into bilateral or multilateral agreements to ban those imports. The agreements can last for no longer than five years, but they can be renewed. It is preferred that other "market" states impose similar restrictions. At this writing, the President has concluded almost 20 such agreements, and renewed a number of them, sometimes only after nudging the other state to more effectively prosecute robbers of archaeological sites.

Documenting the danger to a nation's cultural patrimony is usually not difficult, given the broad definition permitted by the treaty of a country's patrimony. Examples where archaeological sites are bulldozed with no regard to the loss of the educational value of the context in which the artifacts are found, or where artifacts or the buildings to which they are attached are damaged in order to remove them tend to establish that.

Proving concerted action can be more difficult. The Convention does not require universal action, but requires that the action be sufficiently concerted to be effective in reducing the damage to the country's cultural heritage. Thus, if the majority of those artifacts end up in the United States and the United Kingdom, action by those two countries should be sufficient concerted action, because in addition to states that might impose an ad hoc import ban, Australia bans the import of any item of cultural heritage illegally exported, and Canada does the same for exports from countries that are states parties to the UNESCO Convention.

CCPIA also provides that cultural property documented as part of the inventory of a museum or religious or secular monument which is stolen after the effective date of the Convention in both countries (April 1983 for the United States) may not be imported, with the result that it is subject to forfeiture. 19 U.S.C. §§ 2606–2607. It might be thought that these provisions are unnecessary, given the existence of the National Stolen Property Act, but NSPA requires that the importer know that the property is stolen. There is no knowledge requirement in CCPIA. CCPIA was enforced in a straightforward way in *United States v. An Original Manuscript ... Bearing the Signature of Junipero Serra, Located at Sotheby's...*, 1999 U.S. Dist. Lexis 1859 (S.D.N.Y.) The case highlights the expedited nature of the forfeiture process. The government proved by a scholar's declaration that the manuscript had been in the Californias collection at the Mexican National Archives as early as 1956, and that it was listed on a microfilmed inventory dated 1993. In fact, it had disappeared from the Archive no later than early 1992. Based on this evidence, the court found that the government had established a *prima facie* case that the document was part of the Archive's inventory, and that it was stolen after 1983. This shifted the burden of proving otherwise to the manuscript owner, which he was unable to sustain.

It should be noted that although the statute refers to the facility's inventory, the legislative history makes it clear that the term is not used in a formal sense; any way by which the facility keeps track of its possessions is satisfactory. But it appears that it is not enough to prove from outside sources that the item was in the facility, so the statement of the scholar might have been insufficient without the microfilmed inventory of the Archive. There is dictum to the contrary in a concurring opinion suggesting that a publication by a third party listing the item as in the collection of the institution is sufficient. *Autocephalous Greek-Orthodox Church of Cyprus v. Goldberg and Feldman Fine Arts, Inc.*, 917 F.2d 278 (7th Cir. 1990).

The *Junipero Serra* case demonstrates the superiority of the forfeiture route over the foreign government suing for conversion. In *Government of Peru v. Johnson*, 720 F.Supp. 810 (C.D. Cal. 1989), Peru argued that the property was excavated in Peru during the time when Peruvian law would have established government ownership, but was unable to prove by a preponderance of the evidence either the time or the place of excavation. Similar items had been found in Inca settlements in Bolivia and Ecuador. By contrast, a forfeiture action under NSPA requires only a *prima facie* case that the item was stolen; it would not be relevant whether it was stolen from Peru, Bolivia or Ecuador. That question might be relevant if one of those countries lacked an effective law vesting property in the state, and it would certainly be relevant to the subsequent determination by the United States of how it should dispose of the forfeited property in case of a conflict, but the latter question would not stay the forfeiture. In addition, the United States government pays the legal fees for a forfeiture action, while the plaintiff pays the legal fees in a suit for conversion. A final consideration is that a plaintiff makes his own litigation decisions, so inducing the attorney general to file a forfeiture action might result in a settlement unsatisfactory to the original owner, or worse, might result in the government deciding after a time to drop the suit, perhaps after the statute of limitations on a conversion suit has expired.

By contrast, sometimes sufficient facts can be established if plaintiff can only survive a summary judgment motion. In *Republic of Turkey v. Metropolitan Museum of Art*, 762 F.Supp. 44 (S.D.N.Y. 1990), the court refused summary judgment based on the statute of limitations and set discovery in motion on the question of laches as well as the substance. Careful comparison of the artifacts in the Met's possession with the claimed original sites established a strong likelihood that they were the source of the artifacts, and minutes of the museum's acquisitions committee raised significant questions about whether the museum was an innocent purchaser. The Met settled by returning the artifacts to Turkey. If there were other aspects to the settlement, they were not made public.

In addition, the statute of limitations for Peruvian recovery would begin to run either from the time its demand was refused, the property was stolen, or under the discovery rule when Peru discovered or should have discovered all it needed to know to file suit. (For more discussion of this, see the chapter on Title above.) The NSPA statute of limitations runs from the date of importation.

iii. Results of the UNESCO Convention

The UNESCO Convention and its implementation by many states, including states that are primarily states where artifacts are marketed, has been extraordinary. In a mere generation, a number of reforms have occurred. There have been serious prosecutions for importing stolen property, and many restitutions. The year 1970 has been set as a baseline for provenance in the community of museums and art dealers, in the sense that it would be rare that a piece would be accepted by a museum or pass in commerce without a provenance dating back to 1970 and showing both that the work was not stolen during that period and that it was not illegally exported since 1970.

4. Non-Legal Remedies: Soft Law, Alternate Inducements and Self-Help

A. Soft Law

While soft law may have minimal impact on individual collectors, it may have a substantial impact on the market. Museums will typically belong to one or more national or international associations of museums. Each of those organizations will have either accrediting rules or a series of "best practices" guidelines. If one of those organizations enacts accrediting criteria that bar a museum from accessioning stolen or illegally imported work, museums are less likely to buy or accept donations of those materials.

Nothing obligates the museums to follow those criteria except the threat of sanctions that might be imposed by the organization. While those are not legal compulsions, most museum directors seek out the good will of directors of similar museums, and would be powerfully influenced to avoid condemnation by these organizations. In recent years, museums have seriously violated organization rules only when financial exigencies threatened them with closure. In each case the violation involved selling museum assets and using the proceeds for improper purposes. The result has usually been wholesale reorganization of the offending museum and a change in key personnel, a result that can have a powerful deterrent effect. I am unaware of any significant violations of rules relating to acquisition of stolen or illegally exported items.

Some museums will push back against these rules, suggesting that they are "only guidelines," and at least one has threatened a defamation suit should its accreditation be publicly threatened on grounds of failure to adhere to the standards. These rules are not a panacea.

Most art and antiquities dealers are members of regional, national or international organizations. Those organizations may also set criteria for accreditation, though they are more likely to set standards for "best practices." Courts sometimes read "best practice" standards as standards imposing liability when best practices are not followed.

In general, dealer standards are likely to be less strict than museum standards, and less likely to be largely observed by the group's members. These standards are evolved as a form of self regulation by the groups concerned. A group that makes its living by selling things is not likely to exclude a class of merchandise that it wants to sell, while a group that sees its primary mission as educating the public might well be willing to exclude items perceived as ill-acquired from its shows and collections.

B. Alternate Inducements

Museums are team players. They are constantly seeking the cooperation of others. Few museums have rich enough collections to mount a successful exhibition without the cooperation of other museums and private lenders. Museums seek financial help in mounting shows from federal, state and local governmental funds for the support of the arts, and from private companies who help sponsor shows. Museums also seek general support and the donation of artworks from the general public. So an underlying goal of museum operations is to portray the museum as a good citizen. It is not always possible to anticipate what the reaction of anyone might be to news that a museum is keeping stolen art, or refusing to return illegally exported art to a country. Since museums are seeking so much cooperation from so many different communities, they tend to behave well.

Dealers frequently do business with each other, as well as with the general public. A dealer's reputation for never dealing in illegally exported artwork may be an important indicator to other dealers or to knowledgeable buyers. One of the arguments made in *Jeanneret v. Vichey*, 693 F.2d 259 (2d Cir. 1982) was that the illegally exported painting was unmarketable because no reputable dealer would buy, sell or be an intermediary for an illegally exported painting, even though it might be owned by the prospective seller. One should not be too optimistic about dealer reputation substituting for positive law.

C. Self-Help

Some countries have resorted to self-help in recovering artworks they consider to be stolen or illegally exported. Most source nations have considerable power to make deals. As they are the principal source of the works of that nation, it may be impossible to mount a show of that nation's art without loans from the source country, which are purely discretionary. The source country could suspend further archaeological digs in their country by institutions from the country in which a museum is refusing to return artwork, thereby inducing other institutions to put pressure on the museum to comply. Carrots may be used instead of sticks. In return for a promise to return the work or an acknowledgment of the right to its return to the source country, the source country might make other loans available, or might agree that the returned work would be exhibited alternately in the two countries. Where works are in need of restoration, joint fundraising might be undertaken.

Purchase is another form of self-help. Recently, a number of Chinese citizens have bought Chinese art from dealers or at auction and returned them to China. When the auction of Hopi Native American artifacts at a Paris auction could not be stopped by litigation, a foundation was the successful bidder at the auction, and returned the items to the tribe.

Checkpoints

- A major reason to restrict the international movement of art is to dry up the market for stolen or illegally exported art. It applies more forcefully to artifacts than to fine art because artifacts are more likely to be unidentifiable and more likely to be damaged, and the loss of knowledge from removal from their findspots more significant.
- Control of artifacts differs from country to country. Most countries combine ownership restrictions with export restrictions. Three approaches involve private ownership, public ownership, and public ownership with a reward for the finder and the landowner.
- Control of fine arts focuses on export restrictions. Some countries have none; in others an attempt to export results in confiscation of the art; in most there is an export license that must be obtained; in some, a purchase or a request to export triggers a right of first refusal in the government to purchase the artwork.
- General free trade treaties allow countries to impose export restrictions on art to protect national treasures as an exception. Export tariffs do not qualify because they do not protect.
- The European Convention on Human Rights contains provisions on rights to property, the right to leave a country, and the right to travel that might be used to permit an individual to export his art.
- National patrimony has no agreed-upon definition, nor is there any requirement that items be designated as part of the national patrimony in advance.
- Cultural heritage of a country is broadly defined by the 1970 UNESCO Convention as any work produced by nationals or residents, or that was produced or ever existed in the country.
- The 1970 UNESCO Convention seeks international cooperation for export control by requiring signatories to develop an export license, prevent their museums from acquiring illegally exported property and prevent the import of property stolen from museums and facilitate its return on payment of just compensation.
- The 1970 UNESCO Convention allows a country whose cultural heritage is endangered to seek and receive concerted international action to prohibit import of endangered property.
- United States implementation of the UNESCO Convention permits forfeiture of stolen property or property on which there has been a false customs declaration. Knowingly receiving stolen property is a crime in all states. The President is authorized to forbid imports as part of an international cooperation effort.
- Museum organization guidelines, international cooperation efforts, and self-help can aid in recovering stolen or illegally exported property.

Chapter 16

Historic Preservation

Roadmap

After reading this chapter, you should understand:

- The National Historic Preservation Act: Requires that before a decision is made on any federal or federally assisted project, the federal official must consider the effect of the project on anything eligible for inclusion in a national register of historic places.
- Eligibility for inclusion depends on the law of the country where the property is located.
- Standing is limited to persons within the zone of protection of NHPA who are likely to suffer injury in fact from the decision.
- Taking of property by eminent domain can be justified to improve blighted areas.
- Restrictions on historic buildings or to create historic districts are constitutional as long as the owner has some economic use of the property under the police power because they promote the public welfare.
- Historic preservation of churches may be unconstitutional if the requirements infringe church doctrine.

1. Introduction: How the United States Protects Its Cultural Heritage

As we have seen above, some countries protect their cultural heritage by restricting its export; others give the country the right to purchase works that are proposed for export; others nationalize items deemed vital to the country's cultural heritage; others provide rewards to the discoverers of cultural heritage; and still others combine two or more of those devices. The United States uses none of them.

United States law protects U.S. cultural heritage in three ways. It encourages historic preservation; it regulates archaeology, ownership and trafficking; and it has special provisions for certain Native American items. It provides incentives, both through the tax systems and by a series of subsidies at federal, and sometimes state and local levels. Governments at all levels collect and disseminate information.

2. National Historic Preservation Act (NHPA)

A. Basics of NHPA

The major federal instrument for historic preservation is the National Historic Preservation Act, 16 U.S.C. §§470-470x-6. NHPA requires that before a decision is made on any federal or federally-assisted project, called an undertaking, the federal official must "take into account the effect of the undertaking" on anything "included in or eligible for inclusion in the National Register [of Historic Places]." As a practical matter, the responsible federal agency must determine whether there is any appropriate property in the area that may be affected by the undertaking, either during construction or in the future. If there is, the federal agency must consult with people likely to have an interest, and prepare a report detailing the potential injury and methods by which it might be mitigated. It must make findings of fact about that in the process of making its final decision to show that the problems were considered.

The sorts of activities that will trigger NHPA might include any construction project, the financing of state or local government activities, war games or actual combat.

NHPA has been held to apply to activities of the federal government outside the United States on an equal footing with activities within its territorial borders.

There is no requirement in either NHPA or most state or local laws that the property be designated in advance as a historic property. It need only be "eligible for inclusion" in such a register. If outside the United States, it is the other country's historic register. Japan listed the Okinawa dugong, a marine mammal, on its register of historic and cultural resources and the court approved the application of NHPA to it, even though an animal would not be eligible for listing in the United States National Register of Historic Places. *Okinawa Dugong v. Gates*, 543 F.Supp.2d 1082 (N.D.Cal. 2008).

A plaintiff who successfully invokes NHPA does not substantively win. NHPA has been interpreted as a procedural statute. It only requires that the federal decisionmaker "take into account" the effect of the decision on historic sites; it does not require that the decisionmaker actually protect those sites. A victory by the challenger results in the project being sent back to the federal administrator for a new decision, which was what happened when the Army Corps of Engineers closed the Kennewick Man archaeological site without following NHPA procedures. *Bonnichsen v. United States*, 217 F.Supp.2d 1116 (D. Or. 2002) "Bonnichsen III."

B. Standing

The occasional case has raised the question of whether anyone other than the affected owner has standing. Such cases usually arise when the government entity has granted the owner of the historic property permission to modify it, and a neighbor objects.

In one case, persons living in a Philadelphia historic district had standing to challenge a grant by the Department of Housing and Urban Development to the city to construct a hotel and parking garage in the district. *Society Hill Property Owners' Ass'n v. Rendell*, 210 F.3d 168 (3d Cir. 2000).

In another, an owner adjacent to a South Carolina antebellum plantation and cemetery, some of which historic area overlapped his property, had standing to challenge a permit issued by the Army Corps of Engineers to the county to fill a wetland and construct a road without considering the impact of that improved access on the historic site. Standing requires that a plaintiff has sufficient stake in the outcome of the case to litigate it properly. He must demonstrate injury in fact. In the Philadelphia case, this involved increased traffic, pollution and noise, impaired use of the historic district, and decreased property values. In the South Carolina case, plaintiffs pointed out that the improved access would lead to increased trespassing and looting in the historic area, even though the proposed road would not cross either plaintiff's land or the historic area. Plaintiffs must also show that they are within the zone of interest of the legislation; specifically, whether the action protested adversely affects the interests intended to be protected by the National Historic Preservation Act, 16 U.S.C. §§470–470w. They must also show that their injuries are caused by the complained-of decision. *Pye v. United States*, 269 F.3d 459 (4th Cir. 2001).

In *Okinawa Dugong*, persons representing the Dugong and several other organizations were denied standing; Okinawans and other organizations were held to have standing.

3. State and Local Law

A. Eminent Domain

There has been little challenge to a state exercising eminent domain to forcibly purchase property it wishes to preserve. In the 1950s, the Supreme Court construed the requirement that eminent domain be exercised for "public use" as meaning for public benefit, and made it clear that the removal of a blighted area was a public benefit. *Berman v. Parker*, 348 U.S. 26 (1954). More recently, the taking by eminent domain of property that is not blighted has been permitted to help finance a scheme to redo a blighted area. *Courtesy Sandwich Shop, Inc. v. Port of New York Authority*, 12 N.Y.2d 379, 190 N.E.2d 402, appeal dismissed 375 U.S. 78 (1963); *Kelo v. City of New London*, 545 U.S. 469 (2005). This is a two-edged sword: while it justifies eminent domain for the sake of historic preservation, it would also justify the use of eminent domain to destroy historic structures as part of a plan to renovate a blighted area, even if the particular structure being destroyed is neither blighted nor in the blighted area.

B. Regulation

Eminent domain requires the actual expenditure of funds. State and local governments usually have many more funding demands than funds, so they prefer to accomplish their goals without spending money. The way to do that is by regulating.

Most states and localities have laws modeled after NHPA. Such state and local laws generally establish procedures and standards for designating a property as historic; once designated, the laws establish procedures and criteria for making changes to the property. This can be more serious than NHPA because states and localities possess zoning power, and are authorized to refuse permission for development on historic preservation grounds.

Historic preservation restrictions have been justified under the state's police power to regulate public health, morals, safety and welfare against claims that historic preservation restrictions result in the taking of property without just compensation. The portion cited is regulation of public welfare, which includes promoting an improved quality of life. *In re Opinion of Justices to Senate*, 333 Mass. 773, 128 N.E.2d 557 (1955). Preservation of the character and desirable aesthetic features of parts of a city were cited as ways of improving the quality of life. But a locality is unwise to rely solely on aesthetics in enacting historic preservation legislation, as some courts have held that the aesthetic views of the local government cannot overcome the aesthetic free expression of the owner to construct what he wants. Other courts have held that aesthetics alone do not provide satisfactory legal standards to prevent the regulation from becoming a taking. *Munns v. Martin*, 131 Wash.2d 192, 930 P.2d 318 (1997). Usually, aesthetic concerns are joined in statutory purpose language with economic and social goals, or history or culture. Such laws are also safer from challenge when applied to a district constructed in the same era than when applied to an individual property standing alone.

Government historic preservation actions have been upheld that refused to allow the owner to demolish historic structures; that required the owner to make significant repairs to historic structures in specific ways consistent with preserving their historic appearance; and that imposed architectural controls on changes in buildings that were not historic structures, but were in historic districts, and similar controls on new construction. *Figarsky v. Historic Dist. Comm'n of City of Norwich*, 171 Conn. 198, 368 A.2d 163 (1976); *Maher v. City of New Orleans*, 516 F.2d 1051 (5th Cir. 1975).

In the typical case, the owner of property wishes to make a change. His request for permission is denied by the local government. He sues, typically alleging that the denial of permission is not permitted by the authorizing law, and further alleging that if the denial is permitted, the authorizing law is an unconstitutional taking. While plaintiffs have occasionally succeeded in showing that the regulation exceeded the authority granted, most plaintiffs have lost on that point. The constitutional point is usually the more serious argument.

There is no litmus test separating the proper use of the police power from an unconstitutional taking in this area. It is clear that historic preservation is a proper use of the police power. It is likewise clear that in a specific case, the regulation can go too far and become a taking. It is not a physical taking where the government actually occupies, or authorizes some third person to actually occupy, the owner's property. It is rather a regulatory taking. The government interferes with the owner's intended use of the property. The application of the constitution in a specific case will depend on the facts of that case, particularly whether the regulation permits any significant economic use of the property and whether it defeats the owners' reasonable economic expectations.

In the leading case of *Penn Central Transp. Co. v. New York City*, 438 U.S. 470 (1987) plaintiff wanted to construct a 50 story building atop its Grand Central Station, which was designated a historic building under New York City's Landmarks Preservation Law. The court noted that the entire property needed to be considered, as plaintiff owned both the station and the air rights above it. The court was even unwilling to concede that the air rights were rendered worthless by the Landmarks Preservation Law, pointing out that only plaintiff's specific proposal was denied, and that did not necessarily mean that more modest proposals with less impact on the historic appearance of Grand Central Station would be denied. It mentioned that while the property would be worth considerably more if the proposed office building could be built atop it, the property was still worth a substantial amount as a functioning railroad station. The court noted that Grand Central had been designated a Landmark before the construction was proposed, so there were no reasonable investment-based expectations that such a tower could be built there. The court also noted that in most historic preservation situations, a particular owner is both burdened and benefitted. He is burdened because what he can do with his property is limited, but he is benefitted by the restrictions placed on neighboring property.

One should not take any of the court's propositions too seriously in future cases, except its statement that a mere diminution in value, as long as there remains some profitable use, is not a taking. It is doubtful that there would have been a different result if Penn Central had sold the air development rights to a subsidiary corporation before the subsidiary requested development permission, even though the air development rights were the "entire property" owned by the owner. Surely the court does not require that an owner present every conceivably profitable development plan and have them rejected before it is willing to concede that the property might be worthless as restricted. And the court has suggested in dictum that the timing of the designation of Landmark status as before or after the purchase is not determinative.

While the constitutionality of such laws has not been successfully challenged under either federal or state constitutions, administrative agencies must be careful not to exceed their statutory authorization. In *United Artists' Theater Circuit, Inc. v. City of Philadelphia*, 535 Pa. 370, 635 A.2d 612 (1993), the court invalidated the city's attempt to preserve the interior of the theater because the legislation only permitted historic preservation of exteriors.

C. Churches and Historic Preservation

A few churches have successfully challenged historic preservation laws on First Amendment grounds, though it is not always clear whether that success is due to the "free exercise of religion" portion or the "freedom of speech" portion of the First Amendment. Cases where churches are successful usually involve regulations prohibiting changes in the physical structure of the worship area that the church can link to church doctrine. *First Covenant Church of Seattle Wash. v. City of Seattle*, 114 Wash.2d 392, 787 P.2d 1352 (1990) *remanded for consideration of a recently-decided case* 499 U.S. 901 (1991). Churches have usually been unsuccessful when the proposed change was primarily to increase income that could be devoted to religious or charitable purposes, such as building a high-rise office building adjacent to the church's community center that would provide better office support for the church as well as rents from commercial tenants. *Rector, Wardens and Members of Vestry of St. Bartholomew's Church v. City of New York*, 914 F.2d 348 (2d Cir. 1990).

A federal statute requires that the constitutionality of an application of land use control, whether for historic preservation or for other purposes, be tested under strict scrutiny, which requires a compelling governmental purpose for the law. It also requires that the regulation intrude as little as possible on freedom of religion in achieving that compelling government purpose. Religious Land Use and Institutionalized Persons Act, 42 U.S.C. § 2000cc.

Checkpoints

- National Historic Preservation Act requires that before a decision is made on any federal or federally-assisted project, the federal official must consider the effect of the project on anything eligible for inclusion in a national register of historic places.
- Eligibility for inclusion in a national register depends on the law of the country where the property is located.
- Standing to invoke NHPA is limited to persons within the zone of protection of NHPA who are likely to suffer injury in fact from the decision.
- Taking of property by eminent domain is justified to improve blighted areas.
- Restrictions on historic buildings or to create historic districts are constitutional as long as the owner has some economic use of the property under the police power because they promote the public welfare.
- Historic preservation of churches may be unconstitutional if the requirements infringe church doctrine.

Chapter 17

Regulating Archaeology

Roadmap

After reading this chapter, you should understand:

- Archaeology on federal land: The Antiquities Act of 1906 required anyone who wished to excavate on federally owned or controlled land (including land of Indian tribes) to first obtain permission from the federal government.
- Damaging or removing artifacts: The Act criminalized damaging objects of antiquity or removing them from federally owned or controlled land.
- Archaeological Resources Protection Act (ARPA) protection from 1979: ARPA protects archaeological resources, defined as at least 100 years old, and remains of past human life or activities of archaeological interest.
- Criminal liability: A person may be criminally liable for violating the ARPA. This violation is a specific intent crime and requires scienter for each element of the crime.
- Sentencing guidelines: If convicted, the sentence may include restitution of actual loss. Restitution cannot be ordered for archaeological value, but archaeological value can be considered in determining the gravity of the crime. Archaeological value is the value of the information that was lost by taking the resource, measured by the cost of a suitable scientific excavation (even though none was planned).
- Trafficking: ARPA adds criminal offenses for trafficking archaeological resources taken from anywhere in violation of any provision, rule, regulation, ordinance, or permit in effect under federal, state or local law.
- State law protection of archaeology: A number of states provide protection for archaeological sites. Most state laws are modeled on ARPA and provide protection only for archaeological sites on land owned or controlled by the state and included on an official list of sites.
- NEPA: When any federal agency contemplates a project, the National Environmental Policy Act (NEPA) requires the agency to complete and consider an environmental impact report, and respond to the information about archaeological sites contained in the report.
- Goals are to encourage the discovery of clues to the knowledge of the past, and to make both knowledge and significant examples of previous artwork available to the widest possible public.

1. Antiquities Act of 1906

A. Archaeology Permitting

Since the Antiquities Act of 1906, 16 U.S.C. §§431–433, anyone who wished to excavate archaeological resources on federally owned or controlled land (including land of Indian tribes) needed to first obtain permission from the federal government. The agency from which permission must be sought is the federal agency that manages the land in question, but all federal agencies are supposed to coordinate their regulations to the extent possible. An application for a permit is quite detailed in order to assure that the archaeology is up to current standards. The permit will provide for the disposition of what is found, usually to universities or museums.

The fact that the permit requirement is limited to land owned or controlled by the federal government means that this provision is asserting the government's role as a property owner. Many states have followed suit, requiring permits issued by state officials to excavate on state-owned and state-controlled land.

The permitting requirement is continued in the Archaeological Resources Protection Act. Having a permit under that act was crucial in giving the scientists standing to sue the United States to establish a misinterpretation of the Native American Graves Protection and Repatriation Act in *Bonnichsen v. United States*, 357 F.3d 962 (9th Cir. 2004).

B. Stealing or Damaging "Objects of Antiquity"

The Act also criminalizes damaging objects of antiquity or removing them from federally owned or controlled land.

Violation of these laws may subject the violator to forfeiture, civil suits and criminal penalties.

That has led to controversy over what an antiquity might be. A man appealed a conviction for violating the act by taking San Carlos Indian masks and other objects. The objects were only five years old but they were used in the same fashion as objects hundreds of years old. Rather than discuss whether an "antiquity" need have a certain age, the Court of Appeals held the statute unconstitutional, as void for vagueness, because it is impossible to determine what an antiquity might be. *United States v. Diaz*, 449 F.2d 113 (9th Cir. 1974). It would have been better judicial procedure to have found the act constitutional, but not applicable to these items because they were not antiquities.

In a later case, a different circuit saw no vagueness where defendants were convicted of excavating 800-year-old Mimbres pottery. It thought that a person of reasonable intelligence should know the pottery was an antiquity, especially because the road accessing the site was posted with warnings about the Antiquities Act, and the fact that defendants may have previously sold a similar bowl to an archaeologist. *United States v. Smyer*, 596 F.2d 939 (10th Cir. 1979).

The *Diaz* case unleashed a potential disaster, as a substantial amount of federal land is governed by the 9th Circuit. To avoid *Diaz*, prosecutors in Arizona charged defendants with stealing and damaging federal property. The District Court dismissed the indictment on grounds that the Antiquities Act was designed to be the exclusive remedy and it had been declared unconstitutional. Reversing, the court applied the general rule that when conduct violates more than one statute, the prosecutor may choose which to use, and held that there was no evidence that the Antiquities Act was intended to repeal the other laws. *United States v. Jones*, 607 F.2d 269 (9th Cir. 1979). It stated that the relics stolen and damaged were property of the United States without justifying that decision. One might speculate that they were fixtures attached to the realty, that the United States had acquired title by adverse possession, or that it was the successor state to the original owners.

2. Archaeological Resources Protection Act of 1979

The Antiquities Act was succeeded by the Archaeological Resources Protection Act (ARPA) of 1979, 16 U.S.C. §§470aa–470mm.

ARPA changes the terminology of the item protected from an antiquity to an archaeological resource. An archaeological resource must have two qualities: it must be at least 100 years old, and it must be a remain "of past human life or activities" of archaeological interest. Archaeologists have complained that the definition excludes fossils of animal or plant life that ARPA should protect.

A. Intent Required for Criminal Liability

A person may be civilly liable for violating one of these acts; he may forfeit the archaeological resources, as well as the vehicles and equipment used; and he may be criminally liable for knowingly violating either act. Potential criminal liability raises some additional issues. While a court has said that these are specific intent crimes requiring scienter for each element of the crime, such as that the person was excavating and that the find was an archaeological resource, *United States v. Lynch*, 233 F.3d 1139 (9th Cir. 2000), another said that defendant need not know he was on federal land as long as he knew he was excavating without a permit and without the permission of the landowner. *United States v. Quarrell*, 310 F.3d 664 (10th Cir. 2002).

The court's holding in Lynch raises particular difficulties. How do you prove that a person knew that the item was at least 100 years old? The skull and bones in *Lynch* would need either carbon dating or the expertise of a very good archaeologist. Coins would be easy if dated. Other material would probably require an experienced archaeologist to know the age of the item. The 23-year-old high-school-educated Lynch would be unlikely to know the age of the item, but he should have known that he was doing something wrong, akin to grave robbing, when he found the skull. He might have only discovered the age of the item when he tried to sell it to a dealer.

There was no such problem in the *Quarrell* case. They stipulated that defendants were familiar with Mimbres archaeology and art.

B. Sentencing Under the Sentencing Guidelines

The sentence may include restitution of actual loss, but cannot include archaeological value in calculating loss for restitution purposes. Archaeological value is the value of the information that was lost by taking the resource, measured by the cost of a suitable scientific excavation (even though none was planned). However, archaeological value can be used to determine the extent of the loss for purposes of the federal sentencing guidelines, at least where the behavior was egregious, and other measures are inadequate. *United States v. Shumway*, 112 F.3d 1413 (10th Cir. 1997); *United States v. Hunter*, 48 F.Supp.2d 1283 (D. Utah 1998).

C. Scope

Federal and state land comprises about 40% of the land mass of the United States, and a much higher percentage in the West. This means that archaeology in 60% of the U.S. is unregulated. Only two states regulate archaeology on private land. There is no case on the constitutionality of that regulation. If there were such a case, it would no doubt be justified on the police power ground of public welfare in preserving archaeological sites and expanding knowledge of previous inhabitants, and opposed on grounds that prohibiting an owner from excavating artifacts is equivalent to prohibiting an owner from removing minerals under his land.

D. Trafficking

ARPA also adds criminal offenses for trafficking archaeological resources taken from federal land without a permit, or taken from anywhere "in violation of any provision, rule, regulation, ordinance, or permit in effect under State or local law." 17 U.S.C. § 470ee. In *United States v. Gerber*, 999 F.2d 1112 (7th Cir. 1993), defendant bought Native American artifacts from a construction worker who had bulldozed them at a Hopewell site and offered them for sale at his artifact show. He contended that there was no violation of ARPA or a comparable state law in obtaining the relics because they were taken on private land. The court upheld the conviction because the artifacts were taken in violation of state trespass and conversion laws, and that was sufficient to support a trafficking conviction under ARPA.

3. State Laws

A number of states provide protection for archaeological sites. Most state laws are modeled on ARPA and provide protection only for archaeological sites on land owned or controlled by the state and included on an official list of sites. In some states owners can voluntarily submit their lands to the protection of these laws, sometimes in return for tax benefits. In a few states, the regulation encompasses all land in the state. Where the statute is not specific, courts sometimes imply that result from other features of the statute. Where the law applies to activities not normally carried out on state land, such as mining, cemeteries or agriculture, the statute was applied to all land in the state. *Whitacre v. State*, 619 N.E.2d 605 (Ind. App. 1993).

4. Incidental Archaeological Protection

Sometimes archaeological regulation comes in strange disguise. When any agency of the federal government contemplates a project, the National Environmental Policy Act (NEPA), 42 U.S.C. §§ 4321–4347, requires the agency to complete and consider an environmental impact report. Some states have similar statutes. California's is the California Environmental Quality Act (CEQA), Calif. Pub. Resources Code § 21050 et seq. In *Society for California Archaeology v. County of Butte*, 65 Cal. App.3d 832, 135 Cal. Rptr. 679 (1977), the court revoked a development permit because the county board did not sufficiently review, comment upon, and respond to the information about archaeological sites contained in the environmental impact report. The court was clear that the environmental impact report mandated neither approval nor disapproval of the project. It did require the decision-maker to address and provide mitigation for the archaeological problems set forth, and that decision would be reviewed only for abuse of discretion. The Code has since been amended to provide: "If it can be demonstrated that a project will cause damage to a unique archaeological resource, the lead agency may require reasonable efforts to be made to permit any or all of these resources to be preserved in place or left in an undisturbed state." There follows a list of what might be considered reasonable efforts. Calif. Pub. Resources Code § 21083.2(b).

One of the reasonable efforts may be an order that the developer employ a certified archaeologist to be present during the excavation portion of construction. The function of such a contract archaeologist is to monitor and manage any construction that might damage archaeological resources, and to care for any resources that are discovered. The precise responsibilities are normally spelled out in the order approving the development and in the contract with the archaeologist. In *The Lummi Nation v. Golder Assocs., Inc.*, 236 F.Supp.2d 1183 (W.D.Wash. 2002), there was a large difference between the contract and its performance. The archaeologist was to inspect all excavations, notify all parties if human remains were found, transport them to a particular place, and consult with the tribe about reburial, which the archaeologist did on the first find. Thereafter, he did not consult, and removed the remains from Washington to Colorado. The court found that although the tribe was not a party to the contract, they were an intended third party beneficiary, as the obligation with respect to Native American remains was inserted especially because of the tribe's concerns.

Another archaeological preservation comes in the mining laws of some states. Indiana requires a permit from the Department of Natural Resources for Mining, but the director of DNR may declare an area unsuitable for strip mining if it would damage "important historic, cultural, scientific and esthetic values and natural systems." In *Dept. of Natural Resources v. Indiana Coal Council Inc.*, 542 N.E.2d 1000 (Ind. 1989), the court upheld the constitutionality of the DNR director's declaration that one percent of defendant's land was unsuitable for strip mining. It consisted of the Beehunter Site, which held four different cultural periods of occupation. The designation could be removed once archaeological studies were completed. The court's two part test resembles that used in *Penn Central*, discussed in the Historical Preservation chapter above. It held that the law substantially advanced a legitimate state interest. Protecting heritage through preserving archaeological sites is a legitimate state use of the police power. Defendant has owned and farmed the land for half a century, and presented no evidence that the purpose of the purchase was for mining, so the director's declaration did not disappoint any expectations that existed when the land was bought. Further, defendant had the power to lift the restriction by funding an appropriate archaeological dig.

5. Evaluation

Turning to an evaluation of this body of law as it impacts artifacts, one might posit that one goal of the law should be to encourage the discovery of clues to knowledge of the past: the lives of previous inhabitants, the flora and fauna of different times, and its geology. A second goal might be to make both that knowledge and significant examples of previous artwork available to the widest possible public.

Where no recovery of an artifact can be made without state approval, as on federal and state lands, whether individuals are sufficiently encouraged to locate artifacts cannot be known without knowing what typical provisions of those permissions might contain. Professors may be encouraged by the prospect of tenure or significant publications, but private citizens might want a state payment or some stake in what they find to justify expending the money, time and effort to locate the artifacts. The greater the investment required, the greater the reward must be to encourage all but the most devoted amateur. The fact that an excavator can keep what he finds on his own land in most states is probably sufficient incentive to get him to dig there.

It is not, however, any incentive to get him to dig in the right way. To learn the most possible from an artifact requires careful, scientific archaeology. The positioning of the artifact, particularly in relation to other artifacts, may be crucial. Archaeologists may not realize how crucial those relationships are for decades until other artifacts are found in similar relationships. Careful archaeology is a slow, expensive process that provides little incentive for persons interested in marketing what they find on their own land. To achieve proper archaeology, the system of federal and state permitting for archaeology on government property, conditioned on the archaeologist having requisite skills and a plan approved by professionals, is greatly preferable.

None of this guarantees that the artifacts will be shown to the public, or that the knowledge gained will be widely disseminated. Restricting archaeology to professionals probably encourages wider dissemination than permitting individuals to dig, but there have been instances where professionals have restricted data to continue their monopoly on its interpretation. Government licensed digs should include conditions on making information public. In the age of the internet, that might even include putting the archaeologist's notebooks for the project online.

Artifacts are more likely to be shown to the public or at least be available to researchers if they are owned by a public entity than if owned by a private individual. However, there is no guarantee of this absent a requirement in the permit authorizing the dig. Most museums have space to show only a fraction of their collection. The rest may be stored off-site under conditions where access is difficult.

Many artifacts in private hands are eventually donated to museums where they may be available for study and appreciation. But there is no guarantee of this, and there have been documented cases where work has not been seen in public for several generations when in private hands.

Checkpoints

- The Antiquities Act of 1906 required anyone who wished to excavate on federally owned or controlled land (including land of Indian tribes) to first obtain permission from the federal government.
- The Act criminalized damaging objects of antiquity or removing them from federally owned or controlled land.
- Archaeological Resources Protection Act (ARPA) from 1979 protects archaeological resources, defined as at least 100 years old, and a remain of past human life or activities of archaeological interest.
- A person may be criminally liable for violating ARPA. This violation is a specific intent crime and requires scienter for each element of the crime.
- If convicted, the sentence may include restitution of actual loss. Restitution cannot be ordered for archaeological value, but archaeological value can be considered in determining the gravity of the crime. Archaeological value is the value of the information that was lost by taking the resource, measured by the cost of a suitable scientific excavation (even though none was planned).
- ARPA adds criminal offenses for trafficking archaeological resources taken from anywhere in violation of any provision, rule, regulation, ordinance, or permit in effect under federal, state or local law.
- A number of states provide protection for archaeological sites. Most state laws are modeled on ARPA and provide protection only for archaeological sites on land owned or controlled by the state and included on an official list of sites. A few include all land in the state.

- When any federal agency contemplates a project, the National Environmental Protection Act (NEPA) requires the agency to complete and consider an environmental impact report, and respond to the information about archaeological sites contained in the report.
- The goals of these laws are to encourage the discovery of clues to the knowledge of the past, and to make both knowledge and significant examples of previous artwork available to the widest possible public.

Chapter 18

Artifacts Found on Land

Roadmap

After reading this chapter, you should understand:

- Ownership of artifacts found on land depends on the law of finds, which categorizes the artifacts as abandoned, lost, mislaid, embedded, or treasure trove.
- Abandoned property: Property that the owner has not used and intends to abandon. Abandoned property belongs to the person who finds it and reduces it to possession.
- Mislaid property: Property that the owner has put down and left, but the owner probably knows the location at which he mislaid the property. The possessor of the property upon which mislaid property was mislaid may keep that property from anyone except the true owner—even the finder. It is unlikely that artifacts will ever be mislaid property.
- Lost property: Property whose location is unlikely to be known by the owner. Lost property can be retained by the finder against anyone except the true owner. It is unlikely that the owner of an artifact will ever reclaim it.
- Embedded property: Property that is in the land in a way that shows it has been there for a considerable period of time. The embedded property belongs to the land. Under the law of waste, the owner is usually preferred to the tenant.
- Treasure trove: Defined as money, or gold or silver bullion or plate concealed by the owner. Special rules gave it to the Crown in England. In the United States it is treated as embedded property.

1. Ownership of Artifacts: Introduction

Law on the ownership of artifacts has proceeded through some transition, and is still confused and unsatisfactory.

The ownership of artifacts found under land is influenced by the doctrine of abandonment, and the law relating to finds, trespass, and mineral rights. The ownership of artifacts found under water is usually governed by the law of salvage.

Under the law of finds, property is classified as either abandoned, lost, mislaid or embedded. (The English rule that treasure trove, gold or silver bullion secreted somewhere, belongs to the Crown, was never applied in the U.S. That would have been a fifth category in England.)

A. Abandoned Property

Abandoned property is property that the owner has not used and intends to abandon. Non-use is easy to prove; proving intent to abandon is very difficult, almost requiring a statement that the owner intends to abandon the property.

Leaving your property under duress does not constitute intent to abandon. *Menzel v. List*, 267 N.Y.S.2d 804 (Sup. 1966). Leaving your artwork in the hands of a gallery owner for more than half a century is not an intent to abandon if from time to time you inquire about it, at least when your contact is interrupted by a World War and the Cold War. *Mucha v. King*, 792 F.2d 602 (7th Cir. 1986). Wrapping coins in paper, placing them in a jar and burying the jar is evidence that you intend to return and reclaim them, not that you intend to abandon them. *Corliss v. Wenner*, 136 Id. 417, 34 P.3d 1100 (App. 2011). Even burying goods was held not to be an intent to abandon, at least when the goods were buried with ancestors. The goods served some spiritual, moral or religious purpose. *Charrier v. Bell*, 496 So.2d 601 (La. App. 1986).

Abandoned property belongs to the person who finds it and reduces it to possession.

B. Lost and Mislaid Property

Mislaid property is property that the owner has put down and left, but the owner probably knows the location at which he mislaid the property. The possessor of the property upon which mislaid property was mislaid may keep that property from anyone except the true owner—even the finder. The reason advanced is that the owner will realize that he has mislaid the property, retrace his steps, and find it with the owner of the place where he mislaid it.

Lost property is other property out of the owner's possession. The owner did not intentionally place the property where it was found. It may have fallen out of his pocket. Lost property belongs to the finder, subject to the superior rights of the true owner. Giving lost property to the finder encourages the finder to report the find. Because the owner does not associate the loss with a particular place, the most likely way to reunite the owner with his property is to encourage the finder to search for the owner by providing him with an incentive: he can keep the property until the owner shows up and, if the owner does not appear after diligent search, the finder keeps the property permanently.

In many states, the distinction between lost and mislaid property has been replaced with a statutory procedure calling for turning over found property to the police and advertising it.

It is often impossible to determine whether found property is lost, mislaid or abandoned, and those categories are usually result-determining. Presumptions have sprung up. No reasonable person would put his property down in a public place and walk away, so property found in a public place must be either lost or abandoned. On the other hand, it is reasonable to assume that an owner who is in a store might put his property down, perhaps to try on the merchandise. So property found in a theater, restaurant or boutique is likely to be classified as mislaid property.

The result in the case of both lost and mislaid property tries to keep the property as close to the true owner as possible so as to facilitate its restoration to the owner. This rationale clearly has no application to archaeological artifacts because the owner is unlikely to appear.

The court in *Favorite v. Miller*, 176 Conn. 310, 407 A.2d 974 (1978), found itself quite unable to decide whether a piece of a pre-Revolutionary War statue left in a marsh was lost or mislaid property because it despaired of trying to ascertain the state of mind of persons two hundred years in the past. It decided the case in part on the fact that the piece of lead statue was embedded ten inches in the soil, so was embedded property.

In general, trespassing finders yield to the owner of the land. That was a second ground for the decision in *Favorite*: the finder was a wilful trespasser. He knew when he entered that he was trespassing and he was warned both before entering and after coming away with the find that it would be wise to locate the property's owner and discuss the matter with him, and was even given the name and address of the owner. However, this rule provides an incentive for the finder to conceal the find. If there is a living owner, that would deprive him of his property, and if there is no owner, as will be the case for most artifacts, it deprives the public of knowledge of the item found and the circumstances of the find.

Not only have the courts tended to favor the landowner over the finder in case of trespass, they have tended to expand trespass beyond its normal scope. Persons invited onto the land as employees are not normally considered trespassers, but courts have held that persons are trespassers if they exceed the implied scope of their invitation. A treasure-seeker with a metal detector was considered a trespasser on public land. He was not engaged in "pleasure or recreation," and was therefore a trespasser because the gift of the park to the public was for those purposes. *Waverley Borough Council v. Fletcher*, [1995] Q.B. 334 (C.A.), 4 All E.R. 756 (1995).

C. Embedded Property

Embedded property is personal property that is in the land in a way that shows it has been there for a considerable period of time. The property need not be totally interred; it is sufficient that it be firmly affixed in the land.

There is one significant difference between the artifact case and the typical lost or mislaid property case. In the artifact case, the true owner of the chattel is both unknown and long dead, and proving who his living heir might be is not possible. The rules for lost and mislaid property operate on the assumption that the true owner of the chattel is ascertainable if the law could only reunite owner and chattel. The true owner of an artifact being unknown and unknowable, all considerations of reuniting the goods with their true owner should disappear. The dispute should be between the finder, who claims by right of discovery and as the person without whose efforts the property would have remained unknown, the possessor of the land who claims because of his right of possession, and the owner of the land.

The personal efforts of the finder in discovering embedded property are thought inadequate to justify giving him the property; embedded property is considered part of the realty, and goes with the realty.

The question then becomes whether the property belongs to the possessor (who may be a tenant) or the owner. The property belongs to the owner of the land, on analogy to the law of waste. If the land has something of value on it, it belongs to the owner unless it can reasonably be said to have been intended that the possessor use it. The "open mine" rule dictates that a tenant can continue working a mine that was open, but cannot open a new mine. Because the owner and the occupier were unaware of the artifact on the land, they could not have intended that the occupier might use it, so the embedded property remains the property of the owner. In *Elwes v. Brigg Gas Co.*, 33 Ch. D. 562 (1886), the court declined to decide whether a boat more than twenty centuries old carved from a single oak tree and buried four to six feet in the ground was a mineral within the meaning of the lease, part of the soil in which it was embedded, or a chattel, but decided that in any of those situations, it belonged to the owner of the land, not the tenant who excavated it. The court began with the premise that at the time of the lease, the boat belonged to the owner of the land because whether mineral, part of the soil, or a chattel embedded in the soil, it belonged to the owner because he had constructive possession of it by his ownership of the land, good against all the world but the true owner, whose identity cannot be established after twenty centuries. It then found no intention in the terms of the lease to convey artifacts discovered on the land to the tenant.

In *Allred v. Biegel*, 240 Mo. App. 818, 219 S.W.2d 665 (1949), a canoe made from a walnut log was found by plaintiffs embedded in land eroded by a change in course of a stream. Plaintiffs bought the rights of the life tenant and sued a subsequent possessor who excavated the canoe. The owner of the remainder intervened and won the day. The court does not seriously consider the possibility that the finder or the excavator might have rights in the canoe, and as between the remainderman and the life tenant, applies the law of waste to hold for the remainderman. The court does not consider that the life tenant has the right to possession of the land which should include the canoe until the end of the life tenancy.

The accidental finder gets nothing, and the purposeful finder would be well advised to enter into an agreement in advance with the landowner dividing the find, else he discover that he has spent his own money, time and effort to unearth something that will belong to the landowner.

These rules have even occasionally displaced the normal law of salvage when the vessel is embedded in land owned by the government. In *Klein v. The Unidentified Wrecked and Abandoned Sailing Vessel*, 758 F.2d 1511 (11th Cir. 1985), an English (presumably non-military) ship embedded in federal land, Biscayne National Park, was held to belong to the United States *ratione soli*, either because of its embeddedness or because of the constructive possession of the owner of the land.

D. Treasure Trove

In England, there was another situation: the finding of treasure trove. Treasure trove was defined as money, or gold or silver bullion or plate. It is not lost property because the owner did not part with it involuntarily. It is not mislaid property because the true owner did not put it down and forget where he placed it. He concealed it. Treasure trove belonged to the crown for its usefulness in helping the crown maintain the coinage.

The doctrine of treasure trove belonging to the state never took hold in the United States. Instead, an odd perversion of the doctrine occurred. Treasure trove, unlike other embedded property, belonged to the finder. Courts did not persuasively support this ruling with reasons, and whatever one might think about the conflict between the finder and the landowner, it is difficult to see any reason to have a different rule for treasure trove than for other embedded property. Most recent cases have rejected a separate rule for treasure trove, and have instead applied the rule for embedded property, giving it to the owner of the realty. *Morgan v. Wiser*, 711 S.W.2d 220 (Tenn. App. 1985); *Corliss v. Wenner*, 136 Id. 417, 34 P.3d 1100 (App. 2011).

2. Relativity of Title

All the above is subordinate to the elemental doctrine of property law, relativity of title. Specifically, the court is not usually deciding who owns the property. It is only adjudicating which of two claimants has superior rights to it.

Checkpoints

- Ownership of artifacts found on land depends on the law of finds, which categorizes the artifacts as abandoned, lost, mislaid, embedded, or treasure trove.
- Abandoned property is property that the owner has not used and intends to abandon. Abandoned property belongs to the person who finds it and reduces it to possession.
- Mislaid property is property that the owner has put down and left, but the owner probably knows the location at which he mislaid the property. The possessor of the property upon which mislaid property was mislaid may keep that property from anyone except the true owner—even the finder. It is unlikely that artifacts will ever be mislaid property.
- Lost property is property whose location is unlikely to be known by the owner. Lost property can be retained by the finder against anyone except the true owner. It is unlikely that the owner of an artifact will ever reclaim it.
- Embedded property is property that is in the land in a way that shows it has been there for a considerable period of time. The embedded property belongs to the land. Under the law of waste, the owner is usually preferred to the tenant.
- Treasure trove is defined as money, or gold or silver bullion or plate concealed by the owner. Special rules gave it to the Crown in England. In the United States it is treated as embedded property.

Chapter 19

Artifacts Found under Water

Roadmap

After reading this chapter, you should understand:

- Underwater artifacts are usually governed by the law of salvage. If the item has been abandoned, the law of finds gives ownership to the first person to reduce it to possession. If the item has not been abandoned, the owner retains title, but the admiralty court determines an award for the salvor.
- Salvor's award is determined considering the labor spent, the skill and energy in salving, the value of property used in the rescue effort and the degree of danger to which it was exposed, the risks incurred by the salvors, the value of the property saved, the degree of danger to which it was exposed, and the extent to which the salvors protected historical and archaeological value.
- Embedded in owned bed: Some courts have abandoned the law of salvage where the property is embedded in the bed of a watercourse that is owned.
- Abandonment requires non-user for a long period and intent to abandon. Intent to abandon by the federal government or a foreign state must be express.
- The Abandoned Shipwreck Act: Grants ownership of abandoned ships to the federal government and transfers ownership to the state on whose territorial waters the ship is found. It has been largely unused because of the difficulty of finding abandonment.
- Admiralty jurisdiction v. Eleventh Amendment: There is a conflict between exclusive admiralty jurisdiction in federal courts and the eleventh amendment, providing that states cannot be sued in federal court.
- UNESCO Convention on the Protection of the Underwater Cultural Heritage: There is a UNESCO Convention providing protection of underwater cultural heritage, but it is unlikely to be influential because it has not been widely adopted and the U.S.A. is not a member.

---

1. Salvage

Underwater finds march to a somewhat different drummer than artifacts found on land. The governing law is normally the law of salvage, which is administered as part of the admiralty jurisdiction of the federal courts. The salvor is comparable to the finder, though he usually invests much more in technology to enable his finds. There usually is no landowner, because the find is often on the ocean floor. If the artifact is found within the territorial waters, the landowner then becomes either the federal or state government.

With some underwater items, there is an identifiable ship owner. Alternatively, there may be artifacts strewn along the ocean floor without any indication of their source. Underwater artifacts may be moved by the current; covered by it; and uncovered by it. So an artifact that is embedded one day may a week later sit on the ocean floor a mile away.

If the property has been abandoned, the law of finds applies. The finder becomes the owner unless the property is embedded in owned land, in which case the owner of the land becomes the owner.

A. Salvor's Award

A salvor is a person who intentionally rescues a vessel or its cargo from maritime danger. Underwater vessels are presumed to be in danger of further loss. The salvor saves the vessel or cargo for the true owner. The salvor does not receive title to the property, but is entitled to an award from the owner for his services. The admiralty court determines the amount of the award by considering the labor spent, the skill and energy in salving, the value of property used in the rescue effort and the degree of danger to which it was exposed, the risks incurred by the salvors, the value of the property saved, the degree of danger to which it was exposed, and (most recently) the extent to which the salvors protected historical and archaeological value.

The award must be high enough to encourage rescue and recovery, and also high enough to assure that the salvage is reported, rather than stolen. It is not unusual for the award to amount to 70% of the value of the property saved.

Determining the award is set forth in some detail in *Columbus-America Discovery Group v. Atlantic Mutual Ins. Co.*, 56 F.3d 556 (4th Cir. 1995).

The model for the law of salvage is the boat menaced by sinking in a storm that is rescued by the salvor, but that law also applies to wrecks centuries old, like Nuestra Señora de Atocha, which sunk in the Carribean in 1622. *Treasure Salvors, Inc. v. Unidentified Wrecked and Abandoned Sailing Vessel ... Believed to be the Nuestra Señora de Atocha*, 569 F.2d 330 (5th Cir. 1978). The crucial move in that case was that the parties stipulated that the ship was abandoned, and it rested on unowned land, so the salvor, being the first one to take possession, became the owner.

B. Embedded Property

Another case where the traditional law of salvage was completely abandoned was *Klein v. The Unidentified Wrecked and Abandoned Sailing Vessel*, 758 F.2d 1511 (11th Cir. 1985). Plaintiff discovered the exact whereabouts of an abandoned English (presumably non-military) ship in Biscayne National Park. The court denied the finder property rights. It held that property in the ship vested in the United States (even though the United States did not know the ship's precise location) because it was embedded in United States soil. The court then denied a salvage award on the ground that just because the ship on the ocean bottom cannot be located does not mean that it is endangered. The Fifth Circuit has held otherwise. *Treasure Salvors, Inc. v. Unidentified Wrecked and Abandoned Sailing Vessel... Believed to be the Nuestra Señora de Atocha*, 569 F.2d 330 (5th Cir. 1978).

C. Abandoned Shipwrecks

If the shipwreck has been abandoned and it is not embedded in owned land, the salvor, as the first possessor, receives title to the property under the rule for abandoned property in the law of finds. But that rule is challenged by a common law rule, often confirmed by state statute, that the state owns abandoned ships and their abandoned cargo, as well as flotsam and jetsam. The sovereign ownership rule seems to apply if the ship ends up within the territorial waters of a state that has such a statute or has adopted the common law. *State of Florida by Ervin v. The Massachusetts Co.*, 95 So. 2d 902 (Fla. 1956).

Courts have been reluctant to find that a shipwreck has been abandoned. The burden of proof on abandonment lies with the party alleging abandonment. Long periods of non-use do not constitute abandonment without intent to abandon. No abandonment was found even after the ship had rested for more than a century at the bottom and even when the owner cannot produce ownership records. Ordinary property law provides that when an insurance company pays the claim, it is subrogated to the policy-holder's rights in the property, so we are no longer dealing with the original owners but with their subrogees. Indeed, one of the arguments against abandonment is that the technology did not exist at the time of the wreck to raise it, which explains the owner's failure to try. *Columbus-America Discovery Group v. Atlantic Mutual Ins. Co.*, 974 F.2d 450 (4th Cir. 1992); *People ex rel. Illinois Historic Preservation Agency v. Zych*, 186 Ill.2d 267, 710 N.E.2d 820 (1999). In the latter case, the court was impressed by the fact that the insurance company had preserved the documents for more than a century, and had immediately asserted its rights when it discovered that the Lady Elgin had been found. So generally at common law, the finders are limited to the salvor's award. That award may be substantial. In one case, it was ninety percent of the gold found, and each individual insurer had to prove its ownership claim. *Columbus-America Discovery Group v. Atlantic Mutual Ins. Co.*, 56 F.3d 556 (4th Cir. 1995).

However, where no one claims ownership of the vessel, implied abandonment can be found if there is clear and convincing evidence of that intent. In *Northeast Research, LLC v. One Shipwrecked Vessel*, 729 F.3d 197 (2d Cir. 2013), abandonment was found where the vessel was nearing the end of its expected life, its cargo would have been ruined by water, and the owner made no attempt to locate or salvage it for many years after salvage became technologically feasible.

Difficulty of proving abandonment is especially true of ships owned by the federal government. The Constitution grants Congress power to dispose of property belonging to the United States. It has been interpreted to prohibit any implied abandonment, even where the confederate ship Alabama lay at the bottom of the English channel for more than a century and no efforts were made to recover it. Thus neither a diver who recovered the ship's bell, nor any good faith purchaser from the diver or his successors in interest, was able to acquire title to the bell. It remained the property of the United States. *United States v. Steinmetz*, 973 F.2d 212 (3d Cir. 1992). Ironically, in 2002, French divers discovered the wreck of the Alabama, with its bell still intact, so the bell in *Steinmetz* was not authentic and did not belong to the United States government. Fed. R. Civ. Proc. 60(b), which permits reopening decisions for newly discovered evidence, limits the reopening to one year.

The wreck of the battleship Massachusetts was abandoned by a telegram from the Secretary of the Navy announcing that the federal government had abandoned the ship. *State of Florida by Ervin v. The Massachusetts Co.*, 95 So. 2d 902 (Fla. 1956). Express abandonments are effective.

The express abandonment standard applies equally to military ships belonging to foreign nations. This may be derived from the legislative history of the Abandoned Shipwreck Act, or from Article X of the United States' Treaty of Friendship and General Relations with Spain of 1902. In *Sea Hunt, Inc., v. Unidentified Shipwrecked Vessel or Vessels*, 221 F.3d 634 (2000), the Spanish naval vessels had reposed on the ocean floor for 200–250 years.

It seems clear that the only prudent way for a salvor to deal with submerged naval vessels is to enter into a salvage agreement with the owner government detailing who will do what and who will own what at the end of the day.

2. Abandoned Shipwreck Act

In the Abandoned Shipwreck Act, 43 U.S.C. §§ 2101–2106, an attempt was made to stay the application of the law of finds and the law of salvage. That act grants the federal government ownership of abandoned or embedded ships, which ownership the act transfers to the state that owns the land in which the ship is embedded. Following the Act, some states have enacted systems to permit private persons to explore for and recover abandoned shipwrecks, in which case ownership is determined by the permit conditions. Some states require permits for any underwater archaeology, imposing tests of professional competence, and granting the exclusive right to examine specified areas, often in return for the state's right to keep artifacts of historical or artistic significance, to evaluate all artifacts recovered, and to take a percentage of any treasure found. This system has been largely frustrated by the unwillingness of courts to find that a ship has been abandoned. The test for an abandoned ship under the act is the same as the test for an abandoned ship in admiralty law. *California and State Lands Commission v. Deep Sea Research, Inc.*, 523 U.S. 491(1998).

A further constitutional conundrum awaits anyone requiring court action under the Abandoned Shipwreck Act. On the one hand, the constitution places exclusive jurisdiction over admiralty matters in the federal courts, so such matters cannot be litigated in state courts. On the other, states are not subject to suit in the federal courts. Nonetheless, cases have proceeded in federal court under the Abandoned Shipwreck Act where no one raised this issue, or where the case was decided without reaching the issue. U.S. Constitution art. 3 § 2, and amendment 11. The latest precedent narrows that rule, and permits a federal court to proceed *in rem*, at least when the *res* is not in the actual possession of the state. *California and State Lands Commission v. Deep Sea Research, Inc.*, 523 U.S. 491(1998).

The real limitation of the Eleventh Amendment lies when the salvor seeks a salvage award for a ship subject to the Abandoned Shipwreck Act. When the Act was passed, property in all abandoned shipwrecks covered by the Act passed to the federal government and an instant later to the appropriate state. A salvor is always beginning his salvage operation after title has passed to the state, but the Eleventh Amendment prohibits such an action unless the state has waived its sovereign immunity. *Zych v. Unidentified, Wrecked and Abandoned Vessel .. "Seabird,"* 19 F.3d 1136 (7th Cir. 1994). Again, the remedy for the prospective salvor is to negotiate in advance with the state concerned how the wreck will be salvaged and to include in the agreement a waiver of the state's sovereign immunity.

3. UNESCO Convention

There is a UNESCO Convention on the Protection of the Underwater Cultural Heritage signed in Paris 2 November 2001. In 2020, it has 63 parties, the most significant being Argentina, France, Hungary, Iran, Italy, Libya, Mexico, Morocco, Nigeria, Portugal, Spain, Tunisia and Ukraine. The United States is not a state party and is unlikely to become one.

The key definition is underwater cultural heritage. To qualify, it must be a trace of human existence at least partially under water periodically for at least a century, but it does not include pipelines, cables or installations still in use, like drilling platforms. Because of that definition, it would not include plant or animal fossils, nor would it include items underwater due to earthquake or river shifts within the past century. As time passes, some items that are not covered will satisfy the century requirement and become underwater cultural heritage.

Article 2 gives priority to preserving heritage *in situ*. It also provides that it will not be commercially exploited. Responsible non-intrusive access to observe or document *in situ* underwater cultural heritage shall be encouraged to create public appreciation except where that is incompatible with its protection.

These provisions eliminate the possibility of private sector investment in locating and recovering underwater cultural heritage, which requires significant investment. It is unclear whether the prohibition on commercial exploitation would extend to documentary movies relating to the discovery of the heritage.

Article 4 suspends the law of salvage and the law of finds unless the country authorizes it, it conforms to the treaty, and ensures that what is recovered is given maximum protection. Since the law of salvage provides for an award to the salvor out of what is recovered, it appears that such a reward would be inconsistent with the treaty and therefore prohibited.

Article 14, 17 and 18 require States Parties to prevent the import or possession of items recovered in violation of the treaty, or illicitly exported, to provide sanctions, and to provide for their seizure and return.

Throughout the convention, there is much emphasis on providing notice to potentially interested states and consulting with those states.

4. Evaluation

For the underlying purposes of art law, learning as much as possible from the remains of the past and making artifacts available for public study and view, the addition of archaeological care as a criterion for determining the amount of a salvage award is welcome. It is unclear how significant that criterion will be in focusing the behavior of salvors on preserving archaeological value, sitting among six other criteria, until more cases are decided.

A second hopeful sign is the refusal to easily find abandonment of government ships, as well as according rights to the states to abandoned ships. Both cases are likely to lead to negotiated agreements between the government concerned and the salvor in advance of the salvage. This provides the government concerned with the opportunity to insist on having a qualified archaeologist on board who assures that nothing is moved before the archaeology is done. A typical agreement, such as was eventually reached in *Deep Sea Research* after remand, provided that the state would receive a certain number of gold coins and all the non-monetary archaeological artifacts, while *Deep Sea Research* received a salvage award equal to a percentage of the fair market value of everything recovered. That left the archaeological artifacts available for display by the state.

Checkpoints

- Underwater artifacts are usually governed by the law of salvage. If the item has been abandoned, the law of finds gives ownership to the first person to reduce it to possession. If the item has not been abandoned, the owner retains title, but the admiralty court determines an award for the salvor.
- Salvor's award is determined considering the labor spent, the skill and energy in salving, the value of property used in the rescue effort and the degree of danger to which it was exposed, the risks incurred by the salvors, the value of the property saved, the degree of danger to which it was exposed, and the extent to which the salvors protected historical and archaeological value.
- Some courts have abandoned the law of salvage where the property is embedded in the bed of a watercourse that is owned.
- Abandonment requires non-user for a long period and intent to abandon. Intent to abandon by the federal government or a foreign state must be express.
- The Abandoned Shipwreck Act, which grants ownership of abandoned ships to the federal government and transfers ownership to the state on whose territorial waters the ship is found, has been largely unused because of the difficulty of finding intent to abandon.
- There is a conflict between exclusive admiralty jurisdiction in federal courts and the eleventh amendment, providing that states cannot be sued in federal court. States cannot be sued in state court unless they waive sovereign immunity.
- There is a UNESCO Convention providing protection of underwater cultural heritage, but it is unlikely to be influential because it has not been widely adopted and the U.S.A. is not a member.

Chapter 20

Native American Remains and Artifacts

Roadmap

After reading this chapter, you should understand:

- Native American remains, historically, have not been privileged by common law or statutes. Common law held that there was no property right in dead bodies but allowed next of kin a right to properly bury the body. States enacted laws that criminalized disinterring and grave robbing.
- Cemetery establishment: A cemetery may be established formally through a documented planning process or informally through dedication where a property owner permits burials on the property.
- Courts have found implied cemetery dedications and the establishment of private burial grounds. This enabled the court to order visitation rights for descendants and to prevent grave desecration. Courts have suggested these private burial grounds constitute either a trust or an easement.
- Cemetery disestablishment: If a family no longer visits a burial ground and the burial ground's condition is such that the general public cannot discern that it is a cemetery, the burial ground is abandoned. No case has conclusively ruled on who has standing to challenge the desecration of a grave.
- Unmarked graves: Generally, proper disposition of remains in an unmarked grave must be made before the land may be developed. Laws vary on whether this disposition allows a landowner to rebury the remains elsewhere or whether the remains must remain in the burial place.
- Lawful disinterment: Common reasons to disinter a body are for religious reasons, to rebury remains closer to where descendants live, to rebury remains in better maintained burial grounds, to establish the true identity of a body, to gather evidence or medical samples, or to solve historical mysteries. A court has found that a cemetery has standing to oppose exhumation of a body where the cemetery has an obligation to follow the wishes of those who buried the body and when there is no one else to oppose the exhumation.
- Native American burials: Native Americans often buried their dead with goods as part of religious practices in graves without permanent markers. Disturbing these graves raised the question of whether an objecting tribe could recover

and courts decisions varied. State laws did not apply to Native American burial sites because they were often neither marked nor enclosed.

- Courts have also found differently on the question of whether artifacts buried with Native American remains are abandoned or not. The Antiquities Act and Archaeological Resources Protection Act provide some protection of Native American burial sites from looters, but have exceptions that allow approved institutions to remove items for study and preservation.
- Native American Grave Protection and Repatriation Act (NAGPRA): In 1990 NAGPRA provided Native Americans ownership of human remains and burial goods discovered on federal or tribal lands after 1990.
- NAGPRA requires repatriation of human remains, associated funerary objects, unassociated funerary objects, sacred objects, and cultural patrimony from any federally funded museums and federal agencies and universities, whether or not the objects were discovered after 1990 or in any specific location.
- NAGPRA also prohibits trafficking human remains and cultural items.
- Native American defined: NAGPRA protects remains and artifacts of ancestors of a recognized tribe; items must have some cultural affiliation with an existing tribe to be Native American.
- An exception to the repatriation right exists for items that are indispensable to a scientific study that will be a major benefit to the United States. The items must still be repatriated to the tribe after the study is finished.
- Repatriation: Items that are found to be Native American and have a cultural affiliation will be repatriated. Lineal descendants receive human remains and associated funerary objects. If the items are independent, they will go to the tribe with the closest cultural affiliation or to the tribe on whose land they were discovered.
- Standing: NAGPRA provides the return of remains at the request of a lineal descendant or the tribe of the decedent, who has suffered injury in fact, not individuals outside these relationships. The deceased does not have standing.
- Trafficking: NAGPRA prohibits trafficking in Native American goods, including objects that have ongoing cultural importance to a tribe and goods that are considered to be communally owned.
- NAGPRA procedure: Federally funded museums must inventory their collections and provide information about whether items are Native American and with which tribe they are affiliated. If the affiliated tribe requests repatriation, the items should be returned to the tribe.
- If the Interior Department's Bureau of Land Management determines items are not Native American or not affiliated with a tribe, this conclusion should be publicized and open to responses from other tribes. These responses should be considered in further determining whether the items are Native American or tribe affiliated.
- The NAGPRA Review Committee may be asked to review the Bureau's decision; the Committee is advisory but its conclusions must be considered by the Bureau.

- Other federal laws: Many statutes give special treatment to Native Americans. Equal protection-based challenges to these statutes have failed because the statutes have been viewed as creating a political or cultural classification rather than a racial classification. This removes the statutes from strict scrutiny and instead requires only a rational government interest.
- State laws: Some states have enacted laws similar to NAGPRA that apply to items found on state land or in state-funded museums. Others have laws that address discovering remains while building public improvements. These laws often have narrowly defined acceptable interested parties and exceptions that allow removal of the remains.
- Courts have held that forcing remains to stay in a location or forcing their removal does not abridge the free exercise of religion for tribes because it does not interfere with their religious practices or force them to give up their beliefs.
- Tribal laws: Tribal ordinances may require permission from the village council in order to buy, trade, or remove tribal artifacts from a village. Tribal members are bound as a matter of tribal law, but whether persons outside the tribe are bound by the ordinances is a matter of federal law.
- Intellectual property: Copyright protection and patent law may be difficult to apply to Native American customs and practices because of difficulty in determining authorship of works arising from a tribe or a tribe's failure to obtain rights under patent law. Causes of actions for defamation, misappropriation, privacy, and trademark laws may be more successful when a Native American's name has been branded on products.

1. History

Until recently, the law created no special provisions for Native American artifacts, but did create special law for Native American remains. Neither situation favored the assertion of rights by Indian Tribes.

The starting point is Chief Justice John Marshall's holding that the doctrine of discovery gave the discovering nation "an exclusive right to extinguish Indian title of occupancy, either by purchase or by conquest." This meant that the land rights of Native American tribes would be governed by United States law. *Johnson v. M'Intosh*, 21 U.S. (Wheat.) 543 (1823).

A. Common Law and Statutory Law on Dead Bodies and Disinterment

In the 1760s, Blackstone opined that there was no property in a dead body. William Blackstone & St. George Tucker, Blackstone's Commentaries on the Laws of England (1803). Though there was no property right, the courts recognized a right in the next of kin to proper burial of the body, but refused to extend that right in *Smialek v. Begay*, 104 N.M. 375, 721 P.2d 1306 (1986) to persons who were siblings but not next of kin to sue for an unlawful autopsy.

The growing demand for bodies for medical dissection made the disinterment of fresh corpses a profitable enterprise, which *Rex v. Lynn*, 100 Eng. Rep. 394 (K.B. 1788) held to be a misdemeanor. In most states, statutory crimes, often felonies, were created for disinterring or grave robbing. *People v. Baumgartner*, 135 Cal. 72, 66 Pac. 974 (1901) held that simply opening the coffin without raising it from the grave in order to search for money buried with decedent was not the felony of disinterring the body. Escape from the harshness of a similar statute proscribing grave robbing was accomplished on the dual grounds that the bodies, which had lain in the ground for 125 years, had decayed to the point where they no longer qualified as bodies, but skeletons, and that defendant, a real estate developer, did not remove the remains with a nefarious purpose. She engaged an undertaker to remove the remains on land she was developing, and applied for, but never received, a required permit from the local government. *State v. Glass*, 27 Ohio App.2d 214, 273 N.E.2d 893 (1971). In *State v. Redd*, 954 P.2d 230 (Utah App. 1998), the court upheld the dismissal of a case against a Native American artifact collector accused of disinterring bodies on the grounds that there was no evidence that the bodies had ever been interred, a decision reversed on appeal at 199 Utah 108, 992 P.2d 986 (1999).

B. Common Law and Statutory Law on Cemeteries

The American cemetery as we know it today with its sweeping lawns and well-groomed bushes and trees is a product of the 19th century romantic movement reviving Roman custom.

Burial practices differed (and still do) in Europe, where they also differed according to place and time. In poor areas, the place of burial was normally the parish churchyard, where a ditch would be dug in October. The bodies of those who died before spring were dressed in shrouds and placed in the ditch, which was covered in spring. (Most people who died in those areas did so in winter.) The area of each ditch was marked, and after a length of time sufficient for the flesh to decay, the ditch was re-opened, the bones were removed to an ossuary, and the ditch was re-used.

The famous or the wealthy might be buried in marked graves in or under the church, or on property they owned. Alternatively, the family might lease a family plot in a cemetery. A deep grave might accommodate all the members of a single generation and, by the time the next generation was ready for burial, both the flesh and the caskets would have sufficiently decayed to allow room for the next generation to be buried on top of them. A large marker would indicate the family, while small plaques along the side or top of the sarcophagus might memorialize the individuals buried there. The family would retain the plot as long as the rent continued to be paid. When the rent was not paid, the bones were removed to an ossuary and the plot was available for lease to a new family.

i. Establishment

In the United States, a cemetery may be established formally or informally. Formal establishment through a planning process provides a documentary trail. It is also possible to establish a cemetery by dedication, where the landowner commits the land to cemetery use by permitting burials there. The crucial element is whether the land has been permanently devoted to cemetery use. Opinion 87-31 of the New Mexico Attorney General of July 15, 1987, declares that the battlefield of Glorietta is not a cemetery requiring court approval for disinterment. The bodies of the Confederate fallen were interred there, but the land is neither formally declared a cemetery nor dedicated to the permanent interment of human dead by the owner.

Positively, an implied dedication was found where the tract was used as a burial ground by the entire neighborhood with the consent of the owners for thirty years, and an injunction issued to permit relatives to visit and to restrain the owner from desecrating the burial ground. *Roundtree v. Hutchinson*, 57 Wash. 414, 107 Pac. 345 (1910). There is no mention of preserving rights to future burials. *Mingledorff v. Crum*, 388 S.2d 632 (Fla. App. 1980), becomes much more technical about requirements. It denies that a dedication can occur to anyone but the general public, and finds no dedication in the case because burials were limited to persons tied to the owner by blood, marriage, friendship or residence in the neighborhood. It does find that a private burial ground has been established, and suggests that this constitutes either a trust or an easement. Without choosing between those theories, the court decrees a right of visitation and maintenance as well as a right to be buried there in descendants of those already interred. Those rights were made subject to protecting the owner's rights of quiet enjoyment and to the relatives continuing to perform their maintenance duties. *Hines v. State*, 126 Tenn. 1, 149 S.W. 1058 (1911), confirms the same confusion between implied easement theory and trust theory, and enforces the same duties on the landowners, this time in the context of a criminal charge of desecration of a grave.

ii. Disestablishment

No case truly rules on who has standing to contest the desecration of a grave. It might be only the owner of a fee interest in the burial plot, but if so limited, most of the cases above would have been dismissed for lack of standing; it might be the heirs of the decedent; or it might be any descendant of the decedent. *Sanford v. Vinal*, 28 Mass. App. 476, 552 N.E.2d 579 (1990) raises these possibilities, but does not decide them because it proceeds to find that the family has abandoned the burial ground. Passage of time or the cessation of burials is not enough to establish an intent to abandon, but where family no longer visits and the condition so deteriorates that the general public cannot make out that it is a cemetery, there is abandonment. In this case, there were fragments of stones from the 1700s but scientific exploration was unable to discover any burials in the vicinity of the fragments.

C. Unmarked Burial Statutes

Within the past generation, almost half the states have passed legislation protecting unmarked graves. These laws seem to have in mind respectful treatment of those buried there. Some apply specifically to both public and private land, while others are not specific, but have been interpreted to do so. In general, these laws prohibit development of the land until appropriate disposition of the remains is made. Some statutes expressly grant the owner the right to disinter and rebury the remains; others seem to assume that the bodies must remain in place; most are ambiguous on this point.

D. Lawful Disinterment

One should not believe it impossible to open graves to disinter bodies. It is done frequently, normally by descendants requesting a court order authorizing the action. Mark Rothko's children had him removed from one cemetery and reburied in another, where they hoped to rebury their mother, his divorced wife. Having failed to reconcile their parents during life, they are attempting to do so post-mortem. The most common reasons to rebury the dead are religious, to place the burial near where descendants live, or because the cemetery of the original burial is not being maintained. For an interesting survey, see Michael Kammen, Digging Up the Dead (2010).

The most widely publicized reasons for disinterment are to determine the true identity of the person in the grave, to gather evidence for criminal prosecution, to obtain medical samples that might be useful in litigation, especially paternity cases, or to solve historical mysteries. Generally, the cemetery opposes disinterment, seeing its role as defending the deceased's right to repose. Occasionally, a petition to disinter a famous person for reburial elsewhere looks like a contest between two localities to locate a tourist attraction within their borders.

In *Kline v. Green Mount Cemetery*, 110 Md. App. 383, 677 A.2d 623 (1996), collateral descendants of John Wilkes Booth, a great-great-niece and a first cousin twice removed, sought his exhumation for tests to determine if the person buried was really Booth. Their theory was that Booth escaped to Texas, and someone else was buried there to cover up military incompetence. The cemetery opposed on grounds that the exact location of Booth's unmarked grave is unknown, other graves are likely to be disturbed in finding him, and even if found, a positive identification is unlikely, given an absence of dental records. Each of these contentions was found proven by the court. It was not clear whether any of them alone would justify refusing the exhumation, but it is clear that their conjunction was sufficient. The court held the cemetery had standing to challenge the disinterment, in part on grounds that the cemetery has a continuing obligation to fulfill the wishes of the people who buried the person, and in part because under the circumstances of this case, there was no one else to argue against disinterment.

E. Native American Burials

While particular custom varied from tribe to tribe, in general Native Americans buried their dead in plots without permanent markers; they often buried goods with the dead; and they often considered both the remains and the goods as part of their continuing religious practices.

When Native American graves were disturbed, a threshold question was often whether the tribe objecting was an appropriate person to recover. It was argued that the objecting tribe could not establish a genealogical connection between itself and the persons buried. In one case, it was held that the tribe was an appropriate descendant despite the fact that there had been significant intermarriage with other tribes. The court did not require plaintiff to prove that any existing member of the tribe was descended from anyone buried there, proof that might be possible (but expensive) today with the availability of DNA analysis. *Charrier v. Bell*, 496 S.2d 601 (La. App. 1986). In another case, the complaining tribe was held not to be appropriate, as the tribe whose members lay buried had been driven out of the area. *Wana the Bear v. Community Construction, Inc.*, 129 Cal. App. 3d 536, 180 Cal. Rptr. 423 (App. 1982). (To the contrary, it is settled law that a person who is prevented by force or threats from taking his property with him has not abandoned it. *Menzel v. List*, 267 N.Y.S.2d 804 (Sup. 1966).) *Wana* motivated its own statutory reversal by the enactment of an unmarked grave statute, which was construed in *People v. Van Horn*, 218 Cal.App.3d 1378, 267 Cal. Rptr. 804 (1990).

State laws preventing interference with burial sites or religious structures were not applied to Native American sites because they were usually neither marked nor enclosed, which was required for protection.

As to artifacts, the argument that they had been abandoned was sometimes successful on the grounds that burying anything on land you do not own is evidence of intent to abandon. Other courts held that interring them with the dead was a continuing use of the artifacts and not abandonment. In a dispute between the excavator and the tribe, neither party was interested in arguing that the property was embedded property, as it would then go to the landowner.

Enactment of the Antiquities Act and the Archaeological Resources Protection Act may have helped slow the destruction of Native American sites by looters, but those statutes permitted the federal government to authorize qualified institutions to gather objects for study and permanent preservation in museums. The tribes wished to leave the sites undisturbed.

2. NAGPRA

1990 saw the enactment of the Native American Grave Protection and Repatriation Act (NAGPRA), 25 U.S.C. §§ 3001–3013, in response to the perception that Native American graves were being robbed and desecrated in ways that violated both Native American and modern American cultural and religious beliefs. NAGPRA gives Native American tribes ownership of human remains and burial goods discovered on federal or tribal lands after 1990, reversing Blackstone's statement about property in dead bodies. It further provides for the repatriation of five kinds of items from federally-funded museums, federal agencies and universities, regardless of the date or place of discovery. Those five items are: (a) human remains; (b) associated funerary objects; (c) unassociated funerary objects; (d) sacred objects; and (e) cultural patrimony. NAGPRA also prohibits trafficking in human remains and cultural items. Native Americans lobbied heavily for anti-trafficking because they hoped it would remove financial incentives to pillage gravesites for re-salable items.

Jurisdiction over NAGPRA cases lies in the federal courts. In *Pueblo of San Ildefonso v. Ridlon*, 103 F.3d 936 (10th Cir. 1996), plaintiff, a federally recognized tribe, sued the discoverer of a piece of pottery, as well as the Bradbury Museum of the University of California, where the pottery had been kept since its discovery in 1978. The district court had dismissed the case as not within federal jurisdiction, but the court of appeals reversed due to the plain meaning of the statute placing subject matter jurisdiction in the federal courts. The court stated that there was no right in the tribe to obtain the item based on the place or time of discovery, as it was not discovered on federal land, nor was it discovered after the effective date of NAGPRA. It pointed out that those limitations do not apply to the repatriation-from-museums part of NAGPRA. Indeed, read literally, the artifact need not even be owned by the museum; it need only be in the museum's possession. 25 U.S.C. § 3005(a). Regulations clarify that the test is whether the possessor has sufficient legal interest to lawfully treat the objects as part of its collection. Loaned objects do not qualify. 43 C.F.R. § 10.2(a)(3). It is probably because of doubts that the museum met the test of possession that the tribe also named Ridlon, the finder of the pottery, as a defendant. Ridlon had recovered a money judgment for conversion against the museum, the payment of which should have assured the museum of a legal right to add the pottery to its collection. But that judgment was overturned to allow the Pueblo to assert its rights to the pottery, so it was unclear that the museum possessed the pottery.

The major issues confronted thus far involve what is covered, to whom it needs to be repatriated, who has standing, and the proper procedure under NAGPRA. Where private property is being taken, one must also confront constitutionality.

A. Native American

While it has been contended that "Native American" refers to any remains pre-dating European settlement, in its definition as "of, or relating to, a tribe, people, or culture that is indigenous to the United States," the court rejected a broad definition and placed special emphasis on the use of the word "is," a verb in the present tense. It said the purpose of the statute is to protect the remains and artifacts of the ancestors of existing tribes. A skeleton 9,000 years old that was physically dissimilar to any of the four tribes asserting rights was, in an age pre-dating DNA analysis, held not to be Native American. It should be noted that the plaintiff in the case was a group of scientists who wished to study the remains, thus setting up the classic conflict in NAGPRA cases between tribes seeking traditional burials for their ancestors and scientists seeking knowledge of the past. *Bonnichsen v. United States*, 367 F.3d 864 (9th Cir. 2004). The scientists should have been able to study the remains whether they were Native American or not, as there is an exception to the repatriation right for items "indispensable for completion of a specific scientific study, the outcome of which would be of major benefit to the United States." 25 U.S.C. § 3005(b).

It is possible that the scientists were uncertain that their study was specific enough, or whether they could prove that the outcome would be of major benefit, to meet the requirements of the exception. Alternatively, they may have been unwilling to comply with the further requirement that the remains be repatriated to a tribe within ninety days of the completion of the study for reburial, which would preclude further study.

The second problem lies in determining a "cultural affiliation" between the item and the tribe. While the statute allows a broad range of evidence—"geographical, kinship, biological, archaeological, anthropological, linguistic, folkloric, oral tradition, historical or other relevant information or expert opinion"—some affiliation must be shown. The claim of a tribe that never used wampum to wampum found in a museum near the tribe's current reservation may not be enough.

The sense of *Bonnichsen* is that the definitions of "Native American" and "cultural affiliation" are conflated; without some cultural affiliation to some recognized tribe, the item is not Native American.

NAGPRA adds two additional obligations to the requirement of a federal permit for excavation: consultation with an appropriate tribe or, if the excavation is on Indian land, approval of the tribe.

B. What is a Museum? What is Return?

NAGPRA defines a museum as "any institution or State or local government agency (including any institution of higher learning) that receives Federal funds and has possession of, or control over, Native American cultural items." In *Thorpe v. Borough of Thorpe*, 770 F.3d 255 (3d Cir. 2014), a grandson of the Native American Olympic medal winner Jim Thorpe sued to force the Borough in which he had been buried by his surviving wife to disinter his body and turn it over to the tribe to which he belonged, in accord with the NAGPRA provision requiring its "return". While the court talks at length about whether a cemetery operated by a government that receives federal funds is a museum, its decision ultimately rests on the general intent of the statute, which was to return the items to the tribe from which they were taken. In this case, the remains were never with the tribe, and were buried in the cemetery by the person who held the burial right, so the court held that NAGPRA did not apply.

C. Defining the Items Covered

Of the five items subject to repatriation, human remains is a term that probably needs no definition, and it has none.

Associated funerary objects are items reasonably believed to have been placed with the remains, or are exclusively made for burial purposes, and are in the possession of the same institution that possesses the human remains.

Unassociated funerary objects are the same objects as associated funerary objects but are not in the possession of the same institution that possesses the human remains. Unassociated funerary objects must be shown to be related to specific individuals or families, or to specific known human remains, or to have been removed from a specific burial site of an individual currently affiliated with a specific tribe. In other words, items without provenience will not be unassociated funerary objects.

Sacred objects are items needed by current Native American religious leaders to practice their traditional religions. The legislative history adds that this includes items necessary to revive discontinued religious practices of that tribe.

Cultural patrimony is an item with ongoing historical, traditional or cultural importance central to the group or culture. It must be an item that was considered by the tribe to be inalienable by any individual at the time it left the tribe's possession.

However, there are exceptions for scientific study, discussed above; for items the original acquisition of which was voluntarily consented to by a person duly authorized to convey them; where there is a conflict of rights to the item; and where repatriation might be unconstitutional, described below.

In *Pueblo of San Ildefonso v. Ridlon*, 103 F.3d 936 (10th Cir. 1996), the tribe, having won its point on federal jurisdiction, abandoned the field. One can only speculate about the reasons. It might have been a significant doubt that it could prove that the pottery was either a sacred object or cultural patrimony. To prove that it was a sacred object, the tribe would need to reveal to the court, perhaps with more precision than it would care to disclose, exactly how the pots were used in the tribe's religion. To prove that it was cultural patrimony, the tribe may have doubted that it could establish sufficient historical, traditional or cultural importance, or that it was ongoing, or that it was central to the group, or that it was inalienable under tribal law. Alternatively, it may have decided that it could not retrieve the pottery because it was owned by Ridlon, or that obtaining the pots would cost more in legal fees than they were worth. The museum returned the pots to Ridlon.

D. To Whom Will It Be Repatriated

Once it is determined that the item is Native American and there is a cultural affiliation, it must be determined to whom it will be given. Human remains and associated funerary objects go to the lineal descendants; if there are none or if the items are independent, they go to the tribe on whose land the discovery took place; or to the tribe with the closest cultural affiliation.

NAGPRA demands that federally funded universities and museums (which means all of them) spend resources in identifying its possessions of Native American source, catalogue them, notify appropriate tribes, and return possessions to those tribes.

E. Standing

Only a person who has suffered injury in fact has standing. Injury in fact requires that the person suing suffer the loss of a legally protected interest that is concrete and particularized, and that is actual or imminent, rather than conjectural. In *Idrogo v. United States Army*, 18 F.Supp.2d 25 (D.D.C. 1998), plaintiff individual and an organization dedicated to Geronimo sued for the repatriation of the body of Geronimo. NAGPRA specifically mentions that the remains should be returned at the request of a lineal descendant or the tribe of the decedent. Neither of the plaintiffs was a tribe, nor had either offered proof of lineal descent from Geronimo. Their *pro se* case was dismissed for lack of standing.

Likewise, the deceased himself does not have standing, despite the fact that in tribal belief, human remains are spiritual beings that have all the traits of a living person. NAGPRA fails to list human remains as "persons" or as an entity with a legally protected interest. It would not have common law standing because it has not suffered an injury in fact. *Na Iwi O Na Kupuna O Mokapu v. Dalton*, 894 F.Supp. 1397 (D. Hawaii 1995).

F. Trafficking

NAGPRA significantly expands the prohibition on trafficking in Native American goods in two ways. It includes objects that are not old, but which have ongoing cultural importance to a tribe. It also includes goods that are not considered owned by individuals, but communally owned. Criminally punishing trafficking in goods that are part of Native American "cultural patrimony" has been challenged as unconstitutionally vague because of various interpretations of the term held by different Native American experts. Those challenges were unsuccessful, in part because of the egregiousness of defendants' conduct in each case, and the fact that all defendants were professional artifacts dealers. *United States v. Corrow*, 119 F.3d 796 (10th Cir. 1997); *United States v. Tidwell*, 191 F.3d 976 (9th Cir. 1999). Whether a criminal conviction would be upheld if the seller were a novice collector who decided that his first Native

American artifact did not give him the pleasure he anticipated, and sold it to engage in philately has yet to be decided. The lack of written scholarship on whether a particular item was cultural property might also hamper the prosecution's case. Thus far, prosecutors have successfully relied on testimony from Native Americans about the importance of the items in the traditions of their tribes.

It has been suggested that spirituality or religion infuses every part of Native American life. This might make every object sacred, a result that might be surprising to persons outside that culture.

G. Procedure

The NAGPRA process begins by obligating covered museums to inventory their collections. This may require that the museum undertake studies to properly classify items, but it does not authorize new studies to obtain information not required for the inventory or decisions about whether the item is covered by NAGPRA or the tribe with which it is affiliated. *Na Iwi O Na Kupuna O Mokapu v. Dalton*, 894 F.Supp. 1397 (D. Hawaii 1995). The museum provides the information it has about whether each item is a Native American item and, if so, to which location or tribe it is affiliated. The tie between the item and a group can be established by evidence that is geographical, kinship, biological, archaeological, anthropological, linguistic, folklore, oral tradition, historical or other information or expert opinion. The museum is urged to consult with any tribe to whom the item may likely be repatriated. If the museum determines that the item is affiliated with a particular tribe and the tribe requests repatriation, the item should be repatriated. If the inventory submitted to the Interior Department's Bureau of Land Management concludes that the item is not Native American, or is not affiliated with a particular tribe, it is to be publicized, which provides an opportunity for responses from interested tribes. Once responses are received, the Bureau makes a decision about whether the item is Native American, to which tribe it is affiliated, and whether it should be repatriated. A person dissatisfied with the Bureau's decision may request consideration by the NAGPRA Review Committee. The Review Committee is appointed by the Secretary of the Interior from among persons nominated by Native American tribes. The opinion of the Review Committee is advisory, but the agency must explain why it is ruling as it is, discussing the evidence presented and the conclusions of the Review Committee. In *Fallon Paiute-Shoshone Tribe v. United States Bureau of Land Management*, 455 F.Supp.2d 1207 (D. Nev. 2006), the court held that the Bureau had failed to demonstrate that it had considered the evidence provided by the tribe and the conclusions of the Review Committee in reaching its decision that the remains were unaffiliated, and remanded the case to the Bureau.

H. Constitutionality

NAGPRA requires the transfer of bodies and some artifacts, and prohibits trafficking in artifacts. Other federal statutes prohibit trafficking in migratory birds. If a person owned the item before enactment of the statute, can the statute be applied to that person consistent with the constitution's takings clause? In *Andrus v. Allard*, 444 U.S. 51 (1979), the court held constitutional provisions of the Bald and Golden Eagle Protection Act (BGEPA), 16 U.S.C. §§ 668–668d, and the Migratory Bird Treaty Act (MBTA), 16 U.S.C. §§ 703–711, prohibiting trafficking in the items. It said that denial of one property right, the right to sell, was not unconstitutional as long as other property rights,. such as the right to possess and the right to transport, were retained. A reduction in value is not a taking. The court suggests that an alternate economic use might be to display the feathers for an admission charge.

I. Evaluation

The extent to which the law related to Native American remains and artifacts complies with the general goals of art law is mixed. There can be no doubt that the law, along with the establishment of the National Museum of the American Indian, has spurred museums to study their Native American artifacts and remains, though not as quickly as the law requires nor as much as the National Association of Tribal Historic Preservation Officers would like. Problems identified have been a lack of resources and failure of government agencies to appoint persons whose sole responsibility is enforcement of NAGPRA. Estimates are that less than half the items held in collections have been thoroughly examined. If these items are removed from dead storage in museums, that is a plus both for discovery of information and for public education. This is especially true if tribes are encouraged to establish museums celebrating their past. But if Native American items are buried or kept privately within a tribe so that they are not subject to scientific study, there will be neither an increase in knowledge about the tribe nor increased public awareness of significant artwork produced by these cultures.

3. Other Federal Laws Touching Native American Assets

There are also a number of statutes giving preferential treatment to Native Americans or tribes, whether it be to provide for use of feathers of eagles and migratory birds, set standards for what goods can be marketed as "Indian made," or to limit who can sell goods in certain Native American-related places. In each case of challenge on equal protection grounds as being race-based, the statute was upheld as creating a political or cultural, rather than a racial, classification, because it applied to persons not based on their race but based on being a federally recognized tribe or its members. That found, the courts need not subject the regulation to strict scrutiny; they need only find a rational government purpose for the rule. Legitimate governmental interests were found in protecting consumers from counterfeit goods, or in promoting entrepreneurship among Native Americans. *Livingston v. Ewing*, 455 F.Supp. 825 (D.N.M. 1978), aff'd 601 F.2d 1110 (10th Cir. 1979); *Native American Arts, Inc. v. Mangalick Enterprises, Inc.*, 633 F.Supp.2d 591 (N.D.Ill. 2009). While there are certainly less restrictive ways of protecting consumers from counterfeit goods, abandoning strict scrutiny meant that the regulator need not use the least restrictive method.

Embezzlement from Native American tribes and theft of tribal assets have been made federal crimes.

4. State and Tribal Laws

A few states have enacted laws comparable to NAGPRA applying to items found on state property and items in state-supported museums.

Other recently enacted state laws deal with the common problem of the discovery of Native American graves in the process of building public improvements, most frequently highways. In *State ex rel. Comm'r of Transp. v. Eagle*, 63 S.W.3d 734 (Tenn. App. 2001), the court confronted the discovery of Native American graves in the process of widening a highway. The state sought permission of the court to move the graves to a more appropriate place. The Tennessee Commissioner of Indian Affairs and fifteen Native Americans opposed relocation. In the course of holding that none of them was an interested person within the meaning of the statute, the court stated that it would look after the interests of all persons in the exercise of its equitable jurisdiction. It pointed out that the general rule was undisturbed repose, but there was a common law exception for situations where the burial place is no longer cared for. The court then found this codified in a statute permitting a court to close the burial ground if it is abandoned, neglected, and unsuitable for burial use, if arrangements are made for reburial and the removal and reburial are done with decency. The statute is clear that interested parties are persons with interest in the realty and the next of kin of the persons buried there, but none of the parties proved that they fell in either classification. The Commissioner of Indian Affairs and the Native American members of the Archaeological Advisory Commission are entitled to statutory notice of the discovery of Native American remains, but careful reading of the statute does not support the view that receipt of notice means that they are interested parties. There are several other purposes for the notice. Further, it would not have been an abuse of discretion to permit the Native Americans to participate in the litigation as *amici curiae*, as one of the most important situations in which *amici* can be useful is where only one side of a litigation is represented.

More generally, state laws may protect graves, which might include forbidding construction close to graves in order to protect the graves. In one such case, developers bought a farm and subdivided it. One lot had at its center an Indian burial mound located so that no construction could occur on the lot. The developers repurchased the lot from the buyer and sued, alleging that they had been subject to a regulatory taking. There is no right to compensation if the regulation substantially advances a legitimate state interest unless it is a physical taking, which this was not, or unless it denies the owner all economic use of the land. While it is questionable and was not the route taken by the court in *Penn Central* discussed above in the Historic Preservation chapter, the court discussed the case as though this were the only lot owned by plaintiff. The court held that the state did not deprive the landowners of a property right because they never had the property right to build on a lot with that proximity to graves. The statute protecting graves was in effect at the time that the landowners bought their land. *Hunziker v. Iowa*, 519 N.W.2d 367 (Iowa 1994). Alternatively, the court could have proceeded on the theory that the developers did not buy a fee simple, but a fee simple subject to an easement. Had it proceeded on the easement theory, it would have had to confront the question of abandonment of the easement, as discussed in *Sanford v. Vinal*, 28 Mass. App. 476, 552 N.E.2d 579 (1990).

One might also argue that either permitting removal or forcing bodies to remain in an unsuitable location might abridge the free exercise of religion of the tribe. *State ex rel. Comm'r of Transp. v. Eagle*, 63 S.W.3d 734 (Tenn. App. 2001), held that a statute permitting the closing of a burial ground and reburial of remains was a general regulation that did not have as its purpose suppressing religion, so it was not subject to strict scrutiny. It found that the law does not require Native Americans to abandon any beliefs, penalize them, or interfere with their practices, as there was no evidence that this location was inextricably connected to religious practice. The statute had the legitimate government purpose of balancing the interest in progress against the interest of repose of the dead. A similar balance was noted in *Snyder v. Holy Cross Hospital*, 30 Md. App. 317, 352 A.2d 334 (1976), where the court denied a request for an injunction to prevent an autopsy in violation of his religion on the plaintiff's son, who died suddenly and without apparent reason. The court distinguished another case where decedent had died in an auto accident and the medical examiner wished to autopsy the body to discover which trauma was the cause of death. It found that there was a compelling state interest in establishing the cause of death in the first case, but no interest in knowing which part of the auto accident had caused the death in the second.

Some tribes have enacted ordinances designed to protect tribal artifacts. One such ordinance prohibited persons from entering the village to buy, trade or arrange the removal of artifacts without the permission of the village council. There may also be an ordinance prohibiting the removal of artifacts without the approval of the village council. That those ordinances bind members of the tribe as a matter of tribal law is without question. The question is whether they bind persons outside the tribe as a matter of federal law. This is particularly important because where a case is properly brought in federal court on federal question jurisdiction, state law claims can also be litigated related to the same occurrence. In *Chilkat Indian Village v. Johnson*, 870 F.2d 1469 (9th Cir. 1989), the court held that an attempt to enforce the village ordinance against an outsider who induced members of the tribe to deliver four carved posts and a rain screen to him off tribal land was a matter of federal law that could be litigated in the federal courts, as could the pendant claims of conversion.

5. Aboriginal Practices and Intellectual Property

American (and most western) law fits poorly with native customs and practices. American law is mostly individualistic; native customs provide much scope for the communal and tribal. American law tends to focus on the written; tribal practices focus on personal communication.

Questions about these conflicts can be raised in a number of ways. One relates to the branding of products or athletic teams that refer to Native American tribes or individuals. Sometimes these matters can be fit into western legal categories. For example, in *Estate of Witko v. Hornell Brewing Co.*, 156 F.Supp.2d 1092 (D.S.Dak. 2001), the estate of Crazy Horse and his tribe sued a brewer for naming his beverage "The Original Crazy Horse Malt Liquor," despite Crazy Horse's lifelong opposition to the use of liquor. There were causes of action for defamation, misappropriation, privacy, violation of the Indian Arts and Crafts Act, and trademark laws.

Copyright protection becomes difficult because of the difficulty in determining the author when the work arises out of a shared community. One case where the artist recovered in copyright but the tribe did not is *Bulun Bulun v. R & T Textiles Pty Ltd*, 157 Australian L. Rep. 193 (Fed. Ct. 1998), containing a discussion of the artist's legal relationship to his community under community law.

Patent law is equally difficult. Some medicines may be designed based on aboriginal folk cures, but the tribes concerned obtain no rights under the patent law.

Checkpoints

- Historically, common law and statutory law addressed human remains. At common law there was no property in dead bodies but there was a right of proper burial for a body's next of kin. Statutory laws made grave robbing and disinterment felonies.
- A cemetery can be established through a formal process or informally through dedication. When a landowner allows burials on his property and the land is permanently committed to being a cemetery, a cemetery has been established. The law becomes more complicated when it comes to implied dedications and private burial grounds. Courts have ordered visitation rights and prohibited grave desecration by landowners in these instances.
- To show intent to abandon a cemetery, more than the passage of time and the ending of new burials are needed. Where a family ceases to visit the grounds and the public cannot make out the grounds as a burial site, the cemetery is abandoned.
- Laws that protect remains in unmarked graves generally require disposition of the remains before the land may be developed. The appropriate disposition of the remains varies with different state laws and many of these laws are ambiguous.
- A body may be disinterred with court permission. This is often requested by descendants. Reasons for disinterment include identifying the remains, gathering evidence or medical samples, or to solve mysteries. Religious reasons may motivate reburial of remains as well. Not every request to exhume a body will be granted, and courts have found that cemeteries may have standing to oppose such requests.
- Native Americans often buried their dead with goods in graves without permanent markers, creating litigation over whether an objecting tribe can recover for disturbed graves and whether goods in the graves are abandoned.

Courts have held differently, sometimes based on a tribe's ability to establish a genealogical connection between the tribe and the remains.

- NAGPRA provides that Native Americans own any human remains or burial goods discovered after 1990 on federal or tribal grounds. It also prohibits trafficking in human remains and cultural items. NAGPRA requires repatriation of items from federally funded museums and federal agencies and universities.
- The items to be repatriated are human remains, associated funerary objects, unassociated funerary objects, sacred objects, and cultural patrimony. These items need not be discovered within any time period or location and the federal establishments need only be in possession of the objects to require repatriation.
- Scientists often wish to study remains to discover information about the past while tribes wish to maintain the burials of their ancestors. An exception to repatriation exists when the items are indispensable to a scientific study whose results would be a major benefit to the United States.
- NAGPRA defines "Native American" narrowly, requiring the remains or artifacts to have a cultural affiliation with an existing tribe.
- Items that are declared Native American with a cultural affiliation will be repatriated to either lineal descendants, tribes with the closest cultural affiliation, or tribes whose land the items were discovered on, based on what type of item it is. NAGPRA requires federally funded universities and museums to identify its Native American possession and return them to tribes if possible.
- Lineal descendants or the tribe of decedents may request the return of remains under NAGPRA if they have suffered injury in fact. Plaintiffs falling outside these definitions may have their cases dismissed for lack of standing.
- Native American goods that are old or have ongoing cultural importance to a tribe and goods that are both individually and communally owned may not be trafficked under NAGPRA. Testimony from Native Americans is often relied on in determining the significance of items to different tribes.
- The NAGPRA procedure begins with museums inventorying their collections and providing information to the Interior Department's Bureau of Land Management to determine if items are Native American or affiliated with a tribe. If the affiliated tribe requests repatriation, items are to be returned. If the Bureau concludes items are not Native American or affiliated with a tribe, they must publicize this and be open to responses from other tribes. The Bureau is then to consider these responses and make another determination accompanied by an explanation for its ruling. The opinion of the advisory NAGPRA Review Committee may also be requested.
- Statutes that give preferential treatment to Native Americans have been successful against equal protection challenges because courts have considered the statutes as providing cultural or political classifications instead of prohibited racial classification. The statutes are therefore only subject to a rational governmental interest review and do not require the statute to use least restrictive means.
- NAGPRA applies in federal courts but some states have enacted laws similar to NAGPRA for items found on state property or items in state-funded museums.

These laws encounter similar issues of who may be an interested party to remains or artifacts discovered. Some state laws address remains discovered while constructing public accommodations, providing exceptions that permit the removal and reburial of remains. Property owners of land with Indian burial sites that prohibit land development may try to sue claiming their land was subject to regulatory taking. These arguments may fail if there is no physical taking or denial of all economic uses of the land.

- Courts have found that removing remains or requiring remains to stay in their burial site do not abridge the free exercise of religion for the Native American tribes because the tribes are not penalized or required to abandon their religious beliefs.
- Some tribes have enacted ordinances that prohibit buying, trading, arranging, and removing tribal artifacts without permission of the village council. Members of the tribe are bound by these ordinances as a matter of tribal law but whether persons outside the tribe may be bound by the ordinances is a matter of federal law.
- American law does not fit well with Native American custom, which focuses on oral communications and the collective tribe. Often copyright protection is difficult because of trouble determining an author of a work that comes from a shared community. Likewise, tribes may fail to obtain rights under patent law. Causes of action for defamation and similar actions that arise from branding of products based on Native Americans may be more successful.

Chapter 21

International Litigation For Art Lawyers

Roadmap

After reading this chapter, you should understand:

- Assertion of jurisdiction must conform to applicable law, and satisfy due process requiring that defendant have sufficient minimum contacts with the jurisdiction that litigating the case there would not offend fair play and substantial justice.
- Minimum contacts are usually satisfied if defendant performs significant business activities in the state on a continuous basis.
- Fair play and substantial justice are usually satisfied where the suit relates to the minimum contacts defendant has with the state. Factors considered might include the defendant's potential burden in defending in the forum, the convenience of the forum for taking evidence, the difficulties plaintiff would experience in finding an alternate forum, or the interest of the state in regulating the conduct.
- Where the case brought relates to defendant's continuing business in the state (specific jurisdiction), both minimum contacts and fair play and substantial justice are usually satisfied.
- Where the case brought does not relate to defendant's activities in the state (general jurisdiction), defendant must usually be domiciled in the state, incorporated in the state, or have his principal place of business there to satisfy fair play and substantial justice.
- *In rem* jurisdiction is always constitutional because the case relates to property located in the state.
- Defendant's consent gives the court jurisdiction over him, whether that consent is contained in a contract or derived from subsequent conduct.
- Without consenting to jurisdiction, defendant may appear to challenge the jurisdiction at the beginning of the suit.
- Immunity from seizure for loans of art work may be procured through the State Department. Immunity from state court seizure may be automatically provided by statute.
- Foreign sovereigns are immune from jurisdiction in the United States and their property is immune from seizure unless an exception applies.

- A foreign sovereign can be sued in the United States if it waives sovereign immunity, or if the suit relates to a commercial activity carried on in the United States, an act in the United States in connection with a commercial activity elsewhere, or an act in connection with a commercial activity elsewhere that has a significant effect in the United States.
- A foreign sovereign can be sued in the United States if rights in property taken in violation of international law are in issue, and the property, or property exchanged for it, is present in the United States in connection with a commercial activity carried on here by the foreign state, or the property, regardless of location, is owned or operated by an agency or instrumentality of a foreign state engaged in commercial activity in the United States.
- Under the Act of State doctrine, United States courts will not call into question the official acts of a currently recognized foreign state performed within its borders.
- *Forum non conveniens* results in the dismissal of some suits where there is an alternate forum that is more convenient for the litigation, especially if both plaintiff and defendant are nonresident aliens.
- Choice of law is constitutional as long as it has a significant relation to the parties or the transaction so that application of the law is neither arbitrary nor fundamentally unfair. In the absence of a choice-of-law clause, most courts select the law of their own jurisdiction.
- Choice of law in federal court for diversity cases is the law that the state court would have applied. For federal question cases, it is federal common law, which is usually the Second Restatement's significant contacts rule.
- Public policy of the forum may cause a court to disregard its normal choice of law rules, and courts generally do not enforce foreign criminal or tax laws.
- Proving foreign law is subject to special rules requiring notice, giving the court broad latitude about what to consult, and holding that the proof is a matter of law.

1. Introduction

While most of art law work is transactional, there is a substantial amount of litigation. Much of it is international in nature. This is not a book designed to help you master the law of Civil Procedure, so no attempt is made to provide a comprehensive discussion of international litigation law. This chapter discusses the litigation issues that arise frequently in international art law cases.

2. Jurisdiction

Much art law litigation involves claims over the ownership of artworks, especially artworks that changed hands in the period 1933–1945. Three typical claims occur frequently. In one, the artwork is outside the United States in private hands. In a second, the artwork is outside the United States in the possession of a museum owned either directly or indirectly by a foreign government. Third, the artwork is normally outside the United States, but is present in the United States temporarily on loan. In each of these situations, the case is likely to be lodged in federal court because a United States citizen or resident is suing a foreign citizen or foreign government. This creates diversity of citizenship jurisdiction in the federal courts if the value of the artwork exceeds the statutory amount of $75,000.

No lawsuit can begin unless the court has jurisdiction over defendant.

United States law used to recognize three forms of jurisdiction.

Personal jurisdiction was where the court had adjudicatory jurisdiction over a person for all purposes and in unlimited amounts. Personal jurisdiction can now be divided between general jurisdiction, in which defendant can be made to answer for any cause of action, and specific jurisdiction, in which defendant is only liable for causes of action arising out of the activities that form the basis for jurisdiction.

Quasi-in-rem jurisdiction, based on the attachment of property owned by defendant within the jurisdiction, gave the court limited personal jurisdiction over defendant. The court could render judgment against defendant for an amount that could be realized from the property, but for no more. It is doubtful that *quasi-in-rem* jurisdiction exists today.

With *in rem* jurisdiction, the court acquired adjudicatory jurisdiction over property attached within the state sufficient to decide its ownership. The court did not have jurisdiction over the owners of the property with respect to any claim unrelated to the property.

While the same constitutional rules apply today to each of these kinds of actions, their application is sufficiently different that it is still worthwhile talking about them separately. Those constitutional rules have become stricter over the years.

In each case, the first step in analysis is to construe the statute conferring jurisdiction to determine whether the defendant is intended to be included in the jurisdictional scope of the statute. The second step requires the court to determine whether the statute is constitutional as applied to this defendant under the circumstances of the case. The constitutional standard to be used is whether the defendant has sufficient "minimum contacts" with the forum state so that "fair play and substantial justice" would not be offended if defendant were forced to litigate this case there. *International Shoe Co. v. Washington*, 326 U.S. 310 (1945); *Shaffer v. Heitner*, 433 U.S. 186 (1977).

A. Personal Jurisdiction

Regardless of whether the case is brought in federal or state court, jurisdiction is determined according to the statute of the state in which the court sits unless there is a specific federal statute to the contrary, such as the Foreign Sovereign Immunities Act. Fed. R. Civ. Proc. 4(k)(1)(A), (D).

i. State Long Arm Statutes: General Description

State laws conferring jurisdiction over persons or entities not physically present within the state are called long arm statutes because the law's arm must reach outside the state. These laws do not usually differentiate between citizens of other states of the United States and citizens of foreign countries.

In some states, the law provides as broad a jurisdiction as is constitutionally permissible. In that case, step one, determining the reach of the statute, is eliminated. All that one need determine is whether the assertion of jurisdiction is within permissible constitutional limits in the case at bar.

Other states provide a list of situations where the court will assert adjudicatory jurisdiction. Typical on the list would be torts committed within the state, contracts to be performed within the state, doing business within the state, or real property located within the state whose ownership is the subject of the suit.

ii. State Long Arm Statutes: Constitutionality

A statute conferring jurisdiction is constitutional if it satisfies the due process clause of the Fourteenth Amendment, which requires that two tests must be met. Defendant must have minimum contacts with the state, and those contacts must be sufficient that fair play and substantial justice would not be offended if defendant were forced to litigate this case there.

a. Minimum Contacts

A defendant usually satisfies the minimum contacts test if defendant intentionally performs significant activity in the state, so as to invoke the protection of the state. Usually, the contact with the state is continuous, rather than a one-shot contact. Where a defendant did not sell its product in the state, but the product was sufficiently mobile that it was reasonable to anticipate that some customer at some time might take the product into the state, that was insufficient to constitute the required minimum contacts with the state. *World-Wide Volkswagen Corp. v. Woodson*, 444 U.S. 286 (1980). The Supreme Court has evenly divided on whether knowing that you are placing your goods in a stream of commerce that might possibly result in their arriving in the state is sufficient, or whether defendant needs to know that his goods will be in the state. *Asahi Metal Indus. Co., Ltd. v. Super. Ct. of Calif., Solano County*, 480 U.S. 102 (1987). An intermediate case would be where a business seeks to profit from a state's residents and acts in a way that it knows will do so. Thus, where defendant establishes an auto dealership in Arlington, Virginia, just across the river from the District of Columbia, and defendant knows that many D.C. residents buy cars there because the sales tax is lower in Virginia, I believe there would be sufficient minimum contacts with D.C. to support jurisdiction in D.C. over a suit arising from a defective vehicle sold at the Arlington dealership.

b. Offending Fair Play and Substantial Justice, Applied to Specific Jurisdiction

It is often difficult to know whether the court is talking about minimum contacts or about offending fair play and substantial justice. Fair play and substantial justice often seem more about other things than contacts with the state. Factors considered might include the defendant's potential burden in defending in the forum (which seems particularly acute where defendant is a nonresident alien or a foreign corporation not doing business in the United States, as in *Asahi*), the convenience of the forum for taking evidence, the difficulties plaintiff would experience in finding an alternate forum, or the interest of the state in regulating the conduct. The latter factor was also important in *Asahi*, which involved a foreign plaintiff and defendant.

A case is more likely to not offend fair play and substantial justice if it involves specific, rather than general, jurisdiction. Specific jurisdiction is where the case arises out of defendant's contacts with the state. In *Singer v. Walker*, 15 N.Y.2d 443, 209 N.E.2d 68, 261 N.Y.S.2d 8 (1965), jurisdiction was proper where plaintiff was injured by a product bought in the stream of commerce within the state.

A California purchaser of a print from a California domiciliary who later moved to Mexico can sue the seller for breach of warranty of genuineness in California. A business entity that regularly and continuously does business in a state is normally required to register with the state and sometimes appoint an agent for service of process there, and an entity registered to do business in a state can constitutionally be sued there about business done there. Likewise, an entity that is doing substantial business within the state, or whose business has substantial effects within the state, is within constitutional limits if the suit relates to that business.

A California art owner can sue an out-of-state auction house that has a permanent office in California to solicit business for breach of the agency relationship formed as a result of solicitation from the California office.

Alternatively, imagine a case where a resident of the state contacts a London auction house about selling his painting. The auction house has no office in the state and does not solicit business there. The parties contract for the sale of the painting at a London auction. If the contact between the owner and the auction house were the only contact the auction house had with the state, it is doubtful that the auction house has sufficient minimum contacts with the state, and even more doubtful that the court would hold jurisdiction over defendant to be fair play and substantial justice. But if the contract had been negotiated or signed in the state, or the art delivered in the state, or had auction house engaged in a pattern of solicitation in the state, it is likely that the court would hold that there are sufficient minimum contacts and that taking specific jurisdiction would not offend fair play and substantial justice. *Burger King Corp. v. Rudzewicz*, 471 U.S. 462 (1985); *Afram Export Corp. v. Metallurgiki Halyps, S.A.*, 772 F.2d 1358 (7th Cir. 1985).

c. Offending Fair Play and Substantial Justice, Applied to General Jurisdiction

General jurisdiction is much more limited. General jurisdiction exists, for an individual, where the individual is domiciled. For a corporation, general jurisdiction exists where the corporation is at home. A corporation is at home where it is incorporated, and where it has its principal place of business. It may be at home in another place, but it is not at home in every state in which it does a significant amount of business. The court has not given any examples of other places where defendant may be at home. One can speculate that it might be a state where defendant has an exceptionally large concentration of business, but that would be only speculation until the case arises. *Daimler AG v. Bauman*, 134 S. Ct. 746 (2014).

In *Shaffer v. Heitner*, 433 U.S. 186 (1977), a shareholder brought a derivative suit on behalf of his corporation, incorporated in Delaware but with its principal place of business in Arizona, against officers and directors, in Delaware, for violations of laws done outside Delaware. The directors had no contact with Delaware. The court held that they could not reasonably expect to be sued in Delaware and there was a suitable alternative forum, Arizona, available, so asserting general jurisdiction over the officers and directors in Delaware was unconstitutional.

Where defendant did not market its tires directly in the state, but had sporadic sales of tires in North Carolina, the court would not take general jurisdiction over a case alleging wrongful death in France from tires bought in Europe manufactured by defendant's subsidiaries. *Goodyear Dunlop Tires Operations, S.A. v. Brown*, 564 U.S. 915 (2011).

Assume that a state statute provides for all constitutionally possible jurisdiction. If a London-based auction house regularly and successfully solicits sales of art in the state, an art owner who entrusted his work to the auction house as a result of that direct solicitation would meet the state's grounds for minimum contacts through doing business on a continuing basis there. The fact that defendant is regularly doing business in the state of the same kind as involved in the case makes it unlikely that assertion of jurisdiction would offend notions of fair play and substantial justice. It would be a logical forum for plaintiff, who resides in the state. Defendant cannot claim surprise when it purposefully avails itself of the state in order to profit by doing business there when it is sued on a question arising in the course of that business. That would be specific jurisdiction.

However, another resident of the same state contacted at his vacation home in London whose dealings with the auction house were carried on entirely in London might confront a different result. Defendant would meet the constitutional minimum contacts standards because continually doing business in the state is a sufficient minimum contact. Whether it would offend notions of fair play and substantial justice is a closer question. On the one hand, the evidence in the case is likely to be located in London, rather than in the state. Defendant is not at home because it is incorporated and has its principal place of business in London. On the other hand, it would not seem burdensome for defendant to defend in the state because its solicitation in the state is likely to result in other suits based on similar facts that it must defend there. Again, it is a logical forum for plaintiff, a resident of the state, who may spend only a short time (vacation) in London. It is the sort of case that is formally general jurisdiction, but is as close to specific jurisdiction as is possible.

Thus, in the first case posed earlier, art in private hands (including private museums) outside the United States, there would be no personal jurisdiction over defendant unless defendant was a U.S. domiciliary, or was incorporated in the United States or had its principal place of business here.

d. Aggregating United States Contacts for Federal Question Cases

Occasionally, a foreign defendant is sued in the United States on a cause of action that invokes federal question jurisdiction but defendant does not have sufficient contacts with any individual state to constitutionally justify personal jurisdiction in any state. Nonetheless, if the suit involves a federal question, the defendant's contacts with all states in the United States may be aggregated to find sufficient contacts with the United States to justify jurisdiction. Fed. R. Civ. Proc. 4(k)(2). This is intended to insure that foreign defendants who have significant contacts with the United States can be sued somewhere in the United States, just as resident defendants may.

B. *Quasi-In-Rem* Jurisdiction

Quasi-in-rem jurisdiction allowed plaintiff to attach property in the jurisdiction in order to establish jurisdiction over defendant. If plaintiff claimed ownership of a $20 million Picasso kept in England and owned by defendant who also owned a $10 million yacht that docked in California, plaintiff could attach the yacht to gain *quasi-in-rem* jurisdiction to support his action to recover the Picasso. If successful, plaintiff's recovery was limited to the proceeds of the yacht.

The same requirements that we saw for personal jurisdiction apply to *quasi-in-rem* jurisdiction. State law must authorize jurisdiction over defendant, and plaintiff must comply with its requirements. Plaintiff must also meet the same constitutional requirements of defendant's contacts and reasonableness to defendant. *Shaffer v. Heitner*, 433 U.S. 186 (1977), indicates that simply finding defendant's personal property in the jurisdiction is no longer enough. The personal property must relate to the cause of action sufficiently that defendant should have known that suit was reasonable in the jurisdiction. *Quasi-in-rem* jurisdiction still might be possible where the property seized is real estate even though the lawsuit does not concern the realty because defendant substantially invokes the protection of the state in buying real estate there. It is much more likely that attaching defendant's property will not meet the constitutional standards of reasonableness where the property seized is unrelated to the cause of action.

In the paradigm cases where art located outside the United States is possessed by an individual or private museum outside the United States, other property belonging to that possessor cannot be attached to form a jurisdictional basis for determining ownership of the art.

C. *In Rem* Jurisdiction

In rem jurisdiction is jurisdiction over a specific piece of property. It is usually established by attaching the property within the state in order to determine something about the property, usually its ownership or the effect of a security interest in it. Since the litigation must relate to the property attached, there is usually no constitutional problem with *in rem* jurisdiction. The property's presence is the minimum contact with the state. Litigating in the state does not offend fair play and substantial justice because defendant sent the property into the state, so can reasonably contemplate trying a dispute over its title there. If plaintiff claimed foreign defendant's Matisse and defendant lent the painting to the San Diego Museum of Art without a grant of immunity, plaintiff could have the painting attached and proceed with his suit on the basis of *in rem* jurisdiction.

One can imagine a situation where an exercise of *in rem* jurisdiction would offend fair play and substantial justice. Where defendant lends his painting to the San Diego Museum of Art but the plane carrying the painting is forced down in Oklahoma by bad weather, it is likely that a court would find an assertion of *in rem* jurisdiction by the Oklahoma court to be outside the reasonable expectations of defendant, the evidence elsewhere, and the forum not particularly convenient for either party.

D. Consenting to Jurisdiction

A defendant may have consented to personal jurisdiction by including a choice-of-forum clause in a contract. Such clauses are valid, even against consumers, unless they are unreasonable. *Carnival Cruise Lines, Inc. v. Shute*, 499 U.S. 585 (1991). Unreasonableness would include that the chosen forum is in fact unavailable for this litigation, corrupt, or so seriously inconvenient that plaintiff will be deprived effectively of his day in court. Note that this is consent to specific jurisdiction, as the forum clause would only include matters related to the contract.

It was held that a state could prohibit a nonresident corporation from doing business within its borders. Many states took that opportunity to condition the ability of a nonresident corporation to do business within its borders on consenting to jurisdiction in the state and appointing someone as its agent for service of process. These implied consent statutes only applied to specific jurisdiction for suits related to the business the corporation was doing in the state.

A defendant's free consent to personal jurisdiction at any time obviates any constitutional concerns, even if defendant is consenting to general jurisdiction. It is unlikely that an implied consent to general jurisdiction would be found. Consent can only create personal jurisdiction; it cannot create subject matter jurisdiction.

E. Special Appearances

The United States uses the adversary system where the court relies on each party to persuade the court that it is correct. If a case is brought based on personal jurisdiction, defendant may wish to challenge the assertion that jurisdiction exists. To permit that challenge but to recognise that further activity may be an implied waiver of the objection to personal jurisdiction, some states have established the special appearance. A state may require a defendant who wishes to challenge the court's jurisdiction to enter a special appearance to challenge jurisdiction before answering the complaint on the merits.

Under the federal rules and state rules that have copied them, defendant may challenge the jurisdiction either in a pretrial motion to dismiss or, if defendant makes no pretrial motions, in the answer. Fed. R. Civ. Proc. 12.

In both situations, the failure to first challenge the jurisdiction operates as a waiver of that defense.

The challenge to the jurisdiction may fail in the trial court. In that case, if the state has a provision for interlocutory appeals, defendant must take an interlocutory appeal before defending on the merits, or is deemed to have waived the jurisdiction objection. Most states and the federal courts do not have interlocutory appeals. In that case, defendant's jurisdiction objection is preserved even though he disputes the merits, and it can be argued on appeal.

Alternatively, defendant can choose to not appear in the litigation. A default judgment will likely be entered. Defendant's sole remedy thereafter will be a collateral attack on jurisdiction, probably when plaintiff seeks to enforce the default judgment.

If defendant challenges jurisdiction in the initial action and loses, he cannot collaterally attack the court's jurisdiction in an enforcement action.

F. Immunity from Seizure

Some states have statutes authorizing immunity from seizure for artwork. State provisions vary considerably. New York's immunity provision, probably the most important because of the number of works loaned to museums there, provided automatic immunity without filing any paperwork from both civil and criminal attachment for works of art temporarily within the state for exhibition purposes at nonprofit organizations. New York Arts and Cultural Affairs Law § 12.03; *In the Matter of the Grand Jury Subpoena Duces Tecum Served on the Museum of Modern Art*, 719 N.E.2d 897 (N.Y. 1999). That law was amended in 2000 to apply to civil proceedings only.

Federal law is different. The Immunity from Seizure Act, 22 U.S.C. § 2459, provides that the President may determine that an object to be imported into the United States from abroad under an agreement between the owner and the United States or a cultural organization in the United States for temporary display without profit is an object of cultural significance and its display is in the national interest. That declaration made before import, the object is immune from judicial process by any federal or state court that would deprive the organization or the carrier of the object. The law does not distinguish between civil and criminal proceedings.

To receive such a declaration, an application must be made to the Secretary of State describing the item(s), a list of expected places and dates of exhibition, a statement that the exhibition is without profit to the exhibiting organization(s) (including an estimate of the admission charges, costs of the catalogue or other items offered for sale in connection with the display, and an explanation of why those revenues are not anticipated to exceed the costs of the endeavor), a statement that the United States organization(s) has researched the provenance of the item and presenting the results of that research showing that the item is not subject to a dispute over its ownership, or if it is subject to a dispute, the nature of the competing claims, and a scholarship report supporting the proposition that the item is of cultural significance. The application must be accompanied by supporting documents, such as all agreements between any of the parties involved in the loan or the exhibition and the Internal Revenue Code § 501(c)(3) determination letters of the exhibiting organizations. In short, substantial expense is involved in applying for federal immunity.

There is no reason to believe that the procedure for federal immunity was intended to pre-empt state laws on the same subject with respect to purely state law consequences. One could argue that the foreign relations power of the United States is placed in the President's hands, so any attempt by a state to deal with imports or exports would be unconstitutional, but such a ruling is far beyond the state of the law.

Where the artwork is owned by a foreign government, it will be protected from seizure under the same circumstances that the foreign sovereign is immune from jurisdiction in the United States.

3. Foreign Sovereign Immunity

Many foreign governments have vast collections of artwork held either directly by the government or by one of its instrumentalities. A United States person claiming to own one of those artworks may claim it in the foreign country, but may prefer to sue in the United States.

The common law was absolute: a foreign government could not be sued in the United States because it had sovereign immunity. Then the habit grew of permitting the State Department to opine on whether the particular foreign government was a foreign sovereign and whether the facts of the case were appropriate for a grant of sovereign immunity. The courts treated those State Department suggestions as conclusive. In the 1952 "Tate letter," the State Department announced that it would only suggest sovereign immunity for the governmental acts of a foreign sovereign, but not for its commercial acts.

A. General Rule: Foreign Sovereigns Are Immune from Some Suits in the United States

The Foreign Sovereign Immunities Act of 1976 (FSIA), 28 U.S.C. §§ 1330, 1332, 1391(f), 1441(d), 1602-1611, removed State Department suggestions from the process. It placed courts squarely in charge of determining whether the foreign entity was entitled to immunity. It established the general rule that foreign sovereigns are immune from suit in the United States. It also carved out a number of exceptions where the foreign sovereign can be sued in the United States. One might well think that the exceptions are so numerous and so broad as to have become the general rule.

There is no definition of the term "state" in FSIA. Foreign sovereign immunity is not limited to states recognized by the United States, though states that are not recognized cannot sue, as East Germany discovered in *Kunstsammlungen zu Weimar v. Elicofon*, 678 F.2d 1150 (2d Cir. 1982). However, the views of the State Department are likely to be important to a court trying to determine whether a defendant is a state or not. The entity presumably must control territory and a population, and have at least some of the powers that are attached to most states, such as taxation, police power, eminent domain, and the ability to engage in relations with other states.

FSIA does define an "agency or instrumentality" of a state. It is an entity with separate legal personality from the state and either constitutes an organ of the state or one of its subdivisions, or is majority-owned by the state or one of its subdivisions. 28 U.S.C. § 1603(a)(3).

There are both substantive and procedural differences between suing a state and suing its agency or instrumentality, discussed below.

FSIA not only confers personal jurisdiction. It also establishes a new subject matter of federal jurisdiction. So FSIA suits are not suits based on diversity of citizenship (although that may exist). One consequence is that an alien can bring a suit against a foreign government if the suit qualifies for one of the exceptions. A second consequence is that the federal court is not bound by either the choice of law rules or the substantive law of the state in which it sits, as it would be in a suit based on diversity of citizenship.

B. Exception for Waiver

A foreign state can always waive its sovereign immunity. Like a private citizen, it can submit itself to the jurisdiction of the court. While this could happen after the suit is brought by express statement or by pleading to the merits, it is often expressed in a contract or a bond indenture. Waiver can also be implied where the foreign state has included a choice of forum agreement selecting a United States court as the forum for dispute resolution. It is less clear that a choice of U.S. law is an implied waiver, but some courts have so held because U.S. courts are more likely to properly apply U.S. law than non-U.S. courts. *Eckert Int'l v. Fiji*, 32 F.3d 77 (4th Cir. 1985). Many plaintiffs have argued that when a foreign state enters into a treaty with the United States that requires certain conduct, this constitutes a waiver of sovereign immunity for private suits for failure to abide by the treaty. Courts have uniformly declined to find this a waiver of sovereign immunity. *Foremost-McKesson, Inc., v. Islamic Rep. of Iran*, 905 F.2d 438 (D.C.Cir. 1990). So the many international agreements that the United States has concluded about the return of art stolen in the Holocaust will not confer on our courts jurisdiction over a foreign sovereign.

Waiver of sovereign immunity from jurisdiction does not imply waiver of sovereign immunity from execution.

C. Exception for Commercial Activity

An important exception to sovereign immunity for art lawyers is the commercial activity exception. The foreign state is not immune if it is a suit arising out of a commercial activity carried on in the United States, an act in the United States in connection with a commercial activity elsewhere, or an act in connection with a commercial activity elsewhere that has a significant effect in the United States. 28 U.S.C. § 1605(a)(2).

Whether an activity is commercial or not does not depend on the reason for the activity; it depends on the nature of the activity. Any activity that could be engaged in by a private person is a commercial, rather than a governmental, activity. Where a government issued bonds to stabilize its currency, clearly a governmental purpose, this was a commercial activity because any private corporation could have issued bonds. *Rep. of Argentina v. Weltover, Inc.*, 504 U.S. 607 (1992). This means that the definition of a commercial activity is very broad.

But there are limits. In *Aschenbrenner v. Conseil Regional de Haute-Normandie*, 851 F.Supp. 580 (S.D.N.Y. 1994), an artist lent glass sculpture to a show in Rouen sponsored by a French local government agency. The sculpture was broken when returned, either through inadequate packing or handling. The court weighed the commercial aspects of the arrangement, the fact that the defendant promised to facilitate the sale of the sculpture, against the non-commercial aspects, the fact that admission to the show was trivial, that defendant would not profit if the work was sold, and the fact that there was no negotiation about sales, to conclude that this activity was more educational than commercial. At the same time, plaintiff gave defendant photographs of his work to be published in a book that appeared two years after the show closed. The court found that the book was a commercial venture, but because it was not a catalogue for the show or otherwise tied to the show (such as if the sculpture had been shipped to France to be photographed for the book), the cause of action for damage to the sculpture did not arise in connection with the commercial activity.

The jurisdiction over the foreign state provided by the commercial activity is specific, not general. FSIA is specific in stating that the claim sued upon must arise from the commercial activity with the United States contact. Thus, in most contexts, this exception from foreign sovereign immunity will not be useful for persons seeking recovery of artwork because the suit to determine title to the work did not arise from the commercial activity. However, in several cases, courts have held that publishing a book in the United States with the painting that is the subject of the suit on the cover constitutes a commercial activity in the United States. *Altmann v. Rep. of Austria*, 317 F.3d 954 (9th Cir. 2002); *Cassirer v. Kingdom of Spain*, 616 F.3d 1019 (9th Cir. 2010). There is no holding that the property in either case meets the commercial activities exception, as each case was tried under the takings exception.

D. Exception for Takings in Violation of International Law

The most important exception for art lawyers is the takings exception.

This exception is a bit complicated. The first requirement for this exception is that rights in property taken in violation of international law are in issue.

The statute does not specify that the property needs to be taken by the foreign government being sued, though that will most frequently be the case. However, one can also imagine art taken by one state in violation of international law, and sold on the open market to a private citizen who later donated it to a museum operated by a government. That was close to the actual facts in *Cassirer v. Kingdom of Spain*, 616 F.3d 1019 (9th Cir. 2010), where a Pissarro confiscated by Germany in 1939 was sold several times and finally purchased by Baron Thyssen-Bornemisza in the 1970s. The Spanish government bought the Baron's collection in 1993. The court held that this action met the takings exception even though the country that took the property was not the defendant in the lawsuit.

When property is taken by a government, the taking usually does not violate international law unless it discriminates against aliens. Taking the property of your own citizens does not qualify. *Chuidian v. Philippine Nat. Bank*, 912 F.2d 1095 (9th Cir. 1990). Also, taking the property of aliens does not qualify if similarly situated citizens are similarly expropriated. The German government's seizure of degenerate art was a seizure from all persons in Germany, including museums operated by the German government and its states. If there is discrimination against aliens, the taking is a violation of international law if it either does not serve a public purpose or if it is not accompanied by prompt just compensation to the owner. Given the broad interpretation attached to the concept of public use in United States as synonymous with public benefit, it is unlikely that a taking would fail to meet this test. The taking would fail to meet the just compensation test if there were no compensation, if the compensation were ludicrously below the property's fair market value, or if the payment of the compensation were unreasonably delayed.

However, there is one situation where a country's actions with its own citizens violates international law—genocide. *Philipp v. Federal Republic of Germany*, 894 F.3d 406 (D.C.Cir. 2018) held that the taking of art disguised as a 1935 sale for 35% of its value was genocide because designed to deprive their owners of the ability to earn a living and therefore maintain themselves because of their religion.

A taking in violation of international law is not enough to invoke this exception. One of two additional commercial activity tests must be met. Either the property, or property exchanged for it, must be present in the United States in connection with a commercial activity carried on here by the foreign state, or the property, regardless of location, must be owned or operated by an agency or instrumentality of a foreign state engaged in commercial activity in the United States. 28 U.S.C. § 1605(a)(3).

In *Altmann v. Rep. of Austria*, 317 F.3d 954 (9th Cir. 2002), plaintiff's uncle Ferdinand Bloch-Bauer, a Czech citizen, owned six paintings by Gustave Klimt. When Ferdinand fled Austria, a Nazi lawyer appropriately named Fuhrer took possession of the paintings, some of which he sold, others of which he exchanged for other work and one of which he retained in his collection. All resided at the time of suit in the collection of the Austrian Gallery. In discussing whether the takings exception was met, the court pointed out that the property, which was taken for the private benefit of Dr. Fuhrer, would not be a public benefit, and no compensation was received. Ferdinand was an alien in Austria. The court without discussion conflated the actions of Fuhrer, the Nazi party and the Austrian government into a governmental taking. It was admitted that the Austrian Gallery was an agency or instrumentality of the Austrian government. The main issue was whether the Gallery was engaged in a commercial activity in the United States. A commercial activity is defined as either a regular course of commercial conduct, or a particular commercial transaction. The operation of the Gallery was a commercial activity, but that commercial activity was not carried on in the United States. The Gallery did prepare two books in English that were published and sold in the United States, one by Yale University Press, that included the works in question, one being a monograph on Klimt's women and the other being a guide to the Gallery. The Gallery advertised its shows in the United States. The court held that this constituted commercial activity in the United States, and this holding was reaffirmed on similar facts in *Cassirer v. Kingdom of Spain*, 616 F.3d 1019 (9th Cir. 2010).

It is not enough to find a statutory exception permitting the exercise of jurisdiction over a foreign sovereign. That exercise is subject to the same constitutional standards discussed above of sufficient contacts and reasonableness. The *Altmann* court stressed that the promotion of the books and the Gallery in the United States constituted sufficient contacts, and the fact that the paintings in question in the suit were among the works promoted in the books made it reasonable for the Gallery to be forced to defend its title in the United States.

The court also noted that it was not deciding and need not at that stage of the litigation decide whether the foreign government had actually violated international law. The allegations of plaintiff are taken as true (subject to the requirement that they be proved at the later trial). All the court need determine is that the claim is not frivolous.

E. Exception for Actions Related to Rights to Property in the United States Acquired by Gift or Succession, or Rights in United States Immovable Property

Another exception grants jurisdiction over a foreign sovereign to adjudicate rights in property located in the United States that the foreign sovereign acquires by gift or succession. Presumably, succession includes disposition by will, as a foreign government is unlikely to be an heir under an intestacy statute, and also unlikely to acquire property in the United States by escheat. This provision would apply both to tangible property such as paintings, and to intangible property such as the United States copyright in paintings.

The exception also grants jurisdiction to resolve rights in United States immovable property. Immovable property would include a museum building, or a statue that had been affixed to the museum in such a way as to become a fixture and thus part of the realty.

F. Other Aspects of FSIA

There are other exceptions to sovereign immunity contained in FSIA, but none likely to arise in the context of controversies about art.

FSIA is not only a law conferring and denying jurisdiction and the power to attach. It has important provisions that can affect the outcome of the case.

If there is federal court jurisdiction, it is not exclusive jurisdiction, so a foreign sovereign not entitled to immunity can be sued in a state court. However, FSIA allows the foreign sovereign to remove the case to a federal court. 28 U.S.C. § 1441(d). Perhaps the most important of those provisions bars jury trials, 28 U.S.C. § 1441(d), and punitive damages against foreign governments (but not their instrumentalities). 28 U.S.C. § 1606.

What FSIA does not do is create any new cause of action. Plaintiff must seek elsewhere in the law to justify liability.

Though the Tate letter was not issued until the 1950s and FSIA was not enacted until 1976, the provisions of FSIA apply to all actions brought after its enactment, regardless of when the underlying events occurred leading to the action. This means that FSIA is applicable to all cases arising out of World War II takings currently brought. *Rep. of Austria v. Altmann*, 541 U.S. 677 (2004). However, the court noted that the State Department is not prevented from filing papers noting that continuation of any particular suit would be detrimental to the foreign relations of the United States.

The fact that a foreign sovereign may be subject to suit in the United States does not mean that its property located in the United States may be attached. Pre-judgment attachment is permissible only when the foreign state has explicitly consented to it. Pre-judgment attachment cannot be used as a means of securing jurisdiction. 28 U.S.C. § 1609, 1610(d).

Post-judgment, the property of a foreign sovereign can be attached to satisfy the judgment where the foreign sovereign has explicitly or implicitly consented; where, if jurisdiction was based on the commercial activity exception, the property was used in the commercial activity; where, if jurisdiction was based on the takings exception, the property to be attached is the property taken or property exchanged for it; where, if jurisdiction was based on adjudicated rights in property in the United States, the property to be attached is the property subject to the adjudication, but not property used for diplomatic purposes; and where the property is an insurance policy payable to the foreign government to indemnify it for the matter in litigation. 28 U.S.C. § 1610(a). Greater scope is allowed for post-judgment attachment of the property of an agency or instrumentality of the foreign government. 28 U.S.C. § 1610(b).

4. Act of State

A United States court will not call into question the validity of public acts done by a foreign government on its own territory that do not violate treaties. This means that if a plaintiff challenges the confiscation of artwork by the government in its territory in a suit against the current possessor, a private individual, the court will not entertain an argument that the confiscation was invalid, either under the law of the foreign state or under international law. *Stroganoff-Scherbatoff v. Weldon*, 420 F.Supp. 18 (S.D.N.Y. 1976) involved the confiscation of a van Dyck and a Houdon by the U.S.S.R. in Russia. The paintings were then sold at auction in Berlin. The court refused to permit the suit to proceed under the Act of State doctrine.

The origin of this doctrine was probably comity, but it is now based more on the fact that the constitution entrusts the foreign relations power to the federal executive, so the courts, both federal and state, should abstain from pronouncing on the validity of such acts for fear of embarrassing the president's conduct of foreign relations. But other countries that do not have the same separation of powers as the United States also have similar doctrines.

In *Menzel v. List*, 267 N.Y.S.2d 804 (Sup. Ct. NY County 1966), plaintiffs owned a Chagall in Brussels. When they fled to avoid the advancing German army, they left it in their Brussels apartment, where it was confiscated by the *Einsatzstab der Dienststellen des Reichsleiters Rosenberg*, who conveniently left a receipt for it. After the war, defendant List purchased it in good faith from a New York gallery that had bought it from a Paris gallery. Plaintiffs challenged the validity of the confiscation, and defendant invoked the Act of State doctrine.

The court thought that there were four requirements that List needed to meet to succeed with his Act of State argument. He needed to prove that the act was by a foreign government. The court thought the taking was by Rosenberg representing the Nazi party, not a government. Generally, courts have required that the act be a formal act by the government, not an act of an official that was not formally authorized. One court suggested that it must be a statute, decree, order or resolution of the state. *Alfred Dunhill of London, Inc. v. Republic of Cuba*, 425 U.S. 682 (1976). The *Menzel* court did not look at the interrelationship of the Nazi party and the German government.

What is an "Act of State"? It cannot be a classification decision by a minor official, especially if it is an error, as in giving the painting to Rieger instead of Bondi in *United States v. Portrait of Wally, A Painting by Egon Schiele*, 2002 U.S.Dist.LEXIS 6445 (S.D.N.Y.). One court suggested that it must be a statute, decree, order or resolution of the state. *Alfred Dunhill of London, Inc. v. Republic of Cuba*, 425 U.S. 682 (1976). *Von Saher v. Norton Simon Museum of Art*, 897 F.3d 1141 (9th Cir. 2018) adds judicial and administrative decisions, as well as the settlement of lawsuits, to the list of acts that can be Acts of State, and declares that advisory opinions are not because they are recommendations, not decisions.

List needed to establish that the taking occurred within the territory of the foreign government. This taking occurred in Belgium. Though the German army at the time occupied Belgium, this did not extinguish the Belgian government, which the United States continued to recognize in exile. Again, the court read the requirements as *de jure* rather than *de facto*.

List also needed to prove that the foreign government was a government in existence and recognized by the United States at the time of the suit. The court reasoned that if the government no longer existed or was not recognized, judicial decisions about its acts would not embarrass non-existent foreign relations with it. The court decided that the Third Reich no longer existed, thereby raising important questions about state succession that it did not need to answer because of its negative conclusions about the other requirements. *Konowaloff v. Metropolitan Museum of Art*, 702 F.3d 140 (2d Cir. 2012), took a different tack when it was argued that the U.S.S.R., which had confiscated the art, no longer existed. It pointed out that the successor government, the Russian Federation, did not disavow the confiscatory acts, and rejected plaintiff's challenge to the confiscations on Act of State grounds.

Finally, the court stated that the actions of confiscating the artwork violated several of Germany's treaty obligations. Some were treaty obligations that made the war illegal; more specifically, there were prohibitions on both pillage and confiscation of private property. The court did not discuss whether the more general obligations were sufficient to meet this requirement.

Arguments have been advanced for a number of exceptions to the Act of State doctrine, but none have been largely adopted. It has been argued that Act of State should not apply to an act of state in a commercial operation, to a situation where the State Department certifies that an adverse decision would not disrupt the foreign relations (the Bernstein exception), and the counterclaim exception. Whether these are exceptions, factors to be considered, or nonstarters, is not yet clear.

There is an apparent conflict between the Act of State doctrine, and the granting of jurisdiction over a foreign government under the takings exception. There is no actual conflict. The Act of State doctrine will not apply where the act of the foreign government violates its treaty obligations. Also, while the two rules may overlap if the suit is against a foreign government, Act of State also applies to suits between private parties.

5. *Forum Non Conveniens*

Even though the court has jurisdiction, it may decline to hear a case on *forum non conveniens* grounds. In cases where the more convenient forum is another United States court, dismissal on *forum non conveniens* grounds is likely to mean litigation with the same procedural rules and often the same substantive rules. Where the alternate forum is outside the United States, both procedural and substantive law can be radically different.

Plaintiffs, especially tort plaintiffs, love to litigate in the United States because the risks are lower and the potential rewards are higher. The United States has low filing fees, allows lawyers to work under contingent fee contracts, permits extensive discovery, allows jury trials, habitually returns higher verdicts for successful plaintiffs, permits punitive damages, and does not usually require fee shifting to the loser. (The latter rule is not advantageous to plaintiff if he wins.) In addition, if defendant has substantial assets in the United States on which the judgment can be executed, litigating here avoids the necessity of persuading a court to recognize and enforce a foreign judgment.

In order to succeed with a *forum non conveniens* motion, defendant must show that there is an alternate forum available, that the alternative forum is adequate, and that the weight of convenience strongly favors the alternate forum.

As the decision on this motion is discretionary with the trial judge, it can only be overturned if the trial judge has abused his discretion.

The availability of an alternate forum is normally determined on a theoretical, rather than a practical, basis. An alternate forum is not available if the statute of limitations on the cause of action has run, or if the alternate forum lacks jurisdiction over defendant. If these objections may be overcome by defendant's consent, the court may condition its *forum non conveniens* dismissal order on defendant giving that consent. If the objections cannot be waived, there is no alternate forum.

The alternate forum must be adequate. A forum is not adequate if it is corrupt, if its procedures are unfair or if it regularly delays decisions for too long a time. *Bhatnagar v. Surrendra Overseas Ltd.*, 52 F.3d 1230 (3d Cir. 1995) (potential 25 year delay). A forum is not adequate if the potential remedy there is inadequate. The fact that the remedy is not the same does not make the remedy inadequate. To be inadequate, the remedy must be similar to denying plaintiff his day in court; it must be no remedy at all. Neither changes in procedure, discovery nor substantive law necessarily make the remedy inadequate. Nor does a habit of rendering smaller judgments in similar cases.

If he finds an alternate adequate forum, the judge must weigh the conveniences and inconveniences of litigating in the other forum. Those factors include both public factors and private factors. The public factors frequently mentioned are burden on congested courts and jurors, difficulty of establishing foreign law, the advantage of having localized disputes settled at home, and the strength of the interests of the different jurisdictions in having their own courts decide the dispute. Private factors include ease of producing witnesses and documents (including translation costs), convenience for appearance of the parties, availability of process to compel the testimony of witnesses, availability of discovery, contingent fees, a jury trial, and non-compensatory damages. A most significant factor seems to be the nationality or residence of the plaintiff. There are few cases in which the plaintiff was a U.S. national or permanent resident where the court has dismissed for *forum non conveniens.* The feeling seems to be that United States taxpayers are entitled to the services of our courts in resolving their disputes.

A good illustration of the law is *Altmann v. Rep. of Austria*, 317 F.3d 954 (9th Cir. 2002). The court stated that the fact that the filing fee to sue in Austria was $350,000 did not disqualify Austria as an alternate adequate forum; nor did the statute of limitations, as it appears that one of Altmann's causes of action was not subject to the statute of limitations, the statute might not have expired because of fraudulent concealment, and Austrian law empowered the government to provide relief despite the statute of limitations. On the balancing of conveniences, most witnesses and all documents were located in Austria and the documents were in German, and Austrian law would apply. The court was persuaded that, because Altmann was a U.S. citizen who had resided here for more than sixty years, was elderly and would have difficulty and additional expense if she litigated in Austria, the district court did not abuse its discretion in denying the *forum non conveniens* motion.

Where *forum non conveniens* is granted, it is common to condition the dismissal on defendant's consent to service of process and jurisdiction of the foreign court, as well as waiver of technical defenses like the statute of limitations. These conditions have been accepted, but conditions such as submitting to discovery abroad under the Federal Rules of Civil Procedure, or an agreement to satisfy any money judgment of the foreign court, have been struck down, the first because it mandated how a foreign court would conduct its business, the second because it deprived defendant of rights to contest the validity of the judgment and whether it should be enforced in the United States. *In re Union Carbide Corp. Gas Plant Disaster at Bhopal, India*, 809 F.2d 195 (2d Cir. 1987).

6. Choice of Law

A. In General

Choice of law can be determinative of many art law cases. The laws of most United States jurisdictions are relatively similar, though as we saw in the chapter on Title, the rules on when a cause of action accrues can be quite different. Art travels easily over international borders. The laws of countries differ from each other more than the variations between states or provinces within the same country.

i. Constitutional Restraints

The constitutional limits on courts and legislators choosing the law of the forum or another jurisdiction have not been burdensome. The due process clause requires, unless the parties have otherwise agreed, that the law chosen have some relationship to the transaction or parties at issue. In a series of cases, the Supreme Court has stated that the choice of law must have a significant relation to the parties or the transaction so that the application of the law is neither arbitrary nor fundamentally unfair. But it has not insisted that the relation be very significant. *Allstate Ins. Co. v. Hague*, 449 U.S. 302 (1981); *Phillips Petroleum Co. v. Shutts*, 472 U.S. 797 (1985); *Home Ins. Co. v. Dick*, 281 U.S. 397 (1930). The requirements for assuming jurisdiction described above are much stricter than those for making a choice of law. The Uniform Commercial Code requires that the state whose law is chosen have an appropriate relation to the situation litigated. UCC § 1-301(b).

ii. Choice of Law by Case or by Issue

A single choice of law may be made for all issues in a case, or the court may choose the law of different jurisdictions as applicable to different issues. In *Itar-Tass Russian News Agency v. Russian Kurier*, 153 F.3d 82 (2d Cir 1998), United States law was applied to determine whether plaintiff's copyright was violated. Russian law was applied to determine who the original owner of the Russian copyright was and what legal significance transfers of the copyright within Russia had.

iii. Parties Choose the Applicable Law

If the litigation involves a planned transaction, the parties may have chosen a law to apply to disputes. There are few litigated art law cases where this has happened. One of the purposes of a choice of law clause is to eliminate litigation about what jurisdiction's law should apply.

Where there is a choice of law clause, the first duty of the court is to interpret the clause to give effect to its meaning.

A commonly litigated question of meaning is whether the choice of law is meant to select only the substantive law of the jurisdiction, sometimes known as internal law, or whether it is intended to include the choice of law rules of the jurisdiction, the whole law. The presumption is that the clause is intended to refer to the internal law because few persons would choose a state's law if they knew that the law of that state would refer them to the law of another state. They would have chosen the law of the referred-to state directly.

Another commonly litigated question of meaning is whether a choice of law clause is intended to apply to all issues, or only certain issues. A clause that says the contract is "governed" by California law may result in California law being used to interpret the contract. If the question is whether the contract is valid, California law might not apply to that question if the court does not believe that the parties intended the choice of law to extend to anything but interpretation and remedies.

iv. Federal or State Choice of Law Rules

Choice of law rules are regarded as procedural rules, so the rules of the forum where the litigation is held determine what choice of law rules are applied. Most art law cases are litigated in federal courts. The federal courts apply two different sets of choice of law rules.

If the case is in federal court because of federal question jurisdiction, the court applies federal common law choice of law rules.

If the case is in federal court because of diversity jurisdiction, the court applies the choice of law rule that it believes the state in which the court sits would have applied, whether the choice is between the law of different states, or the law of a state and a foreign country. *Klaxon Co. v. Stentor Elec. Mfg. Co., Inc.*, 313 U.S. 487 (1941); *Day & Zimmerman, Inc. v. Challoner*, 423 U.S. 3 (1975).

A situation still unresolved is where the case is in federal court because of the Foreign Sovereign Immunities Act. FSIA establishes both personal and subject matter jurisdiction, but it creates no new cause of action. Whether there is a cause of action depends on other rules of law. Accordingly, one circuit does not believe this to be true federal question jurisdiction, but a closer analogy to diversity jurisdiction, so it applies the conflicts rule that the comparable state court would apply. *Barkanic v. General Admin. of Civil Aviation of PRC*, 923 F.2d 957 (2d Cir. 1991). By contrast, in *Liu v. Republic of China*, 892 F.2d 1419 (9th Cir. 1989), the court used federal common law to determine its choice of law.

B. Federal Choice of Law

i. A Typical Forfeiture-on-Import Case

Consider a typical forfeiture-on-import case: X, a U.S. national and French resident, imports a statue into the United States. Customs intercepts the statue at the port of New York and sues to forfeit the statue under the National Stolen Property Act, 18 U.S.C. § 2315. Customs contends that the statue was stolen from an Egyptian museum (EM). X purchased the statue from an art dealer (AD) in France, and has held it in France for fifty years.

The question to be resolved is whether the statue is stolen. X will win if customs fails to prove either that the statue was stolen from EM, or that the purchase by AD did not give AD good title as a good faith purchaser, or that the purchase by X did not give X good title as a good faith purchaser, or that X's holding the statue for fifty years did not give X good title by prescription.

Each of these four questions require resolution of questions of law and questions of fact. What jurisdiction's law applies to each question? Why does it matter?

ii. Why Choice of Law May Be Determinative

Substantive law on ownership differs from jurisdiction to jurisdiction. It is common in the developing world for laws to provide that artifacts discovered after a fixed date, and artifacts not registered with the government by that date, belong to the state. In some countries of the developed world, artifacts found after a certain date belong to the state, but the finder and the owner of the property on which the artifacts are found are entitled to an award that may be as much as the fair market value of the artifact. In still other jurisdictions, the artifact may belong to a non-trespassing finder, or to the owner of the property on which it is found.

In most legal systems, transfer of rights to property must occur by abandonment, gift, bequest, intestacy, escheat, lease, bailment or sale. But the details about what makes each of these forms of transfer valid vary from jurisdiction to jurisdiction.

Whether a good faith purchaser acquires title confronts a sharp split. In the United States, a good faith purchaser never acquires title to stolen property. In some countries where the legal system follows Roman law, which is most of continental Europe, a good faith purchaser may acquire title to stolen property. What is required to be a good faith purchaser may differ, as may the exact conditions of acquisition.

The law on acquisition of title by expiration of the statute of limitations likewise differs. In most United States jurisdictions, it depends on when the cause of action accrues, and there are a variety of rules on that question. The law here tends to be owner-centered. In most European countries, there are absolute statutes of limitation that depend on the person's possession for a specified number of years. That number of years is often smaller if the person acquired the property in good faith.

iii. Federal Choice of Law Resolution

The choice of law questions in the forfeiture-on-import case would be resolved under federal common law because an action under the National

Stolen Property Act is federal question jurisdiction. In *United States v. Schultz*, 333 F.3d 393 (2d Cir. 2003), the parties argued the case as though it were agreed that Egyptian law applied to the question of whether the art was stolen. Schultz argued that the statues he imported were unowned property under Egyptian law when the builder from whom he acquired them in Egypt discovered them. Written Egyptian law provided that any artifact discovered after 1983 became the property of the state. The court applied the Egyptian law, after an inquiry in which it determined that the Egyptian law not only existed in law books, but also was applied in Egypt. The court declared the statues stolen even though they had never been in the possession of the Egyptian government or any of its officials. There was no suggestion that the law of any United States jurisdiction should be applied to determine ownership of the statues. Ownership of the property and whether the property was stolen was determined under the law of the jurisdiction where the property was located at the time of the alleged theft. That was the traditional common law choice of law, the law of the situs.

It is less clear how federal common law would resolve the bona fide purchaser and statute of limitations questions because we have no cases in point. The traditional common law choice of law rule is that a transfer's validity is measured by the law in force at the time and place that the transfer occurred. *Green v. Van Buskirk*, 72 U.S. (5 Wall.) 307 (1866), 74 U.S. (7 Wall.) 139 (1868). Likewise, the traditional choice of law (unchanged by the Second Restatement) rule for determining whether a party had ownership by adverse possession is the law of the place where the property was located during the period the adverse possession is claimed. RESTATEMENT SECOND CONFLICT OF LAWS § 246 (1971).

C. *Lex Loci* Criticized

The traditional choice of law rule was *lex loci.* Under this rule, one determined the territory in which the crucial event occurred, and all the legal questions in the case were decided using the law of that jurisdiction. The sole determinant was territoriality.

Specific rules were set forth for torts, criminal law, contracts, property, corporations and succession cases.

In the 1960s, the rigidities of lex loci were subject to serious criticism for their inflexibility, mostly in tort cases, and especially for their failure to account for situations where the place seemed to have little relevance to the dispute, such as when two New Yorkers were involved in an auto accident in Ontario Canada. While it was appropriate to use Ontario law to determine whether either driver had violated the rules of the road, it seemed inappropriate to determine their liability to one another entirely by Ontario law when it sharply conflicted with New York law in similar situations.

The result was that many jurisdictions sought more flexibility, either by adopting the most significant contacts rule, a governmental interest methodology, or injecting more flexibility into a fixed rule.

D. The Second Restatement: Most Significant Contacts

More states have adopted some version of the most significant contacts rule of the Second Restatement than any other rule. In deciding which state's law to apply to a particular issue in a contracts dispute, courts look for the state with the most significant relationship to the transaction and the parties. Courts may consider the place of negotiation, the place where the contract was finalized, the place of performance, or the place where the subject matter of the contract is located in determining the place of most significant contact to the transaction, and the nationality, residence, domicile, place of incorporation, or principal place of business of the parties for the most significant contacts to the parties. Some of these contacts may be purely fortuitous or easily manipulable, such as place of negotiation or place of signing; others may be harder to change and of more substance, such as the place of performance or the place where the subject of the contract is located. The contacts are not simply counted; they are weighed to determine their significance to the issue to which the law is to be applied. Some contacts may be purely fortuitous or easily manipulable, such as the place of negotiation, the place of signing, or the residence of a plaintiff who has recently moved. Others may be harder to change and of more substance, like the place of performance or the residence of either party at the time of contracting. The state with the most significant contacts may differ depending on the issue. If the question is whether a contract exists, the parties and the places of negotiation and finalizing may be most significant; if the question is whether the contract has been breached, the place of performance assumes more importance.

E. Interest Analysis

Another modern method of choice of law is interest analysis, of which there are several varieties. They all share a desire to reduce the number of choice of law questions by eliminating those cases where only one state has an interest in applying its own law. A state has an interest in applying its own law when, considering the facts of the case and the substance and policy of its law, the application of the state's law would significantly improve the situation of someone whom the state has an interest in protecting, or the state's other interests. It is not only plaintiff and defendant that the state has an interest in defending. A state has an interest in regulating conduct within its borders, and in assuring the security of transactions that take place in it. In a typical stolen art case, the state where the art is allegedly stolen has an interest in determining what constitutes theft; any state in which that art is subsequently sold has an interest in determining the effect of the sales transaction on title to the art. The state where the art has been during a claimed period of acquisition by prescription or adverse possession has an interest in determining whether title has thusly been acquired. In addition to other states, the forum has an interest in determining whether plaintiff is barred from suing by the statute of limitations or laches.

If each state has an interest in applying its own law, the court must decide which state has the stronger interest, given the facts of the case.

In a well-reasoned opinion involving whether Spanish or California law applied to the question of whether defendant had acquired the property by acquisitive prescription, Judge Walter first said that both Spain and California were interested in applying their law because the possession occurred in Spain, Spain had an interest in certainty of title, in protecting defendants from stale claims, and in encouraging plaintiffs not to sleep on their rights, especially since defendant was Spanish, and Spanish law would protect defendant. California also had an interest in applying its law because of the difficulties faced by owners in discovering artwork, even when held openly. California law encourages purchasers to determine the true owner of property before buying, and protects the "rightful owner" over subsequent possessors. As plaintiff was a California resident, he was within the group intended to be protected by California law.

On the matter of which law had the stronger interest, Judge Walter said that California recognized that a prime interest in regulating conduct lay in the place where the conduct occurred, which was Spain. Though California had an interest in applying its law, that interest only arose long after the painting was lost by plaintiff's ancestor, and resulted from a fortuitous choice to move to California. It was held that Spanish law applied. Cassirer v. Thyssen-Bornemisza Museum, 153 F.Supp.3d 1148, 1154 (C.D.Calif. 2015) *rev'd & remanded on other grounds* 862 F.3d 951 (9th Cir. 2017).

F. Fixed Rule with Flexibility

Some jurisdictions have opted for a fixed rule with flexibility in exceptional cases. A good example is the European rule for contracts choice of law in Regulation 593/2008 of the European Parliament and the Council of 17 June 2008 on the law applicable to contractual obligations, J.O. L 177/6 4 July 2008. Article 3 permits the parties to choose their law. Article 4 says that in the absence of choice, the law used will be the law of the seller's, provider's, or the person providing the characteristic performance of the contract's principal place of business. But then it states, "3. Where it is clear from all the circumstances of the case that the contract is manifestly more closely connected with a country other than that indicated in paragraphs 1 or 2, the law of that other country shall apply." Article 6 then states that the law applicable to contracts between professionals and consumers is the law of the place where the consumer has his habitual residence if the professional pursues his business in that country. The European rule provides fixed rules with an escape clause in articles 4(3) and 6.

G. Application of Forum Law

Most frequently, courts have chosen to apply forum law to art law cases, and to all contested issues in the case. Sometimes the application of forum law is appropriate; in other cases, it is not.

Sometimes forum law is appropriately applied by default. Take *Autocephalous Greek-Orthodox Church of Cyprus v. Goldberg & Feldman Fine Arts, Inc.*, 717 F. Supp. 1374 (S D IN 1989), *aff'd* 917 F.2d 278 (7th Cir. 1990), where suit was brought to recover a mosaic admittedly stolen in Turkish Cyprus, kept in Germany, and sold to defendant Indiana resident in a transaction negotiated while the parties were temporarily in the Netherlands and delivered in a dutyfree warehouse at a Swiss airport. The question was whether defendant was a good faith purchaser and, if so, whether that gave her ownership rights superior to plaintiff original owner. No one argued that Cyprus law should apply. That is appropriate because the sale transaction had no contact with Cyprus. No one argued for German law, although the subject of the contract was in Germany at the time of the conclusion of the contract. No one argued for Dutch law, as the negotiation in Holland was purely fortuitous and dependent on defendant being temporarily there on a buying trip. Defendant argued for the application of Swiss law, but the location of delivery seemed to have little relationship to the transaction except as a place that would not impose significant charges on the transaction or restrict its re-export. In fact, the fiction of the dutyfree warehouse is that the item has not entered Switzerland, even though the warehouse is located physically on Swiss soil. Given that state of affairs, the only rational state left whose law might be applied was Indiana, the residence of both defendant and of the lender whose security interest would be wiped out if plaintiff's suit succeeded. The case nicely illustrates that forum law may be applied either when no party advocates the application of another jurisdiction's law, or when the other jurisdiction seems to have less significant contact than the forum does.

A second case where forum law might properly be applied is where the forum uses interest analysis. Under interest analysis, where no state can be found to have an interest in having its law applied to the issue in the controversy, forum law can appropriately be applied. That might also have justified application of Indiana law in *Autocephalous*, as the law of Cyprus might not have protected the original owner, and the law of Indiana certainly protected neither the purchaser nor the bank. In the case where two or more states have an interest in applying their law, some versions of interest analysis would choose the law of the forum.

One situation where forum law should not be applied is where the only connection with the forum is the presence there of the artwork in controversy. The forum does have an interest in regulating ownership and commerce within its borders. It certainly has an interest in assuring that items stolen within its borders are restored to their rightful owner, if that is what forum law provides. But the forum's interest in using its own law to determine whether property was stolen when it arrived at the forum seems negligible compared to the interests of the states where the property was allegedly stolen, was sold to a good faith purchaser, or was kept for a long period of time.

For instance, one of the issues in *Kunstsammlungen zu Weimar v. Elicofon*, 678 F.2d 1150 (2d Cir. 1982), was whether defendant New York resident, when he purchased two stolen drawings by Albrecht Dürer in New York from an American soldier selling them door-to-door, was a good faith purchaser. The court appropriately applied New York law to determine whether he was a good faith purchaser and what legal consequences might follow from that.

A recent case illustrates facts where forum law should not be applied. A palimpsest on which writings by Archimedes were softened to permit them to be overwritten with a Greek liturgical text disappeared from plaintiff's library either in Jerusalem or Istanbul after 1908. It came into the hands of a French civil servant in the 1920s, and was kept in Paris until being sent to New York in the 1990s to be auctioned. The Frenchman died in the 1950s. No evidence of how he acquired the palimpsest was available. The question of whether the Frenchman and his heirs had acquired title by prescription during the seventy years that the palimpsest was in France was properly decided under French law, rather than New York law. *Greek Orthodox Patriarchate v. Christie's, Inc.*, 1999 U.S. Dist. LEXIS 13257 (S.D.N.Y. 1999)

A print stolen in Austria, then sold by a Belgian resident to a Swiss art gallery, resold to a New York gallery, then resold to a New York collector, presents different problems. New York law might well be applied to the question of whether the collector was a good faith purchaser and the legal significance of the New York transfer. It is inappropriate to apply New York law, as the court did, to determine whether the work was stolen in Vienna, or whether either of the two sales in

Switzerland were to good faith purchasers, and what the legal significance of those sales might be. *Bakalar v. Vavra*, 619 F.3d 136 (2d Cir. 2010). The Second Circuit was obligated to apply New York choice-of-law rules, but the only stolen art cases it could cite for those rules did not litigate choice-of-law questions.

H. Fundamental and Public Policy Limits

There are two important exceptions to any choice of law analysis.

If the parties choose a law that violates the fundamental policy in the forum and forum law would apply in the absence of such a choice, the parties' choice will be ignored and forum law applied. I am guessing that where a jurisdiction has legislation providing that when a resident artist consigns his work to a dealer a trust relationship is created, that relationship cannot be defeated by a choice of law clause that selects the law of a state that does not provide for a trust relationship. In Europe, such a situation is called mandatory law.

Even in the absence of a choice of law clause, a court may override its normal choice of law rules if it finds that a provision of the foreign law that would normally be chosen violates the public policy of the forum.

7. Enforcing Foreign Penal, Tax and Public Law

In the absence of treaty authorization, one country generally does not enforce the tax or criminal laws of another country. That enforcement can come in two ways. A choice of law rule can call on the courts of a state to apply the law in a case before it, or a judgment rendered in the country that adopted the law can be brought to the United States in hopes of its being recognized and enforced. The usually stated reason for either type of non-enforcement is separation of powers. The foreign relations power is granted to the President, and the courts do not wish to interfere with it either by upholding or refusing to uphold the foreign law. Another infrequently stated reason is that national tax and criminal laws represent such a delicate balance of substantive law, procedural law and actual practice such as plea bargaining and settlements that an attempt by a foreign court to replicate the actual enforcement conditions in the enacting country would be fruitless.

It is also often stated that the public law of one country will not be enforced in the courts of another country, but that statement must be qualified by the infrequency of attempts and a diversity of results. In *United States v. Schultz*, 333 F.3d 393 (2d Cir. 2003), the court without discussing the question of whether it could enforce the public law of another state, applied Egyptian law providing that artifacts discovered after 1938 became the property of the state in order to convict defendant of importing stolen property. One might regard the Egyptian law as public law, just as law authorizing the taking of property by eminent domain would be public law. Alternately, one could see this law as private law, doing no more than regulating the ownership of property between persons, one of whom happens to be the state.

English law provides an interesting contrast. In *Attorney-General of New Zealand v. Ortiz*, [1982] 3 All E. R. 432 (C. A. Civil), New Zealand law provided that the export or attempted export of historically significant property would result in the property being forfeited to the state. The court found this to be a public law, as only sovereigns could regulate imports and exports, thereby drawing a distinction between governmental acts that might be engaged in by private parties and those normally only within the power of governments. The court commented that British courts will not enforce such laws, and suggested that the appropriate remedy for the future would be conclusion of a treaty.

A quarter century later, Iran sued an antiquities dealer in Britain to recover artifacts it claimed to own under Iranian law that provided that discovered antiquities would be the property of the state, subject to payment of a finders fee, a law similar to the one in effect in Britain. The court held that this was not a public law, but private law governing property ownership. *Government of the Islamic Rep. of Iran v. Barakat Galleries*, [2007] EWCA Civ 1374, [2008] 1 All E.R. 1177, [2009] Q.B. 22 (Ct. App. Civ. Div.).

8. Proving Foreign Law

At common law, a party who wished foreign law to be applied had the burden to prove the substance of that law as though it were a fact.

The federal rules now provide three points about foreign law in Fed. R. Civ. Proc. 44.1. First, a party who intends to raise foreign law must give reasonable notice. Second, the court may consider any relevant material, including testimony, to determine the substance of foreign law. That material need not be submitted by a party, nor need it be admissible under the Federal Rules of Evidence. Third, the court's determination is treated as a ruling on a question of law.

Each of the three rules raises legal questions, thus far unsettled because the volume of litigation is not great.

How specific must the notice be that a party plans to raise foreign law? The purpose of giving notice must be to permit opposing counsel and the court to plan their own interpretation of foreign law. So presumably the notice must be sufficiently detailed to permit an examination of the general area of the foreign law to be applied, but not necessarily specific cases or legislation.

What is the sanction for failing to give notice, or failing to give adequate notice? That may vary, presumably being more severe the later in the case the party wishes to raise foreign law for the first time. The court might refuse to consider foreign law; it might refuse to consider the offer of proof by the party who failed to give notice, but appoint its own expert to advise it on foreign law; or it might apply forum law.

Fed. R. Civ. Proc. 44.1 gives the court great leeway in considering the evidence to be received on the question of the content of foreign law. Normally, foreign law is proven by the testimony of experts on that law. Like other expert testimony, it will be discounted by the fact that the expert might be paid by one party or another, and enhanced by the expert's experience with the foreign law. In *United States v. Schultz*, 333 F.3d 393 (2d Cir. 2003), defendant's expert was accorded less credibility than plaintiff's on Egyptian law because he did not practice in Egypt and his first contact with the provision was when he was asked to be an expert witness. This despite the fact that plaintiff's witnesses were employed by the Egyptian government, which would be the ultimate beneficiary if the statue were forfeited.

Should the court confine itself to foreign law in the books, or should it also demand evidence that the law is usually applied? In all countries, there may be a gap between law in the books and what actually happens on the ground. In *Schultz*, the court heard evidence both about Egyptian law and its enforcement.

The rule seems to grant the federal court absolute discretion about the evidence it will entertain to determine foreign law. In *Bodum U.S.A., Inc. v. La Cafetière, Inc.*, 621 F.3d 624 (7th Cir. 2010), the court refused to entertain any evidence of French law other than that which was in English and readily available in United States libraries. While at first blush this seems consistent with the wide discretion given courts by the rule, that wide discretion was intended to expand, not to contract, the scope of evidence that the court could consider in determining what foreign law provides. Works written in a language other than the native language of the law in question and published in a foreign country are often highly general treatments by persons from outside that country designed to provide a bit of information about the law for readers who are unlikely to practice in the country. Judge Diane Wood's concurrence, suggesting that it would be prudential to admit a wider range of evidence, is more persuasive.

A court's inquiry into the meaning of foreign law is not definitively foreclosed even by an affidavit from the foreign government unit responsible for administering that law, because rule 44.1 was intended to permit the judge to consider all evidence before making a decision. *Animal Sci. Prods. v. Hebei Welcome Pharm. Co.*, 138 S. Ct. 1865 (2018).

There is an apparent contradiction between the fact that one proves foreign law and the statement that the court's determination shall be treated as a conclusion of law. The purpose of this provision seems to be twofold. It is intended that the initial decision about foreign law not be made by the jury, which would determine questions of fact. It is also intended that the trial court's decision about foreign law be reviewable by the appeals court in the same manner as decisions on points of United States law, rather than on a basis that gave priority to the trier of fact on grounds that the trier of fact had heard the witnesses.

It does, however, leave one with the question of whether the court, if it examines a provision relating to foreign law from a source not presented to it by the parties, must give notice to the parties and an opportunity to argue about the true meaning of the source. While this may be a good idea to assure accurate decision-making, there is no indication of this requirement in the rule or its history. Treating foreign law as though it were a determination of law, which would not require notice to the parties or opportunity to explain, argues against a notice requirement.

Similar rules have been enacted in many states.

For further guidance, see Peter Hay, Patrick J. Borchers, Symeon C. Symeonides & Christopher Whytock, Conflict of Laws (6th ed. 2018).

Checkpoints

- Assertion of jurisdiction must conform to applicable law, and satisfy due process requiring that defendant have sufficient minimum contacts with the jurisdiction that litigating the case there would not offend fair play and substantial justice.
- Minimum contacts are usually satisfied if defendant performs significant business activities in the state on a continuous basis.
- Fair play and substantial justice are usually satisfied where the suit relates to the minimum contacts defendant has with the state. Factors considered might include the defendant's potential burden in defending in the forum, the convenience of the forum for taking evidence, the difficulties plaintiff would experience in finding an alternate forum, or the interest of the state in regulating the conduct.
- Where the case brought relates to defendant's continuing business in the state (specific jurisdiction), both minimum contacts and fair play and substantial justice are usually satisfied.
- Where the case brought does not relate to defendant's activities in the state (general jurisdiction), defendant must usually be domiciled in the state, incorporated in the state, or have his principal place of business there to satisfy fair play and substantial justice.

- *In rem* jurisdiction is always constitutional because the case relates to property located in the state.
- Defendant's consent gives the court jurisdiction over him, whether that consent is contained in a contract or derived from subsequent conduct.
- Without consenting to jurisdiction defendant may appear to challenge the jurisdiction at the beginning of the suit.
- Immunity from seizure for loans of art work may be procured through the State Department. Immunity from state court seizure may be automatically provided by statute.
- Foreign sovereigns are immune from jurisdiction in the United States and their property is immune from seizure unless an exception applies.
- A foreign sovereign can be sued in the United States if it waives sovereign immunity, or if the suit relates to a commercial activity carried on in the United States, an act in the United States in connection with a commercial activity elsewhere, or an act in connection with a commercial activity elsewhere that has a significant effect in the United States.
- A foreign sovereign can also be sued in the United States if rights in property taken in violation of international law are in issue, and the property, or property exchanged for it, is present in the United States in connection with a commercial activity carried on here by the foreign state, or the property, regardless of location, is owned or operated by an agency or instrumentality of a foreign state engaged in commercial activity in the United States.
- Under the Act of State doctrine, United States courts will not call into question the official acts of a currently recognized foreign state performed within its borders.
- *Forum non conveniens* results in the dismissal of some suits where there is an alternate forum that is more convenient for the litigation, especially if both plaintiff and defendant are nonresident aliens.
- Choice of law is constitutional as long as it has a significant relation to the parties or the transaction so that application of the law is neither arbitrary nor fundamentally unfair. In the absence of a choice-of-law clause, most courts select the law of their own jurisdiction.
- Choice of law in federal court for diversity cases is the law that the state court would have applied. For federal question cases, it is federal common law, which is usually the Second Restatement's significant contacts rule.
- Public policy of the forum may cause a court to disregard its normal choice of law rules, and courts generally do not enforce foreign criminal or tax laws.
- Proving foreign law is subject to special rules requiring notice, giving the court broad latitude about what to consult, and holding that the proof is a matter of law.

Master Checklist

Chapter 1 · What is Art? Why Does Anyone Care?

- ☐ There is no universal definition of "art" or "artist"; courts define these terms differently depending on the purpose for which the term is being defined.
- ☐ One definition of art is creativity of a human being that is fixed in tangible form.
- ☐ Tariff law defines art as requiring handmade creativity because such items are unlikely to compete with domestic products.
- ☐ Copyright law requires less creativity, permits mass-produced items, and does not necessarily exclude functional items in determining what is entitled to a copyright monopoly.
- ☐ First Amendment law requires that a work express a message to be entitled to constitutional protection as speech.
- ☐ Housing law may exclude commercially successful artists and amateurs to benefit artists whose income is low by allowing only professional fine artists to reside where they may both live and work.
- ☐ Income tax considers the originality and uniqueness as well as the aesthetic value of an item in considering whether its maker is an artist.
- ☐ Five reasons have been advanced justifying different rules for art and artists than for others. Art is aesthetically pleasing, conveys messages, and educates about past societies. Artists are often treated specially because they suffer from unequal bargaining power, and because there is often market failure in the art market.

Chapter 2 · Freedom of Expression

- ☐ There are five main policy reasons behind the First Amendment: Communication to further self-governance; to seek truth and allow ideas to compete on the open market; to help humans reach their full potential; to help balance stability and change; and to promote tolerance.
- ☐ Rational Basis Scrutiny is applied to a law that does not infringe a fundamental right. The government need only show that there is some rational basis for the law. If rational basis scrutiny is applied, laws are usually held constitutional.

- ☐ Strict Scrutiny applies to laws that infringe a fundamental right. The government must show a compelling interest the law serves and that there is no less restrictive means to achieve the law's purpose. Reasonable restrictions on the time, place and manner of expression are constitutional.
- ☐ Speech is oral or written communication of ideas. Conduct is speech when it is expressive. Neither obscenity nor child pornography is speech protected by the First Amendment.
- ☐ A work of art is obscene only if: (1) "the average person, applying contemporary community standards" would find that the work, taken as a whole, appeals to the prurient interest, and (2) the work depicts or describes, in a patently offensive way, sexual conduct specifically defined by the applicable law, and (3) the work, taken as a whole, lacks serious literary, artistic, political, or scientific value.
- ☐ The government has a compelling interest in protecting the health and safety of children. Child pornography may be defined as the depiction of a child's sexual organs or of a child engaged in sexual activity.
- ☐ The government can limit sale and display of artwork through licensing and sign ordinances, but its limits must be content-neutral. The government can place reasonable time, place and manner restrictions on display and sale.
- ☐ The government can limit expressive activity in a public forum if the law is either a content-neutral time, place and manner restriction, or the law passes strict scrutiny. A public forum is a space traditionally available for speech and assembly, such as public streets, sidewalks, and parks. A limited public forum is a space not traditionally available for speech and assembly, but made available for that purpose by government decision, and is subject to the same rules as long as it is made available. A nonpublic forum is any other space, and persons have no right to use it.
- ☐ The government can sometimes limit display of art when it is acting in a managerial capacity, when necessary to keep traffic moving or to prevent exposure in passageways.
- ☐ The government need not provide funds for the arts, but it cannot use its position as funder or landlord to dictate the content of the art displayed.
- ☐ Programs in which the government gives grants to fund museums and artists may take into account "general standards of decency and respect for the diverse beliefs and values of the American public" in making grants as long as those criteria do not constitute an absolute bar that would eliminate protected speech.
- ☐ There are no constitutional limits restricting the government's choice of subject matter or content when it purchases art.

Chapter 3 · Defamation

- ☐ A defamation action lies for statements of fact communicated to third parties about another person that are false and cause injury. This may include statements falsely attributing or denying credit to the creator of an artwork, or any statement detrimental to reputation or status.

- ☐ Opinions, either spoken or communicated through art, are not defamatory.
- ☐ Libel and slander per se allow for general damages because proving actual damages can be difficult.
- ☐ Other forms of defamation require proof of special damages to recover.
- ☐ Defamation per se arises from allegations of: criminal activity involving moral turpitude or crimes punishable by imprisonment; a loathsome disease; unfitness for his business; and sexual misconduct.
- ☐ Defamation of a private person by someone other than the media requires no proof of fault.
- ☐ Defamation of public officials or public figures, or defamation by the media, require proof of fault.
- ☐ The Single Publication Rule forces recovery from a defamatory statement to be addressed in a single lawsuit.
- ☐ A defendant who communicates information to a person with a need to know has a qualified privilege unless communicated with actual malice.
- ☐ Statements made by persons in legal proceedings have an absolute privilege.
- ☐ Public officials and public figures may be criticized unless there is actual malice.
- ☐ Defending a defamation case is expensive and seldom covered by insurance that most artists have.

Chapter 4 · Publicity and Privacy Rights

- ☐ The right of publicity and privacy are often confused; the right of publicity involves the right to control commercial use of your name and image whereas the right of privacy focuses on the right to prevent undue intrusion or disclosure. The right of publicity aims to provide recovery for someone whose valuable image has been used without out permission or compensation.
- ☐ Some states' rights of publicity require that a person's appropriated image have a special value in order to bring a lawsuit, while others only weigh special value in calculating damages.
- ☐ In states that extend the right of publicity to deceased persons, the longevity of that right can range from a few years to unlimited years. This post-mortem right is often dependent on plaintiff proving that the deceased person's appropriated image was valuable at the time of death.
- ☐ A statement that attaches another person's image to something requires consent of that person to avoid a right of publicity action, regardless of the statement's truth.

- ☐ One must secure the consent of someone with a right of publicity before using a photograph of him commercially. One court has held that the First Amendment bars the application of the right of publicity to a work of art.
- ☐ Exceptions to the right of publicity include a fair use type defense and express statutes that exclude the media's use of photos of famous people at "newsworthy" events. These exceptions arise out of a concern of First Amendment infringements. While "newsworthiness" is an exception to the right, determining what is newsworthy can be a challenge.
- ☐ Several tests balance the right of publicity and the First Amendment. These include determining if art that involves an image of a celebrity is transformative. If so, it may implicate the First Amendment and shield the art from right of publicity claims. Another test requires use of an image in a piece of work to have artistic relevance and to not mislead the viewer of the work about the content or source of the work.
- ☐ Some tests consider art pure expression that supersedes any right of publicity claims.
- ☐ The right of privacy aims to protect individuals from undue disclosure of his image to the public.
- ☐ The right of privacy contains the right to be free from unreasonable intrusions on one's seclusion. This is available if the invasion, trespassory or not, would be highly offensive to a reasonable person.
- ☐ Individuals also have a right to not be publicized in a false light. Often violations of this privacy right constitute defamation as well.
- ☐ The most important privacy right is the right to be free from unreasonable publicity given to one's private life. A broad exception to this right is the publication of newsworthy things which is often left to the discretion of publishers.
- ☐ Celebrities are protected from overly interfering behavior. While photographs of public figures in public places may be freely published, California imposes serious penalties on those who harass children of celebrities. Europe has also created privacy for celebrities which prevents publishing their daily life activities unrelated to their celebrity functions.

Chapter 5 · Copyright

- ☐ Federal copyright law is authorized by the Constitution. Courts have granted copyright ability to artists and artwork, although the Constitution only refers to authors and writing.
- ☐ Copyright is designed to encourage the production of copyrightable works by providing the author with a monopoly on the work for a period of time.
- ☐ Copyright grants exclusive rights for the period of the copyright to reproduce the work; to use it to prepare a derivative work; to sell, lease, or lend it; and to publicly display it.

- ☐ The first sale doctrine permits the owner of the physical item, even if he does not own the copyright, to sell, lease, lend and display that physical item.
- ☐ Copyright is now automatic if the work is an original work in a copyrightable subject matter that is fixed in a medium of expression.
- ☐ The work needs to be a creation of the author and at least minimally creative. Facts cannot be copyrighted.
- ☐ Ideas cannot be copyrighted; all that can be copyrighted is the expression of an idea.
- ☐ The scènes á faire doctrine prevents the necessary steps in expressing an idea from being protected by copyright.
- ☐ Functional elements of a design are not copyrightable; only the expressive element of the design can be copyrighted.
- ☐ The United States government may not be an original copyright holder, but state and foreign governments may. A copyright may be transferred to the federal government.
- ☐ All authors of a joint work are tenants in common of its copyright.
- ☐ If a work is made by an employee in his scope of employment, it is a work made for hire and the copyright belongs to the employer. Certain agreed works produced by an independent contractor are also works made for hire.
- ☐ Transferring a work does not transfer the copyright in it unless such an intent is expressed; transferring the copyright does not transfer the work unless such an intent is expressed.
- ☐ A suit for infringement may not begin until the copyright is registered.
- ☐ Infringement is copying a work's protected expression.
- ☐ Plaintiff must prove that defendant had access to the copyrighted work and that a copyrightable portion of it was copied.
- ☐ Minimal copying may not violate copyright laws.
- ☐ Vicarious infringement occurs when a person has the right to control the action of another and fails to prevent infringement when he profits by it.
- ☐ Derivative work must be done with permission of the copyright holder. Derivative works may be copyrighted if they demonstrate sufficient originality.
- ☐ Fair use is not infringement. Purposes of fair use include criticism, comment, news reporting, teaching, scholarship, and research.
- ☐ To determine if a use is fair, consider the purpose of the use, the nature of the copyrighted work, the proportion of the copyrighted work that is used and the effect of the use on the potential market for the copyrighted work.
- ☐ A successful plaintiff is entitled to ordinary damages, an injunction, and costs. Statutory damages and attorneys' fees may be awarded if the copyright is registered before the infringement.

Chapter 6 · Trademark and Related Actions

- ☐ The Lanham Act protects the investment the business makes in presenting the product or service to the public; prevents deception of the public about the source of goods or services, protects the owners of famous marks from having the meaning of their trademarks diluted; and prevents misrepresentations in commercial advertising.
- ☐ Marks must be distinctive, non-functional and used in the ordinary course of business. Names and descriptions are weak marks unless they have acquired secondary meaning attached to products.
- ☐ The basic trademark violation is use of a mark on a product not made by the mark owner that results in public confusion about the product's source.
- ☐ Artists and art institutions marketing work might wish to trademark their products to prevent others from marketing similar goods with the same mark.
- ☐ It is a trademark violation to blur or tarnish a nationally-known mark by using it on wildly different products or with unsavory connections.
- ☐ Where the appearance of a product has acquired a secondary meaning indicating the product's source, it can be a trademark violation to imitate the packaging or appearance in a way that causes confusion about the source of the goods.
- ☐ The fair use defenses to confusion requires that the mark not be used to identify a product. Descriptive fair use is where the use of another's mark describes the producer, the product or its geographic origin. Nominative fair use is where another's mark is used only to identify the product.
- ☐ If the use does not designate the source of goods, it may be a valid fair use defense to dilution to comparatively advertize, parody, criticize or comment on another's trademarked product.
- ☐ It is a defense to trademark infringement that the use of the mark has artistic relevance in the artwork in which it is used.
- ☐ It is a defense to trademark dilution that the use is noncommercial. Noncommercial use is any use more than selling a product, like parody, satire, or editorializing.
- ☐ Remedies for trademark violation include injunction, actual damages, and up to treble damages. Attorneys' fees may be awarded in exceptional cases.

Chapter 7 · Moral Rights

- ☐ Moral rights are non-waivable rights artists have in the physicality and reputation of their works, while economic rights in those works such as property rights, resale rights and copyright involve only payments for use or ownership.
- ☐ Moral rights group together four distinct rights: the right of paternity or attribution, the right of integrity to prevent modification or destruction of the work, the right of divulgation to decide when the work is finished, and the right to repent or to retake the work.

- ☐ The right of divulgation and the right to repent are not protected in any U.S. jurisdiction.
- ☐ The right of paternity or attribution allows the artist to insist that his name be attached to works that he created, to remove his name from works he did not create, and to remove his name from works he created but that have been modified. It probably does not permit the artist to insist that the work be anonymous or pseudonymous.
- ☐ The right of integrity allows the artist to prevent the modification or destruction of his work.
- ☐ The terms "prejudicial to his or her honor or reputation" and "work of recognized stature" which are necessary to find violation of the right of integrity are easily satisfied, but do require that the work have some public recognition, though not necessarily praise from art professionals.
- ☐ A mental state is required for modification or destruction to be actionable. It must be intentional or, in the case of destruction, grossly negligent, or, in the case of modification during conservation, grossly negligent.
- ☐ Fair use is a defense to a moral rights action.
- ☐ A work that is attached to a building but can be removed without damaging the work is subject to a special rule. If the owner gives the artist 90 days notice to remove the work and the artist removes it, the work belongs to the artist. If the artist does not remove the work, the owner may destroy it.
- ☐ A single work is modified if its elements are placed in different relationships with each other, but whether a work with multiple pieces is a single work or many works is a question of fact. A site-specific work is not modified by being moved to another site or put in storage.
- ☐ Federal moral rights protect only "works of visual art," a limited class of artistic work that includes only paintings, drawings, and certain prints, sculptures and still photographs produced in limited quantities. Works of visual art must be copyrightable. Prints, sculptures and photos done in multiples must be signed and numbered by the artist, and photos must be produced for exhibition purposes.
- ☐ A work made for hire is not a "work of visual art," so it carries no moral rights.
- ☐ Useful items like advertising, containers, posters, maps, globes, charts or technical drawings are not works of visual art.
- ☐ Moral rights are personal to the artist. They cannot be transferred, and it is difficult to waive them.
- ☐ Federal law preempts state moral rights law during the lifetime of the artist for "works of visual art" only.
- ☐ The First Amendment guarantee of free speech may prohibit liability for moral rights where the work is modified or destroyed to communicate a message.

Chapter 8 · Re-Sale Royalties

- ☐ Artists whose artwork is not reproduced do not receive a stream of copyright royalties. A re-sale royalty entitles an artist to a portion of the resale price.
- ☐ No United States jurisdiction has a re-sale royalty.
- ☐ Where there are re-sale royalties, artists are usually given a percentage of the re-sale price of an art work or a portion of the net profit of the resale. After an artist's death, the re-sale royalty may extend to the artist's survivors for a period of time. Foreign artists may not be entitled to re-sale royalties or there may be certain residency requirements to be entitled to receive the royalty.
- ☐ Re-sale royalties do not always apply; a sale under a set minimum price may be exempt. Some jurisdictions require the sale price to exceed the purchase price while others do not, thereby increasing the seller's loss. Likewise some jurisdictions calculate the seller's expenses in determining what percentage artists receive while other jurisdictions do not.
- ☐ The royalty may apply to all sales or be limited to sale through art professionals like auctions, dealers and galleries.
- ☐ Re-sale royalties can be hard to enforce. It may be difficult to determine when a sale has occurred, and its price, and it may be hard to actually collect the royalties, particularly in private sales. Art professionals are required to withhold re-sale royalties before giving the seller the purchase price which alleviates some enforcement issues.
- ☐ There are two justifications for the re-sale royalty. Artists struggle to make money and are easily exploited by buyers to sell their work below fair market value; the royalty gives the artists a portion of the seller's later profit. Also, the value of art work is influenced by the artist's behavior and later work, so the artist should share any increase in value.

Chapter 9 · Taxes and the Art World

- ☐ Income tax deductions are only available for taxpayers with profit-seeking motivation. A taxpayer best demonstrates that motivation who has objectively manifested activities that show he is engaged in the world of art for profit, or by showing a profit in 2 of the previous 5 years.
- ☐ To be engaged in a trade or business, an artist must be engaged in regular activity for profit. Factors such as an artist's marketing activity, past sales, and time spent on art help determine if an artist has a profit-seeking motive.
- ☐ Only itemized deductions are available for investors or collectors who claim their activity as an investment, rather than a trade or business, and they are not available 2018–2025. A lack of sales or a collection kept in a private residence may distinguish an investor from a hobbyist.
- ☐ When a taxpayer exchanges like kind property with another, he can defer income tax because there is no money received to tax, no substantial change in taxpayer's investment and no currently recognized loss or gain.

- ☐ If an artist has a home studio where a room is used exclusively as the principal place of business, to meet clients, or is located in a separate structure, the expense of maintaining this studio may be deductible.
- ☐ Congress has made an exception for artists to the rule that inventory is nondeductible, allowing them to deduct current cost of preparing artwork.
- ☐ Expenses incurred on business travels related to an artist's business are deductible.
- ☐ The passive activity loss rules prevent offsetting passive business losses against income generated from other activities. There are safe harbors available for taxpayers meeting certain requirements concerning the taxpayer's time spent on such activities which most active artists can satisfy.
- ☐ Quick and frequent sales indicate a taxpayer is engaged in a trade or business, subjecting art sales to ordinary income rates. One who buys art or a copyright as an investment is taxed at capital gains rates for collectibles.
- ☐ The fair market value of property gifted to charity may be deducted from most taxpayers' income tax.
- ☐ Fair market value of property is a question of fact that is usually established by testimony of expert witnesses. There may be discounts from fair market value when a supply of an artist's work greatly increases.
- ☐ When comparing sales of artwork to determine an artwork's price, size, condition and changes in the market may alter its value. If a work is illegally exported or lacks good title, the artwork's fair market value may be lowered.
- ☐ Comparable sales that support an appraised price and the expert's knowledge of the artist or work may increase the persuasiveness of the appraisal. Not all appraisals are credible, particularly when the expert is a friend or business associate of the artwork's owner.
- ☐ Fraud and valuation errors on tax returns subject a taxpayer to penalties.
- ☐ Notes from the I.R.S. Art Advisory Panel about an expert witness' views are generally discoverable, but any disclosure is limited to matters related to the determination of the value of that specific artwork.
- ☐ Tax shelters to reduce the income taxes of wealthy taxpayers include the sale of art masters such as silkscreens or lithograph plates. Courts have limited and denied these types of deductions and Congress has made an effort to reduce these opportunities.

Chapter 10 · Authenticity

- ☐ Authenticity of an art work may relate to the period in which it was produced, its condition, its state of restoration, and whether it was created by the named artist.
- ☐ Scientific evidence based on the materials used presently cannot prove which artist made a work but can conclusively establish that the work was not made by an artist if the materials were not used until after the artist's death.

- ☐ Provenance helps prove authenticity by showing the whereabouts of a work over time. It can be difficult to establish because records may be lost, never made, or fraudulent, and copies of the work may be made by the owner himself.
- ☐ Connoisseurship is the evaluation of a work by experts who compare its similarities or differences to other works reliably attributed to an artist.
- ☐ Buyers may recover damages from their sellers if purchasing a misattributed work through common law tort or contract recoveries and sales law statutes.
- ☐ To recovery under fraud, a buyer must prove the seller made a representation he knew was untrue, the seller knew a reasonable buyer would rely on that representation, and that the buyer actually relied on it. A negligent misrepresentation action has the same requirements except the buyer only needs to prove the seller was negligent in making the representation, not that the seller knew it was untrue. The buyer must also prove the seller owed the buyer a duty which does not typically exist between seller and buyer.
- ☐ If a seller promises to deliver a work and then delivers something else and the buyer reasonably relies on the seller's representation, the seller is liable. It is reasonable for a buyer to rely on a representation of fact but it is unreasonable to rely on an opinion. Courts may distinguish between representations made before and after a purchase.
- ☐ Both the Uniform Sales Act and the Uniform Commercial Code hold sellers liable for breach of warranty for misattribution if buyer reasonably relied on the attribution.
- ☐ Buyers may include clauses in bills of sale expressly stating buyer reliance on seller's representations to assure that they have valid warranties. If buyer had an expert examine the work before sale, buyer is precluded from claiming reliance on an express warranty if the defect is one such an expert should have noticed.
- ☐ The statute of limitations to sue for breach of present warranty is four years from the time of delivery.
- ☐ A promise of future action is not breached and the statute of limitations does not begin to run until the future performance is due and not performed.
- ☐ The statute of limitations does not run if defendant fraudulently conceals the defect.
- ☐ When a seller is involved in a continuing course of action, the statute of limitations does not begin to run until the last action occurs.
- ☐ The doctrine of inherently unknowable injury, which extends the running of the statute of limitations until a plaintiff discovers or should have discovered an injury, has been extended to the recovery of property. Cases conflict on whether the discovery rule applies to buyers who purchase misattributed works.
- ☐ United Nations Convention on Contracts for the International Sale of Goods (CISG) is governing law for sales between residents of different countries that

participate in the treaty. Auction sales are exempt, as are sales for personal, family, or household uses unless seller is unaware the buyer purchased the work for those reasons.

- ❑ CISG does not require reliance or being part of the bargain. It has no statute of limitation though the buyer must notify the seller of the specific lack of conformity to the contract within a reasonable time of when buyer should have discovered it but in all cases within two years after delivery in order to contest the quality of the goods and recover.
- ❑ Many states have enacted art legislation to protect consumers. They generally do not require plaintiff to show that the attribution was part of the basis of the bargain, but may limit liability to situations where seller's representations were without a reasonable basis in fact at the time they were made.
- ❑ Auction houses often include provisions in their contracts that allow an auctioneer to rescind a sale if it determines it might be subject to liability from the sale, even without establishing lack of authenticity.
- ❑ The Federal Trade Commission (FTC) can sue to stop unfair and deceptive trade practices, even if the practices are truthful but deceptive to reasonable consumers. Past violations justify a preliminary injunction to prevent fraud before the trial ends.
- ❑ A person who knowingly sells inauthentic artwork may commit state or federal criminal offenses including mail fraud, wire fraud, and obtaining money by false pretenses.
- ❑ Scholars and appraisers are often used to prove or disprove authenticity. They may be liable for misattribution and subject to actions for malpractice, defamation, or product disparagement.
- ❑ Authenticators are liable to their clients for malpractice if they fail to use the special knowledge or skills they advertise. Appraisers are only liable to third parties if a duty of care to that party exists. Some states find a duty to anyone that the appraiser can reasonably foresee would be given the appraiser's appraisal.
- ❑ For an appraiser to be liable to a third party for defamation, the third party must prove an appraiser's attribution is false and was reasonably understood by the public, causing damage to the reputation of the third party. The appraiser may defend himself on freedom of speech grounds.
- ❑ For an appraiser to be liable to a third party for product disparagement, the third party must prove the appraiser's speech or conduct was false, the appraiser acted with malice, the appraiser communicated the falsity to another party, and it reduced the value of his property.
- ❑ Courts have held owners of misattributed work and their lawyers liable for compensatory and punitive damages for abuse of process and malicious prosecution when they unreasonably sue an appraiser and the suit is dismissed but the appraiser incurred substantial legal costs.

- ☐ Risk of suit has caused many experts to create exculpatory or indemnity clauses to shield themselves from lawsuits. These are usually ineffective against gross negligence and wilful misconduct allegations. There is no obligation to authenticate unless there is a contractual obligation.
- ☐ An artist's moral rights may be violated if anyone destroys or defaces a forgery.
- ☐ To succeed in an antitrust action against an authenticator, an owner must prove the work of the artist is the relevant market, that the defendant attempted to monopolize the market or there was an agreement among defendants to restrain trade in the market, and that the monopolization attempt or agreement caused damages.
- ☐ Trademark protects the goodwill of sellers. A plaintiff suing under the Lanham Act must prove a false designation of origin or false description or advertisement of fact, and must show that public confusion is likely.

Chapter 11 · Title

- ☐ Sale of an artwork carries with it a warranty of title unless title is disclaimed.
- ☐ A buyer receives good title if his seller had good title, or if he is a good faith purchaser and seller either had voidable title, or is a merchant who deals in goods of the same kind who was entrusted possession by the true owner and the buyer buys in the ordinary course of his seller's business.
- ☐ A buyer of stolen art does not receive good title in the U.S. In some civil law countries, a buyer receives good title to stolen art if he buys in good faith or if he buys at a government-sponsored auction.
- ☐ Art is not stolen if it has been abandoned, gifted, willed or sold. Each of those transfers must be voluntary.
- ☐ A person who is in open and continuous possession as owner of artwork for the period of the statute of limitations is the owner of it.
- ☐ The cause of action for recovery of artwork accrues in one jurisdiction when the owner demands its return and is refused; others use the discovery rule which provides that the cause of action accrues when the owner discovers or should have discovered the facts necessary to sue if the owner has exercised due diligence; still others when the art is stolen.
- ☐ Despite the expiration of the applicable statute of limitations, through the end of 2026 the owner may sue within six years of actually discovering the facts needed to sue.
- ☐ The statute of limitations is tolled when the artwork is out of the jurisdiction or when it is being fraudulently concealed.
- ☐ If the statute of limitations has not expired, the owner may be barred by laches if he delays bringing suit and the defendant is disadvantaged by that delay, such as by the death of witnesses.

- ☐ Civil Law jurisdictions have acquisitive prescription statutes giving a long-time possessor title, and some have a shorter period for a good faith purchaser to acquire title by prescription.

Chapter 12 · Commercial Art Relationships

- ☐ Contracts commissioning art should be in writing to fix what is to be produced, define the warranty, provide security for performance, specify a time of completion, and provide for dispute resolution.
- ☐ Buying existing art is a sale of goods requiring compliance with the statute of frauds for sales.
- ☐ Agency relationships are established when an artist sells through a dealer. The dealer must observe a duty of loyalty to the artist that forbids conflicts of interest.
- ☐ Art consignments are bailments at common law imposing different duties of care on the agent depending on whether the bailment is for the benefit of one of the parties or for mutual benefit.
- ☐ Special art legislation often provides that consignee is absolutely liable for loss or damage to the consigned goods.
- ☐ When a buyer pays the consignee the buyer has no further obligation at common law, leaving the consignor as a general creditor. Special art legislation often gives consignor priority by establishing a trust relationship.
- ☐ Creditors of consignee prevail over consignor under the UCC unless consignor takes special steps to label his goods. Recent UCC amendments exempt consumer goods from this rule. Special art legislation often gives consignor priority.
- ☐ Agency agreements are normally construed according to the contract. Default rules require that the agent exercise a duty of loyalty and a duty of care to the principal.
- ☐ Friends and business acquaintances of artists may be asked to undertake other duties, such as executors of wills or trustees of foundations. The standards applicable to them will be different than if they were just friends or business acquaintances, as they will be judged by the standards of executors or trustees.
- ☐ Auctions create agency relationships that are usually successfully modified by the specific terms of the auction house's contract.

Chapter 13 · Museum Law

- ☐ Museums may be organized as any business form, but they are most commonly organized under state nonprofit corporation laws for educational purposes. They usually qualify as § 501(c)(3) organizations for tax purposes. They are not permitted to distribute profit to any individual.
- ☐ Museums are subject to supervision by the state attorney general, which may include requiring the submission of periodic reports.

- ❑ Museums usually do not pay income or property taxes, and contributions to museums are usually deductible from income, gift or estate tax liability. Obtaining property tax exemption is usually the most difficult.
- ❑ A museum is taxed on its unrelated business income, defined as income from operating a business that is not related to its exempt purpose. A restaurant and a bookstore are both businesses, but they are related to a museum's exempt purpose if the restaurant is primarily for employees and guests, and if the bookstore sells only books about artwork.
- ❑ If a museum is a private foundation because supported by a few individuals, special rules apply evidencing more supervision and a shorter life span.
- ❑ Museums are governed by a board that chooses the major officers and sets general policy. Members of the board owe a duty of loyalty and a duty of care to the museum.
- ❑ The duty of loyalty is defined by the purposes of the museum, and requires that the board members not engage in self-dealing or take advantage of any conflict of interest they may have. Purposes may be determined from the museum's charter or from the requirements the law imposes on charitable organizations.
- ❑ When changes have occurred since the museum was established that make the achievement of its purposes impractical, a court may order a change in museum purposes to the nearest practical charitable use if the person who established the museum had a general charitable intent. Likewise, the court can order a deviation from mandated administrative matters for impracticability.
- ❑ The duty of care requires reasonable care and diligence in the management of the museum's assets. Trustees are judged under the business judgment rule which provides no liability if the trustee exercises reasonable business judgment.
- ❑ Enforcing trustee duties is left largely to the state attorney general. A taker in default of a gift may have enforcement powers, as may the donor of a gift under some circumstances.
- ❑ Museum acquisitions should be the subject of a policy according to museum association guidelines so that museums acquire ownership of authentic works. Acquisition guidelines generally do not distinguish between purchases, gifts and loans, though there are obvious practical differences.
- ❑ Restoration of works in the collection is a duty of the museum. In unusual cases, a restorer may have a claim for unjust enrichment against the owner of the artwork.
- ❑ Museum de-accessions are limited by the general duties of loyalty and care. Most museum organizations have accreditation standards that limit de-accession to generating funds for future purchases, but prohibit it for operating expenses or building improvement.
- ❑ Museum labor law contains no special rules because the employer is a museum. It is subject to normal rules about union bargaining, specific contracts and at will employment.

- ☐ Termination of employees covered by union contracts, civil service or individual contracts will be governed by the terms of the contracts. At will employees can be terminated for any reason, but cannot be terminated for a prohibited reason such as race, sex, national origin, disability, age, or in retaliation for the exercise of some protected right, such as refusal to violate the law, the exercise of a government duty like jury service, whistle-blowing, or the exercise of a right in connection with employment, such as filing a worker's compensation claim.
- ☐ Federal and state laws frequently prohibit employment discrimination, including discrimination in pay, on grounds of race, sex, national origin, disability, or age.

Chapter 14 · Art in War

- ☐ The sources of law on the treatment of art in war are mainly the Hague Convention, its Second Protocol, and national regulations or training manuals.
- ☐ Distinguishing the Hague Convention from its Second Protocol is important because twice as many countries have adhered to the Convention as have joined the Second Protocol, and the U.S. is not a member of the Second Protocol.
- ☐ The Hague Convention calls on nations during peacetime to plan to protect art in case of hostilities. The Second Protocol is more specific, calling for a national inventory, appointment of an official in charge, protection of art from fire or collapse in the event of war, and locating cultural items away from military targets.
- ☐ The Hague Convention prohibits reprisals against cultural property, or targeting cultural property except when waived for military necessity. The Second Protocol specifies that waiver can only be by a person of high rank, and places additional conditions on the waiver.
- ☐ The Hague Convention requires a country to prevent or put a stop to vandalism against cultural property.
- ☐ A country can take booty, items useful in prosecution of the war, from private citizens in the other state, and use it for its own purposes. Other items would be pillage if taken, and they cannot be taken.
- ☐ The Second Protocol prohibits illegal export or transfer of ownership of art during occupation. It severely restricts archaeology.
- ☐ There is no prohibition on seizure of enemy-owned property without compensation that is located within the territory of the seizing state.

Chapter 15 · Restricting the Movement of Art Across National Borders

- ☐ A major reason to restrict the international movement of art is to dry up the market for stolen or illegally exported art. It applies more forcefully to artifacts than to fine art because artifacts are more likely to be unidentifiable and more likely to be damaged, and the loss of knowledge from removal from their find-spots more significant.

- ☐ Control of artifacts differs from country to country. Most countries combine ownership restrictions with export restrictions. Three approaches involve private ownership, public ownership, and public ownership with a reward for the finder and the landowner.
- ☐ Control of fine arts focuses on export restrictions. Some countries have none; in others an attempt to export results in confiscation of the art; in most there is an export license that must be obtained; in some, a purchase or a request to export triggers a right of first refusal in the government to purchase the artwork.
- ☐ General free trade treaties allow countries to impose export restrictions on art to protect national treasures as an exception. Export tariffs do not qualify because they do not protect.
- ☐ The European Convention on Human Rights contains provisions on rights to property, the right to leave a country, and the right to travel that might be used to permit an individual to export his art.
- ☐ National patrimony has no agreed-upon definition, nor is there any requirement that items be designated as part of the national patrimony in advance.
- ☐ Cultural heritage of a country is broadly defined by the 1970 UNESCO Convention as any work produced by nationals or residents, or that was produced or ever existed in the country.
- ☐ The 1970 UNESCO Convention seeks international cooperation for export control by requiring signatories to develop an export license, prevent their museums from acquiring illegally exported property and prevent the import of property stolen from museums and facilitate its return on payment of just compensation.
- ☐ The 1970 UNESCO Convention allows a country whose cultural heritage is endangered to seek and receive concerted international action to prohibit import of endangered property.
- ☐ United States implementation of the UNESCO Convention permits forfeiture of stolen property or property on which there has been a false customs declaration. Knowingly receiving stolen property is a crime in all states. The President is authorized to forbid imports as part of an international cooperation effort.
- ☐ Museum organization guidelines, international cooperation efforts, and self-help can aid in recovering stolen or illegally exported property.

Chapter 16 · Historic Preservation

- ☐ National Historic Preservation Act requires that before a decision is made on any federal or federally-assisted project, the federal official must consider the effect of the project on anything eligible for inclusion in a national register of historic places.

- ☐ Eligibility for inclusion in a national register depends on the law of the country where the property is located.
- ☐ Standing to invoke NHPA is limited to persons within the zone of protection of NHPA who are likely to suffer injury in fact from the decision.
- ☐ Taking of property by eminent domain is justified to improve blighted areas.
- ☐ Restrictions on historic buildings or to create historic districts are constitutional as long as the owner has some economic use of the property under the police power because they promote the public welfare.
- ☐ Historic preservation of churches may be unconstitutional if the requirements infringe church doctrine.

Chapter 17 · Regulating Archaeology

- ☐ The Antiquities Act of 1906 required anyone who wished to excavate on federally owned or controlled land (including land of Indian tribes) to first obtain permission from the federal government.
- ☐ The Act criminalized damaging objects of antiquity or removing them from federally owned or controlled land.
- ☐ Archaeological Resources Protection Act (ARPA) from 1979 protects archeological resources, defined as at least 100 years old, and a remain of past human life or activities of archaeological interest.
- ☐ A person may be criminally liable for violating ARPA. This violation is a specific intent crime and requires scienter for each element of the crime.
- ☐ If convicted, the sentence may include restitution of actual loss. Restitution cannot be ordered for archaeological value, but archaeological value can be considered in determining the gravity of the crime. Archaeological value is the value of the information that was lost by taking the resource, measured by the cost of a suitable scientific excavation (even though none was planned).
- ☐ ARPA adds criminal offenses for trafficking archaeological resources taken from anywhere in violation of any provision, rule, regulation, ordinance, or permit in effect under federal, State or local law.
- ☐ A number of states provide protection for archaeological sites. Most state laws are modeled on ARPA and provide protection only for archaeological sites on land owned or controlled by the state and included on an official list of sites. A few include all land in the state.
- ☐ When any federal agency contemplates a project, the National Environmental Protection Act (NEPA) requires the agency to complete and consider an environmental impact report, and respond to the information about archaeological sites contained in the report.
- ☐ The goals of these laws are to encourage the discovery of clues to the knowledge of the past, and to make both knowledge and significant examples of previous artwork available to the widest possible public.

Chapter 18 · Artifacts Found on Land

- ☐ Ownership of artifacts found on land depends on the law of finds, which categorizes the artifacts as abandoned, lost, mislaid, embedded, or treasure trove.
- ☐ Abandoned property is property that the owner has not used and intends to abandon. Abandoned property belongs to the person who finds it and reduces it to possession.
- ☐ Mislaid property is property that the owner has put down and left, but the owner probably knows the location at which he mislaid the property. The possessor of the property upon which mislaid property was mislaid may keep that property from anyone except the true owner—even the finder. It is unlikely that artifacts will ever be mislaid property.
- ☐ Lost property is property whose location is unlikely to be known by the owner. Lost property can be retained by the finder against anyone except the true owner. It is unlikely that the owner of an artifact will ever reclaim it.
- ☐ Embedded property is property that is in the land in a way that shows it has been there for a considerable period of time. The embedded property belongs to the land. Under the law of waste, the owner is usually preferred to the tenant.
- ☐ Treasure trove is defined as money, or gold or silver bullion or plate concealed by the owner. Special rules gave it to the Crown in England. In the United States it is treated as embedded property.

Chapter 19 · Artifacts Found under Water

- ☐ Underwater artifacts are usually governed by the law of salvage. If the item has been abandoned, the law of finds gives ownership to the first person to reduce it to possession. If the item has not been abandoned, the owner retains title, but the admiralty court determines an award for the salvor.
- ☐ Salvor's award is determined considering the labor spent, the skill and energy in salving, the value of property used in the rescue effort and the degree of danger to which it was exposed, the risks incurred by the salvors, the value of the property saved, the degree of danger to which it was exposed, and the extent to which the salvors protected historical and archaeological value.
- ☐ Some courts have abandoned the law of salvage where the property is embedded in the bed of a watercourse that is owned.
- ☐ Abandonment requires non-user for a long period and intent to abandon. Intent to abandon by the federal government or a foreign state must be express.
- ☐ The Abandoned Shipwreck Act, which grants ownership of abandoned ships to the federal government and transfers ownership to the state on whose territorial waters the ship is found, has been largely unused because of the difficulty of finding intent to abandon.

- ☐ There is a conflict between exclusive admiralty jurisdiction in federal courts and the eleventh amendment, providing that states cannot be sued in federal court. States cannot be sued in state court unless they waive sovereign immunity.
- ☐ There is a UNESCO Convention providing protection of underwater cultural heritage, but it is unlikely to be influential because it has not been widely adopted and the U.S.A. is not a member.

Chapter 20 · Native American Remains and Artifacts

- ☐ Historically, common law and statutory law addressed human remains. At common law there was no property in dead bodies but there was a right of proper burial for a body's next of kin. Statutory laws made grave robbing and disinterment felonies.
- ☐ A cemetery can be established through a formal process or informally through dedication. When a landowner allows burials on his property and the land is permanently committed to being a cemetery, a cemetery has been established. The law becomes more complicated when it comes to implied dedications and private burial grounds. Courts have ordered visitation rights and prohibited grave desecration by landowners in these instances.
- ☐ To show intent to abandon a cemetery, more than the passage of time and the ending of new burials are needed. Where a family ceases to visit the grounds and the public cannot make out the grounds as a burial site, the cemetery is abandoned.
- ☐ Laws that protect remains in unmarked graves generally require disposition of the remains before the land may be developed. The appropriate disposition of the remains varies with different state laws and many of these laws are ambiguous.
- ☐ A body may be disinterred with court permissions. This is often requested by descendants. Reasons for disinterment include identifying the remains, gathering evidence or medical samples, or to solve mysteries. Religious reasons may motivate reburial of remains as well. Not every request to exhume a body will be granted, and courts have found that cemeteries may have standing to oppose such requests.
- ☐ Native Americans often buried their dead with goods in graves without permanent markers, creating litigation over whether an objecting tribe can recover for disturbed graves and whether goods in the graves are abandoned. Courts have held differently, sometimes based on a tribe's ability to establish a genealogical connection between the tribe and the remains.
- ☐ NAGPRA provides that Native Americans own any human remains or burial goods discovered after 1990 on federal or tribal grounds. It also prohibits trafficking in human remains and cultural items. NAGPRA requires repatriation of items from federally funded museums and federal agencies and universities.
- ☐ The items to be repatriated are human remains, associated funerary objects, unassociated funerary objects, sacred objects, and cultural patrimony. These

items need not be discovered within any time period or location and the federal establishments need only be in possession of the objects to require repatriation.

- ☐ Scientists often wish to study remains to discover information about the past while tribes wish to maintain the burials of their ancestors. An exception to repatriation exists when the items are indispensable to a scientific study whose results would be a major benefit to the United States.
- ☐ NAGPRA defines "Native American" narrowly, requiring the remains or artifacts to have a cultural affiliation with an existing tribe.
- ☐ Items that are declared Native American with a cultural affiliation will be repatriated to either lineal descendants, tribes with the closest cultural affiliation, or tribes whose land the items were discovered on, based on what type of item it is. NAGPRA requires federally funded universities and museums to identify its Native American possession and return them to tribes if possible.
- ☐ Lineal descendants or the tribe of decedents may request the return of remains under NAGPRA if they have suffered injury in fact. Plaintiffs falling outside these definitions may have their cases dismissed for lack of standing.
- ☐ Native American goods that are old or have ongoing cultural importance to a tribe and goods that are both individually and communally owned may not be trafficked under NAGPRA. Testimony from Native Americans is often relied on in determining the significance of items to different tribes.
- ☐ The NAGPRA procedure begins with museums inventorying their collections and providing information to the Interior Department's Bureau of Land Management to determine if items are Native American or affiliated with a tribe. If the affiliated tribe requests repatriation, items are to be returned. If the Bureau concludes items are not Native American or affiliated with a tribe, they must publicize this and be open to responses from other tribes. The Bureau is then to consider these responses and make another determination accompanied by an explanation for its ruling. The opinion of the advisory NAGPRA Review Committee may also be requested.
- ☐ Statutes that give preferential treatment to Native Americans have been successful against equal protection challenges because courts have considered the statutes as providing cultural or political classifications instead of prohibited racial classification. The statutes are therefore only subject to a rational governmental interest review and do not require the statute to use least restrictive means.
- ☐ NAGPRA applies in federal courts but some states have enacted laws similar to NAGPRA for items found on state property or items in state-funded museums. These laws encounter similar issues of who may be an interested party to remains or artifacts discovered. Some state laws address remains discovered while constructing public accommodations, providing exceptions that permit the removal and reburial of remains. Property owners of land with Indian burial sites that prohibit land development may try to sue claiming their land was subject to regulatory taking. These arguments may fail if there is no physical taking or denial of all economic uses of the land.

- ☐ Courts have found that removing remains or requiring remains to stay in their burial site do not abridge the free exercise of religion for the Native American tribes because the tribes are not penalized or required to abandon their religious beliefs.
- ☐ Some tribes have enacted ordinances that prohibit buying, trading, arranging, and removing tribal artifacts without permission of the village council. Members of the tribe are bound by these ordinances as a matter of tribal law but whether persons outside the tribe are bound by the ordinances is a matter of federal law.
- ☐ American law does not fit well with Native American custom, which focuses on oral communications and the collective tribe. Often copyright protection is difficult because of trouble determining an author of a work that comes from a shared community. Likewise, tribes may fail to obtain rights under patent law. Causes of action for defamation and similar actions that arise from branding of products based on Native Americans may be more successful.

Chapter 21 · International Litigation for Art Lawyers

- ☐ Assertion of jurisdiction must conform to applicable law, and satisfy due process requiring that defendant have sufficient minimum contacts with the jurisdiction that litigating the case there would not offend fair play and substantial justice.
- ☐ Minimum contacts are usually satisfied if defendant performs significant business activities in the state on a continuous basis.
- ☐ Fair play and substantial justice are usually satisfied where the suit relates to the minimum contacts defendant has with the state. Factors considered might include the defendant's potential burden in defending in the forum, the convenience of the forum for taking evidence, the difficulties plaintiff would experience in finding an alternate forum, or the interest of the state in regulating the conduct.
- ☐ Where the case brought relates to defendant's continuing business in the state (specific jurisdiction), both minimum contacts and fair play and substantial justice are usually satisfied.
- ☐ Where the case brought does not relate to defendant's activities in the state (general jurisdiction), defendant must usually be domiciled in the state, incorporated in the state, or have his principal place of business there to satisfy fair play and substantial justice.
- ☐ *In rem* jurisdiction is always constitutional because the case relates to property located in the state.
- ☐ Defendant's consent gives the court jurisdiction over him, whether that consent is contained in a contract or derived from subsequent conduct.
- ☐ Without consenting to jurisdiction defendant may appear to challenge the jurisdiction at the beginning of the suit.
- ☐ Immunity from seizure for loans of art work may be procured through the State Department. Immunity from state court seizure may be automatically provided by statute.

- ☐ Foreign sovereigns are immune from jurisdiction in the United States and their property is immune from seizure unless an exception applies.
- ☐ A foreign sovereign can be sued in the United States if it waives sovereign immunity, or if the suit relates to a commercial activity carried on in the United States, an act in the United States in connection with a commercial activity elsewhere, or an act in connection with a commercial activity elsewhere that has a significant effect in the United States.
- ☐ A foreign sovereign can also be sued in the United States if rights in property taken in violation of international law are in issue, and the property, or property exchanged for it, is present in the United States in connection with a commercial activity carried on here by the foreign state, or the property, regardless of location, is owned or operated by an agency or instrumentality of a foreign state engaged in commercial activity in the United States.
- ☐ Under the Act of State doctrine, United States courts will not call into question the official acts of a currently recognized foreign state performed within its borders.
- ☐ *Forum non conveniens* results in the dismissal of some suits where there is an alternate forum that is more convenient for the litigation, especially if both plaintiff and defendant are nonresident aliens.
- ☐ Choice of law is constitutional as long as it has a significant relation to the parties or the transaction so that application of the law is neither arbitrary nor fundamentally unfair. In the absence of a choice-of-law clause, most courts select the law of their own jurisdiction.
- ☐ Choice of law in federal court for diversity cases is the law that the state court would have applied. For federal question cases, it is federal common law, which is usually the Second Restatement's significant contacts rule.
- ☐ Public policy of the forum may cause a court to disregard its normal choice of law rules, and courts generally do not enforce foreign criminal or tax laws.
- ☐ Proving foreign law is subject to special rules requiring notice, giving the court broad latitude about what to consult, and holding that the proof is a matter of law.

Index